Impact of Web Technologies on Digital Transformation

Arnaldo Santos
https://orcid.org/0000-0001-5139-6728
Universidade Aberta, Portugal

Henrique S. Mamede
https://orcid.org/0000-0002-5383-9884
Universidade Aberta, Portugal

IGI Global Scientific Publishing
Publishing Tomorrow's Research Today

Vice President of Editorial	Melissa Wagner
Director of Acquisitions	Mikaela Felty
Director of Book Development	Jocelynn Hessler
Production Manager	Mike Brehm
Cover Design	Jose Rosado

Published in the United States of America by
IGI Global Scientific Publishing
701 East Chocolate Avenue
Hershey, PA, 17033, USA
Tel: 717-533-8845 | Fax: 717-533-7115
Website: https://www.igi-global.com E-mail: cust@igi-global.com

Library of Congress Cataloging-in-Publication Data

LCCN: 2025033248 (CIP Data Pending)
ISBN13: 9798337351674
Isbn13Softcover: 9798337351681
EISBN13: 9798337351698
British Cataloguing in Publication Data
A Cataloguing in Publication record for this book is available from the British Library.

Table of Contents

Detailed Table of Contents

In today's digital economy, the web has transcended its original role as a communication medium to become a foundational infrastructure for digital transformation. This chapter examines the strategic role of web technologies in enabling scalable, agile, and interoperable systems that support innovation across sectors. It integrates conceptual insights with real-world case studies in government, retail, education, and healthcare to illustrate how the web empowers organizations to enhance customer experience, streamline operations, and enable rapid prototyping. The discussion covers core web technologies—cloud platforms, APIs, frontend frameworks, and backend architectures—and future trends including Web3 and Web 5.0. It also addresses challenges such as legacy integration, cybersecurity, and digital inequality, offering frameworks such as digital maturity models and agile-DevOps approaches for mitigation. By aligning web capabilities with organizational strategy, institutions can create resilient, user-centered ecosystems essential for long-term competitiveness in a connected world.

This chapter explores the convergence of theoretical frameworks and practical methodologies in modern web technologies. By integrating models such as the Technology Acceptance Model (TAM), Human-Centered Design (HCD), Systems Development Life Cycle (SDLC), Hypertext Theory, and Actor-Network Theory (ANT), the chapter demonstrates how theory informs and enhances practices like responsive web design, RESTful APIs, and Progressive Web Apps (PWA). Supported by real-world case studies from education, healthcare, governance, and digital business, it highlights how theoretical foundations drive innovation, user

This chapter emphasizes that the rapid growth of e-business has intensified digital exclusion for people with disabilities, making web accessibility a strategic and ethical necessity. Using WCAG 2.2 as a framework, it analyzes key barriers across disability types and how inclusive UI/UX, assistive technologies, and global regulations (ADA, AODA, EN 301 549) shape accessible e-commerce. The chapter argues that accessibility improves customer experience, SEO, conversion rates, and brand trust, especially within the "purple economy." It concludes that accessibility must be embedded into digital transformation to ensure inclusive, resilient, and future-ready e-business ecosystems.

Web technologies have taken over as they are instrumental to cultural heritage preservation and promotion. This chapter discusses the uses of digital storytelling and participatory platforms to be engaged with communities, to share historical knowledge, and to promote cultural expression. It searches the tools and approaches of developing interactive and immersive environments that help users to become connected to heritage content. The chapter also talks of the benefits of participatory platform where users can come with their stories, pictures and share their local history and therefore preserving the culture is a collaborative and participatory process. Examples of good practice in the digital humanities are found at case studies in museums, archives and grassroots initiatives. The problem of digital access, content authenticity, and long term preservation is also touched upon. Finally, the strategies are proposed on how it is possible to develop culturally sensitive, user friendly, and sustainable digital heritage projects through the usage of web technologies.

As digital ecosystems expand, securing web-based systems becomes critical to safeguarding identity, trust, and resilience. This chapter presents a multi-layered cybersecurity architecture that integrates Zero Trust principles, SSL/TLS encryption, DevSecOps practices, and decentralized identity models. It emphasizes regulatory and ethical compliance, showcasing how secure architectures mitigate risks such as phishing, session hijacking, and data exfiltration without compromising scalability or user accessibility. Case studies from government and healthcare demonstrate real-world efficacy, with measurable improvements in breach prevention, trust metrics, and system performance. The chapter concludes with strategic recommendations and future research directions, advocating adaptive AI-driven security, privacy-preserving identity, and quantum-resilient frameworks. This comprehensive approach supports equitable and sustainable digital transformation in the web era.

Vivit Rosmayanti, Universitas Negeri Makassar, Indonesia

This chapter examines how online tools and platforms enhance collaborative English as a Foreign Language (EFL) learning, drawing on social-constructivist theories. It reviews platforms like Google Classroom, Edmodo, Padlet, Slack, Google Docs, Zoom, and Kahoot, alongside wikis and discussion boards, highlighting their roles in communication, resource sharing, and task-based collaboration. Practical applications include peer review, shared storytelling, online forums, and joint problem-solving. The chapter also addresses challenges such as digital access inequality and participation imbalances, offering strategies for inclusive virtual classrooms. It forecasts future advancements with AI, VR, and AR for adaptive, immersive learning, aiming to equip educators with insights for creating dynamic, globally connected EFL environments.

S. Rohith, Vellore Institute of Technology, Chennai, India
Benedict Johnson, Vellore Institute of Technology, Chennai, India
K. R. Rohinth, Vellore Institute of Technology, Chennai, India
D. Kavitha, Vellore Institute of Technology, Chennai, India

As the digital era continues to reshape how individuals approach health and fitness, there is an increasing need for platforms that offer a holistic and accessible fitness experience. IgniteFit is a comprehensive web-based solution designed to meet this demand by providing a unified platform for those seeking to start or advance their fitness journey. Unlike traditional fitness applications, IgniteFit brings together various fitness resources into one centralized website, ensuring users can find all the tools they need to succeed in their fitness goals. The platform focuses on simplicity, personalized user experience, and effective guidance, catering to diverse fitness levels and needs. By consolidating multiple fitness services, IgniteFit aims to eliminate

and visionary policies. The web of the future must be not only smart, but also fair, ethical, and humane.

Preface

Web technologies have evolved from a medium for publishing and connectivity into a foundational layer of modern economies and societies. Today, the Web is not only a channel for communication and service delivery, but also a platform for organisational redesign, data-driven decision-making, new business models, learning ecosystems, and digitally mediated identities. As organisations and institutions pursue digital transformation, the Web increasingly becomes the "operating environment" where strategy, processes, data, applications, trust, and human experience converge.

The purpose of this book—Impact of Web Technologies on Digital Transformation—is to provide a timely and multidisciplinary perspective on how Web technologies enable, shape, and sometimes complicate transformation efforts. Across nineteen chapters, the authors explore how Web-based platforms support organisational maturity and innovation, how cloud and analytics infrastructures unlock real-time value, how Web technologies reshape education and learning organisations, and how emerging societal challenges—such as surveillance, identity construction, and accessibility—must be addressed to ensure transformation is inclusive and ethically grounded.

A distinguishing feature of contemporary digital transformation is that it is inseparable from issues of cybersecurity, identity, trust, and resilience. As Web ecosystems become more distributed and interconnected, ensuring secure access, robust architectures, and intelligent detection and response capabilities becomes central to sustaining transformation at scale. Equally, the Web is shaping the future of work and learning through collaborative platforms, adaptive learning agents, and AI-supported knowledge management systems that redefine how organisations create, share, and apply knowledge.

The chapters in this volume combine conceptual frameworks with applied research and case-driven contributions. The book therefore serves multiple audiences: researchers seeking current advances and research directions; practitioners and decision-makers aiming to design resilient and scalable Web-enabled transformations; and educators and students exploring the broader implications of Web technologies for organisations and society. By bringing together perspectives from information systems, cybersecurity, education, analytics, cultural heritage, and digital society studies, this volume aims to stimulate both critical reflection and practical action.

We would like to thank all contributing authors for their work and collaboration, as well as the reviewers and editorial team for helping shape the coherence and quality of the volume. We hope this book supports ongoing research and practice, and helps readers navigate the opportunities and responsibilities created by the Web as a central driver of digital transformation.

CHAPTER OVERVIEW

Chapter 1: The Web as an Enabler of Digital Transformation examines the strategic role of web technologies in enabling scalable, agile, and interoperable systems that support innovation across sectors. It integrates conceptual insights with real-world case studies in government, retail, education, and healthcare to illustrate how the web empowers organizations to enhance customer experience, streamline operations, and enable rapid prototyping. The discussion covers core web technologies—cloud platforms, APIs, frontend frameworks, and backend architectures—and future trends including Web3 and Web 5.0. It also addresses challenges such as legacy integration, cybersecurity, and digital inequality, offering frameworks such as digital maturity models and agile-DevOps approaches for mitigation. By aligning web capabilities with organizational strategy, institutions can create resilient, user-centered ecosystems essential for long-term competitiveness in a connected world.

Chapter 2: Theoretical Frameworks and Practices in Web Technologies explores the convergence of theoretical frameworks and practical methodologies in modern web technologies. By integrating models such as the Technology Acceptance Model (TAM), Human-Centered Design (HCD), Systems Development Life Cycle (SDLC), Hypertext Theory, and Actor-Network Theory (ANT), the chapter demonstrates how theory informs and enhances practices like responsive web design, RESTful APIs, and Progressive Web Apps (PWA). Supported by real-world case studies from education, healthcare, governance, and digital business, it highlights how theoretical foundations drive innovation, user experience, and ethical system design. Future trends such as AI-augmented UX, ethical design integration, and semantic web advancements are also examined to illustrate ongoing transformations in web development.

Chapter 3: Digital Transformation Frameworks, Maturity, Sectoral Studies, Organizational Change and Leadership comprehensively examines its key enablers: strategic, organizational, and leadership dimensions. Its purpose is to synthesize current understanding, offering actionable insights. The chapter dissects prominent digital transformation frameworks, analyzing components and applicability. It then explores various digital maturity models, demonstrating utility in assessing capabilities and charting enhancement roadmaps. For practical insights, sectoral case studies (e.g., finance, manufacturing, healthcare) are presented, highlighting diverse strategies, challenges, and lessons. Furthermore, the chapter analyzes transformation's impact on organizational change, emphasizing effective change management to foster adoption and innovative cultures. Finally, it details leadership's pivotal role in steering digital transformation, outlining essential competencies for vision, empowerment, and uncertainty navigation. This chapter provides holistic insights for building resilient, digitally-enabled organizations.

Chapter 4: Innovation Strategy and Digital Maturity of Organizations explores how innovation strategies can align with digital maturity stages to drive sustainable transformation. Using frameworks like Three Horizons, Open Innovation, and Design Thinking, it outlines strategic approaches for innovation based on digital readiness. Case studies from Siemens, ING Bank, and Estonia illustrate how these strategies work in real-world settings. Common barriers such as legacy systems and cultural resistance are addressed alongside practical solutions. The chapter also highlights the role of innovation metrics in guiding progress. Ultimately, it positions innovation as both a result and a catalyst of digital maturity, enabling organizations to adapt and lead in an increasingly disruptive environment.

Chapter 5: E-Business and Web Accessibility emphasizes that the rapid growth of e-business has intensified digital exclusion for people with disabilities, making web accessibility a strategic and ethical necessity. Using WCAG 2.2 as a framework, it analyzes key barriers across disability types and how inclusive UI/UX, assistive technologies, and global regulations (ADA, AODA, EN 301 549) shape accessible e-commerce. The chapter argues that accessibility improves customer experience, SEO, conversion rates, and brand trust, especially within the "purple economy." It concludes that accessibility must be embedded into digital transformation to ensure inclusive, resilient, and future-ready e-business ecosystems.

Chapter 6: Web Technologies for Cultural Heritage: Digital Storytelling and Participatory Platforms discusses the uses of digital storytelling and participatory platforms to be engaged with communities, to share historical knowledge, and to promote cultural expression. It searches the tools and approaches of developing interactive and immersive environments that help users to become connected to heritage content. The chapter also talks of the benefits of participatory platform where users can come with their stories, pictures and share their local history and therefore preserving the culture is a collaborative and participatory process. Examples of good practice in the digital humanities are found at case studies in museums, archives and grassroots initiatives. The problem of digital access, content authenticity, and long term preservation is also touched upon. Finally, the strategies are proposed on how it is possible to develop culturally sensitive, user friendly, and sustainable digital heritage projects through the usage of web technologies.

Chapter 7: Web-Based Cybersecurity Architectures: Safeguarding Identity, Trust, and Resilience in the Digital Era presents a multi-layered cybersecurity architecture that integrates Zero Trust principles, SSL/TLS encryption, DevSecOps practices, and decentralized identity models. It emphasizes regulatory and ethical compliance, showcasing how secure architectures mitigate risks such as phishing, session hijacking, and data exfiltration without compromising scalability or user accessibility. Case studies from government and healthcare demonstrate real-world efficacy, with measurable improvements in breach prevention, trust metrics, and system performance. The chapter concludes with strategic recommendations and future research directions, advocating adaptive AI-driven security, privacy-preserving identity, and quantum-resilient frameworks. This comprehensive approach supports equitable and sustainable digital transformation in the web era.

Chapter 8: Web-Based Tools and Platforms for Collaborative English Language Teaching examines how online tools and platforms enhance collaborative English as a Foreign Language (EFL) learning, drawing on social-constructivist theories. It reviews platforms like Google Classroom, Edmodo, Padlet, Slack, Google Docs, Zoom, and Kahoot, alongside wikis and discussion boards, highlighting their roles in communication, resource sharing, and task-based collaboration. Practical applications include peer review, shared storytelling, online forums, and joint problem-solving. The chapter also addresses challenges such as digital access inequality and participation imbalances, offering strategies for inclusive virtual classrooms. It forecasts future advancements with AI, VR, and AR for adaptive, immersive learning, aiming to equip educators with insights for creating dynamic, globally connected EFL environments.

Chapter 9: IgniteFit A Comprehensive Web Application for Fitness Solutions explores the development of IgniteFIt, its unique features, and its potential impact in providing a seamless, all-encompassing fitness solution for individuals worldwide.

Chapter 10: Digital Surveillance and Identity Construction on Web-Based Platforms explores Web-based platforms have brought about fundamental changes in the ways individuals create identities, maintain social relationships, and represent themselves. The development of internet infrastructure and social networks since the 1990s has enabled individuals to establish an online presence without being tied to a physical location. In this context, the concept of "digital identity" refers to a multi-layered structure shaped by strategies individuals employ to reveal, conceal, and establish connections in the online environment. Social media posts, professional profiles, and online performances demonstrate that individuals develop multiple, fragmented, fluid identity strategies. Furthermore, virtual reality environments deepen identity experiences and presentation forms, making digital identity visible not only as screen-based but also interactive and spatial. However, the formation process of digital identity is based not only on individual preferences but also on the ways digital surveillance mechanisms monitor, direct, and categorize individuals' behaviors.

Chapter 11: The Future of Web Technologies and Their Implications for the Digital Society describes the development of web technology from Web 1.0 to Web 5.0 has revolutionized the way humans interact digitally, influencing identity, autonomy, employment, government, education, and culture. The modern web is now intelligent, contextual, and emotional, powered by AI, IoT, blockchain, and quantum computing. Digital identities are evolving towards decentralized models such as Self-Sovereign Identity (SSI), while governance is beginning to implement Decentralized Autonomous Organizations (DAOs). The world of work is changing through the gig economy and the token economy, although it comes with challenges in the form of digital divides and algorithmic manipulation. Education and cultural preservation are also digitized through adaptive learning and immersive technology. With this great opportunity also arises the issue of ethics, digital rights, and the need for inclusive and visionary policies. The web of the future must be not only smart, but also fair, ethical, and humane.

Introduction

Web technologies have moved far beyond their original role as a global publishing and hypertext medium. Today, the Web is the dominant environment through which organisations deliver services, interact with customers and citizens, coordinate value chains, manage knowledge, and increasingly, automate decision-making. As a result, digital transformation is rarely a standalone "IT modernisation" effort; it is a systemic change in how organisations operate and create value, and it is often executed through web-enabled platforms, cloud infrastructures, data-driven services, and continuously evolving digital ecosystems.

The aim of this book—*Impact of Web Technologies on Digital Transformation*—is to examine how web technologies enable, accelerate, and shape digital transformation across sectors and domains. Across its chapters, the volume adopts a multidisciplinary lens: it considers foundational perspectives on web technologies and transformation frameworks, applied architectures and analytics, the organisational conditions that support innovation and maturity, and the societal and ethical implications that emerge as the Web becomes embedded in everyday life. The contributions therefore speak to different audiences—from researchers investigating emerging architectures and intelligent systems, to practitioners designing transformation roadmaps, to educators exploring new learning environments, and to policy-minded readers concerned with trust, identity, and societal impact.

A central theme in the book is that digital transformation is inseparable from questions of *trust, identity, and resilience*. As organisations migrate to cloud-based services, integrate third-party platforms, and adopt AI-enabled web applications, the attack surface expands and security becomes a strategic prerequisite rather than a technical afterthought. This volume addresses these challenges through chapters that explore web-based cybersecurity architectures, deep learning approaches for identity management and threat detection, and the design of secure systems in environments such as smart campuses. These contributions highlight that sustainable transformation depends not only on innovation speed, but on the capacity to protect users, data, and services against evolving threats.

Another major theme is the role of the Web as an enabler of *data-intensive, real-time value creation*. Web-centric architectures now connect front-end interactions with back-end analytics, enabling organisations to respond rapidly to changes in demand, customer behaviour, and operational conditions. The book includes work on scalable cloud-based analytics for real-time retail insights and on e-business capabilities, while also acknowledging that transformation must be inclusive—hence the importance of web accessibility as both a compliance requirement and a strategic driver of broader digital participation.

The volume also explores how web technologies are reshaping *learning and capability development*, both in educational institutions and in learning-oriented organisations. Web platforms support collaboration, community, and adaptive learning at scale. Chapters on web-based tools for language teaching, intelligent digital learning systems, and AI-enabled agents for adaptive learning show how the Web supports new pedagogical models and more personalised learning pathways. Complementing these perspectives, the book addresses AI-supported knowledge management, emphasising that digital transformation requires not only new technologies, but also new ways to create, curate, and mobilise organisational knowledge.

In addition, the book presents concrete examples of web applications designed to improve quality of life and wellbeing, demonstrating how digital transformation reaches beyond productivity and efficiency. Contributions such as WellBeing360 and IgniteFit illustrate how web applications can support mental health and fitness, respectively, while also raising questions about data sensitivity, user trust, and ethical design—issues that connect back to the security and governance themes that run throughout the volume.

Finally, the book recognises that the Web is not a neutral technology: it has profound implications for society, identity, and power. Digital surveillance, identity construction on web-based platforms, and the broader future of web technologies are addressed explicitly, encouraging readers to consider the consequences of web-enabled transformation for privacy, autonomy, democratic participation, and social cohesion. In this sense, the volume aims not only to document progress and innovations, but also to contribute to a more reflective and responsible understanding of digital transformation.

Taken together, the chapters offer a coherent narrative: from foundational concepts and frameworks, to enabling infrastructures and applications, to trust and resilience, and ultimately to the societal implications and future trajectories of the Web. We hope this book helps readers make sense of a rapidly evolving landscape and provides insights that are both practically useful and intellectually stimulating. Digital transformation is ultimately about people and organisations—yet increasingly it is enacted through web technologies. Understanding their impact is therefore essential for anyone shaping the next phase of the digital society.

Chapter 1
The Web as an Enabler of Digital Transformation

Syifa Maulida Akmalia
https://orcid.org/0009-0008-1319-9043
Universitas Esa Unggul, Indonesia

Kodrat Mahatma
Universitas Teknologi Digital, Indonesia

Gusti Muhamad Sardana
https://orcid.org/0009-0001-4281-2432
Universitas Esa Unggul, Indonesia

ABSTRACT

In today's digital economy, the web has transcended its original role as a communication medium to become a foundational infrastructure for digital transformation. This chapter examines the strategic role of web technologies in enabling scalable, agile, and interoperable systems that support innovation across sectors. It integrates conceptual insights with real-world case studies in government, retail, education, and healthcare to illustrate how the web empowers organizations to enhance customer experience, streamline operations, and enable rapid prototyping. The discussion covers core web technologies—cloud platforms, APIs, frontend frameworks, and backend architectures—and future trends including Web3 and Web 5.0. It also addresses challenges such as legacy integration, cybersecurity, and digital inequality, offering frameworks such as digital maturity models and agile-DevOps approaches for mitigation. By aligning web capabilities with organizational strategy, institutions can create resilient, user-centered ecosystems essential for long-term competitiveness in a connected world.

DOI: 10.4018/979-8-3373-5167-4.ch001

1. INTRODUCTION

In the digital age, the World Wide Web has grown far beyond its initial role as a communication medium to become a core driver of digital transformation across sectors. From government agencies to multinational corporations, organizations are increasingly relying on web technology to adapt to rapid changes in consumer behavior, technological advancements, and global market dynamics. The web's openness and global accessibility make it an ideal foundation for modern digital infrastructure. This transformation is not only technical but also strategic, allowing organizations to redesign their service delivery and operational models.

One of the key drivers behind this transformation is the web's inherent ability to support agility and scalability. Modern web platforms, when combined with cloud technologies, allow businesses to deploy services rapidly and scale them with demand. For instance, e-commerce platforms such as Amazon or Tokopedia use web-based microservices and content delivery networks (CDNs) to serve millions of users concurrently. These capabilities provide flexibility that legacy systems typically lack, making the web a critical component in digital modernization efforts.

The interoperability of web technologies also plays a vital role in facilitating digital transformation. Through standardized protocols like HTTP, WebSockets, and RESTful APIs, different systems can communicate seamlessly, even if they are built on disparate architectures. This interoperability is particularly important in sectors like healthcare or finance, where multiple systems must share data securely and in real time (Fielding, 2000). By enabling system integration, web technologies reduce silos and allow organizations to build interconnected ecosystems that are more resilient and responsive.

Moreover, the web fosters innovation by lowering the barrier to entry for developers and startups. Open-source tools, developer-friendly APIs, and browser-based applications allow innovators to quickly prototype, test, and iterate on new digital services. Companies like Spotify and Netflix, for example, use web-based platforms not only for customer-facing interfaces but also for internal innovation through continuous integration and delivery (CI/CD) pipelines (Fowler & Foemmel, 2006). This culture of experimentation and rapid development would not be possible without the flexible foundation provided by web technologies.

In summary, the web serves as a powerful catalyst for digital transformation by combining technical strengths with strategic adaptability. Its scalability, interoperability, and ability to foster innovation make it indispensable for redesigning workflows, enhancing user experience, and enabling data-driven decision-making. As organizations continue to navigate the complexities of the digital age, understanding and leveraging the full potential of web technologies becomes not just an advantage, but a necessity for sustainable growth and relevance.

2. UNDERSTANDING THE ROLE OF THE WEB IN TRANSFORMATION

In the landscape of digital transformation, the web acts as the primary enabler of system modernization and service innovation. It provides a ubiquitous, platform-agnostic foundation upon which other advanced technologies—such as cloud computing, artificial intelligence (AI), big data, and the Internet of Things (IoT)—can converge and interoperate. Unlike traditional IT infrastructures that are often siloed and rigid, web-based systems are inherently designed for interconnectivity, responsiveness, and adaptability (Brous et al., 2020).

Organizations are increasingly leveraging the web to shift from static, monolithic systems to dynamic and decentralized ecosystems. For instance, traditional customer relationship management (CRM) software has evolved into cloud-native web platforms like Salesforce, which integrates AI-powered analytics, third-party plugins via APIs, and mobile accessibility in real-time. This transition enables businesses to enhance operational agility, personalize customer experiences, and respond faster to market demands (Gartner, 2022).

2.1 Key Capabilities of Web-Based Transformation

To better understand the role of the web, we can categorize its capabilities into four main areas. Table 1 shows the Web as a Central Hub for Digital Convergence.

Table 1. The web as a central hub for digital convergence

Capability	Description	Example Technologies	Transformation Impact
Scalability	Ability to handle growing workloads without major infrastructure changes	Auto-scaling via AWS, Azure, Google Cloud	Supports millions of users during traffic spikes
Accessibility	Global access through web browsers and cloud platforms	Web apps, PWA, cloud-hosted dashboards	Enables remote work, hybrid learning, global service reach
Real-Time Communication	Facilitates immediate data exchange and responsiveness	WebSockets, REST APIs, MQTT, GraphQL	Supports live chats, notifications, IoT streaming
Agility	Promotes rapid development and iterative delivery of services	DevOps, CI/CD, containerization (Docker, K8s)	Faster innovation cycles, lower time-to-market

Below is a conceptual diagram that illustrates how the web integrates various digital technologies into a single transformation-enabling hub. Figure 1 shows The

Web as an Integrative Layer for Digital Transformation. Figure 1 shows The Web as an Integrative Layer for Digital Transformation.

Figure 1. The web as an integrative layer for digital transformation

In this model, the web acts as a unifying interface, enabling seamless interaction between users, data systems, and intelligent applications. Each spoke represents a major technology stack (AI, IoT, Cloud, Big Data), all accessible and orchestrated via web technologies.

2.2 STRATEGIC VALUE OF WEB-ENABLED CAPABILITIES

The strategic value of web technologies lies in their ability to foster organizational resilience, agility, and innovation in the face of digital disruption. As industries face growing uncertainty from globalization, shifting consumer behavior, and technological acceleration, web-enabled platforms offer a foundation for rapid adaptation and continuous reinvention. By integrating key capabilities—such as scalability, real-time access, and API-based interoperability—organizations can not only improve performance, but also unlock new digital value propositions (Porter & Heppelmann, 2014).

2.3 Educational Transformation Through Web Platforms

In the education sector, the COVID-19 pandemic served as a global catalyst for the mass adoption of web-based learning platforms. Institutions quickly transitioned to Learning Management Systems (LMS) like Moodle, Google Classroom, and Canvas, which offer cloud-hosted content delivery, student engagement tools, and performance tracking. These systems support both synchronous (live lectures) and asynchronous (recorded content) modalities, enabling hybrid and remote learning models that are now considered standard practice. The flexibility and scalability of web platforms allow institutions to serve students across geographies, promoting lifelong learning and inclusivity.

2.4 Retail Agility via Headless Commerce

In the retail industry, the shift to headless commerce architectures exemplifies the transformative power of the web. Headless commerce separates the frontend user interface from backend commerce logic using APIs, allowing retailers to deliver consistent omnichannel experiences across web, mobile, smart devices, and even voice assistants. This modularity improves time-to-market for new features and personalizations. For instance, brands like Nike and Sephora leverage React- or Vue.js-based frontends while integrating backends via GraphQL APIs, resulting in faster load times, dynamic pricing, and localized content delivery (Forrester, 2022).

2.5 Real-Time Manufacturing Optimization

In manufacturing, web technologies enable real-time visibility into operations through IoT dashboards and analytics platforms. Devices on the production floor transmit telemetry data (e.g., temperature, vibration, uptime) via web-based protocols such as MQTT and WebSockets. This data is then visualized through responsive dashboards that can be accessed on-site or remotely via any browser. As a result, factory managers can monitor Key Performance Indicators (KPIs), predict failures through machine learning, and optimize workflow—minimizing downtime and improving overall equipment effectiveness (OEE) (Lee et al., 2015). Industry 4.0 initiatives heavily rely on these web-based infrastructures to realize smart factory visions.

Table 2 shows Strategic Benefits of Web Capabilities Across Sectors.

Table 2. Strategic benefits of web capabilities across sectors

Sector	Web-Based Solution	Strategic Benefit	Technology Stack
Education	Google Classroom, Moodle	Hybrid learning, global access, student engagement	Cloud, WebRTC, REST APIs
Retail	Headless commerce (e.g., React frontend + APIs)	Omnichannel experience, personalization, rapid deployment	GraphQL, CDN, Microservices
Manufacturing	IoT dashboards via web protocols	Real-time monitoring, predictive maintenance, reduced downtime	MQTT, WebSockets, Node.js, Edge computing

2.6 Cross-Sector Scalability and Innovation Enablement

Beyond specific sectors, the strategic value of web platforms lies in their horizontal applicability—they empower startups and enterprises alike to build scalable solutions without heavy upfront infrastructure costs. For example, a fintech startup can launch a global payment solution using web APIs and serverless computing, while a hospital can use telemedicine platforms to deliver consultations through secure, HIPAA-compliant web portals. In each case, the web provides a flexible launchpad for experimentation, enabling organizations to innovate faster and at lower risk.

3. CORE WEB TECHNOLOGIES ENABLING TRANSFORMATION

3.1 Cloud-Based Web Platforms

The adoption of cloud computing has revolutionized how organizations deploy and manage web applications. Cloud platforms such as Amazon Web Services (AWS), Microsoft Azure, and Google Cloud Platform (GCP) offer elastic infrastructure, enabling businesses to scale applications automatically in response to fluctuating demand. Instead of maintaining costly on-premises servers, organizations can leverage pay-as-you-go models, reducing capital expenditure and enhancing business agility (Armbrust et al., 2010).

Additionally, cloud-native architectures promote resilience and fault tolerance through automated failover, backup systems, and global content delivery networks (CDNs). For example, Netflix uses AWS to deliver content globally, scaling dynamically to serve millions of users concurrently. Educational platforms like Coursera and Udemy also benefit from cloud elasticity during high-demand periods like enrollment season or course launches.

3.2 Web APIs and Integration

Application Programming Interfaces (APIs) are the glue that binds modern web ecosystems together. They facilitate communication between different applications, systems, and services by exposing data and functionality in a structured, reusable format. Two primary types dominate current web integration strategies:

- RESTful APIs: Follow stateless principles using HTTP protocols. Widely used in web and mobile apps.
- GraphQL: A more flexible query language for APIs that allows clients to request only the data they need, improving performance and efficiency (Facebook, 2015).

APIs enable modular system design, allowing organizations to integrate third-party services (like payment gateways or authentication systems) seamlessly. For instance, Shopify merchants can connect inventory, shipping, and analytics tools using a robust set of APIs, enabling end-to-end business automation.

3.2 Web APIs and Integration

Frontend development has evolved significantly with the rise of modern JavaScript frameworks such as React, Vue.js, and Angular. These frameworks enable developers to create responsive, dynamic, and modular single-page applications (SPAs) that can render quickly and interact seamlessly across devices. For example,Angular, maintained by Google, is often used in enterprise-grade applications with complex business logic.

These frameworks support component-based architecture, promoting reusability, maintainability, and faster time-to-market for digital products. Combined with tools like Tailwind CSS or Webpack, they provide a complete ecosystem for frontend innovation.

3.3 Frontend Innovations

Frontend development has evolved significantly with the rise of modern JavaScript frameworks such as React, Vue.js, and Angular. These frameworks enable developers to create responsive, dynamic, and modular single-page applications (SPAs) that can render quickly and interact seamlessly across devices. For example, React, developed by Meta, powers user interfaces for Facebook, Instagram, and Airbnb, Vue.js.

These frameworks support component-based architecture, promoting reusability, maintainability, and faster time-to-market for digital products. Combined with tools like Tailwind CSS or Webpack, they provide a complete ecosystem for frontend innovation.

3.4 Backend and Middleware

The backend layer has also undergone radical transformation with the rise of serverless computing, microservices architecture, and middleware platforms like Node.js, Express, and Fastify. Node.js, a JavaScript runtime, enables high-performance, event-driven server environments—ideal for real-time applications like chat systems or financial dashboards.

This architectural flexibility allows backend systems to be more agile, scalable, and fault-tolerant, supporting continuous delivery and integration pipelines essential to digital transformation (Newman, 2015). Table 3 shows Key Web Technologies and Their Transformation Impact.

Table 3. Key web technologies and their transformation impact

Category	Technology Examples	Key Benefits	Use Case Example
Cloud Platforms	AWS, Azure, GCP	Scalability, resilience, cost-efficiency	Netflix, Coursera
Web APIs & Integration	REST, GraphQL, OAuth2	Interoperability, data exchange, modularity	Shopify, Stripe
Frontend Innovations	React, Vue, Angular	Responsive UI, component reuse, cross-device access	Facebook, Airbnb, Google Docs
Backend & Middleware	Node.js, Express, Serverless, Microservices	Agility, performance, ease of maintenance	Uber, Spotify, Slack

4. STRATEGIC BENEFITS OF WEB-ENABLED TRANSFORMATION

4.1 Customer-Centricity

In the digital age, customer expectations have dramatically shifted toward instant, consistent, and personalized experiences across multiple touchpoints. Web platforms play a pivotal role in addressing these expectations by enabling omnichannel service delivery—allowing users to engage with brands seamlessly via desktop browsers, mobile apps, voice assistants, smart TVs, and even wearable devices. This shift marks a departure from single-channel models, placing the customer at the center of digital strategies and designing interactions around their preferences and behaviors (Lemon & Verhoef, 2016).

Omnichannel capabilities are empowered by responsive web design, progressive web apps (PWAs), and real-time API integrations. For example, companies like Starbucks and Nike deliver consistent user experiences whether customers interact via their website, mobile app, or in-store kiosks. By centralizing customer data and preferences across platforms, these brands create frictionless journeys that reduce abandonment rates and increase engagement. The convergence of frontend technologies like React with backend microservices and customer data platforms (CDPs) enables this seamless interaction (Gartner, 2022).

A critical component of web-enabled customer-centricity is personalization. Modern web architectures allow for real-time personalization based on user location, behavior, and previous interactions. E-commerce platforms like Amazon or streaming services like Netflix exemplify this by dynamically adjusting product recommendations or content suggestions for each user. This is often powered by AI algorithms integrated with web platforms, which use data collected via web interactions to tailor user experiences on the fly (Pine & Gilmore, 2011).

Moreover, accessibility and inclusivity are enhanced through web technologies that support voice-enabled browsing, screen readers, multilingual content, and adaptive interfaces. Voice-enabled customer service, such as voice commerce through Alexa or Google Assistant, is growing in popularity and expanding access for users with different needs or limitations. This inclusivity strengthens customer trust, brand loyalty, and market reach, especially in diverse and globalized markets.

Ultimately, customer-centricity supported by web platforms is more than a convenience—it is a strategic differentiator. Businesses that can consistently deliver value at every customer touchpoint are more likely to outperform their competitors in customer retention, lifetime value, and brand equity. The web, by enabling personalized, cross-platform, and accessible engagement, acts as a catalyst for this transformation, turning user experience into a key source of competitive advantage.

4.2 Operational Efficiency

Operational efficiency is a cornerstone of successful digital transformation, and web technologies offer a robust foundation for achieving it. At its core, operational efficiency involves maximizing output while minimizing resource use—be it time, cost, or labor. Web-enabled platforms, when integrated with automation tools and real-time analytics, allow organizations to digitize repetitive processes, reduce human error, and accelerate decision-making. These capabilities significantly improve the speed, consistency, and accuracy of internal operations.

Automation through web-based platforms replaces manual workflows with rule-based or AI-driven processes. For instance, in HR departments, tasks such as resume screening, interview scheduling, and onboarding can now be handled by integrated web applications like Workday or BambooHR, which utilize cloud infrastructure and web APIs to sync across departments. In supply chain management, tools like SAP Ariba automate procurement workflows—reducing cycle times and increasing compliance. This not only saves operational costs but also frees up human resources for higher-value strategic work (McKinsey & Company, 2021).

Real-time analytics, another key capability of web platforms, enhances visibility into operational performance. Dashboards built with web tools such as Google Data Studio, Tableau, or Power BI, connect to data streams from multiple sources—ERP systems, CRM platforms, IoT sensors, and customer interactions—providing stakeholders with up-to-the-minute insights. For example, a logistics company can monitor delivery delays live and reroute shipments instantly using analytics powered by web dashboards and APIs, resulting in faster resolution times and higher customer satisfaction.

Moreover, web-based systems foster cross-functional collaboration and process transparency. Cloud-based platforms like Asana, Trello, and Slack offer intuitive interfaces for task tracking, project updates, and internal communication—all accessible via browsers or mobile apps. These tools break down silos between departments, align teams around shared goals, and ensure accountability across workflows. They also support remote or hybrid work environments, a critical factor in maintaining efficiency in post-pandemic operational models (Harvard Business Review, 2021).

In conclusion, by integrating automation and real-time analytics through web platforms, organizations can achieve leaner, faster, and more agile operations. Whether it's managing inventory, processing payroll, or analyzing customer behavior, the web serves as the backbone for continuous improvement and intelligent decision-making. As competition intensifies and markets evolve, operational efficiency—driven by web-enabled technologies—becomes not just a goal, but a necessity for sustaining competitive advantage.

4.3 Innovation Enablement

Innovation is a key differentiator in the digital economy, and web technologies play a central role in enabling organizations to innovate faster, cheaper, and with lower risk. Traditional software development cycles—often slow, costly, and rigid—are being replaced by agile, iterative processes that thrive in web-based environments. The web provides a dynamic sandbox where new ideas, services, and features can be rapidly prototyped, tested, and launched to market. This agility drastically reduces time-to-market, a critical metric in competitive industries like fintech, healthtech, and e-commerce.

Modern web development environments, such as cloud IDEs (Integrated Development Environments) like GitHub Codespaces or Replit, and low-code/no-code platforms such as Webflow or Bubble, democratize innovation by allowing both developers and non-developers to experiment. These platforms eliminate the need for complex local setups and make it possible to deploy prototypes in minutes. For instance, startups can launch MVPs (Minimum Viable Products) using Webflow with Stripe integration and gather early feedback before investing in full-scale development. This iterative, feedback-driven approach aligns with lean startup principles and encourages rapid learning (Ries, 2011).

Beyond just prototyping, web technologies support continuous deployment and integration (CI/CD), allowing organizations to deliver updates and new features frequently without interrupting service. This is essential in industries like SaaS, where customer expectations evolve rapidly and product development must be fluid. Platforms like GitLab, Netlify, and Vercel offer developers the ability to push changes live to staging or production environments with a single command. Companies like Shopify and Zoom exemplify this model by releasing dozens of micro-updates per week, improving user experience while staying ahead of competitors.

Another key enabler of innovation is the use of API-first design and open web standards, which allow businesses to rapidly integrate third-party services or scale new solutions. For example, payment functionality can be quickly added using Stripe's API, or customer support features can be integrated using Twilio or Intercom. These modular tools act as building blocks for innovation, reducing the time and technical debt associated with building everything in-house.

In essence, web technologies transform innovation from a siloed, high-risk endeavor into a scalable, repeatable process embedded within daily operations. They empower organizations to explore ideas, validate assumptions, and launch new offerings quickly—all while remaining responsive to user feedback and market trends. As a result, companies that embrace web-driven innovation are better positioned to disrupt markets, respond to change, and sustain long-term growth.

4.4 Data-Driven Decision Making

In the digital transformation era, organizations that can effectively harness data hold a significant competitive advantage. Web technologies have democratized access to real-time data and analytics tools, enabling decision-makers to move beyond intuition and base their strategies on quantifiable evidence and predictive insight. Through the integration of web-based dashboards, machine learning models, and big data processing, businesses can not only visualize past performance, but also forecast future outcomes and optimize services accordingly.

Modern web platforms provide flexible, browser-accessible dashboards built with tools like Power BI, Google Data Studio, Tableau, or Looker, which can pull live data from various sources including CRMs, ERPs, IoT devices, and social media feeds via APIs. These visualizations help executives monitor key performance indicators (KPIs) in real time—such as sales trends, website traffic, customer satisfaction scores, or inventory turnover. For instance, Amazon Web Services (AWS) provides real-time cloud metrics through its CloudWatch dashboard, allowing infrastructure teams to detect and respond to anomalies instantly.

One powerful benefit of data-driven web platforms is the ability to forecast demand and behavior. By using web-based predictive analytics, retailers can estimate future inventory needs, financial institutions can detect fraud, and healthcare systems can anticipate patient surges. For example, Netflix leverages data analytics through web interfaces to personalize recommendations and predict viewing trends, helping the company make informed content investment decisions (Davenport & Bean, 2018). These decisions are not based on guesswork but are the product of continuous, algorithmically guided insight.

Additionally, web-based analytics enable service optimization by identifying process bottlenecks and customer pain points. For instance, ride-sharing companies like Uber use internal dashboards to track supply-demand mismatches in specific areas and adjust driver deployment accordingly. Similarly, government agencies use open-data dashboards to visualize public service usage, helping improve resource allocation in areas such as transportation, waste management, or emergency response. These examples highlight how web-accessible data systems empower not just private enterprises but also public sector institutions to become more efficient and transparent.

In summary, web technologies facilitate data-driven cultures by making analytics accessible, interactive, and actionable. Integrated dashboards and intelligent algorithms help organizations respond quickly to changes, test hypotheses, and make smarter decisions based on evidence. As businesses grow in complexity and data volumes surge, leveraging web-based decision tools becomes critical to sustaining relevance, efficiency, and innovation in a data-centric world.

5. CASE STUDIES

5.1 E-Government

The application of web technologies in the public sector—commonly referred to as e-government—has revolutionized the way governments deliver services, interact with citizens, and manage public resources. By moving critical services online such as tax filing, licensing, and citizen feedback, governments aim to increase transparency, reduce bureaucracy, and improve efficiency. Web platforms have become key tools to streamline administrative processes, ensure service accessibility, and promote inclusive governance (UN E-Government Survey, 2022).

One of the most prominent examples of successful e-government implementation is Estonia's digital government, where over 99% of public services—from voting to healthcare records—are accessible online through a secure web-based ID system known as e-Residency. Estonians can file taxes in under five minutes, register a business in 18 minutes, and access real-time healthcare data, all via a national web portal. This not only reduces operational costs but also boosts citizen satisfaction and participation (Kalvet, 2012). Estonia's success demonstrates how a strong digital infrastructure, supported by interoperable APIs and secure web platforms, can transform the public sector.

In developing economies, e-government systems are also being leveraged to close the digital divide and reduce corruption. For example, India's Digital India initiative promotes the use of web portals for services like Aadhaar e-KYC, passport applications, land records, and mobile governance. Through platforms like DigiLocker, citizens can store and access official documents digitally, minimizing the need for paper-based verification. These services not only reduce physical queues and inefficiencies but also create digital trails that foster accountability.

Moreover, e-government platforms encourage participatory governance by incorporating features such as online surveys, public feedback systems, and open data dashboards. Tools like UK's GOV.UK and New Zealand's SmartStart not only provide streamlined access to services but also solicit public input on proposed regulations or development plans. Web technologies like content management systems (CMS), RESTful APIs, and cloud-hosted databases support these platforms, making government services more adaptive, transparent, and user-centered (OECD, 2020).

In conclusion, the use of web technologies in e-government initiatives empowers institutions to become more agile, transparent, and citizen-focused. By digitizing service delivery, governments enhance access, reduce costs, and increase operational integrity. As global expectations for responsive and efficient governance continue to rise, web-enabled public administration stands as a crucial pillar of democratic resilience and digital maturity.

5.2 Smart Retail

The retail industry has undergone a massive digital transformation, with web technologies at the heart of what is now known as smart retail. Web platforms serve as the digital foundation that enables retailers to build interactive storefronts, deliver personalized shopping experiences, and manage operations through real-time analytics. By combining cloud computing, APIs, artificial intelligence (AI), and responsive web design, smart retail strategies elevate both customer satisfaction and operational efficiency.

At the frontend, digital storefronts powered by web frameworks like React, Vue.js, or Next.js provide a seamless and engaging user interface across devices. These platforms support fast loading times, personalized content, and dynamic pricing. For example, global fashion brand Zara uses a progressive web app (PWA) for its e-commerce site, allowing customers to shop even in low-connectivity environments with app-like experiences on the web. The integration of secure web-based checkout systems and multi-language support further enhances reach and accessibility for global audiences.

Personalized recommendations are a hallmark of smart retail, powered by AI algorithms embedded in web-based platforms. Retailers like Amazon, Sephora, and Tokopedia utilize web APIs to analyze browsing behavior, purchase history, and user demographics in real time. This data is then used to display relevant products, targeted promotions, and cross-selling opportunities. Tools like Dynamic Yield, Algolia, and Segment are commonly integrated into retail websites to provide machine learning-based personalization through API-driven interfaces (Grewal et al., 2020).

On the backend, real-time inventory management is critical to reducing stockouts, overstocking, and delays in order fulfillment. Web-enabled platforms like Shopify, Magento, and BigCommerce allow retailers to sync inventory across warehouses and stores using real-time APIs and dashboards. For instance, Walmart uses web-connected systems to track demand spikes and reroute inventory through its fulfillment network. These systems are often integrated with IoT sensors and predictive analytics engines to further automate replenishment and supply chain decisions.

In summary, smart retail exemplifies how web technologies act as the nervous system of modern commerce. By integrating user interfaces, recommendation engines, and operational analytics into a cohesive digital ecosystem, retailers can deliver personalized, agile, and data-driven experiences at scale. As customer expectations continue to evolve, businesses that fully embrace web-enabled smart retail will be better equipped to adapt, compete, and thrive in the dynamic global marketplace.

5.3 Education Technology

The digital transformation of the education sector has been accelerated by the development and adoption of web-based education technologies, especially learning management systems (LMS). These platforms enable institutions to deliver hybrid (blended) and fully remote learning models with scalable infrastructure, user-friendly interfaces, and integrated communication tools. As education becomes more global and flexible, web technologies are fundamental in ensuring access, engagement, and efficiency across diverse learner demographics (Means et al., 2014).

Prominent examples of web-based LMS platforms include Moodle, Google Classroom, Canvas, Blackboard, and Edmodo. These systems support various functions such as course content delivery, online assessments, discussion forums, attendance tracking, and real-time feedback. Moodle, for instance, is an open-source platform used by thousands of universities worldwide due to its modularity and multilingual capabilities. Google Classroom, on the other hand, integrates seamlessly with Google Workspace, making it ideal for K–12 institutions with limited IT resources (Almpanis, 2015).

These LMS platforms not only support traditional academic delivery but also facilitate interactive and personalized learning through embedded web tools. Video conferencing (Zoom, Google Meet), quiz engines (Kahoot, Quizizz), and collaboration tools (Padlet, Jamboard) enhance student engagement and foster active learning environments. Furthermore, LMS systems support analytics dashboards that track student participation, progress, and learning outcomes in real time, allowing educators to intervene early and offer targeted support (Ifenthaler & Yau, 2020).

The adaptability of web-based education technologies also promotes educational inclusivity. Web platforms allow students in remote or underserved areas to access high-quality learning materials via mobile devices or low-bandwidth versions of LMS platforms. Initiatives like UNESCO's Global Education Coalition have partnered with ed-tech providers to deliver online education in crisis contexts such as COVID-19 and refugee camps. In this way, the web serves as a powerful equalizer, breaking down geographical and socioeconomic barriers to learning (UNESCO, 2021). Table 4 shows Deferents Fitur LMS Berbasis Web.

Table 4. Deferents Fitur LMS Berbasis web

Platform	Type	Key Strengths	Target Users	Main Weaknesses
Moodle	Open Source	Highly customizable, large community	Universities, large institutions	Requires self-hosting and technical setup
Google Classroom	SaaS (Cloud)	Google Drive integration, simple interface	K–12 schools, SMEs	Limited flexibility for advanced features
Canvas	Cloud / On-Premise	Modern UI, strong analytics tools	Universities	Relatively expensive subscription
Blackboard	Enterprise	Comprehensive features, globally adopted	Large universities	Outdated UI, steep learning curve
Edmodo	Freemium	Soci focus, user-friendly interface	K–12, online courses	Lacks support for advanced features

5.4 Healthcare Platforms

The integration of web technologies in healthcare has redefined how medical services are delivered, particularly through the rise of telemedicine platforms. These platforms leverage the internet and web-based systems to facilitate virtual consultations, remote diagnostics, electronic prescriptions, and real-time patient monitoring. This transformation has not only enhanced accessibility to care—especially in rural or underserved areas—but also improved the efficiency, accuracy, and scalability of health systems (Keesara et al., 2020).

Telemedicine systems such as Teladoc Health, Halodoc, Alodokter, and Amwell enable patients to connect with licensed healthcare professionals via secure web portals or mobile apps. Users can schedule video consultations, upload medical records, receive prescriptions digitally, and access follow-up care—all from their browser or device. For instance, Halodoc, an Indonesian web-based healthcare platform, integrates teleconsultation with pharmacy delivery and lab testing, demonstrating how web ecosystems can support end-to-end healthcare experiences.

Web-based Electronic Health Records (EHRs) systems such as Epic, Cerner, and Kareo further support clinical workflows by centralizing patient data and making it accessible to doctors, nurses, and specialists in real time. These platforms often include APIs for interoperability, allowing seamless data exchange between hospitals, laboratories, pharmacies, and insurance providers. This reduces duplication of diagnostics, enhances decision-making, and facilitates personalized treatment planning (Shickel et al., 2018).

In addition, remote patient monitoring (RPM) is increasingly reliant on web technologies. Devices like smartwatches, glucometers, or heart rate monitors transmit health metrics via the web to centralized dashboards, where clinicians can monitor patient vitals and intervene proactively. During the COVID-19 pandemic, RPM systems helped reduce hospital overcrowding by enabling outpatient care for chronic conditions. For example, Babylon Health combines AI-driven chatbots with web-based telehealth to triage symptoms and guide patients toward appropriate care paths.

Table 5 shows Comparison of Web-Based Health Platforms

Table 5. Comparison of web-based health platforms

Platform	Layanan Utama	Cakupan Pasien	Teknologi Web yang Digunakan	Kelebihan
Halodoc	Konsultasi online, pengantaran obat	Indonesia	Web app, REST API, cloud hosting	Layanan end-to-end, integrasi lab & apotek
Teladoc	Telekonsultasi, EHR integrasi	Global	WebRTC, cloud, API integrations	Multi-specialty, skala enterprise
Alodokter	Chat medis, asuransi, konten edukasi	Indonesia	Web CMS, API, live chat systems	Edukasi berbasis web, integrasi asuransi
Babylon Health	AI triage, monitoring, e-prescription	UK, global	AI, web dashboards, mobile APIs	Chatbot AI, efisiensi triase

Figure 2 shows Ilustrasi dashboard monitoring pasien real-time.

Figure 2. Ilustrasi dashboard monitoring pasien real-time

6. CHALLENGES AND MITIGATION

6.1 Legacy System Integration

One of the most persistent challenges in digital transformation is integrating legacy systems—outdated software or hardware still critical to operations—with modern web-based infrastructures. Many organizations, especially in sectors like banking, healthcare, and government, still rely on monolithic mainframes, COBOL-based programs, or on-premise systems that were never designed for the internet era. These systems often lack support for RESTful APIs, cloud connectivity, and security protocols, posing a barrier to real-time data access and interoperability (Benson & Standing, 2018).

To address these incompatibilities, several mitigation strategies have emerged. The first is the use of API wrappers, where a thin web-service layer is built around the legacy system to expose its data or functionality via modern API protocols. This allows newer frontend applications or microservices to communicate with the old systems without requiring deep changes. For example, banks often use Java or .NET wrappers to connect COBOL-based core banking software to modern mobile banking apps. A second approach is implementing data gateways that sync or replicate data from legacy systems into cloud databases, which can then be used by web applications.

Another long-term strategy is gradual modernization, where legacy systems are broken down and replaced incrementally through microservices architecture or hybrid cloud models. Instead of performing a full system replacement—which is risky and expensive—organizations can replatform parts of their system, such as the customer-facing modules, while maintaining mission-critical legacy cores temporarily. Tools like Strangler Fig Pattern guide this process by allowing new functionalities to gradually "strangle" the legacy code until full transition is achieved.

Table 6 shows Strategi Integrasi Sistem Legacy

Table 6. Strategi Integrasi Sistem legacy

Strategi	Kelebihan	Kekurangan	Contoh Penggunaan
API Wrapping	Cepat diterapkan, tidak ubah core	Terbatas oleh arsitektur lama	Perbankan, Sistem ERP lama
Data Gateway	Data real-time bisa diakses dari cloud	Sinkronisasi bisa lambat dan tidak utuh	E-Commerce, Retail Inventory
Gradual Modernization	Minim risiko, fleksibel	Membutuhkan waktu dan koordinasi kompleks	Rumah Sakit, Sistem Pemerintahan
Full Replacement	Sistem baru bisa disesuaikan sepenuhnya	Biaya dan risiko sangat tinggi	Jarang, kecuali sistem kecil

Figure 3 shows the Visualisasi Diagram arsitektur integrasi: Legacy System → API Wrapper → Web Platform.

Figure 3. Visualisasi Diagram arsitektur integrasi

Integrating legacy systems also involves organizational and cultural challenges. IT teams may resist changes due to fear of breaking existing functionality, and skills required for modernization (e.g., microservices, cloud engineering) may not be readily available. As such, change management, staff retraining, and collaboration between legacy experts and modern developers are critical. Organizations must also invest in testing environments to simulate integration outcomes before full deployment.

6.2 Security and Privacy

As organizations increasingly rely on web technologies to power digital transformation, concerns about security and privacy become more critical. The web's openness and global connectivity—while enabling agility and innovation—also expand the attack surface for cyber threats. These threats range from phishing and cross-site scripting (XSS) to data breaches, ransomware, and denial-of-service (DDoS) attacks. Especially in sectors like healthcare, finance, and education where sensitive data is exchanged, maintaining robust security and compliance is non-negotiable (Zhou et al., 2018).

To mitigate these risks, modern web systems implement a range of security protocols. Secure web communication is ensured through HTTPS (TLS encryption), which protects data in transit between client and server. User identity and session protection are handled via OAuth2 (authorization delegation) and JWT (JSON Web Token) for stateless authentication. These protocols help protect user accounts and APIs from unauthorized access, token forgery, and session hijacking. For instance, platforms like Google, Facebook, and Microsoft Azure all rely on OAuth2 + JWT for managing secure API access across apps and services.

Beyond technical controls, compliance with international data protection laws is equally crucial. In the European Union, the General Data Protection Regulation (GDPR) mandates strict requirements for data consent, retention, and breach notification. Similarly, in the United States, HIPAA governs how patient health information is handled and shared digitally. Failing to comply with such regulations not only results in hefty fines but also damages organizational reputation and user trust. Global platforms like Salesforce Health Cloud and Zoom for Healthcare are examples of services architected with these frameworks in mind. Table 7 shows the Comparison of Common Web Security Technologies

Table 7. Comparison of common web security technologies

Technology/ Protocol	Main Functions	Pros	Usage Example
HTTPS (TLS)	Enkripsi koneksi antara server dan client	Mudah diimplementasi, standar global	Semua platform web modern
OAuth2	Delegasi otorisasi antar aplikasi	Aman untuk SSO dan integrasi pihak ke-3	Google, Facebook login
JWT	Token autentikasi untuk akses API	Stateless, ringan, cocok untuk SPA	REST API, mobile backend
GDPR	Regulasi perlindungan data di Eropa	Kontrol pengguna, transparansi data	Shopify, WordPress Eropa
HIPAA	Perlindungan data medis di AS	Wajib untuk layanan kesehatan digital	Teladoc, Zoom for Healthcare

Figure 4 shows OAuth2 + JWT flowchart for web application authentication.

Figure 4. OAuth2 + JWT flowchart for web application authentication

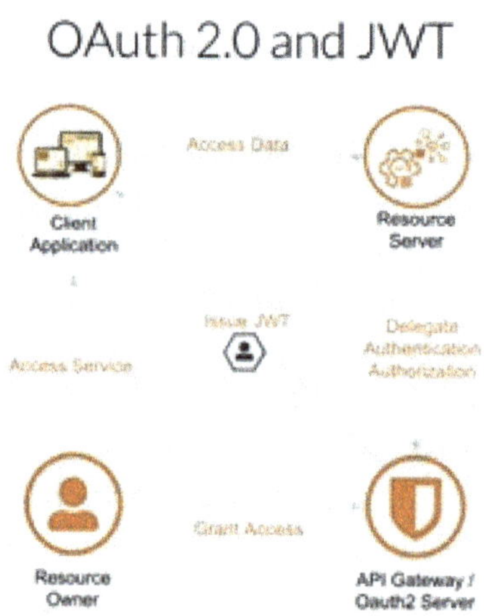

Cybersecurity in the web era also demands a shift toward proactive, layered defenses. Concepts such as Zero Trust Architecture (ZTA), multi-factor authentication (MFA), and security-by-design are gaining traction. Developers now embed security controls directly into web app code (DevSecOps), and organizations use web application firewalls (WAFs), intrusion detection systems (IDS), and runtime protection to defend against emerging threats. Companies like Cloudflare, Okta, and Auth0 provide integrated web security services that are essential for modern infrastructure.

6.3 Digital Divide

One of the most critical challenges in leveraging the web for digital transformation is the digital divide—the gap between those who have access to digital technologies and those who do not. While web platforms offer unprecedented opportunities for innovation, education, healthcare, and commerce, millions of people worldwide remain excluded due to lack of internet access, digital literacy, language barriers, or appropriate devices. Addressing this divide is not only a matter of social justice but a strategic imperative to ensure inclusive and sustainable digital development (van Dijk, 2020).

To overcome these disparities, web transformation efforts must be guided by inclusive design principles. This involves creating websites and applications that are accessible to users with disabilities, older adults, and people using assistive technologies. Frameworks like the Web Content Accessibility Guidelines (WCAG) provide technical standards for creating content that can be navigated by screen readers, voice commands, or keyboard-only users. For example, platforms like BBC and Microsoft have adopted accessibility-first design across their web services, ensuring equal usability for all.

Language diversity is another essential factor. Many global web services still default to English or a limited set of languages, excluding users from non-dominant linguistic backgrounds. Multilingual content, dynamic translation tools (e.g., Google Translate APIs), and localized user interfaces can help bridge this gap. Government portals in India, for instance, provide web services in more than 20 regional languages, while UNESCO recommends offering educational content in both native and second languages to maximize comprehension and engagement (UNESCO, 2022).

Low-bandwidth solutions are equally vital in rural or underdeveloped regions where high-speed internet is not available. Technologies such as Progressive Web Apps (PWA), which load content offline or with minimal connectivity, compressed web formats (like AMP), and text-based interfaces are critical in such contexts. Initiatives like Facebook Lite, Wikipedia Zero, and Google's Android Go demonstrate how web-based services can be optimized for constrained environments without sacrificing functionality or reach (Graham, 2019).

Table 8 shows the Approaches to Overcoming the Digital Divide in Web Transformation.

Table 8. Approaches to overcoming the digital divide in web transformation

Key Challenges	Solution Approach	Implementation Example
Limited internet access	PWA, konten offline, AMP, caching	Wikipedia Zero, Facebook Lite
Language & digital literacy	Multilingual UI, audio-visual learning	India e-Gov multilingual portal
Aksesibilitas fisik	WCAG compliance, UI voice/screen reader	Microsoft Inclusive Design
Device inequality	Mobile-first design, adaptive resolution	Android Go, platform web yang responsif

7. FRAMEWORKS FOR WEB-DRIVEN DIGITAL MATURITY

7.1 Digital Maturity Models

As organizations embark on web-enabled digital transformation, they require structured tools to assess their current capabilities and strategically plan their evolution. This is where Digital Maturity Models (DMMs) play a crucial role. These models provide a framework to evaluate an organization's maturity across several dimensions—technology infrastructure, workforce capability, digital culture, customer engagement, and process agility. A well-defined DMM helps identify gaps, prioritize investments, and align transformation initiatives with long-term goals (Kane et al., 2015).

Numerous DMM frameworks exist, each tailored to different sectors and transformation scopes. Among the most widely adopted are the Deloitte Digital Maturity Model, MIT Center for Digital Business Model, and Capgemini's Digital Transformation Framework. These models typically categorize maturity into five to six levels—from "initial" or "emerging" to "optimized" or "innovative"—and assess progress across pillars like IT architecture, governance, digital skills, data utilization, and customer experience (Westerman et al., 2014). For example, in MIT's model, organizations at the "Digitally Maturing" stage exhibit both a digitally enabled core and continuous innovation across business units.

In the context of web transformation, DMMs can assess how well an organization leverages web technologies such as APIs, cloud platforms, web analytics, agile methodologies, and customer-centric web services. For example, a digitally immature organization may still rely on static websites and manual workflows, while a mature one integrates responsive web apps, real-time dashboards, DevOps, and omnichannel engagement. This kind of benchmarking is essential for tracking digital growth over time and justifying web-based investments. Table 9 shows the Example of a Web-based Organization Digital Maturity Level

Table 9. Example of a web-based organization digital maturity level

Level Maturitas	Key Features of Web-Driven Maturity	Examples of Technology Used
Ad Hoc	Static website, no API integration	HTML static site
Initiated	Start adopting cloud hosting, CMS, and online forms	WordPress, basic CRM
Integrated	Use of APIs, connected data between systems, early use of analytics	REST APIs, Google Analytics
Optimized	Platform web yang responsif, DevOps, pemantauan waktu nyata	React, CI/CD pipeline, Firebase
Innovative	AI-driven personalization, headless web, omni-digital experience	AI API, GraphQL, micro frontends

DMMs not only help in diagnosing the present but also in designing a roadmap for future transformation. They support decision-makers in prioritizing technology upgrades, workforce development, and customer-centric innovations. Organizations often use DMMs in annual digital audits or as benchmarks in digital transformation projects to track ROI, improve operational efficiency, and reduce risk. With web technology evolving rapidly—especially with trends like Web3 and AI-powered web services—DMMs must also be periodically revised to remain relevant.

7.2 Agile and DevOps Integration

In the context of digital transformation, the integration of Agile methodologies and DevOps practices has become a cornerstone for delivering and iterating web solutions with speed, flexibility, and reliability. Traditional software development models—such as the waterfall approach—are no longer suitable for the fast-paced demands of modern digital systems. Agile and DevOps allow organizations to release web applications more frequently, respond to user feedback quickly, and reduce time-to-market for new features or services (Leffingwell, 2016).

Agile emphasizes iterative development through short sprints, user feedback, and continuous prioritization. It is particularly effective for web projects that evolve rapidly based on market needs or customer interaction data. Frameworks like Scrum and Kanban support team collaboration, backlog management, and sprint planning in web development lifecycles. For example, a digital retail platform might use Agile to test new homepage layouts or checkout flows weekly based on real-time user behavior.

DevOps, on the other hand, focuses on the integration of development (Dev) and IT operations (Ops) to create a seamless pipeline for building, testing, deploying, and monitoring web applications. Core DevOps tools such as CI/CD pipelines (e.g., Jenkins, GitHub Actions), infrastructure-as-code (e.g., Terraform), and containerization (e.g., Docker, Kubernetes) automate repetitive tasks and ensure stability in deployments. When paired with Agile, DevOps supports a feedback-driven development loop that optimizes both user experience and technical performance. Table 10 shows the Comparison of Agile and DevOps Practices in Web Development.

Table 10. Comparison of agile and DevOps practices in web development

Aspek	Agile Practices	DevOps Practices	Sinergi dalam Transformasi Web
Main focus	Rapid iteration, team collaboration	Automation, operational reliability	Fast iteration + automatic deployment
General tools	Jira, Trello, Azure Boards	Jenkins, GitLab CI/CD, Docker, Ansible	GitHub Projects + GitHub Actions
Impact on delivery	More adaptive to market changes	High-quality and consistent deployment	Shorter, more stable time-to-market
Metode feedback	User stories, review sprint	Monitoring, logging, error reporting	Integrasi umpan balik pengguna dan sistem teknis
Usage example	Weekly redesign of web application UI	Deploy backend microservices harian	Update UI and backend features in parallel

The integration of Agile and DevOps is particularly beneficial in cloud-native and web-centric environments, where scalability, high availability, and responsiveness are key. Many tech giants—like Amazon, Netflix, and Spotify—have pioneered "Agile at scale" with fully automated DevOps pipelines, allowing them to deploy new code to production hundreds of times a day. For small to medium enterprises, adopting even partial Agile-DevOps integration can result in fewer bugs, happier users, and faster innovation (Kim et al., 2014).

7.3 Capability Mapping

In digital transformation initiatives—particularly those involving web technologies—capability mapping serves as a critical tool for aligning technological investments with strategic organizational goals. It involves identifying core business objectives, mapping them to the necessary digital/web capabilities, and ensuring that IT initiatives are focused on delivering measurable value. Rather than investing in tools or platforms for their own sake, capability mapping enables leaders to prioritize functionalities that directly support goals such as customer engagement, operational excellence, innovation, or data-driven decision making (Ross et al., 2006).

For instance, an organization aiming to enhance customer engagement may require web capabilities such as personalized content delivery, chatbot support, omnichannel user interfaces, and real-time analytics. Meanwhile, an enterprise focused on data intelligence would prioritize capabilities like centralized data lakes, integrated web dashboards, and API-based data pipelines. Capability mapping acts as the bridge between these strategic aims and the underlying technologies such as React frameworks, RESTful APIs, GraphQL, or cloud-native storage systems.

Organizations typically conduct capability mapping by first defining strategic themes (e.g., "Improve customer retention"), then listing supporting processes, followed by the identification of required capabilities and their corresponding web solutions. Tools like heat maps or capability maturity models can then be used to visualize gaps and prioritize development. This helps teams identify whether existing infrastructure is adequate, what capabilities must be enhanced or built, and how investments can be sequenced for optimal impact. Table 11 shows the Example of Capability Mapping in Web-based Digital Transformation.

Table 11. Example of capability mapping in web-based digital transformation

Key Business Strategies	Required Web Capabilities	Example of Web Technology Solution
Increase customer engagement	UI/UX adaptif, sistem rekomendasi berbasis AI	React + Next.js, TensorFlow.js, Firebase
Improving data-driven decisions	Integrasi real-time data, dashboard visualisasi	REST API, Grafana, Apache Superset
Accelerate product innovation	Kotak pasir web, penyebaran otomatis	GitHub Actions, Docker, Feature Flags
Improving self-service	Chatbot, integrated authentication system	Dialogflow, OAuth2 + JWT

Capability mapping also facilitates cross-functional alignment. Business teams gain clarity on how web platforms contribute to broader goals, while technical teams understand why they are building specific components. It creates a shared vocabulary and fosters collaboration across departments like marketing, IT, operations, and finance. For example, when rolling out a new e-commerce platform, marketing may want personalization tools, while IT ensures scalability and cybersecurity. Capability maps help ensure that everyone is building in the same direction.

8. FUTURE TRENDS

8.1 AI-Augmented Web Interfaces

The evolution of the web is entering a new phase with the integration of Artificial Intelligence (AI) into user interfaces (UI), giving rise to what is now referred to as AI-Augmented Web Interfaces. These interfaces leverage AI to provide more personalized, context-aware, and predictive user experiences. Unlike traditional static or rule-based UIs, AI-enhanced interfaces can dynamically adapt to user behavior, preferences, and environmental signals, thereby increasing user satisfaction, engagement, and conversion rates (McKinsey & Company, 2021).

One of the most prominent examples of AI-augmented interfaces is the use of chatbots and virtual assistants. Web-based AI chatbots, such as those powered by OpenAI (ChatGPT), Dialogflow, or Rasa, are capable of handling natural language queries, resolving issues, and even conducting transactions without human intervention. In customer support, these bots can reduce response times by up to 80% while maintaining 24/7 availability. Similarly, recommendation engines—as used by Netflix, Amazon, or Spotify—employ machine learning algorithms to analyze user history and suggest products or content tailored to each individual.

Beyond text interaction, AI also influences visual and behavioral elements of the UI. For instance, predictive UI elements can anticipate what a user might search for, auto-fill forms based on past behavior, or reorder interface elements for improved usability. Technologies such as computer vision, emotion recognition, and voice interface design are pushing boundaries even further. For example, Microsoft's Seeing AI and Google's Lookout use vision-based AI to help visually impaired users navigate web and app content more independently. Table 12 shows the Key Components in AI-Augmented Web Interfaces.

Table 12. Key components in AI-augmented web interfaces

Komponen AI Web Interface	Main Functions	Technology/Tools Commonly Used	Implementation Example
AI Chatbot	NLP-based automated customer service	Dialogflow, Flavor, ChatGPT APIs	Chatbot e-commerce, helpdesk AI
Recommendation Engine	User behavior-based product/ content suggestions	TensorFlow, Scikit-learn, Amazon Personalize	Netflix, Shopee, YouTube
Predictive UI Elements	Anticipate user needs, auto-suggestion	Reinforcement Learning, UX tracking	Google Search, Shopify

continued on following page

Table 12. Continued

Komponen AI Web Interface	Main Functions	Technology/Tools Commonly Used	Implementation Example
Emotion-Aware UI	Display adaptation based on expression/emotion	Affectiva, Microsoft Azure Face API	Customer feedback in banking
Voice-Enabled Web	Web navigation via voice commands	Web Speech API, Alexa SDK, Google STT	Smart home dashboards

The rise of AI-augmented web interfaces also raises questions about privacy, ethics, and transparency. Predictive algorithms must avoid biases, especially in sensitive sectors like healthcare or education. Moreover, the deployment of AI must adhere to regulations like GDPR and emerging AI Acts, which emphasize explainability and accountability. Thus, ethical AI integration is just as important as its technical accuracy. Platforms that practice "human-in-the-loop" validation and offer opt-in personalization controls are leading the way in responsible AI usage.

8.2 Web3 and Decentralization

The concept of Web3, also known as the decentralized web, marks a significant evolution from the current Web 2.0. While Web 2.0 is driven by centralized platforms like Google, Meta, or Amazon, Web3 aims to return control and ownership of data, identity, and transactions to users themselves, using decentralized technologies such as blockchain, smart contracts, decentralized storage, and token-based economics (Buterin, 2020). At its core, Web3 envisions a transparent, open, and permissionless internet where trust is established not by intermediaries, but through cryptographic protocols.

One of the primary technologies powering Web3 is blockchain—a distributed ledger that allows data and transactions to be recorded immutably across a peer-to-peer network. Through smart contracts, blockchain platforms like Ethereum enable autonomous, programmable agreements that execute without human intervention. These capabilities are already being implemented in various industries: Decentralized Finance (DeFi) platforms allow peer-to-peer lending and trading without banks, NFT marketplaces like OpenSea enable digital ownership of art and assets, and DAO (Decentralized Autonomous Organizations) offer community-governed digital entities with no centralized leadership.

In terms of web development, Web3 introduces new architectural models. Applications are no longer hosted on centralized servers but deployed on decentralized networks like IPFS (InterPlanetary File System) or Arweave, ensuring censorship resistance and enhanced data permanence. For user authentication, tools such as MetaMask or WalletConnect replace traditional logins with blockchain-based wallets, giving users ownership of their digital identities. Web3 also introduces token economies, where users can earn, spend, or invest in digital tokens that represent value, access rights, or governance power. Table 13 shows the Key Components of Web3 and its Applications

Table 13. Key components of Web3 and its applications

Web3 Component	Function	Core Technologies	Example Web Applications
Blockchain	Distributed & transparent ledger	Ethereum, Solana, Polygon	Uniswap, Chainlink
Smart Contract	Automated execution without intermediaries	Solidity, Vyper	Compound Finance, Aave
Decentralized Identity	Passwordless login, wallet-based identity	MetaMask, WalletConnect	Lens Protocol, ENS
Decentralized Storage	File & data storage without a central server	IPFS, Arweave, Filecoin	Mirror.xyz, Audius
Tokenization & NFTs	Digital representation of assets or value	ERC-20, ERC-721	OpenSea, Rarible

Despite its promise, Web3 faces several challenges including scalability, regulation, user experience, and energy consumption. Many blockchain networks still struggle with slow transaction speeds and high gas fees, while governments around the world are grappling with how to regulate decentralized finance and token economies. Moreover, onboarding users into Web3 can be complex due to unfamiliarity with wallets, keys, and seed phrases. Therefore, the mainstream adoption of Web3 will depend on both technological maturity and the development of human-centered, intuitive interfaces (Zamfir, 2022).

8.3 Emotionally Intelligent Web (Web 5.0)

As web technologies continue to evolve beyond interactivity (Web 2.0), decentralization (Web3), and intelligence (Web4.0), the future internet—Web 5.0—envisions a more emotionally intelligent and empathetic web. Emotionally Intelligent Web refers to digital systems that can detect, interpret, and respond to human emotions in real time, enabling hyper-personalized and psychologically adaptive interactions. Rather than just reacting to clicks or scrolls, Web 5.0 systems aim to understand how users feel—and respond accordingly—making digital experiences more humane, engaging, and context-aware (Pentland, 2014).

The building blocks of this transformation include advancements in Affective Computing, Artificial Emotional Intelligence (AEI), and Multimodal Emotion

Recognition. Through technologies like facial expression analysis (e.g., Affectiva, Microsoft Emotion API), voice tone analysis (e.g., Beyond Verbal), text sentiment analysis, and biometric input (e.g., eye-tracking, heart rate sensors), web platforms can gauge users' emotional states such as stress, frustration, satisfaction, or boredom. This emotional insight is then used to dynamically adapt the user interface, modify content delivery, or escalate support (e.g., transferring a chatbot to a human agent if emotional distress is detected).

Emotionally aware platforms are already beginning to emerge in e-learning, mental health, e-commerce, and digital marketing. For example, an online learning platform might slow down content delivery if it detects confusion or fatigue from a learner's facial expression. In customer service, emotionally intelligent chatbots can alter their tone, delay timing, or escalate to human agents when negative sentiment is detected. In digital advertising, emotion-detection algorithms can help select visuals or messages that align better with the viewer's mood, increasing engagement and conversions (Picard, 2010). Table 14 shows the Motional Intelligence-Based Web 5.0 Technology Components

Table 14. Motional intelligence-based Web 5.0 technology components

Main Component	Function	Example Technologies	Web Applications
Facial Expression Analysis	Recognizes emotions through users' facial expressions	Affectiva, Microsoft Azure Face API	E-learning platforms, online counseling
Voice Tone Recognition	Detects emotions based on voice tone and speech inflection	Beyond Verbal, Amazon Transcribe	Voice-based customer support
Sentiment Analysis (Text)	Analyzes emotions in written content and comments	IBM Watson NLP, Google Cloud NLP	Social media platforms, review analysis tools
Biometrics and Emotion Sensors	Measures heart rate, pupil dilation, or skin conductance	Empatica, Tobii, Garmin SDK	Wearable UX, mindfulness applications
Emotion-Based UI Adaptation	Adjusts interface appearance or interaction based on detected user emotions	WebGL, React Emotion Librar	Kids' web portals, therapy websites

While the vision of Web 5.0 is promising, it raises serious ethical concerns around privacy, consent, emotional manipulation, and data security. Since emotions are deeply personal, platforms must ensure explicit opt-in consent, secure data handling, and transparent algorithms. There are also risks of AI misinterpreting emotions, especially in multicultural contexts or neurodiverse users. Organizations designing emotionally intelligent systems must therefore prioritize ethical AI, inclusivity, and bias mitigation to ensure fair and beneficial deployment (Cowie et al., 2017).

9. CONCLUSION

The evolution of the web has reshaped the digital economy, transitioning from a basic communication tool into a strategic backbone for digital transformation. In its modern form, the web supports not only connectivity, but also agility, scalability, and real-time decision-making—capabilities essential for organizations navigating a fast-changing, technology-driven environment (Westerman et al., 2014). Whether in government services, commerce, healthcare, or education, web technologies provide the foundation for new ways of working, learning, and delivering value.

Organizations today are not merely digitizing old processes—they are reimagining business models and experiences through web-based platforms and intelligent systems. By leveraging core web technologies such as cloud computing, APIs, modern frontends, and middleware frameworks, institutions can break down silos, enable collaboration, and build resilient infrastructures that respond to customer and market demands (Brynjolfsson & McAfee, 2014). The success stories of e-government, smart retail, and telehealth—highlighted throughout this chapter—demonstrate how web transformation drives tangible improvements in efficiency, accessibility, and personalization.

However, achieving sustainable transformation requires more than adopting the latest tools. As discussed in Chapter 6 and 7, organizations must address critical challenges such as legacy integration, cybersecurity, and the digital divide, while simultaneously building digital maturity through Agile practices, DevOps pipelines, and strategic capability mapping (Ross et al., 2006). Moreover, institutions must stay ahead of emerging trends such as Web3 and Emotionally Intelligent Web (Web 5.0), which promise greater decentralization, transparency, and human-centricity in digital interactions.

To synthesize these insights, the table below summarizes how the web serves as a multidimensional enabler of transformation. Table 15 shows the Web's Strategic Roles in Digital Transformation

Table 15. The web's strategic roles in digital transformation

Strategic Area	Web Capabilities	Example Technologies	Impact
Customer Engagement	Omnichannel delivery, personalized experiences	React, GraphQL, AI chatbots	Improved customer loyalty and satisfaction
Operational Efficiency	Automation, data integration, real-time analytics	REST APIs, cloud databases	Faster workflows and reduced operational costs
Innovation Enablement	Prototyping, agile deployment, DevOps practices	Serverless computing, CI/CD, microservices	Shorter time-to-market and accelerated innovation
Data-Driven Decision Making	Dashboards, big data processing, predictive analytics	BI tools, TensorFlow, Looker	Deeper insights and evidence-based strategic choices
Resilience and Security	Scalable, decentralized, and secure web architecture	HTTPS, OAuth2, blockchain	Reduced risk and enhanced business continuity

Looking ahead, organizations that embed web technologies into their strategic vision will be best positioned to adapt to disruption and harness the full potential of digital change. The web is no longer just a medium—it is a platform for intelligence, collaboration, and value creation. As technology continues to evolve, the institutions that cultivate strategic agility, user empathy, and data fluency will lead the next wave of transformation in the connected world (McKinsey & Company, 2021).

REFERENCES

Armbrust, M., Fox, A., Griffith, R., Joseph, A. D., Katz, R., Konwinski, A., Lee, G., Patterson, D., Rabkin, A., Stoica, I., & Zaharia, M. (2010). A view of cloud computing. *Communications of the ACM*, *53*(4), 50–58. DOI: 10.1145/1721654.1721672

Cowie, M. R., Blomster, J. I., Curtis, L. H., Duclaux, S., Ford, I., Fritz, F., Goldman, S., Janmohamed, S., Kreuzer, J., Leenay, M., Michel, A., Ong, S., Pell, J. P., Southworth, M. R., Stough, W. G., Thoenes, M., Zannad, F., & Zalewski, A. (2017). Electronic health records to facilitate clinical research. *Clinical Research in Cardiology; Official Journal of the German Cardiac Society*, *106*(1), 1–9. DOI: 10.1007/s00392-016-1025-6 PMID: 27557678

Davenport, T. H., & Bean, R. (2018). Big companies are embracing analytics, but most still don't have a data-driven culture. *Harvard Business Review*, *6*, 1–4.

Fowler, M., & Foemmel, M. (2006). *Continuous integration*.

Gartner. (2022). Digital capability frameworks for transformation. Gartner Research

Graham, M. (Ed.). (2019). *Digital economies at global margins*. MIT Press. DOI: 10.7551/mitpress/10890.001.0001

Grewal, D., Kroschke, M., Mende, M., Roggeveen, A. L., & Scott, M. L. (2020). Frontline cyborgs at your service: How human enhancement technologies affect customer experiences in retail, sales, and service settings. *Journal of Interactive Marketing*, *51*(1), 9–25. DOI: 10.1016/j.intmar.2020.03.001

Ifenthaler, D., & Yau, J. Y. K. (2020). Utilising learning analytics to support study success in higher education: A systematic review. *Educational Technology Research and Development*, *68*(4), 1961–1990. DOI: 10.1007/s11423-020-09788-z

Keesara, S., Jonas, A., & Schulman, K. (2020). Covid-19 and health care's digital revolution. *The New England Journal of Medicine*, *382*(23), e82. DOI: 10.1056/NEJMp2005835 PMID: 32240581

Kim, Y., Trimi, S., & Chung, J. H. (2014). Big-data applications in the government sector. *Communications of the ACM*, *57*(3), 78–85. DOI: 10.1145/2500873

Lee, I., & Lee, K. (2015). The Internet of Things (IoT): Applications, investments, and challenges for enterprises. *Business Horizons*, *58*(4), 431–440. DOI: 10.1016/j.bushor.2015.03.008

Leffingwell, D. (2016). *SAFe® 4.0 reference guide: scaled agile framework® for lean software and systems engineering*. Addison-Wesley Professional.

Lemon, K. N., & Verhoef, P. C. (2016). Understanding customer experience throughout the customer journey. *Journal of Marketing*, *80*(6), 69–96. DOI: 10.1509/jm.15.0420

Means, B., Bakia, M., & Murphy, R. (2014). *Learning online: What research tells us about whether, when and how*. Routledge. DOI: 10.4324/9780203095959

Newman, S. (2015). *Building microservices: Designing fine-grained systems*. O'Reilly Media.

OECD. (2020). Digital government in the post-COVID-19 era. *OECD Digital Economy Papers*, (308). Advance online publication. DOI: 10.1787/14e1c5e8-en-fr

Pentland, A. (2014). *Social physics: How good ideas spread-the lessons from a new science*. Penguin.

Picard, R. W. (2010). Emotion research by the people, for the people. *Emotion Review*, *2*(3), 250–254. DOI: 10.1177/1754073910364256

Porter, M. E., & Heppelmann, J. E. (2014). How smart, connected products are transforming competition. *Harvard Business Review*, *92*(11), 64–88.

Ries, E. (2011). *The lean startup: How today's entrepreneurs use continuous innovation to create radically successful businesses*. Crown Currency.

Ross, J. W., Weill, P., & Robertson, D. C. (2006). *Enterprise architecture as strategy: Creating a foundation for business execution*. Harvard Business Review Press.

Shickel, B., Loftus, T. J., Ozrazgat-Baslanti, T., Ebadi, A., Bihorac, A., & Rashidi, P. (2018). DeepSOFA: a real-time continuous acuity score framework using deep learning. *ArXiv e-prints, 1802*.

Westerman, G., Bonnet, D., & McAfee, A. (2014). Leading digital: Turning technology into business transformation. Harvard Business Review Press.

Fielding, N. (2000). The shared fate of two innovations in qualitative methodology: The relationship of qualitative software and secondary analysis of archived qualitative data. In *Forum: Qualitative Social Research* (Vol. 1, No. 3).

Freie Universität Berlin. Brynjolfsson, E., & McAfee, A. (2014). The second machine age: Work, progress, and prosperity in a time of brilliant technologies. W. W. Norton & Company.

World Economic Forum. (2023). Shaping the future of digital economy and new value creation. https://www.weforum.org

World Health Organization. (2022). Telemedicine: Opportunities and developments in member states. https://www.who.int/publications/i/item/9789240027340

Chapter 2
Theoretical Frameworks and Practices in Web Technologies

Fadhil Ezar Rahman
https://orcid.org/0009-0003-4006-7787
Universitas Esa Unggul, Indonesia

Binastya Anggara Sekti
https://orcid.org/0000-0001-5489-4888
Universitas Esa Unggul, Indonesia

ABSTRACT

This chapter explores the convergence of theoretical frameworks and practical methodologies in modern web technologies. By integrating models such as the Technology Acceptance Model (TAM), Human-Centered Design (HCD), Systems Development Life Cycle (SDLC), Hypertext Theory, and Actor-Network Theory (ANT), the chapter demonstrates how theory informs and enhances practices like responsive web design, RESTful APIs, and Progressive Web Apps (PWA). Supported by real-world case studies from education, healthcare, governance, and digital business, it highlights how theoretical foundations drive innovation, user experience, and ethical system design. Future trends such as AI-augmented UX, ethical design integration, and semantic web advancements are also examined to illustrate ongoing transformations in web development.

DOI: 10.4018/979-8-3373-5167-4.ch002

INTRODUCTION

The transformation of web technologies from simple static pages to dynamic, intelligent, and responsive systems has redefined how individuals, organizations, and governments interact with information and with each other. Initially conceived as a medium for linking documents, the World Wide Web has evolved into an intricate ecosystem of applications, services, and user experiences that permeate every aspect of digital life. This evolution is not driven solely by technology, but also by underlying theoretical constructs that help shape the design and delivery of modern web solutions (Francesconi, 2018).

Understanding the theoretical frameworks behind web technologies provides crucial insights into how digital systems can be purposefully developed to meet specific human, organizational, and societal goals. Theories such as Hypertext Theory, Information Architecture, and Human-Centered Design have not only guided the layout and interaction of web platforms but also informed the development of web content that is intuitive, accessible, and context-aware. For example, web accessibility standards such as WCAG are rooted in theoretical principles of inclusivity and universal design, ensuring the web is usable by individuals of all abilities (Dogan & Gogus, 2025)

At the core of this discussion lies the interplay between theoretical models and practical implementation. Concepts such as the Technology Acceptance Model (TAM) and Diffusion of Innovation Theory provide lenses through which user behavior, system adoption, and technology diffusion can be analyzed and predicted. These models are essential in crafting web solutions that align with user expectations and organizational objectives, thereby reducing friction during system adoption and maximizing impact (Verhoef, Kooge, Walk, & Wieringa, 2021). Furthermore, architectural frameworks such as Microservices and Event-Driven Architectures translate these high-level theories into scalable and resilient system designs, which are widely used in digital business and public service platforms.

This chapter provides a structured examination of the key theoretical underpinnings and their manifestations in real-world web applications. By analysing how theoretical constructs, such as Constructivist Learning Theory, inform the development of educational platforms or how Actor-Network Theory supports multi-agent healthcare systems, we can better understand the rationale behind design choices and their implications for system performance and user engagement (Bychkov, et al., 2022). In doing so, the chapter bridges the gap between abstract models and practical tools, highlighting how web technologies serve as socio-technical constructs rather than purely technical artifacts (Rizk, Nasr, & Gheith, 2019).

Ultimately, a theoretical lens allows developers, designers, and decision-makers to transcend ad hoc development practices and build more sustainable, ethical, and inclusive web experiences. As the web continues to evolve with advancements in AI, semantic technologies, and ethical computing, a firm grounding in theory will remain indispensable. The convergence of academic insight and agile practice is essential for shaping the future of digital systems that are not only functional but also meaningful and responsible (Liebig, Güttel, Jobin, & Katzenbach, 2024)

THEORETICAL FOUNDATIONS OF WEB TECHNOLOGIES

The evolution of web technologies is not merely a result of engineering breakthroughs but also of theoretical contributions that have shaped how digital systems are conceived, structured, and refined. Theories from fields such as cognitive psychology, sociology, communication studies, and information science play a central role in guiding the development of web platforms. They provide essential frameworks to interpret user behavior, optimize information flow, and develop interaction models that are contextually meaningful and ethically responsible (Verhoef, Kooge, Walk, & Wieringa, 2021)

Rather than being abstract or purely academic, these theoretical models serve practical purposes: informing UX/UI decisions, shaping system architecture, enhancing personalization, and ensuring inclusivity. For instance, principles from Constructivist Learning Theory guide the design of interactive education platforms, At the same time, Actor-Network Theory sheds light on the socio-technical complexities of healthcare and innovative governance systems. In this way, theory and practice converge, enabling developers and researchers to build systems that are technically robust and socially responsive (Nazarenko, Zazymko, Funderburk, & Klikh, 2024)

Understanding and applying these foundational theories is particularly critical in an era where digital technologies mediate not only commerce and communication, but also education, healthcare, governance, and civic engagement. Below are five theoretical models that have been instrumental in shaping contemporary web development: Hypertext Theory, Information Architecture, Media Richness Theory, Actor-Network Theory, and Constructivist Learning Theory. Each offers unique insights into how digital systems should be structured and how users interact within them, thus ensuring that technological innovation remains anchored in human relevance and societal values.

Hypertext Theory

Hypertext Theory is central to the foundational logic of the web. It postulates that information should be presented in a non-linear manner, allowing users to navigate through related content via hyperlinks (Francesconi, 2018). This theory underpins the way content is interlinked in web platforms, influencing everything from menu structures to content recommendation engines. As a practical example, Wikipedia's hyperlink-rich format exemplifies this theory in action.

Furthermore, with the increasing application of semantic web standards, hypertextuality has evolved beyond simple links, enabling machine-readable relationships between concepts and thus enhancing both user navigation and machine inference (Reyero Lobo, Daga, Alani, & Fernandez, 2023).

Information Architecture (IA)

Information Architecture concerns the structural design of shared information environments. It provides a blueprint for organizing, labeling, and navigating web content to optimize usability and findability (Dogan & Gogus, 2025). IA plays a critical role in UX design, particularly in large-scale platforms such as e-government portals and e-commerce systems, where clarity and structure significantly impact user efficiency and satisfaction.

Studies such as Kim et al. (2024) emphasize the impact of national e-government service design policies that enforce IA principles, ensuring standardized navigation and accessibility across public digital services. Moreover, improved IA supports not only usability but also the sustainability of content delivery in educational platforms (Bezus, Akbilek, & Mekeko, 2021).

Media Richness Theory

Media Richness Theory (MRT) explains the effectiveness of a communication medium based on its capacity to carry information. In the web context, richer media such as video tutorials or interactive dashboards are more effective for tasks that involve ambiguity or complexity (Verhoef, Kooge, Walk, & Wieringa, 2021). MRT influences web design decisions, particularly in e-learning platforms and customer support chat systems where clarity of communication is paramount.

For instance, adaptive multimedia content in digital education systems has been shown to increase learner satisfaction and engagement, particularly when aligned with students' preferences and contextual needs (Chen, et al., 2025). Gazzawe et al. (2022) further support the integration of media-rich design in AI-driven e-learning environments, enhancing cognitive interactivity and accessibility.

Actor-Network Theory (ANT)

Actor-Network Theory views technological systems as the result of networks composed of both human and non-human actors (Bychkov, et al., 2022). In web development, this theory is helpful in for understanding how users, interfaces, APIs, and backend services interact and co-shape the system's function. It's particularly relevant in healthcare and smart city platforms, where multiple stakeholders and technologies are deeply interdependent.

For instance, AI-enhanced healthcare portals that integrate wearable sensors, diagnostic tools, and user-facing dashboards exemplify ANT by treating these entities not as isolated tools, but as collaborative agents contributing to care delivery (Wang, Choo, Ng, Bi, & Wang, 2025). ANT thus becomes instrumental in guiding system designers toward recognizing the systemic consequences of each component's behavior.

Constructivist Learning Theory

Rooted in educational psychology, Constructivist Learning Theory posits that learners construct knowledge through active exploration and interaction. Applied to web technologies, it informs the design of educational platforms that prioritize engagement and personalization, such as LMS with adaptive learning paths or gamified user interfaces (Rizk, Nasr, & Gheith, 2019).

The value of this theory is reflected in platforms that support real-time feedback loops, peer-based learning, and co-creation of knowledge environments. AI-powered educational assistants operationalize constructivist learning by adapting content in response to learner behavior and progress (Nazarenko, Zazymko, Funderburk, & Klikh, 2024). This alignment enables more meaningful knowledge construction, especially in higher education and distance learning contexts.

In addition to these five models, several emerging perspectives are gaining prominence in web design. The application of Crowdsourcing Theory particularly for requirements elicitation in web-based systems is increasingly relevant in participatory platforms and open development environments (Rizk, Nasr, & Gheith, 2019). Similarly, Systemic Thinking and Sociotechnical Systems Theory are essential in managing the interplay between technical infrastructures and societal expectations, especially in large-scale deployments such as national e-governance and pandemic tracking applications (Olca & Can, 2022).

Overall, theoretical foundations in web technologies provide more than intellectual scaffolding they act as practical guides for building digital ecosystems that are human-centered, ethically grounded, and contextually aware. As systems become more intelligent and distributed, the relevance of these frameworks will continue to expand, particularly when paired with emerging approaches like AI-Driven Cross-Platform Design (Eswaran & Eswaran, 2024) and Value-Sensitive Design (Liebig, Güttel, Jobin, & Katzenbach, 2024), ensuring that future web environments are both adaptive and accountable

SYSTEM ARCHITECTURE MODELS IN PRACTICE

The successful deployment of modern web technologies depends heavily on the robustness of their underlying system architecture. Architecture in this context refers to the logical design and structural blueprint that defines how software components interact, process data, and deliver information to users. Much like the foundation of a building, system architecture ensures that web applications possess stable, efficient, and scalable qualities, which are especially critical in today's multi-device, high-demand environments.

As web applications evolve to accommodate more users, process real-time data, and integrate with the cloud, the choice of architecture becomes increasingly strategic. Different use cases ranging from static content delivery to AI-powered personalization demand different architectural solutions. For example, while a small institutional website may operate well on a simple client-server setup, a large e-commerce platform must rely on distributed microservices or event-driven models to maintain speed and reliability under high load.

Over time, several architectural models have emerged, each offering a distinct balance of performance, flexibility, and maintainability. Understanding these models is key to aligning system design with business objectives, user expectations, and technological trends. The following sections explore four of the most prominent system architecture paradigms currently in use: Client-Server, Three-Tier, Microservices, and Event-Driven Architecture (EDA). Each model brings unique advantages and trade-offs that influence how web platforms are built, scaled, and evolved in practice.

Client-Server Architecture

Client-Server Architecture is the foundational model of the early web. In this design, client applications (typically browsers) request services from centralized servers which process the requests and return responses (Alexopoulos, Nikolakis, & Xanthakis, 2022). It provides simplicity in deployment and remains relevant in small-scale applications. However, it can become a bottleneck when scalability or redundancy is required. Despite its limitations, client-server structures remain crucial for lightweight services such as static websites, institutional portals, and local intranets where performance demands are minimal.

Three-Tier Architecture

To improve modularity, scalability, and maintainability, many enterprise-level web applications employ the Three-Tier Architecture, which separates systems into a Presentation Layer, an Application Logic Layer, and a Data Layer. This separation allows developers to independently modify user interfaces, business logic, and data handling processes. For example, in e-commerce platforms like Tokopedia or Shopee, the UI layer renders dynamic content via HTML/CSS, the logic layer handles cart and payment systems, and the data layer manages inventory and customer data (Dogan & Gogus, 2025). This model also aligns well with cloud-native deployment, where each tier may be containerized or deployed across distributed servers to maximize scalability.

Microservices Architecture

As applications became more complex and required faster deployment cycles, the Microservices Architecture emerged. In this model, a web application is broken down into independent, loosely coupled services, each responsible for a specific function. These services communicate via APIs (often RESTful or GraphQL). This modular approach enhances agility, resilience, and scalability, making it ideal for e-commerce platforms and SaaS (Software-as-a-Service) products. For instance, in an online store, different microservices may handle payments, inventory, user authentication, and product recommendations independently (Verhoef, Kooge, Walk, & Wieringa, 2021). The integration of microservices is also central to the architecture of AI-driven systems and federated platforms, as seen in AI-first infrastructures for healthcare and mobile applications (Gazzawe, Mayouf, Lock, & Alturki, 2022). Table 1 Shows the Comparative Overview of Web System Architectures and Their Use Cases.

Table 1. Comparative overview of web system architectures and their use cases

Architecture Type	Key Characteristics	Common Use Cases
Client-Server	Centralized server, thin client	Static websites, small-scale apps
Three-Tier	Separation of concerns across three layers	Enterprise systems, CMS, e-government
Microservices	Distributed, modular services via APIs	E-commerce, FinTech, large-scale platforms
Event-Driven (EDA)	Asynchronous, real-time processing	Messaging apps, IoT dashboards, games

Event-Driven Architecture (EDA)

Event-Driven Architecture enables systems to respond to real-time events such as user actions, database changes, or message triggers. It promotes asynchronous communication and is suitable for applications requiring high interactivity, like financial trading dashboards or real-time notifications (Kesavan, Saravana, Kumar, & Vengatesan K, 2021). EDA complements microservices by improving decoupling and responsiveness. In recent implementations, event-driven systems are further supported by edge computing and streaming services that enhance response latency and concurrency essential for IoT ecosystems, multiplayer gaming engines, and real-time social platforms (Al-Barakati, 2021). Table 2 Shows the Key Benefits of Common Web Architecture Models.

Table 2. Key benefits of common web architecture models

Architecture Model	Key Benefit
Client-Server	Simplicity
Three-Tier	Scalability & Modularity
Microservices	Flexibility & Independent Dev
Event-Driven	Real-Time Responsiveness

The selection of an architecture depends on system requirements, team expertise, and project goals. A hybrid approach is also common, especially in large-scale systems that must balance real-time responsiveness with robust data processing. For instance, Progressive Web Apps (PWA) and AI-enhanced platforms often utilize a mix of event-driven interactions and microservices logic to create responsive, intelligent services (AlDahoul, Hong, Varvello, & Zaki, 2025). Furthermore, decentralized architectures are increasingly considered with the rise of Web 3.0, where peer-to-peer networks and blockchain replace central servers to enhance transparency and control (Eskandarzadeh, 2023). As digital services become increasingly complex and interconnected, understanding and applying the right architecture is essential for delivering performant, sustainable, and future-ready web applications.

WEB STANDARDS AND PROTOCOLS

Web standards and protocols form the foundation of the digital world we interact with every day. These formalized rules and specifications define how web pages are structured, how distributed systems communicate, and how content is rendered across a wide array of devices and platforms. By establishing consistency in data transmission, layout rendering, and user interaction, web standards ensure that the web remains interoperable, inclusive, and adaptable regardless of browser, operating system, or user ability (Dogan & Gogus, 2025). Standards such as HTML, CSS, and JavaScript play a central role in ensuring interoperability, allowing developers to deliver consistent user experiences without reinventing the wheel.

Beyond ensuring technical consistency, these standards also shape the ethical and inclusive dimensions of the modern web. They form the basis for building accessible digital environments, protecting user privacy, and maintaining secure interactions. For example, protocols like HTTPS secured via TLS are vital for encrypting data in transit and ensuring confidentiality in web applications. Similarly, the Web Content Accessibility Guidelines (WCAG) ensure that individuals with disabilities can navigate and engage with content effectively, reinforcing the idea that accessibility is a fundamental right, not a feature (Martins & Duarte, 2024). As the web continues to grow more complex and dynamic, adhering to these evolving standards is not merely about technical compliance it becomes an ethical imperative.

In today's digital ecosystem, conformance to web standards is essential to delivering scalable, responsive, and secure applications. These standards support everything from seamless API interactions using REST and GraphQL (Alexopoulos, Nikolakis, & Xanthakis, 2022), to building inclusive front-end designs and ensuring semantic web compatibility for AI-driven systems (Reyero Lobo, Daga, Alani, & Fernandez, 2023). They also enable progressive enhancement across devices, making the web accessible in low-bandwidth and mobile-first environments. As such, these protocols act as the invisible scaffolding that holds the modern web together. The following sections explore key categories of web standards including front-end technologies, API design protocols, accessibility guidelines, security protocols, and decentralized semantic frameworks each contributing uniquely to the reliability, inclusivity, and ethical resilience of digital ecosystems.

Core Front-End Standards: HTML, CSS, and JavaScript

At the heart of front-end development are HTML (HyperText Markup Language), CSS (Cascading Style Sheets), and JavaScript. HTML structures web content, CSS defines its presentation, and JavaScript enables interactive behavior. Together, these standards allow developers to build responsive, dynamic, and user-friendly interfaces (Dogan & Gogus, 2025). Table 3 Shows the Core Front-End Web Technologies and Their Roles.

Table 3. Core front-end web technologies and their roles

Technology	Role	Example Application
HTML	Content structure	Headings, paragraphs, tables
CSS	Styling and layout	Themes, responsive desigg
JavaScript	Behavior and interactivity	Form validation, animations, dynamic menus

These technologies continue to evolve with specifications like HTML5 and ECMAScript (ES6+), introducing new APIs, semantic tags, and enhanced performance features.

API Protocols: REST and GraphQL

REST (Representational State Transfer) is a widely adopted architectural style for designing networked applications. RESTful APIs use standard HTTP methods to enable interaction between client and server, fostering loose coupling and scalability (Alexopoulos, Nikolakis, & Xanthakis, 2022). GraphQL, on the other hand, is a query language for APIs that allows clients to request only the data they need, improving efficiency and flexibility. In dynamic applications such as recommendation engines or real-time dashboards GraphQL plays an essential role in reducing unnecessary data transfer and improving load times. Table 4 Shows the Comparison of REST and GraphQL API Protocols.

Table 4. Comparison of REST and GraphQL API protocols

Protocol	Approach	Benefits
REST	Resource-oriented	Simplicity, stateless communication
GraphQL	Query-based	Reduced over-fetching, flexible

Both REST and GraphQL support microservices architectures, making them ideal choices for scalable, modular web applications.

Accessibility Standards: WCAG

The Web Content Accessibility Guidelines (WCAG) are a set of recommendations developed by the W3C to ensure digital content is accessible to users with disabilities. WCAG 2.1 emphasizes four principles: Perceivable, Operable, Understandable, and Robust (POUR). These guidelines guide web developers in creating content that accommodates a broad spectrum of user needs. In addition, accessibility is now closely integrated with inclusive design movements and AI-driven personalization, which adapt interfaces in real-time based on user interaction (Martins & Duarte, 2024). Table 5 Shows the WCAG 2.1 Accessibility Principles and Implementation Examples.

Table 5. WCAG 2.1 accessibility principles and implementation examples

Principle	Description	Example
Perceivable	Information must be presented clearly	Alternative text for images
Operable	Interface must be navigable by all users	Keyboard navigation support
Understandable	Content must be readable and logical	Clear error messages
Robust	Content must be compatible with assistive technologies	Use of semantic HTML

Implementing WCAG not only fulfills legal and ethical obligations but also enhances overall usability and SEO performance.

Security Protocols: TLS and HTTPS

Security is a critical component of any web interaction. HTTPS (Hypertext Transfer Protocol Secure) combines HTTP with TLS (Transport Layer Security) to encrypt data transmitted between clients and servers. This prevents eavesdropping, tampering, and impersonation, thus ensuring data integrity and confidentiality (Kesavan, Saravana, Kumar, & Vengatesan K, 2021). The push towards a "secure-by-default" web is further supported by browser policies and the availability of free SSL certificates through services like Let's Encrypt.

Figure 1. TLS handshake process in HTTPS communication

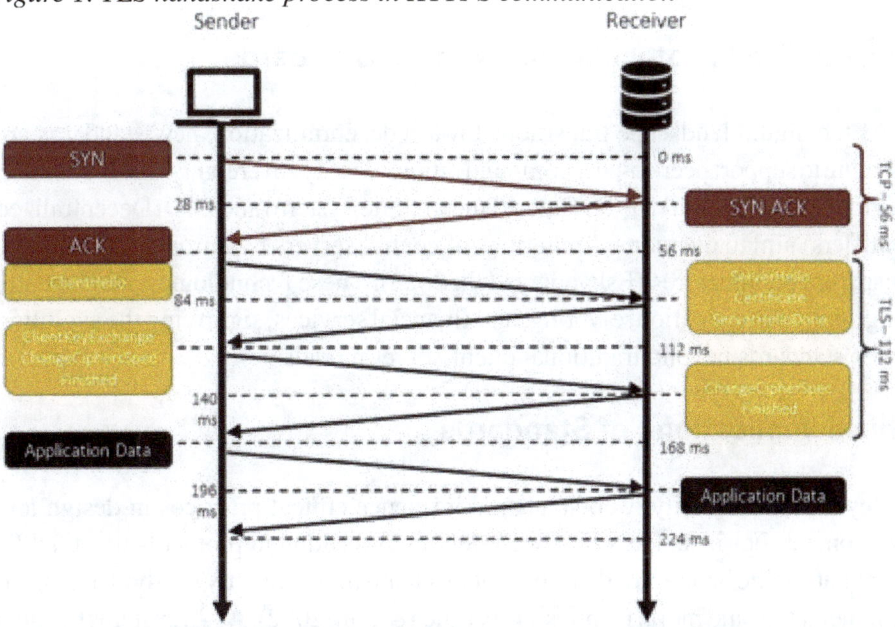

This implementation is mandatory for any site handling sensitive information such as online banking, healthcare portals, or e-commerce platforms and is a baseline expectation for all modern websites.

Semantic Web and Interoperability Standards

Emerging paradigms such as the Semantic Web propose standards that make web content machine-readable and interoperable. Using technologies like RDF, OWL, and SPARQL, systems can share structured knowledge, enabling AI systems to understand and process information more effectively. These standards are especially vital in health informatics, smart city platforms, and digital humanities (Reyero Lobo, Daga, Alani, & Fernandez, 2023). They lay the groundwork for web-based reasoning and automated data linking across systems.

Cross-Platform and Multi-Device Compatibility

With the proliferation of mobile, tablet, wearable, and voice interfaces, ensuring that web standards support multi-platform development is essential. Responsive Web Design (RWD), Progressive Web Apps (PWA), and cross-platform libraries like Flutter or React Native have emerged as practical implementations of W3C and device-agnostic standards (Eswaran & Eswaran, 2024). These ensure consistent UX and performance across a range of screen sizes and interaction methods.

Decentralized Protocols and Web 3.0 Standards

As the digital landscape transitions toward decentralization, new standards are emerging to support peer-to-peer communication, identity sovereignty, and blockchain integration. Protocols like IPFS (InterPlanetary File System) and DID (Decentralized Identifiers) aim to overcome limitations of central servers by introducing resilient, transparent architectures (Eskandarzadeh, 2023). These technologies are currently being applied in education, e-voting, and financial services, signifying the evolution of web standards beyond traditional client-server models.

Ethical Implications of Standards

Beyond functionality, web standards influence ethical practices in design and development. For instance, privacy guidelines embedded in protocols like GDPR-compliant cookie banners or data consent mechanisms tie directly into both technical implementation and moral responsibility (Olca & Can, 2022). As AI systems become more integrated into the web, ensuring ethical AI behavior through standardization becomes a central concern particularly in areas such as federated learning, content moderation, and algorithmic transparency (Nazarenko, Zazymko, Funderburk, & Klikh, 2024). Table 6 Shows the Key Web Standards and Their Technical-Ethical Purposes.

Table 6. Key web standards and their technical-ethical purposes

Category	Standard/Protocol	Purpose
Content Markup	HTML, CSS, JavaScript	Structure, styling, interactivity
API Communication	REST, GraphQL	Data access and integration
Accessibility	WCAG	Inclusive and ethical content delivery
Security	TLS, HTTPS	Confidentiality and integrity of data

By adhering to these standards, web developers ensure cross-platform compatibility, ethical design, and user trust factors that are essential in building modern web ecosystems. The future of web protocols is not just technical, but also social and political, as standards begin to reflect values such as inclusivity, decentralization, sustainability, and algorithmic justice.

USER-CENTERED AND AGILE DESIGN PRACTICES

The success of modern web applications increasingly depends on their ability to align with users' needs, behaviors, and feedback throughout the entire design and development lifecycle. No longer are digital products judged solely by technical robustness or visual appeal; instead, their effectiveness is measured by how well they solve real-world problems across diverse contexts and user demographics. This paradigm shift reflects a broader evolution in software engineering where empathy, adaptability, and inclusivity have become core design values (Dogan & Gogus, 2025). It also reflects a growing understanding that user needs are dynamic, nuanced, and often deeply contextual, requiring iterative and participatory development processes to fully address.

In response to these demands, three interrelated methodologies have emerged as foundational to human-centered digital product development: User-Centered Design (UCD), Agile Development, and Design Thinking. Each methodology offers a unique lens: UCD emphasizes involving real users throughout the design process via observation, feedback, and usability testing; Agile prioritizes iterative, incremental development cycles with continuous user feedback; while Design Thinking fosters creative problem-solving grounded in empathy and ideation. When used independently, each framework offers powerful benefits. However, when integrated holistically, they form a synergistic system that supports the creation of adaptive, responsive, and ethically aligned web technologies (Alexopoulos, Nikolakis, & Xanthakis, 2022).

This section explores how these methodologies work individually and in concert to reshape how we build digital systems. From the structured feedback loops of Agile, to the empathy-driven ideation of Design Thinking, to the data-informed refinement of UCD, these approaches reflect a growing paradigm in web development one that values people over process, iteration over assumption, and inclusion over standardization. In the following sections, we examine each of these practices in detail, showcasing how they support not only usability and performance but also ethical and sustainable innovation in web technologies.

User-Centered Design (UCD)

User-Centered Design is a design philosophy and iterative process where the needs, preferences, and limitations of end-users are given extensive attention at each stage of the design process. UCD involves engaging users through interviews, usability testing, and feedback loops to refine the design over time. According to (Dogan & Gogus, 2025), incorporating direct user input increases engagement and improves learning outcomes in web platforms.

Key techniques in UCD include:

1) Persona development

Representing archetypal users to inform decisions.

2) Scenario writing

Outlining contextual narratives of user interaction.

3) Card sorting

Organizing information architecture based on user logic.

4) Remote usability testing

Enabling feedback collection at scale.

This participatory model ensures that end-products resonate with the users they're meant to serve, reducing friction, abandonment, and confusion in digital interfaces. Table 7 Shows the Core Principles of User-Centered Design.

Table 7. Core principles of user-centered design

Principle	Description	Implementation Example
Understand	Research user context and behaviors	User interviews, personas
Involve	Include users throughout the design process	Usability testing, feedback loops
Iterate	Refine designs based on real user insights	A/B testing, iterative prototyping
Measure	Evaluate effectiveness with quantifiable metrics	Task success rates, error counts

Agile Methodology

Agile methodology promotes an iterative approach to software development, favoring collaboration, adaptability, and customer feedback over rigid planning. In the web development context, Agile enables teams to release frequent updates and respond rapidly to user and market demands. Using sprints, daily stand-ups, and incremental deliveries, Agile empowers cross-functional teams to remain flexible and user-focused (Alexopoulos, Nikolakis, & Xanthakis, 2022).

Key principles of Agile relevant to web technologies include:

1) Incremental delivery

breaking down development into functional pieces.

2) Cross-functional collaboration

involving designers, developers, QA, and product owners.

3) Customer-centric planning

defining product backlog based on user needs.

4) Feedback integration

embedding user stories into sprint cycles.

Figure 2. Agile methodology development cycle

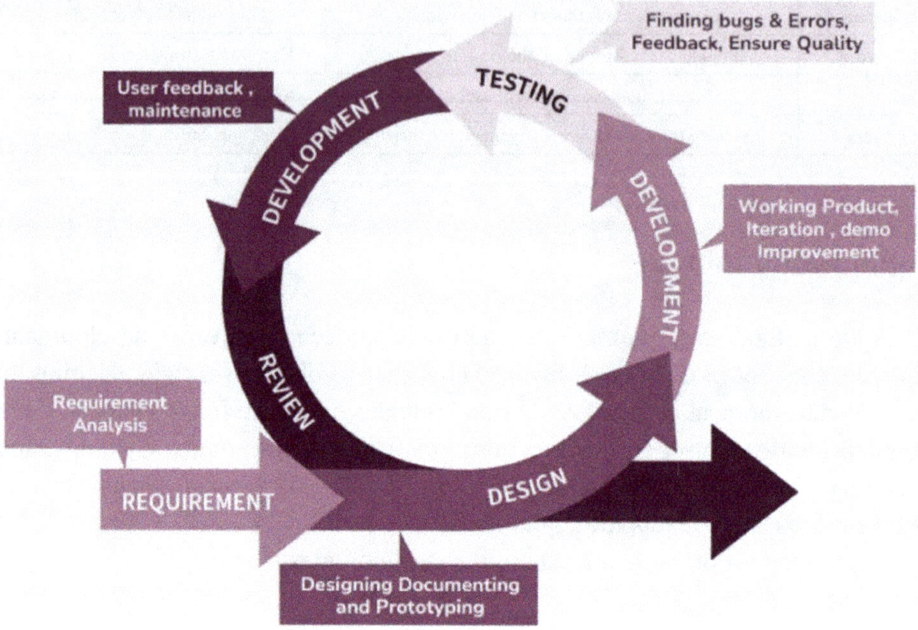

This approach complements UCD by integrating user feedback into the build process, rather than treating user needs as static requirements.

Design Thinking

Design Thinking is a human-centered innovation process that encourages empathetic problem-solving through ideation, prototyping, and testing. It provides a framework to explore creative solutions that align technical feasibility with user desirability. The five stages Empathize, Define, Ideate, Prototype, and Test form the foundation of this iterative, solution-driven methodology.

Unlike traditional linear development, Design Thinking fosters creative exploration and reframing of user challenges. In sectors such as healthcare and digital learning, this mindset opens the door to more intuitive and inclusive systems (Gazzawe, Mayouf, Lock, & Alturki, 2022). Table 8 Shows the Five Stages of Design Thinking and Their Application.

Table 8. Five stages of design thinking and their application

Stage	Purpose	Example Activity
Empathize	Understand users' needs and experiences	User shadowing, empathy mapping
Define	Identify key problems to solve	Problem statements, user journeys
Ideate	Generate innovative ideas	Brainstorming, mind mapping
Prototype	Create early versions of solutions	Wireframes, interactive mockups
Test	Gather user feedback and refine	Usability testing, focus groupus groups

By combining emotional intelligence with design strategy, Design Thinking drives user-centric innovation across sectors like e-learning, healthcare, and e-commerce. This human-first approach ensures that digital products not only solve technical problems but also create meaningful experiences for users. For instance, in the e-learning sector, platforms such as Moodle and Canvas have adopted Design Thinking principles to develop user interfaces that promote engagement and ease of use, making learning more interactive and personalized (Rizk, Nasr, & Gheith, 2019).

Synergy Between UCD, Agile, and Design Thinking

The integration of User-Centered Design (UCD), Agile development, and Design Thinking leads to a robust, adaptive, and human-first approach to web design and development. Each methodology contributes unique strengths:

- UCD anchors decisions in the lived experiences, preferences, and constraints of actual users.
- Agile provides a framework for continuous iteration and collaboration.
- Design Thinking adds creative problem-solving and empathy at the strategic level.

When implemented in synergy, they enable design teams to move from abstract assumptions to validated, scalable solutions with greater speed and precision.

For instance, in healthcare applications where usability, accessibility, and trust are paramount this integration is invaluable. Consider a digital health monitoring app tailored for chronic disease patients. UCD would guide the interface to match patient cognitive abilities, Design Thinking would ensure empathy for their daily struggles, and Agile would support incremental improvements based on ongoing patient feedback. Bychkov et al. (2022) highlight how environmental monitoring systems in healthcare contexts benefit from multi-stakeholder collaboration and technological adaptability, which mirrors the principles of these three methodologies working in tandem.

Example Workflow of Synergistic Integration:

1) Empathize (Design Thinking)

   Engage users (patients, doctors) to uncover real needs.

2) Define (Design Thinking + UCD)

   Translate insights into actionable design requirements.

3) Ideate (Design Thinking)

   Brainstorm with multi-disciplinary teams for creative solutions.

4) Prototype (UCD + Agile)

   Rapidly develop testable mockups.

5) Test and Iterate (UCD + Agile)

   Use usability testing and Agile sprints to refine features.

6) Deliver Incrementally (Agile)

   Launch features in cycles with real-time feedback loops.

The convergence of these methodologies creates a *continuous innovation feedback loop*, where every iteration not only delivers functionality but reinforces the product's alignment with its users. This synergy allows teams to:

- Adapt to change without losing focus on human needs.
- Embed empathy in scalable systems.
- Achieve quicker time-to-market with validated outcomes.

Moreover, this hybrid approach is being widely adopted in sectors such as:

- E-learning

where diverse learners require adaptive, personalized interfaces (Rizk et al., 2019).

- E-commerce

where user behavior data informs rapid UX improvements.

- Smart government services

where accessibility and inclusiveness are mandatory

By combining the strategic creativity of Design Thinking, the rigor of UCD, and the adaptability of Agile, organizations can continuously evolve their digital products to stay relevant, impactful, and user-aligned creating solutions that are not just technically sound but genuinely meaningful.

CASE STUDIES OF THEORETICAL-PRACTICAL INTEGRATION

Web technologies thrive when theoretical principles are successfully translated into practical, real-world implementations. Theories provide foundational frameworks for how digital systems should behave, how information should be structured, and how user interactions can be optimized. However, the true impact of these theories is realized when they are embedded into concrete systems that are scalable, usable, and responsive to contextual needs (Dogan & Gogus, 2025). Whether in the fields of education, healthcare, or public administration, the integration of theory and practice ensures that digital systems are not only efficient but also meaningful, inclusive, and ethically grounded (Kim, Oh, Gim, & Kim, 2024).

Despite their importance, the process of applying theoretical models in practice is rarely straightforward. Theories often begin as abstract constructs, requiring careful interpretation and adaptation before they can shape design decisions or system functionalities. For instance, Constructivist Learning Theory may encourage exploratory, learner-driven digital experiences in educational platforms, while Actor-Network Theory highlights the complex interdependence between technologies and stakeholders in healthcare systems (Wang, Choo, Ng, Bi, & Wang, 2025). In contrast, Information Architecture and Hypertext Theory often dominate in e-government systems, where clarity, navigability, and accessibility are primary goals (Kim, Oh, Gim, & Kim, 2024).

This section presents case studies from three key domains education, healthcare, and e-government to illustrate how theoretical models can shape the architecture, user experience, and functionality of web systems. These examples not only reflect best practices but also demonstrate how academic frameworks, such as Constructivist Learning Theory, Actor-Network Theory, Hypertext Theory, and Information Architecture, are translated into technical structures and interactive workflows. In doing so, they reveal the dynamic and iterative relationship between conceptual thinking and technological execution bridging the often-cited divide between academic theory and industry practice.

Education: Learning Management Systems (LMS)

In the educational sector, Learning Management Systems (LMS) integrate Constructivist Learning Theory to support personalized, active, and exploratory learning. Platforms such as Moodle and Canvas use adaptive content delivery and modular design to allow learners to navigate non-linearly through educational material, reflecting the core tenets of Constructivism and Hypertext Theory.

Additionally, systems like Google Classroom utilize Web 2.0 services to support collaborative activities and integrate multimedia. These tools enable students to construct knowledge interactively rather than passively consume content. As highlighted by Torres Kompen et al. (2019), such environments create more personalized and socially enriched learning experiences that align with constructivist learning outcomes.

Furthermore, Gazzawe et al. (2022) describe the role of AI-enhanced content delivery in mobile e-learning systems, enabling real-time adaptation to learners' progress, difficulties, and preferences an embodiment of Human-Centered Design and adaptive system theories in practice.

Healthcare: Patient Portals and Actor-Network Theory

Actor-Network Theory (ANT) provides a robust lens for examining the interplay between users, technologies, and institutional actors in complex systems, such as healthcare platforms. In patient-facing applications such as MyChart, Halodoc, or Alodokter, ANT is realized through the interdependent activities of digital tools and human stakeholders.

These platforms integrate:

- Wearable device data for passive health monitoring
- Secure electronic health records (EHR) for centralized medical history
- Automated scheduling systems for appointments and reminders
- Chatbots and video consultations for real-time support

Table 9 Shows the Actor-Network Roles in Digital Healthcare Platforms.

Table 9. Actor-network roles in digital healthcare platforms

Actor	Role in the Network
Patient	Data input, appointment interaction
Doctor	Data retrieval, feedback provider
Wearable Device	Passive data collection
Portal System	Information mediator
EHR System	Record storage and analytics

Bychkov et al. (2022) emphasize that the successful implementation of digital healthcare services depends on understanding these dynamic interactions, not merely deploying technology. This perspective encourages co-design methodologies where technical, medical, and user domains intersect continuously.

E-Government: Public Services and Information Architecture

Web-based public service platforms often apply Information Architecture (IA) and Web Accessibility Guidelines (WCAG) to optimize usability and inclusiveness. Government websites like GOV.UK or Indonesia's LAPOR! platform demonstrate well-structured navigation, consistent design, and compliance with accessibility standards to serve diverse populations. These systems embody both Hypertext Theory and User-Centered Design, ensuring citizens from varied backgrounds can find and interact with essential services with minimal friction. Table 10 Shows the Key Information Architecture Principles in E-Government Platforms.

Table 10. Key information architecture principles in e-government platforms

Principle	Implementation Example
Clear Navigation	Mega menus, breadcrumbs
Accessibility	Screen reader support, keyboard navigation
Content Hierarchy	Headings, visual hierarchy
Mobile Optimization	Responsive layout for small devices

Kim et al. (2024) argue that national and regional governments must align their platforms with established standards to maintain digital trust and usability. The application of semantic structure and responsive layouts ensures long-term maintainability, while WCAG compliance fulfills legal and ethical mandates for inclusivity.

Lessons Learned

These case studies demonstrate that the practical application of theoretical foundations whether Constructivist Learning Theory, Actor-Network Theory, Hypertext Theory, or Information Architecture can lead to more functional, inclusive, and responsive web platforms. Successful projects combine:

1) Theory-informed design decisions
2) Cross-functional collaboration
3) Continuous user feedback integration
4) Adherence to technical and ethical standards

Furthermore, integrated digital solutions often evolve more sustainably when guided by established frameworks. As technologies and societal needs advance, the enduring value lies in grounding innovation with theoretical clarity and empirical rigor.

CHALLENGES IN BRIDGING THEORY AND PRACTICE

Despite the growing emphasis on theoretical grounding in web development, several persistent challenges continue to complicate the translation of abstract frameworks into practical, user-facing solutions. Theories such as Human-Centered Design, Actor-Network Theory, and the Technology Acceptance Model provide valuable lenses for understanding user behavior, system relationships, and design logic. However, these models often remain underutilized or superficially applied due to the multifaceted nature of real-world development environments.

One core tension lies in the difference between ideal theoretical conditions and actual development constraints. While theory encourages structured thinking, user empathy, and ethical design, practice demands agility, speed, and compromises. Developers may understand the value of these models, but tight deadlines, insufficient stakeholder buy-in, or infrastructural barriers often hinder their effective integration. This results in digital solutions that are technically functional but may fall short in terms of usability, inclusiveness, or long-term adaptability (Alexopoulos, Nikolakis, & Xanthakis, 2022).

Moreover, the fragmentation between academic research and practical application deepens the divide. Theoretical work tends to operate at a strategic level, while developers and product teams are focused on short-term deliverables and client expectations. Without effective communication channels or interdisciplinary collaboration, opportunities to apply theory meaningfully are frequently lost. This section explores specific barriers both technical and human-centered that obstruct this synergy, and highlights emerging strategies to bridge the conceptual and the actionable in web development practice.

Complexity vs. Usability

Figure 3. Complexity and usability

Many theoretical models are rich in structure and logic but difficult to operationalize in dynamic environments. For example, Actor-Network Theory (ANT) provides a nuanced view of socio-technical relationships, but translating such complexity into an interface can result in cognitive overload or design paralysis (Bychkov, et al., 2022). Designers may struggle to simplify intricate models without oversimplifying or misrepresenting key relationships.

Additionally, high-level theories such as Hypertext Theory advocate for non-linear user pathways, yet in practical application, too many interconnections can confuse users and degrade usability. Balancing theoretical richness with real-world cognitive constraints requires careful UX research and iteration especially in contexts like healthcare and government services, where clarity is essential.

Technological Constraints and Organizational Realities

Even when developers and designers are theoretically informed, practical limitations often obstruct optimal implementation. Constraints such as outdated infrastructure, limited developer skills, or strict budget cycles can push teams to favor quick-fix solutions over theoretically robust designs (Alexopoulos, Nikolakis, & Xanthakis, 2022). Moreover, large-scale organizations may be bound by legacy systems that are incompatible with agile and modular frameworks like microservices.

In many cases, development teams must make compromises between the ideal state envisioned by theory and the constraints imposed by existing systems and policies. This friction is particularly evident in public sector web development, where compliance and procurement procedures often lag behind evolving digital standards (Kim, Oh, Gim, & Kim, 2024). Table 11 Shows the Impact of Technological Constraints on Theoretical Adoption.

Table 11. Impact of technological constraints on theoretical adoption

Theoretical Concept	Ideal Implementation	Real-World Barrier	Compromise in Pratice
Actor-Network Theory (ANT)	Dynamic stakeholder mapping	Legacy systems, fixed roles	Simplified static user types
Microservices Architecture	Modular system integration	Low dev capacity, monolithic backend	Partial API adoption
WCAG Accessibility	Fully accessible UI	Lack of training, tool limitations	Basic compliance without testing
Agile + UCD Integration	Iterative user-driven dev	Tight deadlines, siloed teams	Feedback only at post-launch phase

User Diversity and Cultural Bias in Models

Theoretical frameworks often emerge from Western-centric paradigms and may not fully account for global diversity in user behavior, literacy, access, and cognitive processing. For instance, design principles based on minimalism and linear navigation may alienate users from high-context cultures who rely on visual cues, metaphors, and exploratory interfaces (Kesavan, Saravana, Kumar, & Vengatesan K, 2021).

Likewise, models like the Technology Acceptance Model (TAM) assume access to stable infrastructure, consistent internet connectivity, and baseline digital literacy. However, in regions where these prerequisites are not guaranteed, such models may lead to misleading interpretations of user readiness. This issue has been echoed in studies on e-learning accessibility and mobile education systems in the Global South (Gazzawe, Mayouf, Lock, & Alturki, 2022).

To mitigate these issues, web developers must:

- Localize content and interfaces linguistically and culturally
- Test theories across varied demographics before generalization
- Apply hybrid frameworks that blend empirical evidence with contextual design
- Involve regional stakeholders during the design phase to validate assumptions

Strategic Approaches Forward

Overcoming these barriers demands an interdisciplinary approach. Teams must foster collaboration between theorists, engineers, designers, and end-users. Methods such as participatory design, inclusive research, and continuous feedback integration help ensure that theoretical frameworks remain grounded and adaptable.

Moreover, flexible design systems and modular architectures like Progressive Web Apps (PWAs) offer a compromise between innovation and feasibility allowing teams to apply complex ideas within scalable, maintainable infrastructures (Eskandarzadeh, 2023). By acknowledging limitations without abandoning theory, digital teams can build systems that are not only innovative but also equitable, sustainable, and contextually relevant.

FUTURE TRENDS IN WEB TECHNOLOGIES

The evolution of web technologies is set to accelerate in the coming years, driven not only by breakthroughs in artificial intelligence and data semantics but also by a shift in societal expectations. As users demand faster, smarter, and more personalized digital experiences, web developers and designers must grapple with increasingly complex requirements ranging from technical scalability to ethical responsibility. The web is no longer just a medium for publishing information, but a dynamic ecosystem that must respond adaptively to individual and collective human needs.

This transformation is not solely technological it is deeply intertwined with theoretical and philosophical developments. Human-Centered Design (HCD), systemic thinking, and digital ethics are reshaping the foundations of how we build, test, and maintain web systems. The future of web technologies lies in their ability to reflect human values, social structures, and contextual relevance. This means designing not just for efficiency and performance, but also for empathy, fairness, and long-term impact.

Emerging trends now point toward a convergence between hard science and soft understanding. As AI-driven automation meets ethical frameworks, and as responsive interfaces are reimagined through inclusive design, the next generation of web platforms will be shaped by this duality: intelligent by architecture and humane by design. These paradigms serve as the entry point into key areas of innovation such as the Semantic Web, AI-Augmented UX, and embedded ethical governance frameworks.

Semantic Web and Ontologies

The Semantic Web, a concept championed by Tim Berners-Lee, envisions a web of data that is understandable by machines. It builds on ontologiesformal representations of knowledge that define concepts and relationships within a domain to create meaning-rich, interconnected systems. This movement is central to the next evolution of data-driven applications that rely on automated reasoning, data interoperability, and context-aware systems. For instance, platforms using semantic tagging and linked data enable more accurate search results, dynamic content generation, and smarter navigation structures (Reyero Lobo, Daga, Alani, & Fernandez, 2023).

In legal, healthcare, and education sectors, ontology-driven systems are improving decision support, knowledge management, and service integration especially in multilingual and cross-disciplinary environments (Francesconi, 2018).

AI-Augmented Design and Predictive UX

Artificial Intelligence is rapidly transforming web development from code-based logic to data-informed design decisions. AI-augmented UX refers to using machine learning to automate, enhance, and personalize user experiences based on behavioral data. For example, recommender systems in e-commerce or adaptive learning paths in LMS platforms rely heavily on predictive algorithms rooted in Behavioral Modeling, a theory from cognitive science (Verhoef, Kooge, Walk, & Wieringa, 2021)

In addition, AI techniques such as Natural Language Processing (NLP), sentiment analysis, and generative AI are being embedded into web applications to support intelligent interfaces, conversational agents, and automated content generation (AlDahoul, Hong, Varvello, & Zaki, 2025). Table 12 Shows the AI-Driven UX Features and Their Theoretical Foundations.

Table 12. AI-driven UX features and their theoretical foundations

AI Feature	UX Application Example	Theoretical Backbone
Predictive Search	Auto-suggestions in search bars	Information Foraging Theory
Chatbots & Virtual Agents	24/7 support with NLP	Conversation Theory
Personalization Engines	Adaptive content on dashboards	Constructivist Learning Theory

Ethical Framework Integration in Web Development

With growing concerns around bias, surveillance, and dark patterns, the future of web development must integrate ethical design frameworks from the ground up. This includes:

1) Transparency

   systems must clearly disclose how data is used

2) Fairness (no algorithmic bias)

   algorithms must be audited for bias

3) Accessibility (inclusive by default)

   inclusive design should be the default, not an afterthought

Frameworks like Value-Sensitive Design (VSD), Ethics by Design, and Explainable AI (XAI) are gaining traction in both academic and industry settings (Liebig, Güttel, Jobin, & Katzenbach, 2024). Moreover, the Semantic Web itself is being re-examined through ethical lenses to prevent reinforcement of bias in knowledge graphs and automated reasoning (Reyero Lobo, Daga, Alani, & Fernandez, 2023). Table 13 Shows the Ethical Design Principles and Their Theoretical Foundations in Web Development.

Table 13. Ethical design principles and their theoretical foundations in web development

Ethical Principle	Implementation Technique	Related Theory
Fairness	Algorithmic audits	Justice Theory (Rawls)
Transparency	Consent UIs, open-source models	Ethical HCI
Accountability	Explainable AI (XAI)	Actor-Network Theory

CONCLUSION

Web technologies have evolved beyond mere tools for information dissemination; they are now dynamic, interconnected ecosystems shaped by both technical capabilities and human-centered design philosophies. This chapter has demonstrated that the development of effective, accessible, and scalable web systems cannot rely solely on engineering practices or coding proficiency it requires a deep integration of theoretical frameworks such as Hypertext Theory, Information Architecture, Actor-Network Theory, and Constructivist Learning Theory. These models provide critical lenses through which developers and researchers can interpret user behavior, system interactions, and design outcomes.

However, the translation of these theories into practice is rarely straightforward. As discussed, real-world constraints such as limited budgets, legacy infrastructures, and diverse user profiles often challenge the direct application of ideal models. Nevertheless, through agile methodologies, user-centered design, and iterative prototyping, practitioners can continuously refine their approaches, aligning theoretical insights with practical realities. Case studies from sectors like education, healthcare, and e-government illustrate how this integration can lead to more meaningful, context-aware web solutions that genuinely serve their intended audiences.

As we move toward a future shaped by AI, semantic technologies, and ethical design imperatives, the fusion of theory and practice will become even more vital. Developers must remain critically aware not only of the technical standards and protocols that govern web development but also of the social, cultural, and ethical dimensions embedded within these technologies. Ultimately, embracing a balanced and reflective approach where theoretical foundations inform, but do not rigidly dictate will enable the creation of more resilient, inclusive, and transformative web experiences.

REFERENCES

Al-Barakati, A. (2021). Leveraging Artificial Intelligence-enabled Workflow Framework for Legacy Transformation. *International Journal of Advanced Computer Science and Applications*, *12*(12), 297–303. DOI: 10.14569/IJACSA.2021.0121239

AlDahoul, N., Hong, J., Varvello, M., & Zaki, Y. (2025). Towards a World Wide Web powered by generative AI. *Scientific Reports*, *15*(1), 7251. Advance online publication. DOI: 10.1038/s41598-024-77301-0 PMID: 40021676

Alexopoulos, K., Nikolakis, N., & Xanthakis, E. (2022). *Digital Transformation of Production Planning and Control in Manufacturing SMEs-The Mold Shop Case. Laboratory for Manufacturing Systems & Automation (LMS)*. Department of Mechanical Engineering & Aeronautics, University of Patras., DOI: 10.3390/app122110788

Bezus, S., Akbilek, E., & Mekeko, N. (2021). Web Technologies in Distance Learning: Student Perception on the Advantages and Disadvantages. *2021 IEEE International Conference on Educational Technology, ICET 2021*, 85-89. Retrieved from DOI: 10.1109/ICET52293.2021.9563134

Bychkov, I., Ruzhnikov, G., Fedorov, R., Popova, A., Avid, B., Batgerel, B., & Dulamrchaga, U. (2022). Digital transformation of the environmental monitoring for Lake Khubsugul and Prikhubsugulye. *Journal of Computational Technologies*, 14 - 29. doi:DOI: 10.25743/ICT.2022.27.5.003

Chen, S., Yang, L., Zhang, Y., Zhang, M., Xie, Y., Zhu, Z., & Li, J. (2025). Digital Human Technology in E-Learning: Custom Content Solutions. *Applied Sciences (Basel, Switzerland)*, *15*(7), 3807. Advance online publication. DOI: 10.3390/app15073807

Dogan, B., & Gogus, A. (2025). The Effect of the 'Instructional Technologies' Course on the Competencies of Teacher Candidates in Using Web 2.0 Tools: The Case of Early Childhood Education Program. *Springer Science and Business Media B.*, *30*(2), 883–910. DOI: 10.1007/s10758-025-09842-w

Eskandarzadeh, A. (2023). The future of web 3: A roadmap for the decentralized web. *Concepts, Technologies, Challenges, and the Future of Web 3*, 511-523. DOI: 10.4018/978-1-6684-9919-1.ch025

Eswaran, U., & Eswaran, V. (2024). AI-Driven Cross-Platform Design: Enhancing Usability and User Experience. *Navigating Usability and User Experience in a Multi-Platform World*, 19-48. DOI: 10.4018/979-8-3693-2337-3.ch002

Francesconi, E. (2018). On the future of legal publishing services in the Semantic Web. *Future Internet*, *10*(6), 48. Advance online publication. DOI: 10.3390/fi10060048

Gazzawe, F., Mayouf, M., Lock, R., & Alturki, R. (2022). The Role of Machine Learning in E-Learning Using the Web and AI-Enabled Mobile Applications. *Mobile Information Systems*, *2022*, 1–10. Advance online publication. DOI: 10.1155/2022/3696140

Kesavan, S., Saravana, K., Kumar, A., & Vengatesan K. (2021). An investigation on adaptive HTTP media streaming Quality-of-Experience (QoE) and agility using cloud media services. *International Journal of Computers and Applications*, 431 - 444. DOI: 10.1080/1206212X.2019.1575034

Kim, J., Oh, J., Gim, G., & Kim, Y. (2024). An Empirical Study on E-Government Service Using Web Standard Policy. *Studies in Computational Intelligence*, *1160*, 75–85. DOI: 10.1007/978-3-031-61163-6_7

Liebig, L., Güttel, L., Jobin, A., & Katzenbach, C. (2024). Subnational AI policy: shaping AI in a multi-level governance system. *ZeMKI, Centre for Media, Communication and Information Research*, 1477 - 1490. DOI: 10.1007/s00146-022-01561-5

Martins, B., & Duarte, C. (2024). A large-scale web accessibility analysis considering technology adoption. *Universal Access in the Information Society*, *23*(4), 1857–1872. DOI: 10.1007/s10209-023-01010-0

Nazarenko, V., Zazymko, O., Funderburk, M., & Klikh, L. (2024). Web information educational assistant service with focus on artificial intelligence and smart systems technologies. *CEUR Workshop Proceedings*, *3781*, 175–191. https://www.scopus.com/inward/record.uri?eid=2-s2.0-85207073925&partnerID=40&md5=36acf26d32f0374aaf7fe0aae07e309e

Olca, E., & Can, O. (2022). DICON: A Domain-Independent Consent Management for Personal Data Protection. *IEEE Access*, 95479 - 95497. DOI: 10.1109/ACCESS.2022.3204970

Reyero Lobo, P., Daga, E., Alani, H., & Fernandez, M. (2023). Semantic Web technologies and bias in artificial intelligence: A systematic literature review. *Semantic Web*, *14*(4), 745–770. DOI: 10.3233/SW-223041

Rizk, N., Nasr, E., & Gheith, M. (2019). Enhancing CREeLS the crowdsourcing based requirements elicitation approach for elearning systems using bi-gram evaluation. *ICENCO 2019 - 2019 15th International Computer Engineering Conference: Utilizing Machine Intelligence for a Better World*, 222 - 226. DOI: 10.1109/ICENCO48310.2019.9027371

Verhoef, P., Kooge, E., Walk, N., & Wieringa, J. (2021). *Creating value with data analytics in marketing: Mastering data science.* DOI: 10.4324/9781003011163

Wang, Y., Choo, W., Ng, K., Bi, R., & Wang, P. (2025). Evolution of AI enabled healthcare systems using textual data with a pretrained BERT deep learning model. *Scientific Reports, 15*(1), 7540. Advance online publication. DOI: 10.1038/s41598-025-91622-8 PMID: 40038367

Chapter 3
Digital Transformation Frameworks, Maturity, Sectoral Studies, Organizational Change, and Leadership

Wilson Fabian
https://orcid.org/0009-0007-0886-1912
Universitas Esa Unggul, Indonesia

Qori Halimatul Hidayah
https://orcid.org/0009-0008-7567-4102
Universitas Esa Unggul, Indonesia

Rudi Heri Marwan
Universitas Esa Unggul, Indonesia

ABSTRACT

Digital transformation is critical for modern organizations. This chapter comprehensively examines its key enablers: strategic, organizational, and leadership dimensions. Its purpose is to synthesize current understanding, offering actionable insights. The chapter dissects prominent digital transformation frameworks, analyzing components and applicability. It then explores various digital maturity models, demonstrating utility in assessing capabilities and charting enhancement roadmaps. For practical insights, sectoral case studies (e.g., finance, manufacturing, healthcare) are presented, highlighting diverse strategies, challenges, and lessons. Furthermore, the chapter analyzes transformation's impact on organizational change, emphasizing

DOI: 10.4018/979-8-3373-5167-4.ch003

effective change management to foster adoption and innovative cultures. Finally, it details leadership's pivotal role in steering digital transformation, outlining essential competencies for vision, empowerment, and uncertainty navigation. This chapter provides holistic insights for building resilient, digitally-enabled organizations.

INTRODUCTION

Background and Context of Digital Transformation

The contemporary digital era has fundamentally reshaped industries, economies, and societies across the globe. This profound shift is largely propelled by rapid advancements in technologies such as Artificial Intelligence (AI), the Internet of Things (IoT), Big Data, cloud computing, and blockchain. Consequently, organizations in every sector are now compelled to undertake a comprehensive digital transformation (DT). More than a simple adoption of new tools, DT signifies a holistic reimagining of business models, operational processes, customer engagement strategies, and even the very fabric of organizational culture. This urgent imperative stems from several interconnected forces: the accelerating pace of technological innovation, which quickly renders traditional methods obsolete; the evolving expectations of customers, who now demand seamless and personalized digital experiences; and the intensified global competition, which necessitates greater agility and continuous innovation. As a result, digital transformation has become an undeniable strategic necessity for survival and sustained growth in the 21st century. It guides organizations toward becoming more adaptive, data-driven, and customer-centric entities, capable of flourishing amidst relentless disruption. This chapter, therefore, offers a thorough exploration of the essential frameworks, models, and human elements critical to achieving successful digital transformation.

Figure 1. Stages of the digital transformation journey

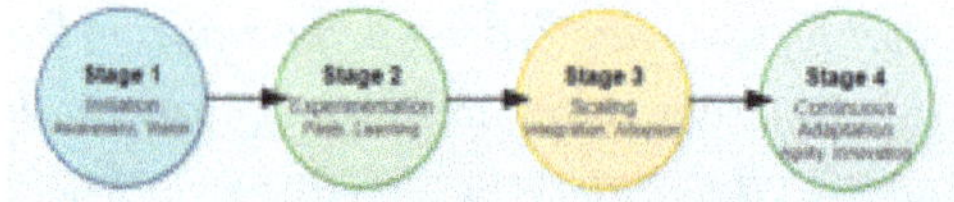

Challenges and Gaps in Digital Transformation Implementation

Even with the urgent need for digital transformation, actually pulling it off successfully often turns out to be quite difficult. Many initiatives, unfortunately, don't quite hit their targets, usually because of a tricky mix of technological hurdles, organizational misalignment, and critical human factors. A significant problem surfaces when companies try to weave new digital technologies into their older, established systems, creating significant technical debt and slowing down the flow of information. Beyond technology, strategic and organizational gaps frequently appear, including a fuzzy strategic vision, insufficient investment, and struggling to scale pilot projects across the enterprise. The biggest hurdles, however, truly lie in the human and cultural aspects; people naturally resist change, and inadequate leadership or risk-averse culture can bring transformation to a halt. Many companies view DT narrowly as solely an IT concern, missing its profound impact on processes and people. The absence of solid measurement tools, such as robust maturity models, further contributes to unsystematic, trial-and-error approaches. To truly tackle these multifaceted challenges, a holistic approach is needed—one that combines strategic foresight with a genuine understanding of organizational dynamics and human behavior.

Chapter Objectives and Significance

This chapter aims to provide a comprehensive, integrated understanding of digital transformation, synthesizing fragmented views into a cohesive, holistic perspective. Specifically, this chapter seeks to:

- Analyze and compare prominent digital transformation frameworks and maturity models, detailing their components and strategic utility.
- Present rigorous sectoral case studies, explicitly linking implementation strategies and lessons learned to the theoretical frameworks and models.
- Critically examine the profound impact of DT on organizational change, leadership competencies, and the cultivation of agile, innovative cultures.
- Integrate discussion on foundational enablers often overlooked, specifically cybersecurity, data ethics, and financial evaluation, offering a more holistic view of the DT landscape.
- Synthesize all key components into a clear model for practical implementation, providing actionable guidance for practitioners and valuable insights for academics.

The chapter's significance lies in its integrative approach, providing a structured narrative that bridges theory with practical application and emphasizes the crucial human dimension. It contributes valuable insights for readers seeking both a deeper theoretical understanding and actionable guidance necessary to build resilient, competitive, and future-ready organizations.

Chapter Structure

This chapter is systematically organized. Following this introduction, Section 2 provides a refined literature review, conceptualizing digital transformation and its dimensions. Section 3 analyzes major digital transformation frameworks. Section 4 explores digital maturity models. Section 5 presents detailed sectoral case studies, linking practice to theory. Section 6 focuses on organizational change management. Section 7 examines leadership's critical role. Finally, Section 8 offers a comprehensive discussion, synthesizing the components, addressing unresolved challenges, and outlining directions for future research. This structured approach guides the reader through a logical progression from foundational concepts to strategic implementation and holistic human-centric considerations.

CONCEPTUALIZING DIGITAL TRANSFORMATION

Definition and Dimensions of Digital Transformation

Digital transformation (DT) is a dynamic, multifaceted concept that profoundly transcends mere technology adoption. It represents a fundamental, strategic shift where digital technologies are strategically leveraged to create new or substantially modify existing business processes, culture, and customer experiences, ultimately meeting evolving market requirements. Influential scholars, such as **Westerman and Kane**, emphasize that successful DT is fundamentally about the strategic integration of technology, people, and processes—a notion critical for separating meaningful change from simple digitization. DT is best viewed as an organizational and cultural change, fully enabled by technology.

Key dimensions consistently emerge as critical pillars for successful DT, often framed around the concept of organizational capabilities:

- **Customer Experience (CX) Transformation:** Focuses on leveraging technology to enhance customer interactions, personalize services, and create seamless, omni-channel experiences.
- **Operational Process Transformation:** Involves digitizing and automating core processes using technologies like Robotic Process Automation (RPA) and the Internet of Things (IoT) to improve efficiency and agility.
- **Business Model Transformation:** Entails fundamentally rethinking how an organization creates, delivers, and captures value, often through new digital products, services, or platform-based ecosystems.

- **Organizational Culture and Capabilities Transformation:** Addresses the human element, requiring the fostering of innovation, agility, collaboration, and continuous learning alongside developing necessary digital skills.
- **Strategy and Vision:** Requires a clear, compelling digital strategy aligned with overall business objectives, guiding technology investments towards purposeful, value-driven initiatives.
- **Data and Analytics:** Central to DT, this dimension focuses on leveraging data as a strategic asset to inform decision-making, personalize offerings, and optimize operations.

These dimensions are deeply interconnected, requiring simultaneous attention for a holistic approach to achieve sustainable digital success.

Figure 2. Key dimension of digital transformation

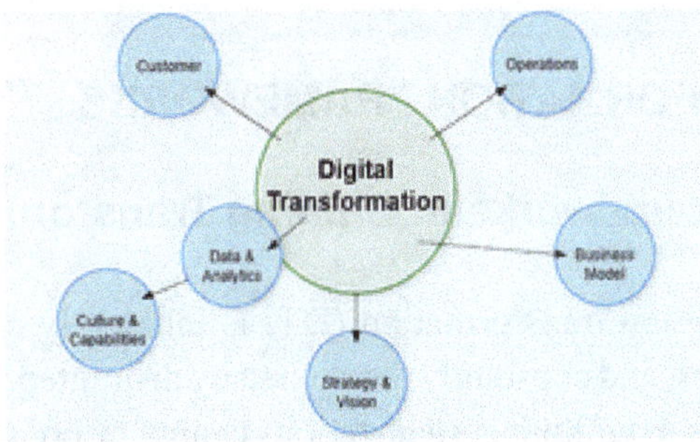

Distinguishing Between Digitization, Digitalization, and Digital Transformation

To fully anchor the DT concept, it is crucial to differentiate it from two related concepts that are frequently misused, as highlighted by works from scholars in the field of information systems:

- **Digitization:** This is the most basic step, referring to the process of converting analog information into a digital format (e.g., paper to PDF). It changes the *form* of data, making it machine-readable, but does not alter underlying processes or business models. It is simply about doing the same things, but electronically.

- **Digitalization:** This involves leveraging digitized information and digital technologies to enable or improve existing business processes. It applies digital capabilities to enhance efficiency or streamline operations (e.g., implementing an ERP system). While it improves processes, it typically avoids radical changes to the business model or culture. It is about doing things digitally.
- **Digital Transformation (DT):** The most expansive concept. It is the comprehensive, strategic, organizational, and cultural change of an entity, leveraging integrated digital technologies to achieve new value propositions and competitive advantage. DT is about transforming the entire business model through digital means.

Understanding this precise distinction is vital for formulating effective digital strategies that move beyond mere technological upgrades toward genuine, sustainable transformation.

DIGITAL TRANSFORMATION FRAMEWORKS

Importance of Frameworks in Guiding Transformation

The journey of digital transformation (DT) is inherently complex, marked by profound uncertainties, and constantly threatened by disjointed, isolated efforts. For an undertaking of this magnitude, organizations cannot afford to proceed without a structured approach. Digital transformation frameworks stand as truly indispensable strategic tools, providing a systematic blueprint that reliably guides organizations through the intricate phases of their transformation journey. These frameworks offer a vital shared language, establish a common organizational understanding, and define a clear, logical sequence of actions, which is crucial for reducing ambiguity and successfully fostering alignment across all departments and stakeholders involved in the change(Yu et al., 2025).

The value derived from adopting a robust framework is multifaceted. Firstly, frameworks provide Structure and Direction by offering a clear roadmap, effectively breaking down the vast scope of DT into manageable phases and defined areas of focus. This approach actively prevents fragmented initiatives and ensures that every effort directly contributes to the overarching strategic vision. Secondly, they guarantee Holistic Coverage by encompassing multiple DT dimensions—such as customer experience, operations, business models, culture, and technology—which prevents the common pitfall of neglecting critical human or strategic elements that are often the true determinants of success. Thirdly, they effectively Facilitate Assessment and

Measurement by often integrating tools or criteria for measuring digital capabilities and progress, allowing for objective evaluation, identification of strengths and weaknesses, and tracking of initiative impact over time. Furthermore, frameworks significantly Reduce Risk and Uncertainty by highlighting industry best practices and potential pitfalls, offering insights that increase the likelihood of successful outcomes. Finally, they strongly Foster Alignment and Collaboration, creating a shared understanding of DT goals that successfully breaks down organizational silos, and actively Promote Continuous Learning and Adaptation, essential for cultivating an agile mindset. In essence, DT frameworks empower organizations to expertly navigate complexity, ensure comprehensiveness, manage risk, and ultimately drive successful, sustainable change toward true digital maturity(J. Liu et al., 2025).

Comparative Analysis of Leading Digital Transformation Frameworks

The diverse landscape of digital transformation (DT) frameworks offers unique perspectives, making a comprehensive comparative analysis crucial for selecting the most suitable approach. These foundational concepts are directly relevant to organizational strategy, as they illuminate distinct contributions and underlying philosophies for navigating digital change. Such an analysis empowers decision-makers to critically evaluate and select a tailored strategy that aligns precisely with their specific strategic goals, organizational culture, and current digital maturity, thereby maximizing their potential for digital success(Zia et al., 2025).

Table 1. Comparative analysis of leading digital transformation frameworks

FRAMEWORK	CORE FOCUS / PILLARS	KEY STAGES / DIMENSIONS	STRENGTHS	CONSIDERATIONS / LIMITATIONS
MIT CISR Digital Business Model Framework	Operational Excellence, Customer Intimacy	Suppliers, Omni-channel Businesses, Digitized Operations, New Digital Businesses (4 models)	Clear focus on business outcomes; Actionable quadrant model for strategic positioning.	Less explicit on broader ecosystem or cultural transformation.
Altimeter Group's Six Stages of Digital Transformation	Evolutionary journey from experimentation to integration	Business As Usual, Present & Active, Formalized, Strategic, Converged, Adaptive & Innovative (6 stages)	Clear, progressive stages for benchmarking; Emphasizes moving beyond isolated projects.	Implied linearity may not fully capture real-world simultaneous efforts.
IBM's Digital Reinvention Framework	Reimagine Customer Experience, Reinvent Core Operations, Build New Business Models	3 core pillars	Comprehensive, action-oriented language; Highlights advanced technologies as enablers.	May require significant initial investment and strong top-down mandate.
Deloitte's Digital Transformation Framework	Customer, Strategy, Technology, Operations, Organization & Culture	5 key areas	Strong emphasis on interconnectedness and holistic approach; Balanced view.	Broadness may require further sub-component drill-down.
Accenture's Digital Transformation Framework	Digital Strategy, Digital Customer, Digital Operations, Digital Technology, Digital Talent & Organization	Multi-dimensional approach (5 dimensions)	Comprehensive and balanced view; Stresses integration and data/analytics as cross-cutting.	Similar to Deloitte, may require deeper dive into specific areas.

Upon reviewing these frameworks, one key insight immediately emerges: while each offers a unique lens, they all collectively underscore the inherently multifaceted nature of digital change. The choice of framework should never be merely a matter of organizational preference. Instead, it must be a strategic decision that meticulously aligns the framework's core emphasis—be it achieving Operational Excellence (e.g., MIT CISR), strategic integration across evolutionary stages (e.g., Altimeter), or radical new business model creation (e.g., IBM)—with the organization's most pressing and immediate digital imperative.

MIT CISR Digital Business Model Framework

The MIT CISR framework is widely cited and influential, serving as a foundational model in DT literature. It fundamentally posits that successful transformation relies on mastering two critical, interconnected capabilities: operational excellence (digitizing and standardizing core processes for efficiency) and customer intimacy (leveraging digital tools for personalized customer interactions). Organizations strive to achieve the ideal state, known as the New Digital Business, by strategically balancing proficiency in both these areas. The framework defines a clear pathway through four business models, making its strength lie in its sharp focus on clear, tangible business outcomes and providing an actionable quadrant model for strategic positioning(Giang & Dung, 2025).

Altimeter Group's Six Stages of Digital Transformation

The Altimeter framework maps the digital transformation process as an evolutionary journey, outlining six sequential stages that progress from initial, isolated experimentation to full organizational integration. The stages range from Business As Usual to the highly adaptive and continuous innovation stage. This model is exceptionally valuable because its clear, progressive structure allows organizations to effectively benchmark their evolutionary progress and clearly understand the necessary steps required to move toward a cohesive, integrated digital strategy, emphasizing the necessity of scaling efforts beyond mere epartmental pilots.

IBM's Digital Reinvention Framework

IBM's model centers its strategic approach on three core, action-oriented pillars: Reimagine Customer Experience, Reinvent Core Operations, and Build New Business Models. This comprehensive framework wisely emphasizes both internal efficiency and external value creation, strategically positioning advanced technologies (like AI and cloud) not as ends in themselves, but as key enablers that unlock profound new organizational capabilities. The framework's structured approach helps organizations focus their significant investment toward measurable outcomes in these three areas.

Success Factors for Framework Implementation

The effective implementation of any chosen DT framework, ensuring it successfully translates into real organizational value, hinges on diligent attention to several key, interconnected success factors. This phase demands strong commitment and meticulous planning across the human and strategic dimensions:

First and foremost, Strong Leadership Commitment and a Clear Vision are non-negotiable. Transformation must be actively driven and sponsored from the highest levels of leadership, ensuring a cohesive and sustained vision that is meticulously aligned with overall business goals. Secondly, maintaining a Holistic Integration strategy is critical; this involves successfully breaking down organizational silos and integrating efforts across technology, process, people, and culture simultaneously to ensure comprehensive coverage. Thirdly, the adoption of Agile Methodologies and Iterative Execution is necessary for quick learning, adaptation, and flexibility in a constantly changing digital environment. Furthermore, a determined Focus on People and Culture through continuous talent investment, skill development, and fostering psychological safety is vital, given that the human element remains the biggest success determinant. Finally, Data-Driven Decision Making must be central for tracking impact, coupled with Adequate Resource Allocation to ensure the sustained financial and technological investment required to realize the full potential of digital efforts.

DIGITAL MATURITY MODELS

Role of Maturity Models in Evaluation and Planning

In the complex landscape of digital transformation (DT), organizations frequently struggle to objectively assess their current digital capabilities, identify critical gaps, and strategically plan their next steps. Digital maturity models (DMMs) are truly indispensable tools, providing a structured framework to evaluate progress along the DT journey. They offer a diagnostic approach to understand an organization's current state ("as-is") and define its desired future state ("to-be"), outlining progressive stages from nascent digital adoption to advanced, integrated capabilities. These models serve to guide resource allocation and investment prioritization(Saari et al., 2025).

The primary roles and benefits of utilizing DMMs include:

- Objective Assessment: DMMs offer a standardized approach to evaluate various dimensions of digital capabilities, such as strategy, technology infrastructure, data analytics, customer experience, operations, and culture. This provides a clear, data-driven understanding of strengths and weaknesses, moving beyond subjective perceptions.
- Gap Identification: By mapping the current state against the ideal characteristics of higher maturity levels, DMMs highlight specific areas where capa-

bilities are lacking. This precise identification enables leaders to prioritize investments and focus efforts on the most impactful areas for improvement.

- Strategic Planning and Roadmap Development: The staged nature of DMMs provides a clear roadmap for transformation. Once assessed, organizations can define realistic and achievable goals for advancing to the next stage, facilitating a structured, phased implementation plan aligned with strategic objectives.
- Benchmarking: DMMs allow organizations to compare their digital maturity with competitors or industry leaders, providing valuable external context to understand their relative position and accelerate efforts to gain competitive advantage.
- Communication and Alignment: DMMs provide a common vocabulary for discussing DT across the organization. This fosters better communication, aligns expectations, and builds a shared understanding of the transformation journey, reducing internal friction.
- Resource Allocation: Insights from maturity assessments guide effective allocation of financial, technological, and human resources, ensuring investments target identified weaknesses for maximum impact and value realization.
- Monitoring Progress and Accountability: DMMs enable organizations to track their progress over time, measuring initiative effectiveness against defined criteria. This continuous monitoring fosters accountability and allows for timely strategy adjustments.

DMMs serve as vital navigational tools in the DT journey, empowering organizations to assess, plan, and execute digital strategies with greater clarity, precision, and a higher likelihood of success.

Classification and Review of Popular Digital Maturity Models

The diverse landscape of DMMs reflects the varied needs of organizations navigating digital change, from broad strategic assessments to granular operational evaluations. Understanding these inherent differences is crucial for selecting the most appropriate model. These models classify digital capabilities and assign a specific maturity level, providing a standardized lens through which to evaluate progress. The sheer proliferation of these diverse models directly reflects the varied needs, strategic priorities, and unique perspectives of organizations actively navigating digital change. Selecting the most suitable model necessitates a careful and deliberate consideration of an organization's precise strategic goals, its unique industry context, the depth of analysis required, and the resources available for conducting the assessment(Zhang et al., 2025).

Comparative Analysis of Popular Digital Maturity Models

The diverse landscape of digital maturity models (DMMs) offers various approaches for assessing an organization's digital capabilities and guiding its transformation journey. While all DMMs aim to provide a structured evaluation, they often differ in their core dimensions, the number of stages they propose, and their specific applicability. This comparative analysis assists organizations in selecting a DMM that best aligns with their strategic objectives and specific needs for assessment and planning(Putri et al., 2025).

Table 2. A comparative overview of popular digital maturity models, highlighting their core focus, typical stages, strengths, and applicability

MODEL	CORE FOCUS / DIMENSIONS	TYPICAL STAGES	STRENGTHS	APPLICABILITY
Capgemini Digital Maturity Model	Digital Customer Experience, Digital Operations, Digital Business Model	Beginner, Fashionista, Conservative, Digirati	Clear focus on three crucial pillars; Intuitive stages for broad assessment.	General organizational assessment; Good for initial understanding.
BCG Digital Acceleration Index (DAI)	Strategy, Customer Experience, Products & Services, Operations, Technology, Organization & Culture	Continuum (e.g., Laggards, Followers, Challengers, Leaders)	Holistic coverage of six building blocks; Granular scoring for detailed insights.	Detailed benchmarking; Identifying specific strengths/weaknesses.
Gartner's Digital Maturity Model	Evolution from traditional to digital enterprise	Analog, Enabled, Enhanced, Digital, Transformational (5 stages)	Clear, progressive path; Emphasizes increasing integration and strategic impact.	Understanding sequential digital journey; Strategic planning for progression.
Deloitte's Digital Maturity Model	Digital Strategy, Digital Capabilities, Digital Culture and Talent, Customer Experience	Often aligned with their framework's dimensions	Practical applicability; Emphasizes leadership and scaling initiatives.	Consulting engagements; Guiding client Assessments.

Capgemini Digital Maturity Model

The Capgemini Digital Maturity Model, a widely recognized model, categorizes digital maturity across three core pillars: Digital Customer Experience, Digital Operations, and Digital Business Model. Organizations are typically rated across four stages: Beginner (limited, fragmented initiatives), Fashionista (experimentation, lacking integration), Conservative (strategic, cautious), and Digirati (fully integrated, continuous innovation). Its strength lies in its clear focus on three crucial areas and intuitive stages, making it accessible for broad organizational assessment and goal setting.

Boston Consulting Group (BCG) Digital Acceleration Index (DAI)

The BCG Digital Acceleration Index (DAI) provides a comprehensive assessment across six key building blocks: Strategy, Customer Experience, Products & Services, Operations, Technology, and Organization & Culture. BCG's DAI often uses a detailed scoring system to place organizations on a continuum, typically categorized into stages like Digital Laggards, Digital Followers, Digital Challengers, and Digital Leaders. Its strength is its holistic nature, covering a wide range of critical dimensions, which allows for detailed scoring and granular insights into specific areas of strength and weakness.

Gartner's Digital Maturity Model

Gartner's Digital Maturity Model often presents a clear, five-stage progression, emphasizing the evolution from a traditional, analog organization to a fully digital enterprise. The stages typically progress from Analog (traditional, manual) to Enabled (basic digital tools), Enhanced (coordinated initiatives), Digital (integrated capabilities), and finally, Transformational (fully agile, digitally native). This model offers a clear, sequential understanding of the digital journey, highlighting increasing integration and strategic impact at each stage(Chirumalla et al., 2025).

Deloitte's Digital Maturity Model

Deloitte's model assesses maturity across areas such as Digital Strategy, Digital Capabilities (Technology, Data, Operations), Digital Culture and Talent, and Customer Experience. It emphasizes the importance of leadership commitment and the ability to scale digital initiatives from pilot projects to widespread adoption. Its strength lies in its practical applicability, often utilized in consulting engagements to guide specific client assessments and roadmapping.

Integrating Maturity Models with Transformation Strategy

The true value of DMMs is realized when they are effectively integrated into an organization's broader DT strategy, serving as the foundational step that guides the entire transformation journey. This integration process typically involves several critical stages. It begins with the Initial Assessment to establish the organization's current maturity level. This leads directly to a Gap Analysis and Prioritization, where the current state is compared with desired higher maturity levels to identify and prioritize specific improvement areas based on strategic importance and potential business impact. These prioritized gaps are then translated into a Roadmap Development, establishing a concrete, phased DT roadmap complete with specific initiatives, timelines, and Key Performance Indicators (KPIs). The insights gained directly inform Resource Allocation and Investment and mandate Continuous Monitoring and Re-assessment to ensure the strategy remains agile and responsive. Finally, clear Communication and Buy-in is essential to align efforts towards

SECTORAL CASE STUDIES: DIGITAL TRANSFORMATION IMPLEMENTATION

Methodology for Case Study Selection

To provide robust and actionable insights into digital transformation (DT) in practice, this section presents a series of sectoral case studies. The selection methodology ensures diversity, relevance, and the ability to extract meaningful lessons applicable across contexts. The key criteria guiding the selection include:

- Sectoral Diversity: Cases are chosen from distinct economic sectors (e.g., finance, manufacturing, healthcare) experiencing significant digital disruption. This allows for comparative analysis of challenges and strategies.
- Demonstrated Holistic DT Initiatives: Selected organizations or industry trends must show clear, documented efforts towards holistic DT, rather than mere technology adoption.
- Publicly Accessible Information: Cases are primarily drawn from publicly available reports, industry analyses, academic studies, and reputable business publications for verifiability.
- Explicit Relevance to Frameworks and Models: Cases illustrate the application, challenges, or implications of DT frameworks and maturity models discussed in previous sections.
- High Potential for Extracted Lessons Learned: Each case offers valuable insights, best practices, or cautionary tales regarding DT implementation, organizational change, and leadership roles.

These case studies offer a practical lens through which the complex theoretical constructs of DT can be better understood, highlighting the nuances and complexities involved in real-world application.

Digital Transformation in the Financial Sector (e.g., Banking, FinTech)

The financial sector has undergone one of the most profound digital transformations, driven by evolving customer expectations and the agile competition posed by FinTech disruptors. Established banks and emerging FinTechs leverage digital capabilities to redefine services, fundamentally altering customer relationships and operational efficiency(Huang et al., 2025).

Traditional Bank Reinvention: Focus on Operational Excellence and CX

Incumbent banks, facing persistent challenges from legacy IT and regulation, typically prioritize strategies that align with Operational Excellence and Customer Intimacy (referencing the MIT CISR framework). Their initiatives focus on:

- **Operational Automation:** Implementing Robotic Process Automation (RPA) for back-office tasks, reducing errors, and accelerating processing times, which directly drives Operational Excellence.
- Customer-Centric Channels: Investing in mobile banking, AI-powered chatbots, and personalized services to create seamless, 24/7 digital experiences, which significantly drives Customer Intimacy.

Success for these banks often involves navigating the lower maturity levels (e.g., Fashionista stage) of models like the BCG DAI, moving decisively to the Strategic level by standardizing core processes before attempting broad innovation. Failures frequently occur when cultural resistance impedes the "Refreeze" stage of change management, resulting in regression to old habits despite new technology.

FinTech Disruptors: Focus on Business Model Innovation

FinTech companies, born digital, inherently embody the highest levels of digital maturity, often starting at the New Digital Business quadrant (MIT CISR) or the Adaptive & Innovative stage (Altimeter).

- **Strategy:** They fundamentally focus on Business Model Transformation, utilizing platforms (e.g., P2P lending) or disruptive technologies (e.g., blockchain) to bypass traditional intermediary roles.
- **Customer Value:** Neobanks, for instance, achieve superior Customer Intimacy through hyper-personalized, digital-only user interfaces, drastically lowering operational costs and enabling rapid innovation.

FinTechs demonstrate high maturity across the technology and business model dimensions but often struggle with the Organizational Change challenge of rapidly building regulatory trust and scaling governance effectively. Their success is distinguished by extreme agility and a culture of continuous experimentation, demonstrating high resilience in uncertain environments.

Digital Transformation in the Manufacturing Sector (e.g., Industry 4.0)

The manufacturing sector's transformation, driven by Industry 4.0, aims to create "smart factories" where physical and digital systems integrate. This transformation requires mastering both technological adoption and systemic organizational change.

Smart Factory Implementation: Holistic Operational and Technological Maturity

Manufacturers are implementing smart factory concepts to optimize production and enable mass customization. Key initiatives include:

- **IoT and AI:** Using sensors and Artificial Intelligence for Real-time Monitoring and Quality **Control** (enhancing Operational Excellence and moving to the Integrated/Digital stage of Gartner's model).
- **Digital Twins:** Creating virtual replicas of physical assets for simulation and predictive maintenance, enhancing strategic decision-making based on data.

This sector's success relies heavily on achieving high technological maturity (Technology pillar of BCG DAI) coupled with strong Leadership commitment to manage the cultural shift towards data literacy and collaboration. Failures typically stem from an inability to overcome the Technical Debt of integrating new IoT systems with aging legacy Operational Technology (OT), resulting in siloed data and limited scalability. Successfully scaling these initiatives requires moving beyond isolated pilots to full enterprise integration.

Digital Transformation in the Healthcare Sector (e.g., Telemedicine, Digital Health Records)

The healthcare sector, historically burdened by complex regulation and privacy concerns, is accelerating its DT journey, primarily focused on improving patient outcomes and service accessibility.(D. Liu et al., 2025)

Telemedicine and EHR: Enhancing CX and Process Integration

Initiatives like Telemedicine and Electronic Health Records (EHR) fundamentally enhance **Customer/Patient Experience** and **Operational Process Transformation**.

- **Customer/Patient Focus:** Telemedicine (virtual consultations, remote monitoring) rapidly improves patient access and convenience (driving Customer Intimacy).
- **Process Integration:** EHRs centralize patient data, enhancing interoperability, reducing medical errors, and supporting data analytics for population health management (driving Operational Excellence and achieving higher maturity in data management).

Analytical Rigor: Healthcare transformation is unique because its success is often measured by patient outcomes and regulatory compliance (e.g., HIPAA). It requires robust Organizational Change Management (Section 6.0) to overcome resistance from medical professionals accustomed to paper-based systems. The transition demonstrates a move from the Analog stage to the Enabled/Enhanced stages (Gartner model), with compliance and data governance being critical success differentiators.

Comparative Analysis and Cross-Sectoral Learnings

The analysis across finance, manufacturing, and healthcare reveals common success factors and challenges, underscoring the universal principles of DT. These cross-sectoral learnings emphasize that while specific applications of technology vary, the underlying success pillars remain constant: unwavering Customer Centricity, Leadership Commitment, the imperative for Data as a strategic asset, and the absolute necessity of Organizational Agility.

Table 3. Comprehensive overview of these key learnings, highlighting their insight and relevance across diverse sectors

LEARNING THEME	CORE INSIGHT	RELEVANCE ACROSS SECTORS
Customer/User Centricity	User at core; Enhances experience, provides value.	Universal Personalization (finance), patient engagement (healthcare), tailored products (manufacturing).
Technology as Enabler	Value unlocked by strategy, organization, culture.	Universal Prevents tech-first failures; Requires human adoption.
Data is the New Currency	Collecting, analyzing, deriving actionable insights from data.	Universal Drives personalization (finance), predictive maintenance (manufacturing), population health (healthcare).
Agility and Experimentation	Agile approaches; Willingness to experiment and adapt.	Universal Essential for rapid response to market shifts and continuous innovation.
Leadership and Culture	Strong, visionary leadership; Supportive culture.	Universal Overcomes resistance, fosters innovation, ensures sustainability.
Ecosystem Thinking	Building partnerships with external entities.	Growing importance Seen in FinTech, smart manufacturing, health tech.
Compliance & Security	Navigating regulations; Robust cybersecurity.	Critical in regulated sectors (finance, healthcare) Relevant across all.
Scaling Beyond Pilots	Moving successful small projects to enterprise-wide adoption.	Universal challenge Requires robust change management and governance.

A key lesson distinguishing success from failure across all three sectors is the ability to integrate the Framework (Direction), the Maturity Model (Assessment), and the Change Management Strategy (Adoption). Success is rarely about technology acquisition alone; it is achieved when the vision (from the framework) is measured objectively (by the maturity model), and the resulting implementation is actively championed and sustained by proactive change leadership.

ORGANIZATIONAL CHANGE FOR TRANSFORMATION

Importance of Change Management in Digital Transformation

Digital transformation (DT) is frequently misconstrued as an exclusively technological undertaking. However, its true essence lies in the profound organizational and cultural shifts it necessitates. The mere implementation of new digital tools or platforms without adequately addressing the human element—the individuals who must adopt, adapt to, and champion these changes—is widely recognized as a common and critical pathway to failure. Consequently, effective change management is not merely a supplementary activity; it stands as an indispensable core component of any successful DT initiative. It provides the structured approach and essential tools needed to support individuals in making the often-difficult transition from their established ways of working to new, digitally-enabled processes and mindsets(Felipe et al., 2025).

The critical importance of robust change management in DT stems from several fundamental factors. Firstly, human beings are inherently predisposed to resist change, particularly when it disrupts familiar routines, creates perceived threats to job security, or demands the acquisition of entirely new skills. DT inevitably involves significant alterations in roles, responsibilities, and workflows, generating considerable anxiety and uncertainty among the workforce. Without a proactive and well-executed change management strategy, this natural resistance can manifest as low adoption rates, decreased productivity, and even active opposition, effectively derailing the entire transformation effort.

Secondly, change management serves as the crucial bridge between technological capabilities and human potential. While technology provides the underlying infrastructure, it is the organization's people who ultimately unlock and realize the true value embedded in digital investments. Effective change management ensures that employees not only comprehend the strategic rationale ("the why") behind the transformation but are also equipped with the necessary skills and intrinsically motivated to embrace new digital tools and processes. This proactive approach is vital for translating technological potential into tangible organizational performance by facilitating widespread and enthusiastic adoption.

Furthermore, large-scale digital transformations are inherently disruptive. A well-implemented change management approach is explicitly designed to mitigate these negative impacts by systematically preparing the workforce, actively managing expectations, and providing continuous support throughout the transition. This stance helps to minimize operational downtime, reduce errors that often occur during periods of significant change, and accelerate the rate at which new systems and processes are fully adopted, enabling the organization to realize its benefits more rapidly. Beyond immediate adoption, change management plays a pivotal role in fostering a new, digital-centric organizational culture. DT demands a shift towards agility, innovation, and data-driven decision-making(Xie et al., 2025). Change management actively cultivates this desired culture by consistently promoting new behaviors, reinforcing emerging values through recognition, and consciously creating an environment where employees feel psychologically safe to learn, iterate, and adapt without fear of punitive consequences. This cultural evolution is fundamental for long-term digital success. Finally, effective change management is instrumental in ensuring strategic alignment and securing broad organizational buy-in. It facilitates clear, consistent, and transparent communication of the transformation's vision, strategy, and anticipated benefits across all levels. This transparency ensures that individual and departmental efforts are cohesively aligned with the overarching digital objectives. In essence, neglecting change management in digital transformation is akin to installing a high-performance engine but neglecting to train the driver; it is the human element that powers the technological vehicle, making change management an indispensable discipline.

RELEVANT CHANGE MANAGEMENT MODELS AND STRATEGIES

To effectively navigate the complexities of organizational change during digital transformation, various established models and strategies can be strategically employed. These frameworks provide structured approaches to understand, plan, and execute change initiatives, significantly increasing the likelihood of successful adoption and desired outcomes by addressing both organizational and individual dynamics(Prosen & Ličen, 2025).

Lewin's Change Management Model (Unfreeze-Change-Refreeze)

Kurt Lewin's classic three-stage model remains a foundational and highly influential framework for understanding the fundamental dynamics of organizational change. The model begins with Unfreeze, which involves preparing the organization for change by creating a compelling awareness of the need for transformation and clearly demonstrating the urgency and potential benefits of the digital shift. In the context of digital transformation, this means highlighting market disruptions, competitive threats, or the inherent inefficiencies of legacy systems. The second stage, Change (Movement), represents the actual implementation phase. Here, new digital processes, technologies, and desired behaviors are introduced alongside comprehensive new information and targeted training programs. Effective and consistent communication is paramount during this stage to manage expectations, address concerns proactively, and guide individuals through the transition. The final stage, Refreeze, aims to stabilize the organization in its newly transformed state. This involves embedding the new digital practices deeply into the organizational culture, reinforcing new behaviors through appropriate reward and recognition systems, and establishing updated standards and policies. This crucial step prevents regression to old habits and ensures the long-term sustainability of the digital transformation. While Lewin's model is strong on preparation and reinforcement, some critics argue its implied linearity may be less suited for the more iterative and continuous nature of digital transformation(Bocean & Vărzaru, 2025).

Kotter's 8-Step Change Model

John Kotter's widely adopted 8-step model provides a detailed and sequential process for leading organizational change, making it highly applicable to digital transformation initiatives. The model begins with Creating Urgency and Forming a Powerful Guiding Coalition to assemble the necessary leadership and momentum. Subsequent steps involve Creating a Vision for Change and ensuring it is Communicated widely to secure understanding and buy-in. As the transformation progresses, leaders must Remove Obstacles (e.g., resistant individuals, outdated systems) and strategically Create Short-Term Wins to maintain enthusiasm and demonstrate tangible progress. The process culminates by ensuring leaders Build on the Change and, finally, that the transformation is Anchored in Corporate Culture, integrating new digital practices into the organizational values and daily operations to ensure long-term sustainability. Kotter's model emphasizes the critical role of leadership, transparent communication, and the strategic importance of generating momentum through early, demonstrable successes.

ADKAR Model

The ADKAR model, developed by Prosci, offers a distinct focus on the individual's perspective of change, providing a practical framework for understanding and enabling individual transitions throughout a digital transformation. ADKAR represents five sequential elements that an individual must achieve for successful change: Awareness of the need, Desire to participate, Knowledge of how to change, Ability to implement skills, and Reinforcement to sustain the change. This model is particularly useful for diagnosing precisely why individuals might be resisting change, allowing leaders and change managers to tailor specific interventions (e.g., training, focused communication) to address precise gaps in individual readiness. ADKAR effectively complements broader organizational change models by providing a granular, micro-level perspective, ensuring that individual readiness for change is systematically addressed, which is paramount for widespread digital adoption(Mahroof et al., 2025).

Overcoming Resistance and Building Adoption

Resistance to change is a natural human reaction and frequently emerges as a significant impediment to digital transformation efforts. Effectively overcoming this inherent resistance and fostering widespread adoption of new digital ways of working requires a proactive, empathetic, and strategically planned set of interventions.

One of the most crucial strategies involves transparent and consistent communication. Leaders must clearly articulate "the why," "the what," and "the how" of the digital transformation, explaining the overarching benefits for individuals, teams, and the organization as a whole. Utilizing multiple communication channels and ensuring consistency in messaging across all touchpoints is vital. Furthermore, creating open forums for dialogue and actively addressing employee concerns helps to build trust and manage expectations. Active leadership sponsorship is equally paramount. Senior leaders must not only visibly endorse the change but also actively participate in the transformation, model desired behaviors, and consistently communicate their unwavering commitment. Their visible involvement signals the strategic importance of the initiative, helping to overcome skepticism and encourage broader participation.

Employee involvement and co-creation are powerful tools for fostering buy-in. When individuals are actively involved in the design and implementation of new digital processes and solutions, their sense of ownership significantly increases, thereby reducing natural resistance. Co-creation efforts can also lead to more practical, user-friendly, and effective digital solutions that are better tailored to the organization's specific needs. To address skill gaps and build confidence, targeted training and skill development programs are essential. These programs should be comprehensive, ongoing, and designed to equip employees with the new digital skills and competencies required for their evolving roles. Directly addressing skill deficiencies reduces anxiety and empowers employees to embrace new tools(Jiang et al., 2025).

Establishing robust support systems and coaching mechanisms is also critical. This includes providing dedicated help desks for technical issues, identifying and empowering "digital champions" within teams who can offer peer-to-peer support, and offering opportunities for one-on-one coaching and mentorship. Such systems help individuals navigate challenges, troubleshoot problems, and adapt more smoothly to new ways of working. To maintain momentum and demonstrate tangible progress, celebrating short-term wins is highly effective. Recognizing and publicly celebrating early successes and milestones, no matter how small, helps to build enthusiasm, provides visible proof of progress, and reinforces the positive impact of the transformation. Finally, reinforcement mechanisms are vital for embedding new behaviors and processes into the organizational fabric. This includes integrating new digital practices into performance management systems and aligning reward structures with desired outcomes.

Role of Organizational Culture in Supporting Transformation

Organizational culture is frequently identified as either the single biggest barrier or the most powerful enabler of successful digital transformation. Defined as the shared values, beliefs, norms, and practices prevalent within an organization, culture profoundly influences how employees perceive, react to, and ultimately adopt new technologies and ways of working. A culture characterized by rigidity, risk-aversion, or deep-seated silos will inherently struggle to embrace the agility, collaboration, and experimentation that are fundamental to digital transformation. Conversely, a supportive and forward-looking culture can significantly accelerate adoption and foster continuous innovation, becoming a powerful competitive advantage.

Several key cultural attributes are particularly crucial for supporting and sustaining digital transformation:

- Agility and Adaptability: A culture that not only tolerates but actively embraces change and is comfortable with inherent ambiguity. This involves the capacity to rapidly pivot strategies, processes, and even organizational structures in response to new information, evolving market dynamics, or technological disruptions. Such a culture stands in stark contrast to traditional, bureaucratic environments that are slow to react and resistant to deviation from established norms.
- Innovation and Experimentation: A culture that actively encourages the generation of new ideas, provides dedicated space and resources for exploration, and crucially, tolerates "intelligent failure." Leaders in such a culture create psychologically safe environments where employees feel empowered to experiment with novel technologies and processes without fear of punishment or blame. This fosters a mindset of continuous improvement, creativity, and proactive problem-solving.
- Collaboration and Cross-Functional Thinking: Digital transformation frequently necessitates breaking down traditional departmental silos and fostering seamless integration across different functions. A collaborative culture promotes interdisciplinary teamwork, encourages open knowledge sharing across the organization, and facilitates integrated problem-solving. This is essential for developing and implementing holistic digital solutions that transcend individual departmental boundaries.
- Customer Centricity: A deeply ingrained cultural value that consistently prioritizes understanding, anticipating, and serving customer needs. In the context of digital transformation, this ensures that all digital initiatives, from new product development to process re-engineering, are ultimately aligned with

creating enhanced customer experiences and delivering superior customer value.

- Learning Mindset: Given the continuous evolution of digital technologies and market demands, a culture that values and promotes continuous learning, upskilling, and reskilling is paramount. Employees are encouraged to actively acquire new digital competencies and adapt to evolving technological landscapes. This supports the ongoing nature of digital transformation and ensures the workforce remains relevant and capable.
- Transparency and Open Communication: A culture that promotes open dialogue, honest feedback, and clear communication about both challenges and successes during the transformation journey. This builds trust among employees, helps manage expectations realistically, and ensures that everyone is informed and engaged. It minimizes rumors and fosters a sense of shared purpose.

Cultivating such a supportive culture requires intentional and sustained effort from leadership. This includes consistently modeling desired behaviors, actively reinforcing new values through organizational policies and practices, and recognizing employees who embody these critical attributes. Without a fundamental cultural shift, even the most advanced technologies and meticulously designed frameworks will struggle to deliver their full potential, rendering digital transformation efforts ineffective(Zhu et al., 2025).

LEADERSHIP FOR TRANSFORMATION

Characteristics and Competencies of Digital Leaders

In the contemporary era of digital transformation (DT), traditional leadership paradigms are demonstrably insufficient. Organizations demand a new breed of leaders with distinct characteristics and competencies tailored to foster innovation, inspire profound change, and guide entire entities through a rapidly evolving digital landscape. These "digital leaders" are not defined merely by their technical expertise; rather, they excel by synthesizing technological understanding with strategic foresight, organizational empathy, and a deep appreciation for human dynamics, effectively bridging the gap between technological capabilities and human readiness.

The unique responsibilities of steering DT mandate several key characteristics and competencies that define effective digital leaders:

- **Visionary Thinking:** Digital leaders possess the crucial ability to articulate a compelling, long-term digital vision. This involves foresight in identifying emerging technologies, accurately anticipating market shifts, and creatively envisioning new value propositions or fundamental reshaping of the business model. This clear vision provides an unwavering anchor for the entire transformation journey and aligns efforts across the organization.
- **Agility and Adaptability:** The digital environment is characterized by persistent change and inherent uncertainty. Effective leaders must be exceptionally agile, capable of rapidly adapting strategies, processes, and even their own leadership style in swift response to new information, market feedback, or sudden technological disruptions. They embrace iterative approaches, learning quickly from setbacks, and confidently leading through pervasive ambiguity.
- **Customer Centricity:** An unwavering commitment to the customer is paramount. Digital leaders actively prioritize leveraging technology to profoundly enhance customer experience, personalize interactions, and build lasting, meaningful relationships across all touchpoints. They are fervent champions of a customer-first mindset throughout the entire organization, ensuring all digital initiatives deliver superior customer value.
- **Technological Fluency:** While not necessarily deep technical experts, digital leaders must maintain sufficient technological fluency. This enables them to understand the fundamental potential and inherent limitations of key digital technologies (e.g., AI, cloud, big data), empowering them to make informed strategic decisions, engage constructively with technical teams, and proactively identify opportunities for digital leverage.
- **Data Literacy and Data-Driven Decision Making:** These leaders are instrumental in championing a culture where critical decisions are consistently informed by robust data and insightful analytics. They understand how to leverage data as a strategic asset, actively promote data literacy across all levels, and rigorously insist on evidence-based approaches to measure progress, assess impact, and validate the effectiveness of digital initiatives.
- **Collaboration and Ecosystem Thinking:** Digital transformation frequently transcends organizational boundaries. Leaders foster a collaborative mindset, actively breaking down internal silos and strategically building external partnerships and ecosystems to co-create value and leverage collective intelligence across the broader market(Feng et al., 2025).
- **Empowerment and Talent Development:** Recognizing that DT is fundamentally a human endeavor, effective leaders empower their teams, delegate necessary authority, and foster an environment of psychological safety where employees feel comfortable experimenting and taking calculated risks. They

prioritize continuous learning, upskilling, and reskilling the workforce to build necessary digital capabilities.

- **Change Management Acumen:** Digital leaders are highly adept at managing organizational change. They understand the human psychology of transition, proactively address resistance, communicate transparently, and build necessary buy-in through consistent engagement, serving as visible role models for the required new behaviors and mindsets(Benlhabib & Berrado, 2025).
- **Resilience and Persistence:** Transformation journeys are often long and challenging. Leaders demonstrate resilience, maintaining focus on the long-term vision despite inevitable obstacles, and inspiring their teams to persist through complexities inherent in large-scale change.

Role of Leaders in Driving Digital Vision and Strategy

The success of any digital transformation initiative hinges significantly on the active, unwavering, and visionary role played by an organization's leaders. They function as the primary architects, catalysts, and sustained drivers of the entire digital journey. Their core responsibilities extend far beyond the realm of mere strategic planning, encompassing the crucial tasks of fostering a conducive organizational environment, strategically allocating vital resources, and inspiring collective action.

Table 4. Digital leader vs. traditional leader competencies

COMPETENCY AREA	DIGITAL LEADER	TRADITIONAL LEADER (CONTRAST)
Vision & Strategy	Bold, adaptive digital vision; New value creation.	Executes established strategies; Optimizes existing value.
Decision Making	Data-driven; Ambiguity-tolerant; Iterative; Risk-tolerant.	Experience-based; Seeks certainty; Linear; Risk-averse.
Organizational Structure	Fosters agile, cross-functional teams; Decentralized.	Relies on hierarchy; Centralized control.
Culture & People	Promotes innovation, learning, psychological safety.	Emphasizes stability, process adherence, compliance.
Technology View	Understands strategic potential; Tech as core business.	Views tech as IT support; Focus on tech cost.
External Engagement	Builds ecosystems, partnerships; Open to collaboration.	Focus on internal capabilities; Limited external collaboration.

One of the most pivotal responsibilities is the articulation of a clear and compelling digital vision. Leaders must meticulously define and effectively communicate an inspiring vision that outlines the organization's ambitious aspirations in the digital age. This vision must be easily understandable, highly motivating, and explicitly link all digital initiatives to broader business objectives and, where applicable, to positive societal impact. Such a clearly defined vision provides an unwavering clarity and direction, ensuring that all efforts are precisely aligned towards a unified common goal.

Building upon this compelling vision, leaders are then directly responsible for setting strategic priorities and developing actionable roadmaps. This involves the meticulous identification of key areas for strategic investment, the precise definition of measurable objectives, and the establishment of a phased roadmap that carefully outlines the sequential progression of initiatives. Leaders ensure that necessary resources—financial, human, and technological—are strategically allocated to robustly support these defined priorities, guaranteeing sustained investment throughout the complex transformation journey(Bian et al., 2025).

Leaders must actively serve as champions and visible sponsors for all digital initiatives. Their visible endorsement and vocal advocacy are paramount in overcoming internal resistance, securing resources, and signaling the profound strategic importance of the transformation across the entire organization. They proactively remove any existing roadblocks, mitigate potential obstacles, and provide continuous support to project teams, empowering them to execute effectively and efficiently.

Effective leaders are responsible for communicating progress and celebrating successes throughout the transformation journey. Regular, transparent, and consistent communication about the progress of digital initiatives, encompassing both achievements and lessons learned, is absolutely essential. Leaders judiciously celebrate short-term wins to build crucial momentum and motivate their teams, while simultaneously maintaining transparency about challenges and necessary adjustments. By fulfilling these critical roles, leaders effectively transform digital aspirations into tangible organizational realities, guiding their organizations through a complex yet ultimately rewarding journey of reinvention and sustained growth(Wang & Zhao, 2025).

Leading Through Uncertainty and Ambiguity

Digital transformation is inherently characterized by high levels of persistent uncertainty and pervasive ambiguity. The relentless pace of technological change, the constantly evolving market demands, and the frequent absence of clear historical precedents mean that leaders are often compelled to operate without a complete picture or a guaranteed, predefined roadmap. Effectively leading in such a dynamic and unpredictable environment demands a distinct set of skills that enable leaders to navigate complexity, maintain strategic focus, and inspire unwavering confidence amidst the unknown. This requires a shift from traditional command-and-control approaches to more adaptive and empowering styles.

- Embracing a Growth Mindset: Leaders must cultivate a personal and organizational growth mindset, viewing challenges, unforeseen obstacles, and inherent unknowns not as debilitating threats but rather as invaluable opportunities for profound learning, continuous development, and strategic adaptation.
- Communicating with Transparency and Honesty: In times of uncertainty, clear and honest communication is paramount. Leaders must be forthright about what is known and what remains unknown, meticulously avoiding any false assurances. This builds deep trust among employees, manages expectations realistically, and fosters a more resilient workforce.
- Fostering Psychological Safety: Leaders must cultivate an environment where employees feel genuinely safe to voice their concerns, admit mistakes, and propose unconventional or nascent ideas without any fear of punitive repercussions. This encourages open dialogue, facilitates rapid identification and resolution of problems, and allows for the emergence of innovative solutions in ambiguous situations.
- Prioritizing and Focusing: In an environment characterized by an overwhelming array of possibilities and constant change, leaders must be exceptionally adept at setting clear priorities and maintaining sharp focus on the most critical strategic objectives. This disciplined approach prevents the dilution of precious resources.
- Empowering Teams and Decentralizing Decision-Making: Faced with ambiguity, centralized decision-making processes can quickly become significant bottlenecks. Digital leaders therefore empower cross-functional teams with the necessary autonomy, resources, and clear boundaries to make rapid decisions and experiment effectively. This strategic decentralization accelerates the pace of adaptation.
- Building Resilience: Leaders must actively focus on building resilience within their teams and the broader organization. This involves fostering a culture that possesses the inherent capacity to absorb unexpected shocks, learn constructively from setbacks, and rapidly bounce back stronger.
- Leveraging Data and Analytics for Insights: While complete certainty remains elusive, leaders can significantly reduce ambiguity by systematically championing the use of real-time data and advanced analytics. They promote data literacy and insist on evidence-based approaches to inform decisions and iteratively adjust strategies.

By mastering these strategies, leaders transform uncertainty from a paralyzing force into a powerful catalyst for organizational learning, continuous innovation, and sustained competitive advantage.

DISCUSSION AND CONCLUSION

Integrated Model: Frameworks, Maturity, and Implementation Synergy

The comprehensive analysis throughout this chapter reveals that successful digital transformation (DT) is achieved not by addressing its components in isolation, but through their synergistic integration. A successful DT journey must translate the abstract direction provided by frameworks into measurable action, which is sustained by effective leadership and cultural change.

This integration process follows a clear, cyclical logic that links theory to practice:

- **Direction (Frameworks):** Organizations begin by adopting strategic frameworks (e.g., MIT CISR, IBM) to define their strategic pillars (e.g., Operational Excellence, Customer Intimacy). This establishes the "what" and "why" of the transformation.
- **Assessment (Maturity Models):** The strategic direction must be measured. Maturity models (e.g., BCG DAI, Gartner) are applied as objective diagnostic tools to assess the organization's current state and capacity across the framework's dimensions. This identifies the precise "where we are" and "what gaps we have."
- **Execution (Organizational Change & Leadership):** The gaps identified by the maturity models are then addressed through targeted initiatives. Implementation is driven by robust change management strategies, actively overcoming resistance, and anchored by committed digital leadership. This addresses the "how to act."

The synergy among these elements—Frameworks providing the direction, Maturity Models offering the objective assessment, Organizational Change facilitating widespread adoption, and Leadership acting as the orchestrator and catalyst—is the ultimate determinant of sustainable digital success. These interdependent pillars must be developed synchronously for organizations to truly thrive in the digital age.

Managerial and Practical Implications

The synthesis of frameworks, maturity models, and cross-sectoral learnings provides several crucial managerial and practical implications for leaders navigating DT:

- **Prioritize Strategy over Technology:** Managers must view DT holistically, integrating technology adoption with fundamental shifts in business models, organizational structure, and culture. Utilise the selected framework as a guiding blueprint to prevent fragmented, technology-only initiatives.

- **Establish Data-Driven Governance:** Regularly assess digital maturity (using DMMs) to provide an objective baseline and inform the development of a phased, data-driven roadmap. This allows for targeted investment and measurable progress tracking, ensuring investments are directed towards closing critical capability gaps.
- **Investment Prioritization (Financial Evaluation):** Leaders must utilize financial evaluation frameworks, moving beyond simple cost-cutting to assess digital ROI holistically. This requires valuing intangible benefits such as enhanced agility, customer lifetime value (CLV), and innovation capacity, rather than just immediate returns on individual technology spend.
- **Cultural Readiness is Non-Negotiable:** Invest heavily in change management strategies and transparent communication to address employee resistance, build digital literacy, and foster a culture of agility and continuous learning. Leadership must actively champion this cultural shift.
- **Adaptive Leadership is Essential:** Leaders must embody the characteristics of the digital leader (visionary thinking, agility, data literacy). They must be prepared to lead through ambiguity and foster psychological safety, acting as the primary catalyst for change adoption.

Foundational Enablers: Cybersecurity, Ethics, and Governance

A realistic portrayal of DT necessitates addressing foundational governance and security enablers that underpin every digital initiative. These areas are not optional but prerequisites for sustained success:

- **Cybersecurity and Data Privacy:** As organizations become increasingly interconnected and reliant on data, robust cybersecurity and adherence to data privacy regulations (e.g., GDPR, CCPA) become foundational enablers. Failure in this area can halt the entire transformation and erode public trust. DT efforts must integrate security by design, ensuring comprehensive protection of customer and organizational data.
- **Ethical AI and Responsible Innovation:** The pervasive integration of AI demands rigorous ethical oversight. Organizations must establish clear guidelines to mitigate algorithmic bias, ensure transparency in decision-making processes, and promote responsible innovation. This addresses the broader societal implications of digital products and is critical for maintaining ethical integrity.

- **Regulatory and Geopolitical Influences:** DT strategies must be designed with flexibility to navigate evolving regulatory landscapes (e.g., data sovereignty, digital taxation) and geopolitical risks. Leaders must anticipate regulatory shifts that could impact data flows, market entry, or competitive strategy.

Remaining Challenges and Future Outlook

Despite significant advancements, digital transformation still faces persistent challenges and offers vast areas for future innovation. Key unresolved issues include effectively scaling digital pilots across the enterprise, accurately measuring the holistic ROI of DT initiatives, and navigating the complexities of cybersecurity and data privacy. Managing the human element, particularly large-scale reskilling and addressing the psychological impact of automation, remains a significant hurdle.

Future research should focus on empirical validation of frameworks and models in diverse contexts, deeper exploration into specific leadership styles and cultural interventions, and continuous investigation into the impact of nascent technologies (e.g., quantum computing) on DT strategies. Developing more robust, holistic metrics for assessing DT value beyond traditional financial measures is also crucial. Addressing these challenges through interdisciplinary research and innovative practices will further enhance our collective understanding and enable organizations to navigate the complexities of digital transformation with greater precision and success.

REFERENCES

Benlhabib, H., & Berrado, A. (2025). Towards a digital platform for performance management and systemic improvement of education systems: Evidence from Morocco. *Discover Education*, *4*(1), 15. Advance online publication. DOI: 10.1007/s44217-024-00317-1

Bian, X., Wang, B., Li, K., & Du, Z. (2025). Navigating ethical decision-making in digital transformation: Ethical climate, digital competence, and person-organization fit in China's banking sector. *Humanities & Social Sciences Communications*, *12*(1), 920. Advance online publication. DOI: 10.1057/s41599-025-05184-1

Bocean, C. G., & Vărzaru, A. A. (2025). Health status in the era of digital transformation and sustainable economic development. *BMC Health Services Research*, *25*(1), 343. Advance online publication. DOI: 10.1186/s12913-025-12498-y PMID: 40045359

Chirumalla, K., Oghazi, P., Nnewuku, R. E., Tuncay, H., & Yahyapour, N. (2025). Critical factors affecting digital transformation in manufacturing companies. *The International Entrepreneurship and Management Journal*, *21*(1), 54. Advance online publication. DOI: 10.1007/s11365-024-01056-3

Felipe, T., Torres de Oliveira, R., Toth-Peter, A., Mathews, S., & Dulleck, U. (2025). Digital transformation in commercial banks: Unraveling the flow of Industry 4.0. *Digital Business*, *5*(2), 100129. Advance online publication. DOI: 10.1016/j.digbus.2025.100129

Feng, Z., Luo, N., Wu, S., & Yan, Z. J. (2025). Trade-in marketing strategies in gaming industry: The effect of digital transformation. *Electronic Markets*, *35*(1), 58. Advance online publication. DOI: 10.1007/s12525-025-00800-z

Giang, H. T. T., & Dung, L. T. (2025). Sharing economy and retailer sustainable performance: The mechanisms via business model innovation and digital capabilities. *Journal of Innovation and Entrepreneurship*, *14*(1), 27. Advance online publication. DOI: 10.1186/s13731-025-00492-x

Huang, R., Shuai, Q., Zhang, Y., Chen, Y., & Zhang, Q. (2025). The impact of digital education on household allocation of risky financial assets in China. *Scientific Reports*, *15*(1), 21840. Advance online publication. DOI: 10.1038/s41598-025-01140-w PMID: 40594050

Jiang, C., Niu, Z., Qu, J., Zhao, Y., & Rezaeipanah, A. (2025). Overlapping community-based fair influence maximization under a multi-transformation optimization algorithm. *Journal of Big Data*, *12*(1), 133. Advance online publication. DOI: 10.1186/s40537-025-01181-y

Liu, D., Sun, N., & Zhu, X. (2025). ESG ratings empower high-quality development of logistics enterprises through digital transformation and green innovation. *Scientific Reports*, *15*(1), 22861. Advance online publication. DOI: 10.1038/s41598-025-06029-2 PMID: 40596363

Liu, J., Jiang, F., Tashiro, S., Chen, S., & Tanaka, M. (2025). A physics-informed and data-driven framework for robotic welding in manufacturing. *Nature Communications*, *16*(1), 4807. Advance online publication. DOI: 10.1038/s41467-025-60164-y PMID: 40410176

Mahroof, J., Rafi, D. A., & Ahmad, D. A. (2025). Talent management during digital transformation: Role of transformational leadership and resistance to change. *Technology in Society*, *83*, 102964. Advance online publication. DOI: 10.1016/j.techsoc.2025.102964

Prosen, M., & Ličen, S. (2025). Evaluating the digital transformation in health sciences education: A thematic analysis of higher education teachers' perspectives. *BMC Medical Education*, *25*(1), 820. Advance online publication. DOI: 10.1186/s12909-025-07420-3 PMID: 40457303

Putri, A. N. A., Hermawan, P., Mirzanti, I. R., Meadows, M., & Sadraei, R. (2025). Unpacking green growth in SMEs: A framework for dynamic capabilities, value co-creation, and sustainable performance. *Sustainable Futures : An Applied Journal of Technology, Environment and Society*, *10*, 100840. Advance online publication. DOI: 10.1016/j.sftr.2025.100840

Saari, A., Sinclair, S., Leshinsky, R., & Junnila, S. (2025). Best practices for blockchain-driven digital transformation in cross-industry settings. *Digital Business*, *5*(2), 100127. Advance online publication. DOI: 10.1016/j.digbus.2025.100127

Wang, J., & Zhao, H. (2025). Enterprise digital transformation and sustainable productivity. *Discover Sustainability*, *6*(1), 308. Advance online publication. DOI: 10.1007/s43621-025-01128-6

Xie, F., Peng, P., Li, D., Xu, Y., & Wu, M. (2025). Uncovering the evolution of digital economy investment networks: A county-level perspective. *Computational Urban Science*, *5*(1), 19. Advance online publication. DOI: 10.1007/s43762-025-00179-9

Yu, P., Abdul Hamid, R., Hakim Osman, L., & Liao, J. (2025). Bridging the digital gap: Empirical insights into agri-food supply chain transformation. *Sustainable Futures : An Applied Journal of Technology, Environment and Society*, *10*, 100810. Advance online publication. DOI: 10.1016/j.sftr.2025.100810

Zhang, H., Li, Y., Zhang, S., Song, L., & Tao, F. (2025). Artificial Intelligence-Enhanced Digital Twin Systems Engineering Towards the Industrial Metaverse in the Era of Industry 5.0. [English Edition]. *Chinese Journal of Mechanical Engineering*, *38*(1), 40. Advance online publication. DOI: 10.1186/s10033-025-01210-0

Zhu, Y., Wan, H., Carlos, L.-A., Ye, J., & Zeng, S. (2025). Evaluating digital maturity in specialized enterprises: A multi-criteria decision-making approach. *The International Entrepreneurship and Management Journal*, *21*(1), 28. Advance online publication. DOI: 10.1007/s11365-024-01051-8

Zia, S., Yildiz-Aktas, I. Z., Zia, F., & Parwani, A. V. (2025). An update on applications of digital pathology: Primary diagnosis; telepathology, education and research. *Diagnostic Pathology*, *20*(1), 17. Advance online publication. DOI: 10.1186/s13000-025-01610-9 PMID: 39940046

KEY TERMS AND DEFINITIONS

Agile Organization: An organization characterized by its ability to adapt quickly and effectively to changing market conditions and customer demands. It embraces iterative approaches, continuous learning, cross-functional collaboration, and rapid experimentation, which are crucial for navigating the dynamic environment of digital transformation.

Business Model Transformation: The fundamental rethinking and alteration of how an organization creates, delivers, and captures value, often enabled by digital technologies. This can involve developing entirely new digital products or services, shifting revenue models, or embracing platform-based ecosystems.

Customer Centricity: A core organizational value and strategic approach that prioritizes understanding, serving, and enhancing the experience of customers. In digital transformation, it involves leveraging digital technologies to personalize interactions, create seamless journeys, and build strong customer relationships.

Digital Leader: An individual who possesses a distinct set of characteristics and competencies, capable of articulating a compelling digital vision, fostering a culture of innovation and experimentation, empowering teams, and navigating complexity and uncertainty inherent in digital transformation. They drive strategic alignment and champion the necessary organizational shifts.

Digital Maturity Model: A structured framework or diagnostic tool used by organizations to objectively assess their current state of digital capabilities and progress across various dimensions (e.g., strategy, technology, culture). These models typically outline progressive stages, guiding organizations in identifying gaps and planning their advancement in digital transformation.

Digital Transformation: A profound and holistic strategic, organizational, and cultural change that leverages digital technologies to create new or modify existing business processes, culture, and customer experiences to meet evolving business and market requirements. It is a continuous journey of adaptation to the digital age, aiming to create new value propositions and fundamentally alter how an organization operates and interacts.

Digitalization: The process of leveraging digitized information and digital technologies to enable or improve existing business processes. It focuses on applying digital capabilities to enhance efficiency, streamline operations, or improve service delivery within an organization, without necessarily a radical overhaul of the business model.

Digitization: The foundational process of converting analog information (e.g., paper documents, physical photographs) into a digital format. This step primarily changes the *form* of information, making it machine-readable, but does not inherently alter underlying business processes or models.

Organizational Change Management: A systematic approach and set of tools applied to support individuals and organizations in transitioning from a current state to a desired future state. In digital transformation, it focuses on mitigating resistance, fostering adoption of new technologies and processes, and cultivating a supportive organizational culture.

Chapter 4
Innovation Strategy and Digital Maturity of Organizations

Ilham Firmansyah
https://orcid.org/0009-0007-6104-9966
Universitas Esa Unggul, Indonesia

ABSTRACT

Innovation and digital maturity are essential pillars for organizational success in the digital age. This chapter explores how innovation strategies can align with digital maturity stages to drive sustainable transformation. Using frameworks like Three Horizons, Open Innovation, and Design Thinking, it outlines strategic approaches for innovation based on digital readiness. Case studies from Siemens, ING Bank, and Estonia illustrate how these strategies work in real-world settings. Common barriers such as legacy systems and cultural resistance are addressed alongside practical solutions. The chapter also highlights the role of innovation metrics in guiding progress. Ultimately, it positions innovation as both a result and a catalyst of digital maturity, enabling organizations to adapt and lead in an increasingly disruptive environment.

INTRODUCTION

In the era of accelerated technological change, digital transformation has become a fundamental imperative rather than a strategic option. Organizations across industries are compelled to redesign their operations, culture, and value propositions in response to shifting customer expectations, disruptive market forces, and emerging digital technologies. However, successful transformation does not begin

DOI: 10.4018/979-8-3373-5167-4.ch004

with technology alone it begins with a clear innovation strategy supported by the organization's digital maturity (Meng et al., 2025).

Digital maturity, in this context, reflects an organization's capability to effectively leverage technology, human capital, and processes to create sustainable value. This capability varies widely across industries and organizations, depending on factors such as leadership commitment, investment in digital infrastructure, employee readiness, and agility in decision-making. Organizations with higher levels of digital maturity tend to demonstrate greater adaptability, speed of innovation, and operational resilience (Raza et al., 2025).

At the same time, innovation strategy defines the organization's approach to generating new ideas, implementing change, and delivering improved outcomes. In digitally mature organizations, innovation is not just isolated in R&D departments; it becomes embedded across all business functions from customer service to product development and supply chain management. Aligning innovation with digital capability allows organizations to unlock new growth opportunities while managing risks associated with transformation (Watson, 2025).

This chapter introduces the critical relationship between innovation strategy and digital maturity. It argues that digital maturity is not merely a technical achievement but a strategic enabler that shapes how innovation is conceived, delivered, and scaled. The chapter will examine established digital maturity frameworks and innovation models that guide organizations in aligning their vision with practical execution (Y. Wang et al., 2025).

Furthermore, this chapter explores how different maturity levels require tailored innovation approaches. For example, organizations in the early stages of digital maturity may focus on digital literacy, leadership alignment, and pilot initiatives, while more advanced organizations may prioritize data-driven innovation, platform ecosystems, and continuous optimization. By contextualizing innovation strategies within the spectrum of digital readiness, organizations can make more informed, realistic, and impactful decisions (Margaretha et al., 2025).

Finally, the chapter highlights key challenges such as legacy systems, fragmented data environments, cultural resistance, and short-termism, which often hinder innovation and digital progress. It also outlines how metrics, benchmarking, and innovation scorecards can be used to measure both digital maturity and innovation performance (Djatmiko et al., 2025).

Through a combination of theoretical insights, strategic frameworks, and real-world case studies, this chapter aims to provide actionable guidance for organizations seeking to align their innovation efforts with their digital capabilities. In doing so, it contributes to the broader discourse on how organizations can thrive in a digital-first economy where resilience, adaptability, and innovation are interdependent forces. As illustrated in Figure 1, innovation strategy and digital maturity share a dynamic and reciprocal relationship, where each element reinforces and shapes the other within the organizational transformation process.

Figure 1. Strategic alignments & feedback loop

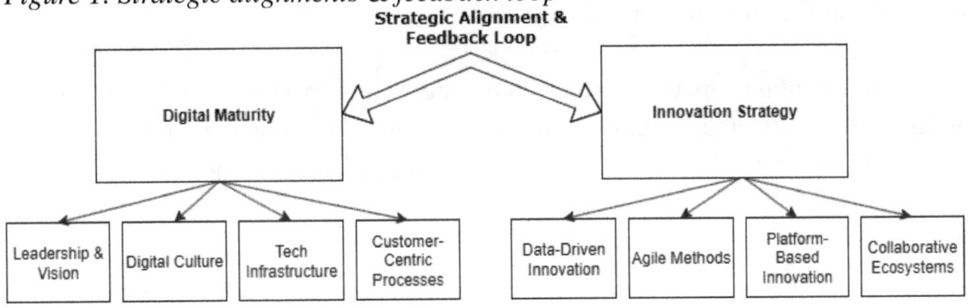

UNDERSTANDING DIGITAL MATURITY

In today's fast-paced digital economy, the concept of digital maturity has emerged as a crucial determinant of an organization's ability to navigate transformation effectively. Digital maturity refers to the extent to which an organization is capable of leveraging digital technologies, data, people, and processes to achieve strategic goals. It goes beyond technology adoption it encompasses leadership, culture, and the organization's capacity to continuously adapt to change (Rongrong & Ismail, 2025).

Digitally mature organizations typically demonstrate high levels of integration between their technological capabilities and business objectives. They use data and automation not only to improve operations but to reimagine products, services, and customer experiences. Conversely, organizations with low digital maturity often struggle with siloed systems, limited digital skills, outdated infrastructures, and lack of agility in responding to disruption (Indravathy & Abd Rahim, 2025).

Key Dimensions of Digital Maturity

Several interrelated dimensions are commonly used to assess digital maturity. These include:

- Leadership and Vision

A strong digital vision led by committed executives is foundational. Digital transformation requires leaders who can align business goals with technology investments, foster innovation, and champion change across all levels of the organization.

- Digital Culture and Capabilities

Cultural readiness influences how teams adopt and experiment with digital tools. A digitally mature organization promotes continuous learning, collaboration, and a growth mindset ensuring that employees are equipped and empowered to innovate.

- Technology Infrastructure

Modern infrastructure such as cloud computing, integrated platforms, and secure data architectures enables scalability, agility, and resilience. Legacy systems, in contrast, often act as barriers to transformation.

- Customer-Centric Processes

Digital maturity includes redesigning processes to be customer-focused, data-informed, and experien ce-driven. Organizations must be able to collect and respond to real-time customer insights across channels.

These dimensions help assess where an organization currently stands and identify areas that require investment or transformation (Alnaser & Elmousalami, 2025).

Digital Maturity Models

To guide assessment and improvement, a number of digital maturity frameworks have been developed by consulting firms and research institutions (Yan & Sun, 2025). Some of the most recognized include:

- Digital Maturity Model (DMM)

Developed by the Digital Standards Initiative, DMM evaluates maturity across five domains: strategy, culture, technology, operations, and governance. Each domain has defined levels of maturity, from nascent to optimized.

- Deloitte Digital Maturity Framework

Deloitte proposes six dimensions: digital strategy, culture, customer experience, technology, organization, and innovation. It helps businesses identify capability gaps and develop roadmaps toward digital leadership.

- Capability Maturity Model Integration (CMMI)

Though originally designed for software engineering, CMMI is widely used to measure process maturity across organizations. Its staged approach provides a structured path from initial awareness to continuous improvement.

Table 1. Comparison of three digital maturity models

Model Name	Domains/Dimensions	Assessment Levels	Primary Focus
Digital Maturity Model (DMM)	Strategy, Culture, Technology, Operations, Governance	5 Levels (e.g., Initial → Optimized)	Comprehensive evaluation across enterprise-wide capabilities
Deloitte Digital Maturity Framework	Strategy, Culture, Customer Experience, Technology, Organization, Innovation	Low, Medium, High	Linking digital capabilities with business value
CMMI (Capability Maturity Model Integration)	Process Management, Measurement, Performance, Quality	5 Maturity Levels (1–5)	Process standardization and continuous improvement

Table 1 provides a comparative overview of widely used digital maturity models, highlighting their focus areas and assessment structures.

These models are not only useful for benchmarking, but also for tracking progress over time. They enable organizations to prioritize initiatives, allocate resources more effectively, and align digital efforts with strategic outcomes (Ozdemir & Zonah, 2025).

From Measurement to Action

Assessing digital maturity is only valuable if it leads to actionable insights. Organizations must not treat digital maturity as a static label, but rather as a dynamic state requiring continuous improvement. Regular assessments can help ensure that digital initiatives remain aligned with business goals as market conditions and technologies evolve (Prajwal et al., 2025).

Moreover, a nuanced understanding of digital maturity allows leaders to tailor their innovation strategies to fit their current capabilities this alignment is central to the rest of the chapter (Afolabi et al., 2025).

INNOVATION IN THE DIGITAL AGE

Innovation is no longer a luxury it has become a necessity for organizational survival and growth in the 21st century. In a rapidly evolving digital environment, the ability to generate new ideas, implement novel solutions, and adapt quickly to change is what separates thriving organizations from those that stagnate. Yet, digital innovation is distinct from traditional forms of innovation; it is driven by data, enabled by platforms, and accelerated through collaboration and agility (X. Zhang et al., 2025).

Digital innovation often takes the form of integrating advanced technologies such as artificial intelligence (AI), cloud computing, Internet of Things (IoT), and big data analytics into business operations and value creation. However, innovation in the digital age is not solely about the tools it is about how organizations rethink their strategies, engage stakeholders, and structure internal processes to deliver sustained impact (Korać et al., 2025).

Platform-Based Innovation

One of the defining features of modern innovation is the use of platforms. Platform-based innovation involves creating shared digital infrastructures such as APIs, developer ecosystems, and open standards that enable external and internal actors to co-create value. Companies like Amazon, Google, and Salesforce exemplify this model by fostering vibrant ecosystems of developers, users, and third-party providers (Murrar et al., 2025).

This approach offers several advantages:

- Scalability: Platforms allow rapid expansion without linear increases in resources.
- Interoperability: Open standards enable integration across diverse systems and partners.
- Speed to Market: Innovation cycles accelerate as partners contribute complementary capabilities.

In many cases, platform innovation becomes a foundation for business model transformation. Rather than delivering value through linear supply chains, platform firms orchestrate complex networks of interaction that amplify innovation at scale (Fu et al., 2025).

Data-Driven Innovation

Data has become a critical asset in modern organizations. Data-driven innovation involves using real-time analytics, machine learning, and predictive modeling to uncover insights that inform decision-making, personalize customer experiences, and improve operational efficiency (Liang et al., 2025).

Organizations that embrace data-driven innovation:

- Monitor key performance indicators (KPIs) across digital channels
- Use algorithms to detect trends, anomalies, and emerging opportunities
- Automate workflows and optimize outcomes based on evidence

The success of data-driven innovation depends not only on technical tools but also on governance structures that ensure data quality, accessibility, and ethical usage (H. Wang & Liu, 2025). This requires investment in data infrastructure and talent with analytical expertise.

Agile and Lean Innovation

Agile and lean methodologies have become essential in enabling innovation under uncertainty. Rather than long development cycles with fixed outcomes, agile innovation emphasizes short, iterative sprints with frequent feedback. This approach allows teams to test ideas, fail fast, and pivot when necessary minimizing risk while maximizing learning (Hernández-Barrera et al., 2025).

Core principles of agile and lean innovation include:

- Customer feedback loops
- Cross-functional collaboration
- Minimum Viable Products (MVPs)
- Continuous improvement and experimentation

Organizations that institutionalize agility are better positioned to respond to market changes, technological shifts, and evolving customer needs.

Collaborative Innovation

The complexity of digital challenges often exceeds the capacity of any single organization. Collaborative innovation refers to partnerships across industries, academia, startups, and even customers to jointly develop and scale solutions. Open innovation models, co-creation platforms, and joint ventures are all manifestations of this approach (Ferhataj et al., 2025).

Collaboration enhances innovation by:

- Accessing diverse perspectives and expertise
- Sharing risks and resources
- Accelerating problem-solving and market entry

In the digital age, innovation ecosystems are replacing isolated efforts. Leading organizations are those that can orchestrate or participate in networks of innovation effectively.

Table 2 provides a summary of four major digital innovation strategies, highlighting their distinct characteristics, examples, and strategic advantages.

Table 2. Types of digital innovation strategies

Strategy Type	Description	Example	Benefit
Platform-Based	Leveraging APIs, ecosystems, and open standards to enable co-creation and integration	Salesforce AppExchange	Scalable innovation ecosystem
Data-Driven	Utilizing analytics, AI, and big data to derive insights and guide decisions	Netflix recommendation engine	Personalized experiences and efficiency
Agile/Lean	Applying short development cycles with rapid feedback and iteration	MVPs in tech startups	Faster adaptation and reduced risk
Collaborative	Partnering across organizations and sectors to innovate jointly	Apple–IBM enterprise solutions	Shared resources and extended reach

Aligning Innovation with Maturity Stages

A successful innovation strategy must be grounded in the organization's current digital maturity level. Misalignment between ambition and readiness can result in wasted resources, failed initiatives, or organizational resistance. Therefore, tailoring innovation efforts to different stages of digital maturity enables organizations to progress realistically while maintaining momentum and stakeholder trust (Chen & Huang, 2025).

Digital maturity is not a binary condition but a spectrum, typically segmented into stages ranging from initial adoption to fully optimized digital integration. Each stage presents distinct capabilities, constraints, and opportunities. As such, innovation must be calibrated accordingly, ensuring that goals and methods are appropriate for the organization's level of readiness.

Initial Stage: Laying the Groundwork

Organizations at the initial stage often rely on manual processes, siloed data systems, and have limited digital expertise. At this level, innovation efforts should focus *on building foundational digital awareness*, creating internal alignment, and cultivating leadership support for transformation (Z. Zhang et al., 2025).

Recommended actions include:

- Establishing digital literacy programs
- Appointing digital champions or innovation sponsors
- Piloting low-risk digital initiatives to demonstrate value

This phase is less about large-scale transformation and more about preparing the organization culturally and structurally to embrace change.

Developing Stage: Experimentation and Early Wins

As organizations progress, they begin adopting digital tools and experimenting with agile methods. The developing stage is characterized by increased investment in technology and initial cross-functional collaboration. Innovation at this level should be *focused, measurable, and agile* (Korać et al., 2025).

Key strategies include:

- Launching Minimum Viable Products (MVPs)
- Applying customer journey mapping and design thinking
- Encouraging collaboration between IT and business units

The goal is to build credibility and internal momentum through quick wins and iterative development.

Defined Stage: Structured Innovation and Integration

Organizations at the defined stage have formalized innovation processes, better-integrated systems, and established digital governance. At this point, innovation efforts *can scale more systematically*, supported by clearer roles, processes, and data assets (Murrar et al., 2025).

Innovation initiatives may involve:

- Embedding innovation labs or cross-functional squads
- Integrating customer data platforms to inform product development
- Expanding digital capabilities to back-office functions (e.g., HR, finance)

This stage enables a shift from isolated experiments to cohesive, organization-wide innovation programs.

Managed Stage: Scaling and Optimization

The managed stage reflects a high level of operational maturity and cross-departmental coordination. Here, innovation strategy should focus on *scalability, automation, and ecosystem partnerships.*

Examples of strategic focus areas:

- Platform-based offerings and digital ecosystems
- Predictive analytics to drive product/service optimization
- Strategic alliances to co-develop new digital capabilities

Organizations in this stage are no longer reactive but are shaping the market through continuous innovation.

Optimizing Stage: Continuous Improvement and Intelligence

At the highest stage, innovation becomes embedded in the organization's DNA. Organizations operate with real-time data, autonomous processes, and an adaptive culture. The focus shifts from delivering innovation projects to sustaining *a culture of innovation and intelligent decision-making* (Fu et al., 2025).

At this level, organizations:

- Utilize AI for predictive innovation management
- Embrace scenario-based strategic planning
- Continuously benchmark, adapt, and evolve through learning systems

Innovation in this phase is not just enabled by digital maturity it actively advances it.

As summarized in Table 3, each stage of digital maturity aligns with distinct innovation priorities and outcomes, enabling a staged yet strategic approach to transformation.

Table 3. Innovation focus by digital maturity stage

Maturity Stage	Innovation Focus	Key Activities	Expected Outcomes
Initial	Building awareness and leadership alignment	Digital literacy programs, pilot initiatives, identifying change champions	Foundational readiness and leadership buy-in
Developing	Agile experimentation and quick wins	MVPs, design thinking, cross-functional collaboration	Early success, internal momentum
Defined	Structured integration and scale-up	Innovation labs, customer data integration, process redesign	Broader innovation capacity, strategic alignment
Managed	Ecosystem collaboration and predictive design	Platform-based innovation, AI-driven insights, partnerships	Market responsiveness, scaled innovation
Optimizing	Continuous learning and intelligent innovation	Autonomous systems, strategic foresight, adaptive culture	Innovation embedded in culture, long-term adaptability

FRAMEWORKS FOR STRATEGIC INNOVATION

To navigate the complexity of innovation in the digital age, organizations need more than ambition they need structure. Strategic frameworks serve as critical tools for aligning innovation with organizational goals, evaluating progress, and reducing uncertainty. These models provide a common language for decision-makers, helping them assess where to invest, how to balance risks, and when to pivot. This chapter introduces four widely recognized frameworks that support innovation planning, execution, and scaling in digitally evolving environments (Liang et al., 2025).

Three Horizons of Growth (McKinsey)

The Three Horizons model helps organizations manage current operations while simultaneously preparing for the future. It divides innovation efforts into three overlapping time frames:

- Horizon 1: Core business improvements incremental innovations in existing products or processes
- Horizon 2: Emerging opportunities extensions of current capabilities or adjacent markets
- Horizon 3: Future bets high-risk, high-reward innovations that may redefine the business

This framework allows leaders to maintain operational performance (Horizon 1), invest in scalable ideas (Horizon 2), and explore disruptive possibilities (Horizon 3). It encourages a *balanced portfolio approach*, ensuring long-term resilience without sacrificing short-term results.

Open Innovation Model (Chesbrough)

Coined by Henry Chesbrough, open innovation emphasizes the use of *external ideas and collaboration* to accelerate internal innovation. Rather than relying solely on internal R&D, organizations create permeable boundaries to allow the inflow and outflow of knowledge (H. Wang & Liu, 2025).

Open innovation can take many forms:

- Joint ventures and strategic partnerships
- Innovation contests or idea sourcing platforms
- Licensing technologies or co-developing with startups

This model is especially relevant in digital contexts *where speed, diversity of input, and platform integration* are essential. Open innovation reduces development costs, accelerates time-to-market, and increases access to breakthrough technologies.

Design Thinking

Design Thinking is a *human-centered, empathy-driven* innovation process that prioritizes the needs, behaviors, and experiences of users. It is particularly effective in addressing complex, ambiguous problems where traditional analytical approaches fall short (Hernández-Barrera et al., 2025).

The Design Thinking cycle typically includes:

- Empathize: Understand user needs and pain points
- Define: Clearly articulate the problem
- Ideate: Generate creative solutions
- Prototype: Develop low-cost, testable models
- Test: Gather feedback and iterate

In digital transformation, Design Thinking helps ensure that technology solutions are not only functional, but also *usable, desirable, and meaningful* to real users.

Digital Capability Framework (DCMF)

The Digital Capability Framework (DCMF) provides a structured method to assess and improve digital readiness across several key areas:

- Strategy and Leadership
- Culture and People
- Technology and Infrastructure
- Processes and Governance
- Customer and Ecosystem Engagement

DCMF helps organizations identify *capability gaps*, prioritize investments, and align innovation initiatives with their maturity level. It acts as a diagnostic and planning tool, enabling digital transformation to proceed in a *coordinated, measurable way* (Ferhataj et al., 2025).

As shown in Table 4, each framework offers a distinct approach to structuring innovation, with applications that span from organizational strategy to product and service design.

Table 4. Summary of strategic innovation frameworks

Framework	Core Focus	Application Area	Primary Benefit
Three Horizons (McKinsey)	Managing innovation across time horizons (now, next, new)	Portfolio planning, resource allocation	Balances short-term gains with long-term growth
Open Innovation (Chesbrough)	External collaboration and knowledge flow	R&D, product development, startup engagement	Accelerates innovation and broadens idea sources
Design Thinking	Human-centered, empathy-driven problem solving	UX design, digital service development	Enhances user relevance and creative solutioning
Digital Capability Framework (DCMF)	Assessing digital readiness and maturity	Transformation planning, capability benchmarking	Aligns innovation with organizational digital needs

CASE STUDIES OF INNOVATION AND DIGITAL MATURITY

While models and frameworks provide structure, it is through real-world applications that the value of innovation strategies and digital maturity becomes most evident. Organizations across various sectors have demonstrated how aligning innovation efforts with digital capabilities leads to measurable impact. This section presents three diverse case studies that illustrate how companies and institutions operationalize innovation through varying degrees of digital maturity (Chen & Huang, 2025).

Siemens: Digital Twin Strategy in Manufacturing

Siemens, a global leader in industrial automation, has embraced a highly mature digital strategy through its implementation of *digital twin technology* virtual replicas of physical systems used to simulate, predict, and optimize performance in real time (Z. Zhang et al., 2025).

Through its *MindSphere platform*, Siemens integrates Internet of Things (IoT) sensors, real-time analytics, and cloud computing to support predictive maintenance and operational efficiency. This approach enables engineers and managers to monitor asset performance, test simulations before deployment, and reduce system downtime.

Key takeaways:

- High alignment between digital infrastructure and innovation goals
- Investment in platform-based and data-driven innovation
- Demonstrates Horizon 2 and 3 innovation focus in a managed/optimized maturity stage

Siemens' case exemplifies how advanced digital maturity allows for the scaling of complex innovation models that fundamentally reshape operational processes.

ING Bank: Scaled Agility and Product Innovation

ING Bank, a prominent European financial institution, undertook a comprehensive digital transformation to enhance customer experience and speed-to-market. The bank adopted a *scaled agile framework (SAFe)*, restructuring its operations into small, cross-functional teams known as "squads" each responsible for a specific customer journey or product line (Cheng & Chen, 2025).

By combining agile methods with data-driven innovation and customer feedback loops, ING was able to:

- Reduce product development cycles from months to weeks
- Increase responsiveness to market shifts
- Foster a collaborative innovation culture across departments

This case reflects *the defined-to-managed* stage of digital maturity, where innovation becomes embedded in organizational design and is supported by data, leadership, and cultural transformation.

Estonian Government: Digital Governance and Public Innovation

Estonia offers a unique example of national-level digital maturity. Over the past two decades, the Estonian government has implemented a digital-first governance model through initiatives *like e-Residency, digital ID,* and *X-Road* a secure data exchange platform connecting all government systems (Ao, 2025).

Key features of Estonia's digital innovation:

- Seamless interoperability between public services
- Secure identity verification and digital signatures
- Citizen-centric design driven by data and transparency

By embedding innovation into its core governance structure, Estonia has achieved:

- Cost savings in public administration
- Increased public trust and civic engagement
- A global reputation as a pioneer in e-governance

This case illustrates a maturity model that extends beyond organizational boundaries, demonstrating how strategic innovation can drive systemic transformation at national scale.

Table 5 summarizes the key insights from the three case studies, illustrating how innovation strategies align with digital maturity stages across different sectors.

Table 5. Case study comparison of innovation and maturity alignment

Organization	Sector	Innovation Strategy	Maturity Stage	Key Outcomes
Siement	Manufacturing	Platform-based innovation, Digital Twin	Managed/Optimizing	Predictive maintenance, operational efficiency, scalability
ING Bank	Financial	Agile methods, Data-driven product design	Defined/Managed	Faster time-to-market, customer-focused product development
Estonian Gov.	Public Sector	Citizen-centered digital services, Open innovation	Optimizing (National-Level)	Integrated governance, digital citizenship, global recognition

BARRIERS TO INNOVATION AND DIGITAL PROGRESS

Despite the growing emphasis on digital transformation and innovation, many organizations face persistent barriers that hinder their ability to evolve. These challenges often stem not from a lack of vision, but from deeply embedded structural, cultural, and technical constraints. Understanding these obstacles is essential for developing effective strategies to overcome them and sustain digital advancement (J. Zhang & Zhao, 2026).

Legacy Systems and Siloed Data

Many organizations, particularly those with long operational histories, are burdened by *legacy IT systems* that are outdated, inflexible, and difficult to integrate with modern technologies (Liu et al., 2026). These systems often operate in silos, preventing seamless data sharing across departments and functions.

Common impacts include:

- Reduced operational agility
- Inconsistent customer data and fragmented insights
- High maintenance costs and slow development cycles

Overcoming this barrier requires modernization strategies such as cloud migration, data integration platforms, and API-based architectures that support interoperability.

Lack of Change Management and Leadership Support

Innovation and digital maturity require not only new technologies but also organizational change. However, many initiatives fail due to weak change management practices or the absence of strong leadership commitment.

Symptoms of this barrier include:

- Unclear communication about transformation goals
- Resistance from middle management
- Lack of sponsorship at the executive level

Effective change management involves aligning stakeholders, providing training and incentives, and establishing governance structures that sustain progress. Leaders must champion innovation efforts and model the behaviors they expect from their teams (Li et al., 2025).

Talent Gaps and Cultural Resistance

Digital transformation demands *new skills, mindsets, and ways of working*. Many organizations struggle to attract or retain talent with digital expertise, such as data scientists, UX designers, and cloud engineers (Singh et al., 2025). At the same time, existing employees may resist new tools or workflows.

Challenges include:

- Skill mismatches and outdated roles
- Fear of job displacement due to automation
- Low engagement in innovation activities

To address this, organizations should invest in *reskilling and upskilling programs*, create psychologically safe environments for experimentation, and embed digital thinking into the organizational culture.

Short-Term Thinking and Risk Aversion

Innovation inherently involves uncertainty and long-term investment. However, some organizations are constrained by short-term financial pressures or a low appetite for risk particularly in regulated industries or volatile markets (Deveci et al., 2025).

Consequences of this mindset:

- Underinvestment in transformative innovation
- Prioritization of incremental improvements over bold ideas
- Failure to respond to emerging threats or opportunities

Building a sustainable innovation culture requires shifting focus from quarterly returns to long-term value creation, supported by balanced innovation portfolios and scenario planning.

Table 6 outlines the major barriers encountered by organizations in their digital innovation journeys, along with their respective impacts and recommended countermeasures.

Table 6. Common barriers to innovation and digital progress

Barrier	Description	Impact	Recommended Response
Legacy Systems & Siloed Data	Outdated IT systems and fragmented data architectures	Poor integration, slow responsiveness, high maintenance costs	Migrate to cloud platforms, use APIs, enable data interoperability
Lack of Leadership & Change Management	Weak executive sponsorship and unclear transformation roadmaps	Organizational resistance, initiative failure	Clear vision, training, change agents, and stakeholder alignment
Talent Gaps & Cultural Resistance	Shortage of digital skills and reluctance to adopt new ways of working	Skill mismatches, fear of automation, low adoption	Upskilling, safe experimentation space, digital culture-building
Short-Term Thinking & Risk Aversion	Focus on immediate ROI and fear of uncertainty	Underinvestment in bold innovation, missed strategic shifts	Balanced innovation portfolio, long-term performance metrics

Measuring Progress and Outcomes

Innovation without measurement is a gamble. For innovation strategies to deliver lasting value, organizations must establish robust mechanisms for tracking progress and evaluating outcomes. Measurement not only provides visibility into what works and what doesn't it also enables alignment between strategic intent and operational execution. However, measuring innovation is inherently complex. Unlike traditional business metrics, innovation often involves long time horizons, intangible value, and high degrees of uncertainty (Yang et al., 2025).

In the context of digital transformation, organizations must measure both *innovation performance* and *digital maturity evolution*, ensuring that innovation efforts contribute to capability growth and strategic differentiation.

Innovation Metrics: Moving Beyond Vanity Indicators

Many organizations rely on surface-level indicators such as the number of ideas generated or projects launched. While these *input* metrics can indicate activity levels, they rarely reflect impact. Effective innovation measurement requires a combination of *input, process,* and *output/outcome metrics*, balanced across short-term and long-term timeframes (Routman et al., 2025).

Examples of Innovation Metrics:

Table 7. Sample innovation metrics by category

Metric Type	Examples
Input	R&D spend as % of revenue, number of new ideas submitted, team diversity
Process	Time to prototype, iteration speed, % of ideas progressing to MVP stage
Output	Number of new products/services launched, % of revenue from new offerings
Outcome	Customer satisfaction (NPS), market share growth, ROI on innovation portfolio

A well-designed innovation dashboard tracks a mix of these metrics, customized to the organization's industry, maturity, and goals. For example, in early-stage innovation, learning velocity (how fast teams gather insights) may matter more than short-term ROI.

Measuring Digital Maturity Over Time

Tracking *digital maturity* is equally important. Organizations should assess how their capabilities evolve over time, ideally using the same framework or model at regular intervals (Binkley et al., 2025). This enables benchmarking, identifies capability gaps, and reveals whether innovation efforts are leading to tangible transformation.

Repeatable maturity assessment tools (like DMM or DCMF) typically evaluate progress across key domains:

- Leadership & Vision: Are executives leading with a digital-first mindset?
- Culture & Skills: Are teams adapting and innovating effectively?
- Technology & Infrastructure: Is the organization moving away from legacy systems?
- Customer Orientation: Is the customer experience becoming more personalized and integrated?

Organizations should not treat these assessments as compliance exercises. Instead, they should become part of a *continuous feedback loop*, embedded in strategy reviews and annual planning cycles.

Linking Metrics to Strategic Goals

Metrics become meaningful only when linked to *strategic objectives*. For example, an organization aiming to increase market responsiveness might prioritize metrics *like time-to-market, customer feedback loop cycles*, or *product iteration frequency*. Those focused on sustainability might track *carbon footprint reductions from process innovations* (Sposato, 2025).

High-performing organizations use "*innovation scorecards*" strategy maps that connect innovation KPIs to enterprise-level performance goals.

A well-aligned measurement system answers critical questions:

- Are we investing in the right types of innovation?
- Are we developing the capabilities needed for future competitiveness?
- Are our innovation efforts improving customer, employee, or societal outcomes?

Integrating Quantitative and Qualitative Insights

While numerical metrics provide structure, *qualitative insights* offer context. Interviews, retrospectives, customer testimonials, and ethnographic studies can capture emotional, behavioral, and cultural dimensions of innovation that numbers often miss (Zeidanloo & Špaček, 2025).

For instance:

- Teams might achieve MVP launch targets but feel creatively constrained
- A digital product may have low adoption due to trust or usability concerns
- Cultural resistance might not show in dashboards but emerge in feedback sessions

Blending hard data with soft signals ensures a holistic view of innovation performance and maturity progression. It also promotes learning and empathy two essential ingredients in any transformation journey.

Feedback Loops and Learning Systems

Measurement should not be the endpoint it must feed into *actionable learning systems*. Feedback loops, where data from outcomes is used to adjust strategies and behaviors, are crucial for adaptive innovation (Meng et al., 2025).

Organizations can embed feedback loops through:

- Agile retrospectives and sprint reviews
- Innovation governance boards reviewing metrics quarterly
- Machine learning systems analyzing user behavior to guide development

FUTURE OUTLOOK AND RECOMMENDATIONS

As digital transformation continues to reshape competitive landscapes, innovation is no longer a peripheral activity it is a core strategic function. The coming years will demand even greater alignment between digital maturity and innovation strategy, with organizations needing to not only adopt emerging technologies but also reimagine their operating models, talent structures, and value creation approaches. This final chapter explores key future trends and offers practical recommendations to guide organizations in building resilient, innovation-ready ecosystems (Raza et al., 2025).

Anticipated Trends in Innovation and Digital Maturity

1. Rise of Generative AI and Autonomous Innovation

Artificial intelligence, especially generative models, is expected to become a central enabler of innovation from product design to customer support and even strategic decision-making. Organizations that integrate AI not just as a tool, but as a collaborator, will unlock new levels of speed and personalization.

2. Platform Ecosystems and Open Collaboration

The future of innovation will be increasingly ecosystem-driven. Businesses will form platforms where partners, developers, and even customers contribute to co-creating value. Digital maturity will be defined not only by internal capabilities but by the ability to orchestrate external networks.

3. Sustainable and Ethical Innovation

Environmental, Social, and Governance (ESG) considerations are evolving from compliance to strategy. Future innovations must address climate impact, social equity, and data ethics. Digital solutions that fail to integrate sustainability may face resistance or irrelevance.

4. Personalized Workforce Enablement

With hybrid and distributed work becoming the norm, future organizations will invest in *digitally augmented workplaces* using analytics, AI, and collaborative tools to create personalized and empowering employee experiences. Innovation will flourish where employees feel enabled and connected.

5. Continuous Maturity Evolution

Digital maturity will no longer be viewed as a static destination but as a *dynamic capability*. Organizations will need to constantly assess, adapt, and evolve their maturity strategies to match the speed of technological and market change.

Strategic Recommendations for Organizations

Based on insights from earlier chapters, the following strategic actions are recommended to support long-term innovation and maturity alignment:

1. Institutionalize Innovation

Embed innovation into governance structures, budgeting cycles, and performance metrics. Make innovation part of everyone's job not just the R&D department.

2. Build Adaptive Digital Capabilities

Invest in scalable, modular technology platforms that allow rapid experimentation, integration, and evolution. Prioritize cloud-native infrastructure, cybersecurity, and data governance.

3. Foster an Innovation-Ready Culture

Create psychological safety, celebrate failure as learning, and encourage cross-disciplinary thinking. Provide continuous learning and career mobility aligned with digital skill demands.

4. Measure What Matters

Develop innovation scorecards and digital maturity assessments that are relevant to business outcomes. Balance financial metrics with human and societal indicators.

5. Engage the Ecosystem

Actively collaborate with startups, academia, governments, and even competitors. Innovation thrives in open, diverse environments. Use platforms and APIs to extend your innovation network.

6. Think Long-Term, Act Iteratively

Adopt a "dual-speed" strategy: maintain short-term agility (via MVPs and sprints) while investing in bold, transformative bets. Use scenario planning to prepare for multiple possible futures.

Final Thought: Innovation As A Maturity Engine

In closing, innovation should not be treated merely as an outcome of digital maturity it is also its most powerful *engine*. The most successful organizations of tomorrow will not be those with the best technologies, but those that consistently adapt, experiment, and evolve. By aligning innovation strategy with evolving digital capabilities, leaders can create organizations that are not only fit for the future but capable of shaping it.

Regional and Industry Differences

While innovation strategies and digital maturity models offer a generalizable framework, their application often varies across regions and industries. Economic, cultural, regulatory, and infrastructural factors shape how organizations interpret and implement innovation and transformation initiatives. Recognizing these contextual differences is crucial for tailoring strategies that are both realistic and effective.

A. Regional Variations: Global North vs. Global South

Organizations in high-income countries often operate in digitally saturated markets, where innovation tends to be incremental, focusing on customer experience, automation, and artificial intelligence. In contrast, many organizations in low- and middle-income countries (LMICs) are engaged in leapfrogging innovation—bypassing legacy systems and adopting newer, more agile technologies.

For instance:

- *Sub-Saharan Africa* has seen a rise in mobile-based innovation, such as digital banking through platforms like M-Pesa.

- *Southeast Asia* demonstrates rapid adoption of e-commerce and fintech due to high mobile penetration and a large unbaned population.
- In contrast, *Western Europe* tends to focus on integrating AI into existing infrastructure, improving sustainability, and aligning with strict regulatory frameworks like GDPR.

These differences imply that a one-size-fits-all model for digital maturity is insufficient. Policymakers, consultants, and leaders must adapt frameworks to regional realities.

B. Industry-Specific Dynamics

Different industries face distinct pressures and innovation imperatives:

- Healthcare: Highly regulated, patient-centric, and slow to adopt. Innovation focuses on telemedicine, AI diagnostics, and EHR integration. Digital maturity is often uneven high in diagnostics but low in interoperability.
- Financial Services: Highly digital and competitive. Innovations like blockchain, digital identity, and AI fraud detection are central. Regulatory compliance (e.g., Basel III, PSD2) shapes how maturity is pursued.
- Manufacturing: Adoption of Industry 4.0, including IoT, robotics, and digital twins, is transforming production. Innovation is driven by operational efficiency and predictive maintenance.
- Public Sector: Innovation faces structural inertia but plays a critical role in citizen services. Digital maturity varies by country and political will, with leading examples in Estonia, Singapore, and South Korea.

C. Implications for Strategy and Maturity Models

These regional and industry differences imply that digital maturity models should not be applied mechanically. Instead, organizations should:

- Customize maturity assessments based on industry benchmarks and regional norms.
- Consider stakeholder readiness, especially in highly regulated or resource-constrained sectors.
- Align innovation goals not only with internal capabilities but also with external enablers like broadband access, skilled workforce availability, and ecosystem maturity.

CONCLUSION

This chapter consolidates the key insights from the discussion on how innovation strategy and digital maturity interact to drive organizational transformation. In the rapidly evolving digital economy, innovation cannot be a side activity it must be embedded in the core fabric of an organization's operations, culture, and leadership.

The book chapter began by exploring the theoretical foundations of innovation and digital maturity, establishing that both are dynamic, interdependent constructs. Through a review of models such as the Three Horizons framework, Open Innovation, and the Digital Capability Maturity Framework, we demonstrated how organizations can structure their innovation efforts based on their maturity level.

The integration of real-world case studies from Siemens, ING Bank, and the Estonian government provided tangible examples of how innovation strategies, when aligned with digital readiness, lead to measurable impact. These cases illustrated that while tools and technologies matter, success ultimately depends on people, governance, and adaptability.

Barriers such as legacy systems, talent gaps, and short-term thinking continue to slow down transformation efforts. However, with the right measurement tools, cultural mindset, and leadership commitment, these obstacles can be transformed into opportunities for learning and reinvention.

Looking ahead, organizations must treat digital maturity not as a fixed destination but as a capability to be continuously developed. Innovation, in turn, must be approached strategically guided by frameworks, informed by data, and empowered by ecosystems. Only by harmonizing both can organizations stay resilient, relevant, and responsible in an era defined by disruption.

REFERENCES

Afolabi, S. O., Malachi, I. O., Olawumi, A. O., & Oladapo, B. I. (2025). Data Process of Net-Zero Revolution for Transforming Earth and Beyond Sustainably. *Sustainability (Basel)*, *17*(12), 5367. Advance online publication. DOI: 10.3390/su17125367

Alnaser, A. A., & Elmousalami, H. (2025). Benefits and Challenges of AI-Based Digital Twin Integration in the Saudi Arabian Construction Industry: A Correspondence Analysis (CA) Approach. *Applied Sciences (Basel, Switzerland)*, *15*(9), 4675. Advance online publication. DOI: 10.3390/app15094675

Ao, J. (2025). Research on the impact of artificial intelligence on corporate sustainability performance and its mechanisms: An empirical analysis based on text analysis. *Discover Artificial Intelligence*, *5*(1), 122. Advance online publication. DOI: 10.1007/s44163-025-00359-w

Binkley, C. E., Bouslov, D., Zaidi, A., Kaye, L., Whalen, R., Sethi, S., & Azar, J. (2025). An early pipeline framework for assessing vendor AI solutions to support return on investment. *NPJ Digital Medicine*, *8*(1), 368. Advance online publication. DOI: 10.1038/s41746-025-01767-z PMID: 40523928

Chen, D., & Huang, Y. (2025). Integrating reinforcement learning and large language models for crop production process management optimization and control through a new knowledge-based deep learning paradigm. *Computers and Electronics in Agriculture*, *232*, 110028. Advance online publication. DOI: 10.1016/j.compag.2025.110028

Cheng, P., & Chen, D. (2025). Cultural gene decoding: Digital protection of intangible paper-cut and construction of gene bank. *Digital Scholarship in the Humanities*, *40*(1), 54–63. DOI: 10.1093/llc/fqaf008

Deveci, M., Pamucar, D., Vasilateanu, A., Datta, G., Goga, N., Marian, C. V., Bratosin, I.-A., & Cali, U. (2025). Prioritization of health distributed ledger technology use cases using fuzzy sine trigonometric based decision-making model. *Expert Systems with Applications*, *294*, 128794. Advance online publication. DOI: 10.1016/j.eswa.2025.128794

Djatmiko, G. H., Sinaga, O., & Pawirosumarto, S. (2025). Digital Transformation and Social Inclusion in Public Services: A Qualitative Analysis of E-Government Adoption for Marginalized Communities in Sustainable Governance. *Sustainability (Basel)*, *17*(7), 2908. Advance online publication. DOI: 10.3390/su17072908

Ferhataj, A., Memaj, F., Sahatcija, R., Ora, A., & Koka, E. (2025). Ethical concerns in AI development: Analyzing students' perspectives on robotics and society. *Journal of Information. Communication and Ethics in Society*, *23*(2), 165–187. DOI: 10.1108/JICES-08-2024-0111

Fu, Y., Shi, K., & Xi, L. (2025). Artificial intelligence and machine learning in the preservation and innovation of intangible cultural heritage: Ethical considerations and design frameworks. *Digital Scholarship in the Humanities*, *40*(2), 487–508. DOI: 10.1093/llc/fqaf034

Hernández-Barrera, E., Alfonso-Francia, G., Badillo-Fernández, M., & Tovar-Arriaga, S. (2025). Advanced AI strategies for accurate detection and localization of retinal nerve fiber layer defects: Employing multifaceted analysis across various color spaces. *Network Modeling and Analysis in Health Informatics and Bioinformatics*, *14*(1), 11. Advance online publication. DOI: 10.1007/s13721-025-00507-3

Indravathy, K., & Abd Rahim, N. (2025). How ambidextrous entrepreneurial leaders react to the artificial intelligence boom. *IAES International Journal of Artificial Intelligence*, *14*(3), 1708–1718. DOI: 10.11591/ijai.v14.i3.pp1708-1718

Korać, D., Damjanović, B., Simić, D., & Pu, C. (2025). Management of evaluation processes and creation of authentication metrics: Artificial intelligence-based fusion framework. *Information Processing & Management*, *62*(6), 104233. Advance online publication. DOI: 10.1016/j.ipm.2025.104233

Li, S., Yang, Y., Han, C., Sun, Y., Attar, R. W., & Gupta, B. B. (2025). Addressing consumer needs: Effects of firms remediation strategies on satisfaction and brand usage intent in AI-powered voice assistant service failures. *International Journal of Information Management*, *85*, 102951. Advance online publication. DOI: 10.1016/j.ijinfomgt.2025.102951

Liang, X., Tao, M., Xia, Y., Wang, J., Li, K., Wang, Y., He, Y., Yang, J., Shi, T., Wang, Y., Zhang, M., & Wang, X. (2025). SAGE: Self-evolving Agents with Reflective and Memory-augmented Abilities. *Neurocomputing*, *647*, 130470. Advance online publication. DOI: 10.1016/j.neucom.2025.130470

Liu, Z., Duan, P., Chu, Q., Kuhlmann, L., Zhang, C., Yue, W., Tang, X., & Zhang, B. (2026). An attributed multiplex network enabled GNN-based stock predictor with observable and non-observable information. *Expert Systems with Applications*, *296*, 129018. Advance online publication. DOI: 10.1016/j.eswa.2025.129018

Margaretha, W., Ariesia, K., & Yustian, O. R. (2025). ARTIFICIAL INTELLIGENCE AND ENTREPRENEURSHIP EDUCATION: INCREASING ENTREPRENEURIAL INTENTIONS AMONG FUTURE ENTREPRENEURS IN BANDUNG CITY. *Journal of Theoretical and Applied Information Technology*, *103*(7), 2813–2824. https://www.scopus.com/inward/record.uri?eid=2-s2.0-105002738499&partnerID=40&md5=bc240b968dd23a1966e8c423140102df

Meng, L., Ding, L., Atli, M., Khan, A. M., Shan, Y., & Farooq, M. U. (2025). Enhancing two dimensional irregular pattern packing using a modified genetic algorithm and image processing. *Engineering Applications of Artificial Intelligence*, *155*, 111040. Advance online publication. DOI: 10.1016/j.engappai.2025.111040

Murrar, A., Paz, V., Batra, M., & Yerger, D. (2025). Strategies for driving customer adoption of AI-powered mobile apps: Insights from structural equation modeling in the water sector. *Journal of Systems and Information Technology*, *27*(3), 343–364. DOI: 10.1108/JSIT-12-2023-0335

Ozdemir, G., & Zonah, S. (2025). Revolutionising Heritage Interpretation with Smart Technologies: A Blueprint for Sustainable Tourism. *Sustainability (Basel)*, *17*(10), 4330. Advance online publication. DOI: 10.3390/su17104330

Prajwal, R., Pawan, S. J., Nazarian, S., Heller, N., Weight, C. J., Duddalwar, V., & Kuo, C. C. J. (2025). A Study on Energy Consumption in AI-Driven Medical Image Segmentation. *Journal of Imaging*, *11*(6), 174. Advance online publication. DOI: 10.3390/jimaging11060174 PMID: 40558774

Raza, H., Raja, M. J. A. A., Mubeen, R., Masood, Z., & Raja, M. A. Z. (2025). Supervised autoregressive eXogenous Networks with Fractional Grünwald–Letnikov finite differences: Tumor Evolution and Immune Responses under Therapeutic Influence fractals model. *Biomedical Signal Processing and Control*, *107*, 107871. Advance online publication. DOI: 10.1016/j.bspc.2025.107871

Rongrong, L., & Ismail, A. I. (2025). AI Innovation in Architectural Design: Enhancing Aesthetic Experience with "Midjourney.". *Journal of Advanced Research Design*, *127*(1), 84–95. DOI: 10.37934/ard.127.1.8495

Routman, J. S., Zhang, E. J., Blocker, J. D., Paiste, J., & Tsai, M. H. (2025). Using Performance Frontiers To Evaluate Non-OR Anesthesia (NORA) Efficiency. *Journal of Medical Systems*, *49*(1), 96. Advance online publication. DOI: 10.1007/s10916-025-02229-5 PMID: 40629210

Singh, J., Sillerud, B., Yednock, J., Larson, C., Steffen, A., & Singh, A. (2025). Healthcare leaders' attitudes and perceptions on the use of artificial intelligence and artificial intelligence enabled tools in healthcare settings. *Journal of Medical Artificial Intelligence*, *8*, 41. Advance online publication. DOI: 10.21037/jmai-24-392

Sposato, M. (2025). Artificial intelligence in educational leadership: A comprehensive taxonomy and future directions. *International Journal of Educational Technology in Higher Education*, *22*(1), 20. Advance online publication. DOI: 10.1186/s41239-025-00517-1

Wang, H., & Liu, M. (2025). Methods and content innovation strategies of digital education in higher vocational colleges under the background of artificial intelligence. *Journal of Computational Methods in Sciences and Engineering*, *25*(3), 2630–2641. DOI: 10.1177/14727978251321337

Wang, Y., Wang, J., & Chu, Z. (2025). Multi-agent large language models as evolutionary optimizers for scheduling optimization. *Computers & Industrial Engineering*, *206*, 111197. Advance online publication. DOI: 10.1016/j.cie.2025.111197

Watson, A. (2025). An imperative to innovate? Crisis in the sociotechnical imaginary. *Telematics and Informatics*, *98*, 102229. Advance online publication. DOI: 10.1016/j.tele.2024.102229

Yan, X., & Sun, T. (2025). Artificial Intelligence Development and Carbon Emission Intensity: Evidence from Industrial Robot Application. *Sustainability (Basel)*, *17*(9), 3867. Advance online publication. DOI: 10.3390/su17093867

Yang, J., Ge, H., & Cui, Y. (2025). An AI framework for counterattack detection and decision-making evaluation in football. *Journal of Big Data*, *12*(1), 91. Advance online publication. DOI: 10.1186/s40537-025-01128-3

Zeidanloo, H. R., & Špaček, M. (2025). Assessing disruptive potential in the IT sector: A framework for evaluating company-to-company impact. *Journal of Innovation and Entrepreneurship*, *14*(1), 82. Advance online publication. DOI: 10.1186/s13731-025-00541-5

Zhang, J., & Zhao, Z. (2026). Corporate ESG rating prediction based on XGBoost-SHAP interpretable machine learning model. *Expert Systems with Applications*, *295*, 128809. Advance online publication. DOI: 10.1016/j.eswa.2025.128809

Zhang, X., Li, F., Hu, X., & Fang, J. (2025). A lightweight deep learning framework for wild berry detection in complex natural environments. *Engineering Applications of Artificial Intelligence*, *154*, 110918. Advance online publication. DOI: 10.1016/j.engappai.2025.110918

Zhang, Z., Li, S., & Yang, Y. (2025). Explorative Policy Optimization for industrial-scale operation of complex process control systems. *Journal of Process Control, 152*, 103471. Advance online publication. DOI: 10.1016/j.jprocont.2025.103471

Chapter 5
E-Business and Web Accessibility

Muhammad Alvin Pratama
https://orcid.org/0009-0000-8009-5246
Universitas Esa Unggul, Indonesia

Binastya Anggara Sekti
https://orcid.org/0000-0001-5489-4888
Universitas Esa Unggul, Indonesia

ABSTRACT

This chapter emphasizes that the rapid growth of e-business has intensified digital exclusion for people with disabilities, making web accessibility a strategic and ethical necessity. Using WCAG 2.2 as a framework, it analyzes key barriers across disability types and how inclusive UI/UX, assistive technologies, and global regulations (ADA, AODA, EN 301 549) shape accessible e-commerce. The chapter argues that accessibility improves customer experience, SEO, conversion rates, and brand trust, especially within the "purple economy." It concludes that accessibility must be embedded into digital transformation to ensure inclusive, resilient, and future-ready e-business ecosystems.

1. INTRODUCTION

The rise of global digital markets has fundamentally rewritten the rules of commerce. It is a story not just of technological change, but of a seismic shift in how

DOI: 10.4018/979-8-3373-5167-4.ch005

the world connects, trades, and creates value. At the heart of this transformation lies e-business the central engine powering contemporary economic exchange.

This digital revolution has dismantled the old barriers of geography and time, giving birth to a dynamic, 24/7 global marketplace. In this new arena, a craftsperson in Jakarta can instantly connect with a customer in Oslo. Information, capital, and goods now flow across borders in seconds, creating an interconnected ecosystem where opportunity is truly global.

E-business has emerged as the central nervous system of this new world, defined by key developments: it has democratized access, empowering small entrepreneurs to compete on the world stage; it is driven by data, enabling hyper-personalized customer experiences; it has redefined supply chains, making them more transparent and responsive; and it has spawned entirely new business models, from the sharing economy to digital subscriptions.

Yet, this rapid integration also brings profound challenges from cybersecurity threats and complex regulations to the ethical imperative of digital inclusion. It is within this complex, fast-paced, and borderless context that businesses must now operate. To build lasting success, they must move beyond simply having an online presence. They must embrace strategic, responsible, and forward-looking principles. And as commerce becomes inseparable from the digital experience, one such principle rises to critical importance: building an e-business that is accessible to all. This is no longer a niche concern, but a fundamental pillar of ethical, resilient, and competitive commerce in the 21st century.

The internet and digitalization are fundamentally changing the way people, businesses, and governments interact. This has led to a new phase of globalization driven by the movement of data across national borders, changing the nature, patterns, and actors in international trade in goods and services (Fayyaz, 2019).While democratizing access to goods and services, this transformation has simultaneously exposed a significant digital divide: the systemic exclusion of individuals with disabilities from full participation in the digital economy. Therefore, the intersection of e-business and web accessibility represents a critical boundary in the evolution of commerce, where technological innovation, ethical imperatives, and commercial strategies converge. The relationship between IT and disability is revealed as a normative phenomenon, providing IT developers with powerful tools to manage those with non-standard bodies consumers with disabilities (Viluckienė, 2015). This chapter explores the crucial integration of web accessibility principles within the e-business ecosystem, arguing that inclusive design is not simply a matter of regulatory compliance but a fundamental component of sustainable, ethical, and profitable digital enterprises.

The need for accessible e-commerce goes beyond legal mandates and is rooted in profound shifts in societal and market expectations. Therefore, building platform legitimacy has become a global concern in recent years (Pan et al., 2023). Through this lens, we will explore how inclusive design principles, when embedded in the core architecture of e-commerce platforms, payment gateways, and customer service portals, can improve usability for everyone, leading to increased conversion rates, reduced bounce rates, and a stronger brand reputation built on principles of equity and inclusion. These effects contribute to social issues such as polarization, reduced creativity, and reduced critical thinking due to algorithmic bias (Balagopalan et al., 2023). Figure 1 shows integrating web Accesibility in E-Business

Figure 1. Integrating web accesibility in e-business

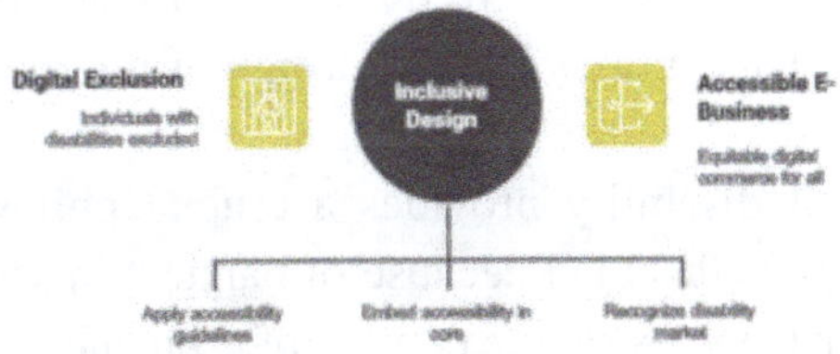

The discussion will be anchored in the established principles of the Web Content Accessibility Guidelines (WCAG), which serve as the international benchmark for accessible web content. We will explore how these technical guidelines translate into tangible design and development practices for e-business, from product discovery and shopping cart functionality to checkout processes and post-purchase support. Furthermore, the chapter will address the economic rationale, highlighting how accessible design opens markets to a demographic with significant purchasing power the global disability community, often termed the “purple pound” or “disability market.” This community, encompassing over one billion people worldwide, represents a vast and frequently underserved consumer base. By creating barriers, e-businesses inadvertently exclude this market; by prioritizing accessibility, they unlock substantial growth potential.

Ultimately, this chapter contends that web accessibility is an integral pillar of modern e-business strategy. It is a multidimensional challenge encompassing technology, design, law, and ethics. By examining the barriers faced by users with diverse abilities, the technological solutions available, and the compelling business case for inclusion, this chapter aims to provide a roadmap for academics, practitioners, and policymakers. The goal is to foster a future where digital commerce is inherently accessible, ensuring that the benefits of the e-business revolution are equitably shared across all segments of society, thereby creating a more inclusive and resilient digital economy.

2. FOUNDATIONS OF E-BUSINESS ACCESSIBILITY

The conceptual foundation of e-business accessibility lies at the intersection of digital commerce, human-computer interaction, and the social model of disability. Essentially, web accessibility refers to the practice of designing and developing websites, tools, and technologies so that people with disabilities can understand, navigate, interact with, and contribute to the web. When applied to e-business, this definition expands to ensure that every aspect of the commercial journey from marketing and product discovery to transaction completion and customer support can be operated by individuals with a wide range of auditory, cognitive, neurological, physical, speech, and visual abilities. Web accessibility emphasizes incorporating the needs of people with disabilities into the design of Internet applications (Koutsabasis, 2010).

The social model of disability provides a crucial philosophical foundation, stating that people become disabled because of barriers in society, not because of their impairments or differences. In the context of e-business, the barrier is not the disability itself, but rather poorly designed websites, incompatible applications, and proprietary digital processes that prevent full participation. For example, an inaccessible e-commerce checkout form is the barrier, not the user's motor impairment that makes using a mouse difficult. This model shifts the responsibility from the individual to adapt, to designers and businesses to create inherently accessible environments. Consequently, e-business accessibility becomes a barrier-removal effort, which demands a proactive approach to design that anticipates and accommodates human diversity. This is fundamental to providing equal opportunities to all web users and enhancing accessible user experiences by offering web services and products with accessibility in mind (Shad et al., 2019).

Figure 2. Achieving e-business accesibility

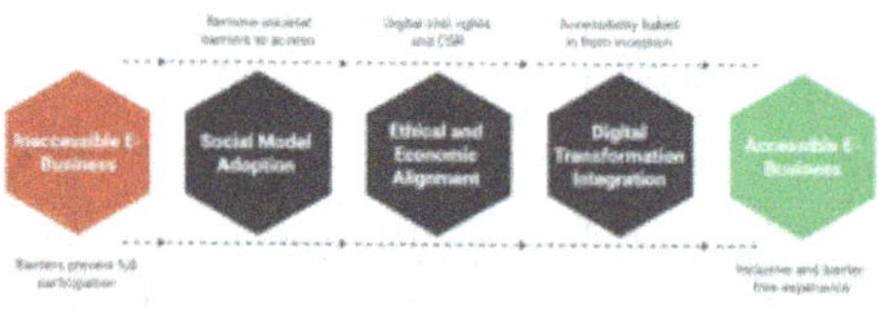

The economic and ethical rationales for inclusive e-business design are powerfully intertwined. Ethically, it is a matter of digital civil rights. The internet has become a fundamental infrastructure for civic and economic life; denying equal access to online shopping, banking, education, and services constitutes a form of digital exclusion with real-world consequences for independence, financial security, and social participation. From a corporate social responsibility (CSR) perspective, investing in accessibility aligns with ethical business practices and sustainable development goals focused on reducing inequalities.

Economically, the argument is compelling. The global market of people with disabilities, along with their families and friends, controls discretionary spending power estimated in the trillions of dollars annually. This "purple economy" is largely brand-loyal to companies that demonstrate inclusivity. Furthermore, accessibility features often create a superior user experience for all customers. Captions on marketing videos benefit users in noisy environments; clear navigation and concise content aid users with cognitive differences and those simply in a hurry; voice-controlled shopping assists hands-free situations. This phenomenon, often called the "curb-cut effect," illustrates how designs created for a specific group (sidewalk ramps for wheelchair users) end up benefiting a much broader population (parents with strollers, travelers with suitcases, delivery workers). In e-business, accessible design frequently translates to better SEO (search engines function similarly to screen readers), reduced site complexity, faster load times, and broader device compatibility all factors that boost overall conversion rates and customer satisfaction.

Finally, accessibility must be understood as an integral component of digital transformation strategy. For businesses undergoing digital transformation, accessibility cannot be an afterthought or a bolt-on feature. It must be "baked in" from the inception of digital projects. This requires a shift in organizational culture, where accessibility is championed at the executive level, integrated into procurement processes for third-party platforms, and embedded in the skill sets of design and development teams. An accessible-first approach to digital transformation ensures that as businesses scale their online presence, they do so in a way that is inclusive by default, future-proofing their operations against evolving regulations and expanding their potential market reach from the outset. This strategic integration positions accessibility not as a cost center but as a catalyst for innovation, risk mitigation, and sustainable growth in the digital marketplace.

3. STANDARDS, POLICIES, AND LEGAL FRAMEWORKS

The operationalization of web accessibility in e-business is governed by a complex interweaving of international standards, national laws, and regional directives. These frameworks provide technical specifications and legal requirements that guide design and development, ensuring a consistent and enforceable foundation for inclusive digital experiences. Understanding this regulatory landscape is crucial for any e-business operating in a global marketplace. The FISE design/methodology/approach was developed through a cross-theoretical conceptual synthesis grounded in prior research and supported by narrative comparisons and visual mapping of accessibility gaps in service environments (Jeseo & Lindsey Hall, 2025).

Figure 3. Navigating web accessibility

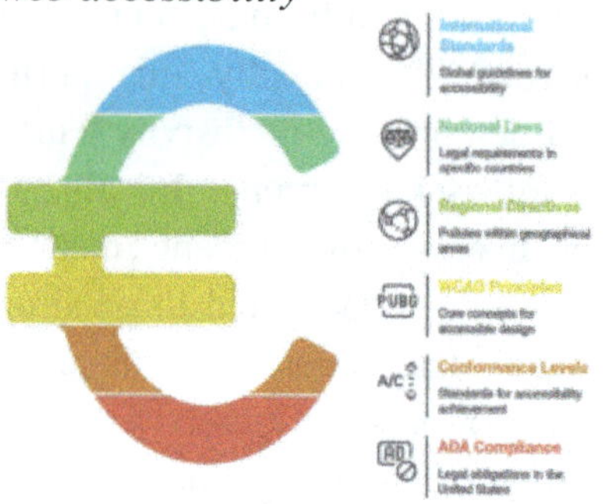

The Web Content Accessibility Guidelines (WCAG), developed by the World Wide Web Consortium (W3C) through its Web Accessibility Initiative (WAI), serve as the universally accepted technical standard. Currently at version 2.2, WCAG is organized around four foundational principles, often remembered by the acronym POUR:

1. **Perceivable:** Information and user interface components must be presentable to users in ways they can perceive. This includes providing text alternatives for non-text content, captions for audio, and content that can be presented in different ways without losing information.
2. **Operable:** User interface components and navigation must be operable. This requires that all functionality is available via a keyboard, users have enough time to read and use content, content does not cause seizures or physical reactions, and users can easily navigate and find content.
3. **Understandable:** Information and the operation of the user interface must be understandable. This means text is readable and predictable, web pages operate in predictable ways, and users are helped to avoid and correct mistakes (crucial for form inputs in checkout processes).
4. **Robust:** Content must be robust enough to be interpreted reliably by a wide variety of user agents, including current and future assistive technologies. This is achieved by maximizing compatibility and using clean, standard-compliant code.

Each principle contains testable success criteria categorized into three levels of conformance: A (minimum), AA (standard and most commonly legally required), and AAA (enhanced). For e-business, achieving WCAG 2.2 Level AA is typically the target for both compliance and meaningful accessibility.

These technical guidelines are given legal force through various national and regional policies:

- **The Americans with Disabilities Act (ADA) in the United States:** Although enacted before the commercial internet, Title III of the ADA, which prohibits discrimination in "places of public accommodation," has been consistently interpreted by courts to include websites and mobile apps. A wave of litigation, particularly in the e-commerce sector, has made ADA website compliance a critical legal and financial consideration for U.S. businesses.
- **The European Union Web Accessibility Directive (2016/2102):** This directive mandates that websites and mobile applications of public sector bodies in the EU member states must be accessible. While primarily targeting the public sector, it establishes a powerful normative and technical benchmark that increasingly influences private sector expectations and procurement requirements across Europe.
- **The Accessibility for Ontarians with Disabilities Act (AODA) in Canada:** AODA requires private and non-profit organizations in Ontario to make their websites and web content accessible according to WCAG 2.0 Level AA. It represents one of the most specific and enforceable digital accessibility laws for the private sector in North America.
- **EN 301 549:** This is a European standard that sets accessibility requirements for Information and Communication Technology (ICT) products and services, including web content. It harmonizes with WCAG and is frequently referenced in public procurement across Europe.

Compliance challenges for online businesses are diverse. The dynamic nature of e-commerce sites, with constantly updated product listings, promotional content, and third-party plugins (such as payment gateways and live chat widgets), makes maintaining consistent accessibility an ongoing process, not a one-time project. Furthermore, legal jurisdictions can overlap and conflict; international online retailers may need to navigate ADA requirements for US customers, AODA for Ontario customers, and potential claims under the UK Equality Act 2010 for UK customers. The financial implications of non-compliance extend beyond potential lawsuits to include reputational damage, lost revenue from excluded customers, and emergency repair costs. Therefore, a proactive, standards-based approach to accessibility, integrated into the agile development and content management cycles of online businesses, is the most effective strategy for managing legal risk and ensuring continued inclusion. A company's ability to keep pace with these changes, assess their potential impact on its business, and develop and implement a plan to adapt to new requirements can be a key factor in its overall success or failure in the European market (Casanova & Savoie, 2019).

4. BARRIERS TO ACCESSIBILITY IN E-BUSINESS PLATFORMS

For users with disabilities, navigating e-commerce platforms can present a series of frustrating obstacles, turning routine online shopping tasks into impossible challenges. These obstacles arise from design choices that fail to consider diverse modes of interaction and sensory processing. Identifying and understanding these common obstacles is the first step towards eliminating them. People with Visual Impairment (PVI) face numerous challenges when engaging in Customer-to-Customer (C2C) e-commerce, particularly in tasks such as product listing, packaging, shipping, and post-sales interactions (Gupta et al., 2025).

Figure 4. E-commerce accesibility

Sensory and Motor Barriers:

- **Visual Barriers:** Users who are blind or have low vision often rely on screen readers (software that converts text and elements to speech or braille). Common barriers include lack of alternative text (alt text) for product images, infographics, and buttons, leaving users unaware of visual content. Inaccessible PDF receipts or product manuals, complex data visualizations without textual summaries, and poor color contrast between text and background render content unreadable for those with color blindness or low vision. Non-descriptive link text like "click here" or "read more" provides no context when read by a screen reader.
- **Auditory Barriers:** Pre-recorded audio content, such as product demonstration videos or promotional messages, without synchronized captions or tran-

scripts exclude users who are deaf or hard of hearing. Similarly, live audio streams for product launches or customer service hotlines without real-time captioning are inaccessible.

- **Motor/Physical Barriers:** Users with limited dexterity, tremors, or paralysis may navigate primarily or exclusively using a keyboard, switch device, or voice control. Barriers include interactive elements like product carousels, dropdown menus, and "Add to Cart" buttons that cannot be reached or activated via keyboard tabbing. Short time limits for completing actions (like entering payment details) or CAPTCHAs that require precise mouse movements can also be prohibitive. Forms with small click targets create difficulty for users with motor control challenges.

Cognitive and Neurological Barriers:

- **Cognitive Barriers:** Users with cognitive, learning, or intellectual disabilities require clarity and predictability. Barriers include overly complex navigation structures, dense blocks of text without clear headings, inconsistent layout across pages, and confusing checkout processes with unexpected steps. The use of jargon, ambiguous instructions on forms, and automatic content that moves, blinks, or updates (like countdown timers or auto-rotating banners) can be distracting or disorienting.
- **Neurological Barriers:** Content that flashes at certain rates can trigger seizures for individuals with photosensitive epilepsy. Similarly, auto-playing videos with sound can be disruptive and difficult to stop for users with attention disorders or sensory sensitivities.

Platform-Specific Barriers in Modern E-Commerce:

- **Mobile Commerce (m-commerce):** The shift to mobile introduces unique challenges. Touchscreen gestures like swiping or pinching may be difficult for some motor-impaired users. Responsive design failures can create zooming or scrolling issues. Voice assistants on mobile devices may not integrate properly with the e-commerce app's native functionality.
- **Digital Payments and Checkout:** The checkout process is often the most critical and most broken stage. Inaccessible iframes from third-party payment processors (e.g., PayPal, Stripe) can break keyboard navigation and screen reader flow. Form fields without proper labels and error messages that are only conveyed by color (e.g., a red border) are not perceivable to all users. Complex multi-page checkouts with poor feedback mechanisms increase cognitive load and abandonment rates.

- **Dynamic Content:** Modern e-commerce relies heavily on dynamic content updates shopping cart totals that update, live inventory notifications, product recommendations that load asynchronously. If these dynamic changes are not programmatically announced to assistive technologies, users relying on screen readers remain unaware of them, leading to confusion and erroneous actions.

These barriers collectively create a fragmented and often unwelcoming user experience. This signals to users with disabilities that their support is not valued, which directly leads to lost sales, negative brand perception, and potential legal action. Recognizing these barriers as fundamental design flaws, rather than user shortcomings, is crucial to building a truly inclusive e-commerce platform from the outset. Ensuring accessibility is essential for e-commerce platforms to create inclusive experiences and equitable access to the digital space (Mishra & Sharma, 2025).

5. DESIGNING INCLUSIVE E-BUSINESS EXPERIENCES

Creating accessible e-business requires the intentional application of inclusive design principles throughout the user experience (UX) and user interface (UI) development cycle. This process goes beyond mere technical compliance to foster an environment where usability and inclusivity become synonymous. We identify usability issues and UX factors early in the development of educational software for users with special educational needs. Furthermore, we present the User Interface (UI) design and its evaluation conducted with experts and students. This UI evaluation has been divided into several phases, using a variety of methods with different actors. Prototyping and usability heuristics are presented as fast and cost-effective yet effective and accurate evaluation methods for user experience with educational software (González et al., 2013).

Figure 5. Building inclusive e-business experience

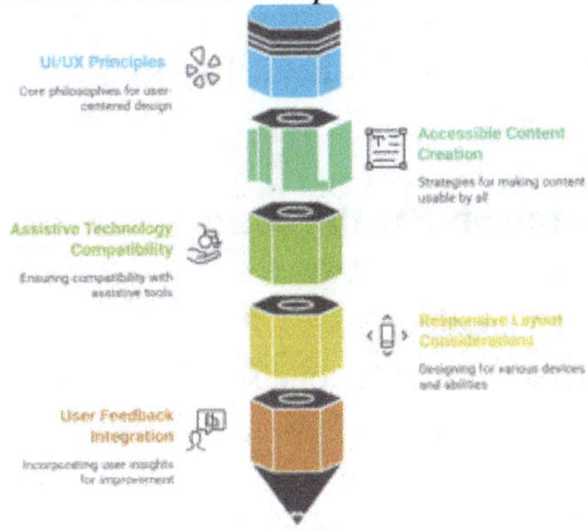

Inclusive UI/UX Principles and Best Practices:

The core philosophy is to design for the broadest possible range of human diversity. Key principles include:

- **Equitable Use:** The design is useful and marketable to people with diverse abilities. For example, providing high-quality product images alongside detailed textual descriptions serves both visual users and those using screen readers.
- **Flexibility in Use:** The design accommodates a wide range of individual preferences and abilities. This includes offering multiple ways to complete tasks (e.g., browse by category or search), allowing user control over time-sensitive content, and providing options for text size and contrast.
- **Simple and Intuitive Use:** The design is easy to understand, regardless of the user's experience, knowledge, language skills, or concentration level. This involves consistent navigation, clear information hierarchy, and plain language.
- **Perceptible Information:** The design communicates necessary information effectively to the user, regardless of ambient conditions or the user's sensory abilities. This is the direct application of WCAG's perceivable principle.
- **Tolerance for Error:** The design minimizes hazards and adverse consequences of accidental or unintended actions. In e-commerce, this means providing clear error identification, suggestions for correction in forms, and easy reversal of actions (like removing an item from a cart).

- **Low Physical Effort:** The design can be used efficiently and comfortably with a minimum of fatigue. This involves minimizing repetitive actions, ensuring keyboard navigation is logical and efficient, and designing large enough clickable areas.

Practical Implementation Strategies:

- **Accessible Content Creation:**
  - **Text Alternatives:** Provide concise, descriptive alt text for all informative images (e.g., "Red wool sweater with V-neck"). Decorative images should have empty alt attributes (alt=""). For complex images like charts, provide a detailed description in the surrounding text or via a linked long description.
  - **Semantic Structure:** Use proper HTML heading tags (H1, H2, etc.) to create a logical document outline. This allows screen reader users to navigate by headings, understanding the page structure at a glance. Use lists (<ul>, <ol>) for list content and proper markup for data tables.
  - **Multimedia:** All pre-recorded audio must have synchronized captions. Video should have audio descriptions for key visual elements not conveyed by dialogue. Provide transcripts for both audio and video content.
- **Assistive Technology Compatibility:**
  - **Screen Readers:** Ensure all interactive elements are programmatically determinable. Use ARIA (Accessible Rich Internet Applications) landmarks and roles sparingly and correctly to enhance semantics where native HTML is insufficient (e.g., for complex widgets). Ensure custom-built components like product sliders or modal dialogs are fully keyboard accessible and announce their state (e.g., "dialog opened").
  - **Keyboard Navigation:** The entire website must be navigable using only the Tab key. The focus indicator (the outline around the currently selected element) must be clearly visible. The tab order should follow the visual and logical flow of the page.
  - **Voice Control:** Design for compatibility with voice recognition software (like Dragon NaturallySpeaking or built-in OS tools). Ensure interactive elements have names that match their visible labels and functions, allowing users to say "click add to cart" reliably.
- **Responsive and Adaptive Layout Considerations:** A responsive design must maintain accessibility at all breakpoints. Navigation menus that collapse on mobile must be operable via touch and keyboard. Touch targets (buttons, links) should be large enough (minimum 44x44 pixels is a common guideline) and have sufficient spacing to prevent accidental activation. Ensure that

zoom functionality is not disabled, as many users with low vision rely on browser zoom to read content.

By embedding these practices into standard workflows—from framework and prototyping to content development and delivery—online businesses can systematically build experiences that are not only standards-compliant but also truly user-friendly and efficient for every user. User feedback is an approach for users to review service processes and plays a crucial role in reviewing service approaches. One such approach is Mobile Government (eGovernment) services, which aim to facilitate government services for public use. As mobile government (mGovernment) services become increasingly important in public service delivery, understanding user insights and feedback is crucial to ensuring service excellence. Using a Systematic Literature Review (SLR), the authors collected and analyzed qualitative studies that explored user perspectives, experiences, and expectations regarding the role of user feedback on online services. This review highlights key areas for service improvement, including user interface design, accessibility, responsiveness, and information accuracy (Desmal et al., 2023).

6. TECHNOLOGICAL SOLUTIONS ENABLING ACCESSIBILITY

Technological advancements provide powerful tools for creating and maintaining accessibility in e-business environments. These solutions range from automated auditing software to sophisticated artificial intelligence (AI) applications, enabling businesses to efficiently scale their accessibility efforts. Accessibility on online platforms is a critical concern in our increasingly digital world, where information and services are largely accessed through the internet. The purpose of this systematic review is to provide a comprehensive overview of the current state of online accessibility technology, focusing on key tools such as sign language recognition, speech-to-text recognition, text-to-speech, and voice recognition. Despite advances in digital inclusivity, many technical limitations remain, limiting the accessibility of online content for people with disabilities (Bercaru & Popescu, 2024).

Figure 6. Accesibility tools range from automated to human-centered approaches

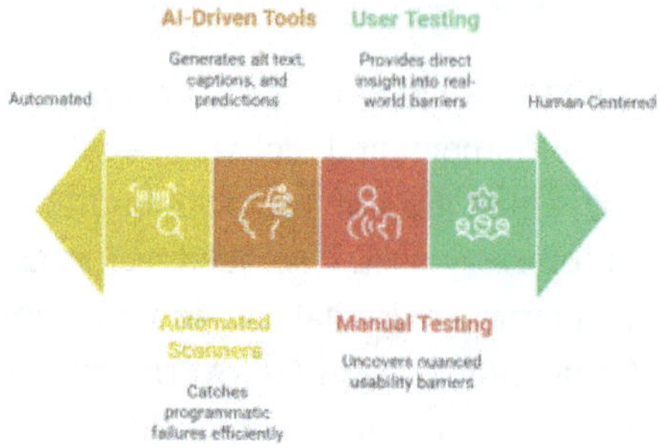

AI-Driven Accessibility Tools:

Artificial intelligence is becoming a transformative force in identifying and remediating accessibility issues.

- **Automated Alt-Text Generation:** Computer vision AI can now analyze images and generate descriptive alt text automatically. While human review is still necessary for accuracy and context (e.g., ensuring a product's key selling point is mentioned), these tools significantly reduce the manual burden of tagging thousands of product images in a large e-commerce catalog.
- **Real-Time Adjustments and Personalization:** AI can power user-facing toolbars or settings that allow individuals to personalize their viewing experience according to their needs. These can include options to increase text size and spacing, change color contrast schemes, pause animations, or utilize a simplified, distraction-free reading mode. Such personalization acknowledges that a one-size-fits-all design may not suit every user's preference or disability.
- **Automated Captioning and Transcription:** AI-powered speech-to-text services have dramatically improved, allowing for the rapid generation of captions for video content and transcripts for audio podcasts or product descriptions. Again, human quality assurance is critical, especially for technical product terms or brand names, but the automation drastically speeds up the process.
- **Predictive Analysis for Barrier Detection:** Machine learning models can be trained on vast datasets of known accessibility issues to predict where new barriers might emerge in a design or codebase, allowing for preemptive fixes during the development phase.

Accessibility Testing Tools and Auditing Frameworks:

Automated testing tools are essential for maintaining accessibility, but they must be part of a broader strategy.

- **Automated Scanners:** Tools like axe-core, WAVE, or Lighthouse can be integrated into development pipelines to run automated tests on every new code commit. These tools are excellent at catching programmatic failures, such as missing alt attributes, insufficient color contrast, or improper heading structures. However, they can only detect about 30-40% of WCAG issues; they cannot assess logical flow, meaningfulness of alt text, or keyboard trap scenarios that require contextual understanding.
- **Manual Testing and Assistive Technology QA:** Comprehensive auditing requires manual testing by knowledgeable experts using the same tools as end-users. This includes navigating the entire site using only a keyboard, testing with multiple screen readers (JAWS, NVDA, VoiceOver), and using voice control software. This human-centric testing uncovers the nuanced usability barriers that automated tools miss.
- **User Testing with People with Disabilities:** The most valuable form of testing involves recruiting users with various disabilities to complete realistic tasks on the e-commerce platform (e.g., "Find a winter coat under $100 and proceed to checkout"). This provides direct, empathetic insight into where real-world barriers and frustrations occur, informing design priorities in a way no automated tool can.

The Role of Personalization and Adaptive Interfaces:

The future of e-business accessibility lies in dynamic systems that adapt to individual user needs. Beyond simple user-controlled toolbars, more sophisticated systems can leverage user profiles (with consent) to automatically present content in the most accessible format. For example, users identified as preferring high-contrast modes and simplified text can be automatically presented with a customized version of a product page. These adaptive interfaces represent the convergence of accessibility, user experience personalization, and machine learning, leading to truly individualized web experiences that respect and respond to human diversity. For e-businesses, investing in these technologies represents an investment in customer-centric innovation, reducing barriers for all users, and building robust, adaptable, and fundamentally inclusive platforms. Personalized service and adaptive interfaces play a crucial role in e-commerce. This paper proposes an adaptive interface to assist customer transactions in e-commerce. Adaptive interfaces aggregate consumer behavior by monitoring customer operations, excluding unnecessary operations, and recognizing behavioral patterns. These interfaces utilize Bayesian belief networks and RBF neural networks to accomplish these tasks (Hsu & Kuo, 2005).

7. ACCESSIBILITY AS A DRIVER OF BUSINESS OUTCOMES

Rather than being a charitable expense, robust web accessibility serves as a powerful commercial engine, driving real business outcomes that impact the bottom line. When implemented effectively, accessibility initiatives yield significant gains across a range of customer metrics, brand equity, and market performance. The Reliability-Aware Web Accessibility Experience Metric (RA-WAEM), a new web accessibility metric that considers the experience of users with disabilities and its reliability in objectively assessing the severity of accessibility barriers. We present an optimization algorithm based on Expectation Maximization to efficiently derive RA-WAEM parameters (Song et al., 2018).

Figure 7. Web accesebility drives busiiness outcomes

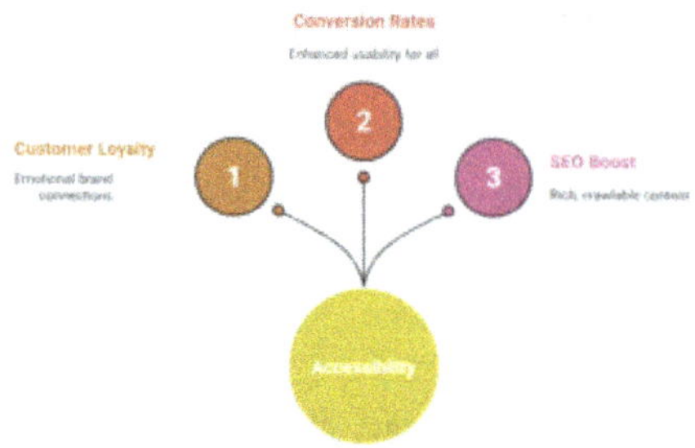

Impact on Customer Experience, Brand Loyalty, and Trust:

A seamless and accessible shopping experience directly impacts customer experience (CX). For users with disabilities, an accessible website is often the difference between frustration and loyalty. When a brand demonstrates inclusivity through its digital touchpoints, it sends a powerful message of respect and appreciation, fostering deep emotional connections and brand trust. These communities are known for their strong brand advocacy; positive accessible experiences are shared within disability networks, leading to valuable word-of-mouth marketing. Conversely, inaccessible experiences can cause lasting reputational damage, with negative reviews and criticism on social media amplifying the damage. In an era where corporate values are under scrutiny, a visible commitment to digital inclusion enhances a company's reputation and aligns with the expectations of socially conscious consumers across all demographics. In recent years, the digital landscape has undergone a remarkable transformation, opening up new opportunities for companies to engage in social responsibility initiatives while simultaneously advancing their marketing objectives (Dundua, 2024).

Increased Conversion Rates and User Engagement:

The technical and design improvements that underpin accessibility inherently enhance general usability, leading to better performance for all users. Key metrics often see direct improvement:

- **Reduced Bounce and Abandonment Rates:** Clear navigation, readable text, and predictable interfaces keep users engaged. A simplified, accessible checkout process with clear error messages directly reduces cart abandonment a critical KPI for any e-business.
- **Improved Search Engine Optimization (SEO):** Many accessibility best practices overlap with SEO best practices. Semantic HTML structure, descriptive headings, meaningful link text, image alt attributes, and transcriptions for video content all provide rich, crawlable content for search engines. This synergy means that efforts to improve accessibility often lead to higher organic search rankings, increasing discoverability and traffic.
- **Enhanced Cross-Device and Cross-Browser Compatibility:** Building with web standards and robust code to support assistive technologies results in a more stable and consistent experience across different browsers, operating systems, and devices (desktop, mobile, tablet). This reliability reduces technical support costs and expands the contexts in which customers can shop successfully.
- **Faster Page Load Times:** Practices like providing proper text alternatives instead of relying on text within images, and writing efficient, clean code contribute to faster loading pages. Page speed is a major factor in user satisfaction, conversion rates, and search ranking.

Case Studies of Accessible E-Business Success:

Several leading companies have publicly documented the benefits of their accessibility investments.

- **Target Corporation:** After settling a landmark class-action lawsuit in 2008 regarding the inaccessibility of its website, Target embarked on a comprehensive accessibility overhaul. The company reported that the improvements led not only to compliance but also to a broader enhancement of the user experience for all customers, contributing to increased online sales.
- **BBC:** The BBC's commitment to accessibility is core to its public service mandate. Its extensive accessibility guidelines and research have made one of the most accessible large-scale websites globally. This focus has cemented its reputation for inclusivity and ensured its content reaches the widest possible audience.
- **Microsoft:** Microsoft has made accessibility a central pillar of its product development philosophy, encapsulated in its "Design for Everyone" ethos. This commitment, visible in products like the Xbox Adaptive Controller and built-in Windows accessibility features, has strengthened its brand as an innovator in inclusion, attracting both consumer and enterprise customers who value these principles.

These examples underscore a fundamental business truth: designing for marginal market segments often improves the experience for mainstream markets. The economic argument for accessibility is clear—it expands market reach, enhances brand perception, improves key performance indicators, reduces legal risk, and drives innovation. For forward-thinking e-commerce businesses, accessibility isn't a compliance checklist; it's a competitive differentiator and the foundation for sustainable growth in an increasingly diverse and digitally dependent global marketplace. E-commerce platforms often neglect the needs of users with color vision impairments and low literacy levels, creating accessibility challenges (Rai et al., 2026).

8. CHALLENGES AND FUTURE DIRECTIONS

Despite the clear ethical and commercial imperatives, the journey towards fully accessible e-business remains fraught with persistent challenges. At the same time, new technologies present both new barriers and unprecedented opportunities to create more inclusive digital commerce experiences. These challenges include changing customer behaviors and expectations for products and services that require a shift in corporate mindsets, the need to build knowledge management and customer relationships, the difficulty in identifying successful models adopted by other companies, competition with companies that already have established e-business models, technological and business expertise, and the difficulty in integrating business and technology components into a single e-business system (Noordin & Othman, 2005).

Figure 8. Inaccesible e-business experinences

Current Implementation Challenges:

- **Balancing Accessibility with Aesthetics and Performance:** A common misconception is that accessible design is visually unappealing or clunky. Designers may perceive requirements for sufficient color contrast or text size as constraints on creativity. Similarly, developers might worry that additional ARIA attributes or semantic markup could impact page load speed. The core challenge is educating teams that beautiful, high-performance, and accessible design are not mutually exclusive but are hallmarks of sophisticated, user-centered craftsmanship. This requires close collaboration between designers, developers, and accessibility specialists from project inception.
- **Resource Allocation and Expertise Gap:** Many organizations, particularly small and medium-sized enterprises (SMEs), lack in-house expertise in accessibility. They may view hiring specialists or conducting thorough audits as prohibitively expensive. The solution lies in integrating accessibility into core professional skills making basic WCAG knowledge a requirement for all web developers, UX designers, and content creators and leveraging the growing ecosystem of affordable auditing tools and consultancy services.
- **Maintaining Accessibility in Dynamic Environments:** E-commerce sites are living entities. Every new product page, marketing campaign, blog post, or third-party widget integration poses a potential risk to accessibility. Sustaining compliance requires procedural integration: making accessibility checks part of the content publishing workflow, procurement requirements for third-party services, and the definition of "done" in agile development sprints.

Future Directions and Emerging Technologies:

The landscape of e-commerce is constantly evolving, bringing new frontiers for accessibility.

- **Voice-Enabled Commerce and Conversational AI:** The rise of smart speakers (Amazon Alexa, Google Home) and voice shopping introduces new paradigms. Ensuring these voice interfaces are accessible means designing for clear, concise, and predictable voice responses, providing non-visual confirmation of actions, and allowing for voice-controlled error correction. The underlying AI must understand a diverse range of speech patterns, including those affected by speech disabilities.
- **Augmented Reality (AR) and Virtual Try-On:** AR applications that allow users to visualize products in their home or on their body pose significant accessibility hurdles. How does a blind user interact with an AR furniture placement tool? Solutions may involve rich auditory feedback, haptic responses, or complementary non-visual methods to convey spatial and aesthetic information. For virtual try-ons, providing detailed textual descriptions of how a garment looks in different contexts becomes even more critical.
- **AI-Powered Hyper-Personalization:** The future points toward AI systems that learn individual user preferences and adapt interfaces in real-time. For accessibility, this could mean systems that automatically detect a user's preferred mode of interaction (e.g., from past behavior) and adjust the UI accordingly—presenting a simplified, keyboard-optimized view to one user while showing a standard view to another. This dynamic adaptation represents the ultimate form of inclusive design but raises important questions about privacy, consent, and the risk of creating separate, unequal experiences if not implemented thoughtfully.
- **Research Gaps and Opportunities:** Significant research is needed in several areas: developing standardized methods for testing the accessibility of AI-driven interfaces and immersive technologies (AR/VR); creating more sophisticated tools for automated cognitive accessibility testing; and studying the longitudinal impact of accessibility investments on customer lifetime value and brand equity. There is also a need for more case studies from diverse e-business sectors (B2B, services, digital goods) to build a more comprehensive evidence base for the business case.

The path forward requires a dual focus: diligently addressing the persistent organizational and technical challenges of today's web, while proactively engaging with the designers, developers, and policymakers shaping the technologies of the future.

By embedding accessibility into innovation processes for voice, AI, and immersive commerce, the e-commerce industry can ensure that the next wave of digital transformation elevates all users, creating a commercial landscape that is not only more advanced but also fundamentally more equitable. As e-commerce continues to grow, ensuring accessibility for all users, including individuals with hearing impairments, is crucial. Current web and mobile platforms often lack support for sign language users, creating barriers to inclusivity (Ramineni et al., 2024).

9. CONCLUSION

The integration of web accessibility into e-business represents far more than a technical checklist or a legal safeguard; it signifies a critical and profound evolution in the very philosophy of digital commerce. This evolution masterfully aligns ethical responsibility with sharp commercial acumen, demonstrating that what is morally right can also be fundamentally profitable. This chapter has charted a comprehensive journey, beginning with the foundational understanding of accessibility as a non-negotiable human-rights issue in our increasingly digital public square. It progressed to recognizing accessibility's potent role as a powerful strategic lever, capable of unlocking innovation, fostering customer loyalty, and driving sustainable business growth. While the frameworks provided by the Web Content Accessibility Guidelines (WCAG) and enforced through global legislation like the ADA, AODA, and the European Accessibility Act establish a crucial technical and legal baseline, true, transformative progress demands that businesses look beyond mere compliance. The future belongs to those who embrace a holistic philosophy of inclusive design a mindset that proactively considers the full spectrum of human diversity from the earliest stages of conception.

The barriers encountered by users with disabilities within e-commerce platforms from navigational impasses and indecipherable forms to transactional roadblocks and multimedia traps are not inherent to the disabilities themselves. They are, unequivocally, created by thoughtless, exclusionary design. The systematic identification and removal of these barriers, achieved through the thoughtful application of universal design principles, semantic and robust coding practices, and seamless compatibility with assistive technologies, constitutes a dual imperative. It is both a moral duty, in upholding the right to equal participation in the digital economy, and a sound, strategic investment with a demonstrable return. The empirical evidence is compelling: this investment yields measurable dividends across key business metrics. It expands market reach into the vast, underserved, and notably loyal disability community, representing a trillion-dollar market segment with considerable disposable income. It enhances brand trust, reputation, and corporate social responsibility, resonating powerfully with all consumers, not just those with disabilities. Furthermore, the technical foundations of accessibility clean code, proper labeling, and text alternatives intrinsically improve Search Engine Optimization (SEO) and overall site performance, leading to faster load times and broader discoverability. Ultimately, these efforts culminate in higher conversion rates and reduced cart abandonment, as the principles of clarity, predictability, and ease of use that benefit users with disabilities create a superior and more frictionless experience for *every* user.

However, it is vital to recognize that this work is never finished; there is no final "accessible" state. The dynamic, ever-evolving nature of e-commerce platforms, coupled with the relentless pace of technological innovation, presents an ongoing series of challenges and opportunities. The continuous balancing act between cutting-edge aesthetics and robust accessibility requires constant vigilance. Maintaining rigorous standards in a fluid content environment, where marketing teams, user-generated content, and third-party widgets are constantly updated, demands robust governance and automated monitoring tools. Moreover, the horizon beckons with new frontiers that must be navigated with inclusion at the forefront: the accessibility implications of voice-activated AI assistants, the immersive worlds of augmented and virtual reality, and the complexities of the Internet of Things (IoT). Preparing for this future requires a sustained, organization-wide commitment. It necessitates ongoing education and the dismantling of silos, making accessibility a core competency rather than a specialist niche. It must become a standard part of the professional toolkit for every designer, developer, content strategist, product manager, and executive involved in the digital value chain.

In final analysis, building a truly accessible e-business is not a destination to be reached but a continuous journey of improvement, learning, and adaptation. It is a living commitment to constructing digital spaces where commerce is genuinely and equitably for everyone a recognition that human diversity in ability, perception, and interaction is not a problem to be solved or a challenge to be overcome, but a fundamental and enriching reality to be designed *for*. By wholeheartedly embracing this commitment, e-businesses achieve far more than just risk mitigation or tapping into a new demographic. They contribute to the foundational work of building a more inclusive, equitable, and resilient digital economy and society. They future-proof their operations against regulatory shifts and technological disruptions. The competitive advantage, in the end, will belong to those organizations that deeply understand a central, immutable truth: in the vast and beautifully varied landscape of human ability, exclusion is always, ultimately, a design failure. Inclusion, therefore, is not just an ethical goal or a business tactic; it is the ultimate benchmark of design excellence and commercial triumph.

REFERENCES

Balagopalan, A., Jacobs, A. Z., & Biega, A. J. (2023). The Role of Relevance in Fair Ranking. *SIGIR 2023 - Proceedings of the 46th International ACM SIGIR Conference on Research and Development in Information Retrieval*, 2650–2660. DOI: 10.1145/3539618.3591933

Bercaru, V., & Popescu, N. (2024). A Systematic Review of Accessibility Techniques for Online Platforms: Current Trends and Challenges. *Applied Sciences (Basel, Switzerland)*, *14*(22), 10337. Advance online publication. DOI: 10.3390/app142210337

Casanova, J., & Savoie, M. (2019). Navigating the EU regulatory landscape for payments. *Journal of Payments Strategy and Systems*, *13*(3), 242–254. DOI: 10.69554/BKTB9869

Desmal, A. J., Alsaeed, M., Zolait, A. H., & Hamid, S. (2023). Feedback for Excellence: Improving mGovernment Services Through User Insights. *2023 International Conference on Innovation and Intelligence for Informatics, Computing, and Technologies, 3ICT 2023*, 181–187. DOI: 10.1109/3ICT60104.2023.10391312

Dundua, E. (2024). Digital Marketing and Corporate Social Responsibility: Strategies for Brand Building and Stakeholder Engagement. *Springer Proceedings in Business and Economics*, 269–282. DOI: 10.1007/978-3-031-66517-2_21

Fayyaz, S. (2019). A review on measuring digital trade & e-commerce as new economic statistics products. *Statistika, 99*(1), 57–68. https://www.scopus.com/inward/record.uri?eid=2-s2.0-85065500011&partnerID=40&md5=786eeace3689f08a2cea99eb55c6dc0b

González, C. S., Toledo, P., Muñoz, V., Noda, M. A., Bruno, A., & Moreno, L. (2013). Inclusive educational software design with agile approach. *ACM International Conference Proceeding Series*, 149–155. DOI: 10.1145/2536536.2536559

Gupta, K., Takaki, K., Tsutsui, A., Teramoto, K., & Ryskeldiev, B. (2025). AccessibleShip: Exploring Packaging and Shipping Barriers for Visually Impaired Users in C2C E-Commerce. *Conference on Human Factors in Computing Systems - Proceedings*. DOI: 10.1145/3706599.3706665

Hsu, C.-C., & Kuo, Z.-H. (2005). An adaptive interface for customer transaction assistant in electronic commerce. *Proceedings of the International Conference on Electronic Business (ICEB)*, 962–966. https://www.scopus.com/inward/record.uri?eid=2-s2.0-84873553119&partnerID=40&md5=7829134c4536d5466065112a16a09cd3

Jeseo, V., & Lindsey Hall, K. K. (2025). A framework for inclusive service experiences (FISE): Bridging the gap between traditional and immersive offerings. *Journal of Service Theory and Practice, 35*(5), 805–831. Advance online publication. DOI: 10.1108/JSTP-12-2024-0468

Koutsabasis, P. (2010). E-Business and Web Accessibility. In *Encyclopedia of E-Business Development and Management in the Global Economy* (pp. 570–577). DOI: 10.4018/978-1-61520-611-7.ch056

Mishra, S., & Sharma, S. (2025). User Experience for Inclusion: Analysis of WCAG 2.2 in Pharmacy App for Visually Impaired Group. *Communications in Computer and Information Science, 2338 CCIS*, 187–201. DOI: 10.1007/978-3-031-80832-6_14

Noordin, M. F., & Othman, R. (2005). Challenges to an E-business model: Pre- and post-adoption. *Internet and Information Technology in Modern Organizations: Challenges and Answers - Proceedings of the 5th International Business Information Management Association Conference, IBIMA 2005, 1*. https://www.scopus.com/inward/record.uri?eid=2-s2.0-84903648466&partnerID=40&md5=fbdc6410f4674496b3d66763f46e79c9

Pan, Q.-H., Luo, W.-P., Wang, J., & Dai, J.-P. (2023). A study of legitimacy building and governance of digital platforms. *Studies in Science of Science, 41*(6), 1076–1084. https://www.scopus.com/inward/record.uri?eid=2-s2.0-85212159063&partnerID=40&md5=ae7a82622eee03b8f512c074157b9fcb

Rai, A., Kumar, A., Vyshnav Kumar, A., & Mercy Rajaselvi Beaulah, P. (2026). Visio-Shop: A Technological Solution for Assisting Visually Impaired People in Retail Settings. *Communications in Computer and Information Science, 2608 CCIS*, 362–372. DOI: 10.1007/978-3-032-02537-1_31

Ramineni, V., Ingole, B. S., Krishnappa, M. S., Nagpal, A., Jayaram, V., Banarse, A. R., Bidkar, D. M., & Pulipeta, N. K. (2024). AI-Driven Novel Approach for Enhancing E-Commerce Accessibility through Sign Language Integration in Web and Mobile Applications. *Proceedings - 2024 IEEE 17th International Symposium on Embedded Multicore/Many-Core Systems-on-Chip, MCSoC 2024*, 276–281. DOI: 10.1109/MCSoC64144.2024.00053

Shad, A., Abdullah, T., & Butt, U. (2019). Web Accessibility Adoption Framework (WAAF) for Businesses and Web Professionals. *Proceedings of 12th International Conference on Global Security, Safety and Sustainability, ICGS3 2019*. DOI: 10.1109/ICGS3.2019.8688028

Song, S., Bu, J., Wang, Y., Yu, Z., Artmeier, A., Dai, L., & Wang, C. (2018). Reliability aware web accessibility experience metric. *Proceedings of the 15th Web for All Conference : Internet of Accessible Things, W4A 2018*. DOI: 10.1145/3192714.3192836

Viluckienė, J. (2015). Digital divide as social inequality in relation to IT users with disabilities. *Filosofija. Sociologija*, *26*(4), 314–321. https://www.scopus.com/inward/record.uri?eid=2-s2.0-84953396407&partnerID=40&md5=425cdbd6c0e9aef2d432cd6ab739f474

Chapter 6
Web Technologies for Cultural Heritage:
Digital Storytelling and Participatory Platforms

Azamat Ali
https://orcid.org/0000-0003-2931-2166
Lovely Professional University, Punjab, India

Ankit Dixit
Lovely Professional University, Punjab, India

ABSTRACT

Web technologies have taken over as they are instrumental to cultural heritage preservation and promotion. This chapter discusses the uses of digital storytelling and participatory platforms to be engaged with communities, to share historical knowledge, and to promote cultural expression. It searches the tools and approaches of developing interactive and immersive environments that help users to become connected to heritage content. The chapter also talks of the benefits of participatory platform where users can come with their stories, pictures and share their local history and therefore preserving the culture is a collaborative and participatory process. Examples of good practice in the digital humanities are found at case studies in museums, archives and grassroots initiatives. The problem of digital access, content authenticity, and long term preservation is also touched upon. Finally, the strategies are proposed on how it is possible to develop culturally sensitive, user friendly, and sustainable digital heritage projects through the usage of web technologies.

DOI: 10.4018/979-8-3373-5167-4.ch006

1. INTRODUCTION

Cultural heritage is a significant aspect of a human being and a collective memory. It consists of material things, including monuments, artefacts, and landscapes, and non-material things, including traditions, languages, rituals. Maintaining this heritage assists in individuals being aware of their past, beliefs and culture. New technologies are altering the way cultural heritage is recorded, stored and made available to other people in the digital age (Masciotta et al., 2023). The emergence of the internet and the web technologies has altered the way we interact, learn and communicate with information. These technologies have become an important part of preservation and promotion of cultural heritage. Previously, the preservation of heritage was predominantly the work of professionals such as historians, archivists and museum professionals. In the modern world, communities and individuals can participate in this process with the help of digital tools. They are able to tell stories, post photographs and contribute to the history of the place online (Roued et al., 2023).

The availability of cultural heritage to individuals worldwide is enhanced by the web technologies. The ability to access collections and acquire knowledge about various cultures in the comfort of one's home can be made by websites, digital archives, and multimedia platforms (Kaur and Rai, 2024). Europeana, Wikimedia Commons, and Historypin are all good examples of platforms. They encourage the nation to share photos, documents and stories and heritage has become more participatory and involving. This aids in the preservation of local knowledge and voices those communities that were usually disregarded in the official accounts. One of the most efficient methods of promoting cultural heritage is with the help of digital stories. It is a combination of text, pictures, sound, and video to make interesting stories (Privitera et al., 2024). StoryMapJS and TimelineJS are web tools that allow the user to create an interactive story about a historical event, place, or personal memory. These narratives can be posted on internet and this will reach individuals in various parts of the world. As an example, a community may use a web site to communicate its oral traditions, festivals or migration history. This forms a good linkage between the past and the present and assists in preserving the cultural traditions.

Also, web technologies enable immersive experiences. Online exhibitions, 3D models and virtual museums enable people to access heritage sites in a different manner. Virtual reality (VR) and augmented reality (AR) products have the potential to make past buildings or events so real, giving learners interactive experiences (Paulauskas et al., 2023). These applications are useful, particularly when a travel to the physical location is infeasible because of distance, money or security issues. They also render the study of history interesting and significant to students and to the masses in general. Conservation of cultural heritage conserves the culture to the future as well. This is assisted by web technologies in digital archiving and cloud storage (Ranjgar et al., 2024). Weaker papers, photographs of past and rare items can be scanned and kept in electronic forms. This information can be organized with the help of metadata and tagging and be easily searched and shared. Such systems also promote interaction among researchers, educators and cultural institutions.

There are challenges however in the use of web technologies in cultural heritage. The internet and access to digital devices is not equally available to all. Such a digital gap can also disenfranchise certain communities by excluding them in online heritage projects. Offline content accuracy, copyright and long-term viability of digital files is also of concern (Peukert and Windisch, 2025). In addition, cultural sensitivities should be observed and sacred materials and traditions should not be misrepresented on the internet. Nevertheless, the cultural heritage work has enormous opportunities with the use of web technologies. They assist teamwork, innovativeness and international reach. They enable professional and laypeople to play a part in conserving and spreading culture. Such a strategy contributes to making heritage more active, participatory, and to have relevance with modern people.

2. DIGITAL STORYTELLING FOR CULTURAL HERITAGE

2.1 Definition and Historical Evolution of Digital Storytelling

A digital story telling is the act of telling stories with digital tools and media. It is a mixture of text, images, sound, video and animation that make interesting stories. These are personal stories, historical stories, educational stories, or cultural stories. Digital storytelling enables users to share their ideas and emotions in multi-media formats, which makes the experience more interactive to the audiences (Hutson, 2024). Digital storytelling was initially coined in the early 1990s. It is commonly attributed to its modern form as developed by Joe Lambert and Dana Atchley at the Center for Digital Stories in California (Hardy & Dobson, 2024). They were also aimed at assisting individuals in sharing personal stories with simple digital tools. With time, the digital storytelling was used not only to tell personal stories. It is applied today in education, medicine, news reporting and culture. Digital storytelling is now a significant tool of preserving and sharing tangible and intangible cultural material in the sphere of cultural heritage (Lian and Xie, 2024). It enables institutions, communities and individuals to communicate their past knowledge, traditional practices, and personal memories in imaginative ways. Digital stories make cultural heritage more approachable, captivating and close to everyone of any age (Da Milano et al., 2023).

2.2 Tools and Platforms for Digital Narratives

There are a great number of resources and platforms to create digital stories. This is achieved through such tools allowing integration of multimedia capabilities and organizing of the same into meaningful stories. The cultural heritage projects use some of the most popular platforms, such as:

- *StoryMapJS:* StoryMapJS is a tool developed at the Knight Lab at Northwestern University that enables the user to construct stories based on geographic maps. The scenes are labelled by the point on the map which is linked to each slide or scene. The tool can be applied to narrate about migration, historical journeys or geographically spread heritage sites.
- *TimelineJS:* created by Knight Lab as well, TimelineJS lets the user create interactive timelines. It is best suited in presenting historical events, individual histories or neighborhood histories. Users have the option of embedding images, videos, audio clips, and maps and create rich storytelling.
- *Omeka:* Omeka is a free and open-source web publishing system commonly employed by libraries, museums and archives. It enables the users to build online exhibits and collections. The system helps in the provision of metadata norms and is applicable in structuring and displaying historical artifacts.
- *Wordpress and Wix:* The two content management systems are popular with digital storytelling blogs and websites. They do not limit design freedom and multimedia content.
- *Adobe Spark, Canva and Microsoft Sway:* The two tools are easy to use and applicable in the design of visual stories, presentations, and short videos. They can be applied in education and community work.

These sites are easy and effective. They allow individuals of limited technical knowledge to engage in heritage narrations. Through this, the digital storytelling process is made more inclusive and participatory.

2.3 Role of Digital Storytelling in Preserving Intangible Heritage

Intangible cultural heritage is a term that denotes generation to generation practices, knowledge and traditions (Scovazzi, 2023). This covers oral histories, music, dance, rituals, languages and culinary practices. The intangible heritage is more prone to loss as compared to the physical objects, especially in terms of modernization and globalization. Online narration is important in the conservation of intangible heritage. It assists in the documentation and exchange of traditions that are often passed orally or by observation. An exemplar is to have a community produce a digital narrative of a local festival, in the form of video clips, interviews, and background music. This enables the future generations to know their cultural background and enjoy it (Hutson, 2024).

Emotions, expressions, and personal experiences are some of the primary strengths of digital stories since they are able to capture them (Jiang, 2024). These factors are needed in discerning the more profound interpretation of cultural practices. Through recording rituals, songs and crafts with video and audio digital storytelling assists in preserving cultural identity of communities. Digital storytelling also has a role in language preservation in most instances. The languages that are in danger of extinction can be recorded with the help of those stories, songs and conversations of the minority language written down. Such recordings can be shared on the websites or social media, and it reaches a broader audience and motivates people to learn a new language. Furthermore, digital storytelling supports intergenerational learning. Digital media allows elders to exchange their experience and stories with young individuals. This forms an interconnection between the present and the past and assists in the formation of a feeling of belonging and pride (Cerezo et al., 2023).

2.4 Case Examples from Museums and Community Projects

Digital storytelling has become popular in many museums and cultural institutions in order to make their collections more interactive and significant. Some of the remarkable ones may be listed below:

- The British Museum (UK): This museum integrates online storytelling within its online exhibitions and learning material. As an example, its digital collection on Ancient Egypt has animated timelines, interactive maps and story based discovery of pieces. With the help of such tools, students and the population can interact with historical topics in an interactive manner (Li et al., 2024).
- Smithsonian Institution (USA): The institution provides digital storytelling projects through the platform of the Smithsonian Learning Lab, which combine cultural content with multimedia storytelling. The museum has enormous digital collections, stories, and digital exhibits that permit teachers and students to craft personal collections, narrations, and digital exhibits (Jia and Guo, 2023).
- Europeana (EU): Europeana is an online resource offering access to millions of objects of European museums, galleries, libraries and archives. It encourages participatory storytelling by projects such as the Europeana Migration in which individuals all around Europe contribute their stories of migration,

photos, and family history online. This assists in creating a common discourse concerning European identity and migration (Capurro & Severo, 2023).

- Museum of New Zealand Te Papa Tongarewa (New Zealand): Te Papa has created a number of digital storytelling collections to present Māori culture and traditions. These are multimedia displays, verbal histories, and computer aided recreations of cultural rituals. The stories are developed together with the native communities such that there is cultural correctness and respect (Naepi et al., 2025).
- Community Archives in India: A number of community archiving initiatives in India employ digital collection as a method of recording local heritage. As an example, the Voices of the Forest initiative gather oral history of tribal societies in the Central Indian region. They are documented in local languages and disseminated using the digital medium to increase awareness and cultural sustainability (Camilleri et al., 2023).

These case studies demonstrate how digital storytelling can turn cultural heritage more interactive, participatory and inclusive. They mention the significance of the cooperation between institutions and communities. Local people are not only subjects as in most projects but also co-creators. This is in order to guarantee authenticity and enforce community ownership of heritage.

3. PARTICIPATORY PLATFORMS AND COMMUNITY INVOLVEMENT

3.1 Understanding Participatory Culture in Digital Heritage

Participatory culture is a culture in which people are active participants in production and distribution of content. Participatory culture encourages users to be contributors and collaborators, unlike the traditional media where the audience is largely a passive consumer. This move has given communities new avenues of telling their cultural stories and knowledge through web-based platforms in the context of digital heritage (Asplund et al., 2024). The rise of participatory culture is strongly associated with the evolution of internet, social media and easy-to-use digital tools. There is no longer a necessity of sophisticated technical ability to share videos, pictures or stories on the web. Consequently, cultural heritage is no longer left in the hands of professionals operating in museums, archives and universities.

Rather, ordinary people and societies are now able to capture, store and market their heritage online (García-Mieres et al., 2024).

This new strategy attaches importance to local knowledge, lived experiences and diversity of views. It gives a view that all people have something of worth to share when it comes to learning of culture and history. The connection between individuals and their heritage also becomes more significant and applicable in everyday life with the help of participatory culture (Aziz et al., 2023). The participatory culture is significant in the digital heritage projects to make the heritage inclusive and dynamic. It promotes transparency and open access and collaboration. When communities play a part in the process of heritage documentation and interpretation, they have a stronger sense of ownership and they are more proud of their cultural identity.

3.2 Crowdsourcing Heritage Data and Stories

One of the major techniques in participatory digital heritage work is crowdsourcing. It is the process of gathering facts, photographs, paper materials or anecdotes of a very many number of individuals, often via the internet. The lending of crowdsourcing enables institutions to develop massive, diversified, and enriched collections that could not be achieved solely by the conventional means (Cui et al., 2024). Crowdsourcing in cultural heritage can be done in numerous ways. It can involve posting vintage photos, labelling historic photos, oral history, translations or mapping of cultural places. Such contributions contribute to the gaps in the official archives and introduce new knowledge of the past and the ordinary life. Crowdsourcing is also more inclusive as it gives people with different backgrounds an opportunity to express their views. It aids in the recovery of stories of underrepresented communities like women, indigenous peoples, migrants, and the rural communities. The stories make our perception of the past more nuanced and make sure that the many voices are represented (Reed and Rudman, 2023).

Crowdsourcing is a trend that is taken by many institutions just to encourage the masses to be involved in digital heritage initiatives. The project of the British Library called Georeferencer, requested users to assist in matching the historical maps with current geographic information. The outcome was an interactive and search-based map archive. In the same way, the Smithsonian Institution has a so called Transcription Center where volunteers are engaged in the process of transcribing written materials to render them searchable and open. These campaigns demonstrate how communal involvement can make cultural heritage resources more accessible and also quality. Crowdsourcing does not only serve the interest of institutions but also enables the participants. It makes them feel that they are involved and contributing. It is also an invaluable opportunity to learn as individuals acquire insights into their history and culture by participating in such projects (Mishra and Maheshwari, 2023).

3.3 Empowering Communities through Digital Contribution

Online spaces enable the communities to narrate their stories through their voices. This is of particular significance to those communities, which have been overlooked, forgotten, or distorted, in the mainstream record. Through participating in digital heritage initiatives, such communities will regain their narratives and transmit them to the subsequent generations (Song et al., 2024). Community involvement in digital heritage fosters cultural pride and social cohesion. It enhances interrelations both in the community and with the larger community. It also assists the youth to associate their past with their new and significant forms. Digital contribution may come in many forms including sharing of photos of family heirlooms, interviewing of the aged, or documenting of local festivals and traditions. Such contributions are usually posted to online media where they can be accessed by other people worldwide (Mustafa et al., 2023).

Empowerment of communities also means making them have the control of how their cultural materials are used and represented. It is also important that in participatory heritage work, we respect cultural protocols, seek consent, and engage local voices in the decision making process. In others, digital archives are established and maintained by communities. This will enable them to keep their heritage in their own hands. It also aids continuity and innovation of culture. As an example, indigenous Australians have developed web-based archives where they record traditional knowledge, language, and art to prevent the disappearance of this knowledge to the generations to come. Community empowerment is also dependent on education and training. Digital storytelling, content creation, and platform workshops can make individuals have the skills to participate in digital heritage projects. These opportunities can be offered with the assistance of partnerships between institutions and local organizations (Mantzou et al., 2023).

3.4 Examples of Participatory Platforms: Europeana, Historypin, Wikimedia Commons

A number of web platforms have been created in order to facilitate participatory methods in digital heritage. These platforms enable people to create and share content, interact with stories and find cultural materials worldwide. Among the most famous platforms there are:

Europeana

Europeana is an online source where millions of cultural heritage objects of European museums, libraries and archives have access. It helps in institutional and public donations. Among its major participatory initiatives is the Europeana Migration project, which engages individuals to submit personal narratives, photographs and objects touching on migration. The contributions form a common digital memory and represent the different cultural European history. Europeana also provides educators, researchers and cultural organizations with tools with which to produce and curate digital exhibitions. Its presence as a free online resource and multiple language interfaces has ensured that it reaches a broad group of people in Europe and further (Marsh, 2023).

Historypin

Historypin is a global interactive with the aim of enabling individuals to share historical photos, tales and recollections pinned on a virtual map. Users have the opportunity to upload old photographs of places and provide information about them like the date, people and the context of the photo. This assists other people in knowing about the history of certain places and people. Historypin promotes the partnerships between communities, schools, libraries and heritage groups. It has been applied in neighbourhood history, oral history, urban change projects. The platform offers personalization of history and place-based connection that assists users to establish a connection with the past (Pernarella & Koed Madsen, 2023).

Wikimedia Commons

Wikimedia Commons is an online storage of media utilized by Wiki projects such as Wikipedia. It contains millions of freely usable video content, audio files and images posted by its users worldwide. A lot of such files are connected to cultural heritage, such as pictures of monuments, artefacts, works of art and practices. Any media can be uploaded to Wikimedia Commons and there are a few guidelines and licensing rules to be followed. The contribution assists in recording and sharing heritage culture in an open and accessible manner. It is also the platform of multilingualism and is popular in education and research. Combined, these sites reveal the merits of participatory digital heritage. They demonstrate how cultural collections can be enriched by the contributions of the public and create comprehension globally (Mantzou et al., 2023).

4. DESIGNING INTERACTIVE AND IMMERSIVE EXPERIENCES

Digital heritage does not just entail content holding and presentation. It is also concerned with designing attractive and worthwhile experiences to the users.

Interactive and immersive technologies enable individuals to relate to cultural heritage. They assist in changing the passive viewing into the active exploration. When properly crafted, these online experiences are informative, entertaining and they stimulate inquisitiveness (Hutson, 2024). In cultural heritage, web-based tools that include AR, VR, 3D modelling and gamification have become common. These technologies make artefacts, stories and historical places come to life. They provide new approaches to studying the past and learning the cultural identity. The following section addresses the application of these tools, the concepts of user experience (UX) design in heritage platforms, and best practice and case studies.

4.1 Web Based Tools for Interactivity and Immersion

Interactive and immersive tools provide the user with the option of interacting with heritage material beyond a mere text or image. The tools replicate real world experiences or provide novel ways of telling stories through the development of digital environments. Some of the most used tools in digital heritage include:

Augmented Reality (AR)

AR introduces digital information to the real-world setting via a tablet or smartphone screen in the form of text, picture, or video. It complements the visits to museums or heritage sites in the real life by giving extra information. An illustration is that by pointing a phone on an old structure, we may see how it was previously. AR is also applicable in printed media where scanning a page can bring out animations or videos (Dargan et al., 2023).

Virtual Reality (VR)

VR is the formation of an entirely digital space in which the user is free to move and interact with objects. VR devices like the Oculus Rift or Google Cardboard enable users to do a virtual tour of heritage sites. They can stroll in the streets of ancient cities, or stand in the buildings of history which do not exist now. VR can serve to open up places that cannot be accessed (Remote locations, 2024) or are blocked off by war or calamities to the general population (Kulkarni & Kulkarni, 2024).

3D Modeling and Reconstruction

In 3D modeling, digital models of artifacts, buildings and landscapes are made true to life. Such models are rotatable, zoomable, and can be looked at in detail, scanned with 3D and recreated using photogrammetry to reconstruct damaged or lost objects. Online exhibitions of museums are presented with the help of 3D models, or they can be used to provide an opportunity to view collections at home (Barszcz et al., 2023).

Gamification

Gamification uses aspects of game design (points, badges, quests, or storytelling) on learning tasks. It makes it more motivating and involving particularly among the younger generation. Heritage apps or games can include historical mystery-solving, gathering online objects, or solving missions in physical locations. This interactive style makes users learn and explore the playfully (Wang et al., 2024).

These tools support learning, exploration, and memory retention. They render heritage more personal by involving the user on an emotive and intellectual level.

4.2 Principles of User Experience (UX) in Heritage Platforms

Technology is not the only way of designing a digital heritage experience. It must also be user-experience-intensive. UX is the feeling and engagement of people with a product or platform. On heritage platforms, good UX implies that end-users are presented with a platform that is simple to operate, meaningful, and respectful of heritage material (Unger and Chandler 2023). Major UX principles of heritage platforms are:

- Usability: Sites are supposed to be easy to navigate. The content should be easily searchable, browsable and interactive. It is significant to have clear menus, instructions and icons.
- Accessibility: Digital heritage should be made accessible to everyone possessing different abilities and needs. This involves the provision of subtitles, alt-text, screen-reader, and mobile support. Various audiences also need multilingual support.
- Interactivity: The content is supposed to be interactive in that users are able to click, drag, select or customize. This makes them feel engaged and they learn in an active way.
- Cultural Sensitivity: The design must be of respect to the cultural aspect of the materials. Pictures, icons and stories should be selected. Consultations with local communities should also be done to guarantee that the representations are proper and correct.
- Engagement: The platform must be curious and interesting to the users. This can be achieved with the help of using storytelling, animation, and elements of gamification.

- Feedback and Evaluation: Feedback should be enabled to be provided by the users and designers should analyse user responses to enhance the experience as they move forward.

Using these principles, the heritage platforms can develop digital spaces that are informative and entertaining.

4.3 Best Practices in Designing Culturally Sensitive Digital Environments

Digital heritage is very sensitive to culture. Communities have values, beliefs and traditions that must be considered when creating interactive experiences to the community. The sacred or meaningful content should not be distorted, over simplified, or turned into a commercialized product of digital tools. Here are some best practices:

- Community Involvement: Designers are to engage in communities at the start. They can direct the design and storytelling and content choice by their voices. This makes it authentic and trust building.
- Informed Consent: Before their cultural content is digitized and shared, communities ought to consent to it. Religious ceremonies or holy places may need to be restricted as sensitive material.
- Representation: The digital platform must demonstrate various opinions. Do not have stereotypes or historical one sided views. As much as possible, have the community narrate its story.
- Contextualization: Offers contextualization on the background of content to enable the user to perceive the cultural connotation behind content. As an example, describe the purpose of a traditional dance or a meaning of an artefact.
- Respect for Language and Identity: Use indigenous languages when appropriate. Understand cultural importance of names, ritual, and oral traditions (Dreyfus & Hellwig, 2023).

Sensitive design designs respectful, inclusive and empowering experiences. It also assists in maintenance of cultural integrity.

4.4 Case Studies of Virtual Museums and Heritage Apps

A number of successful projects demonstrate the roles of interactive and immersive technologies in improving the heritage experience. Below are some examples:

- The Virtual Angkor Project (Cambodia): The project is a 3D model and VR reconstruction of an ancient city of Angkor Wat. Users get to view the city during the 13th century with temples, markets and festivals. It is utilized in the classroom and museums to educate about the history of Southeast Asia (Buragohain et al., 2025).
- The Smithsonian National Museum of Natural History (USA): The museum provides an online tour in which the visitor can navigate through galleries, enlarge objects on display and multimedia resources. It gained fame in the COVID-19 pandemic and still touches the global markets (Meng et al., 2023).
- The British Museum and Google Arts & Culture: With this collaboration, the user is able to view museum collections in 3D and VR. There is a rich user experience with the help of high-resolution images, audio tours, and interactive features (Li et al., 2024).
- CyArk (Global): CyArk is a heritage conservation project that digitises threatened heritage sites through 3D laser scanning and photogrammetry. These comprise ancient temples and caves as well as monuments. Data is applied to education, tourism and conservation. The platform has high immersive touring and visualization (Kumar et al., 2025).
- Staro Selo Mobile App (Serbia): The application enables the user to navigate through the real-world traditional rural architecture by means of AR. In a village, users are able to scan QR code and view how houses used to appear in the past. It also has audio stories of the local residents (Deri et al., 2023).

Through these projects, it is demonstrated how technology and heritage can collaborate to produce potent learning tools. They also demonstrate how technical design should be combined with cultural awareness.

5. CHALLENGES IN DIGITAL HERITAGE PROJECTS

Digital technologies have introduced the possibilities of preservation and sharing of cultural heritage. Digital stories, interactive maps, and 3D modelling are only a handful of tools that allow people to dive into the past in an engaging manner. Nevertheless, there are a lot of difficulties in digital heritage projects too. Such difficulties may have an impact on the quality, reach, and ethical integrity of such initiatives. The challenges should be known to enhance the future digital heritage practice. Four broad areas of concern are discussed in this section, namely: barriers to digital access and inclusion, authenticity and representation, technical limitations and risk of digital preservation, and the challenges of cultural sensitivity, bias and data sovereignty.

5.1 Barriers to Digital Access and Inclusion

The digital divide is one of the largest problems in digital heritage undertakings. Not everyone is equally available to the internet, digital devices, and technical abilities. This gap is between the poor and the rich, the city and the countryside, and even among the various age or education levels (Lian and Xie, 2024). As an illustration, most of the communities in the remote or poverty stricken areas do not have constant access to the internet. They are not able to engage in online cultural content or on digital projects without proper infrastructure. When this happens, digital heritage sites will be closed off to the very individuals that they are supposed to represent or serve.

Although internet access is a possibility, not all people are digital literate to use platforms, post content, or browsing websites. Elderly people, individuals with low education, and individuals with disabilities are usually challenged to use digital tools. Unless such barriers are considered, digital heritage efforts can even leave the very communities they would target out (Baumgartner et al., 2023). Designers have to make digital heritage really inclusive, easy to use, multi-lingual and accustom able to people with disabilities. The gap can also be closed with the help of offline access, mobile friendly versions, and training programs. Ideally all planning and design should be inclusive.

5.2 Concerns about Content Authenticity and Ethical Representation

The other significant issue of digital heritage is the authenticity of the content. Information might be wrong or false when the people post pictures, narrations, or perceptions. Unless examined carefully, wrong data may propagate and harm the reputation of digital archives (Moss et al., 2023). Historical pictures can be uploaded, say, with the incorrect date or location. Personal accounts can be given in only one view point without the inclusion of key facts or background. In the worst scenario, cultural traditions can be misinterpreted or be out of context. This may result in the mistrust of the users, researchers, and members of the community.

Ethical representation is an issue as well. Materials of culture are usually significant to the communities concerned. Rituals, symbols, or artefacts that are regarded to be sacred must not be communally shared. Unauthorized publication of such content by the platforms may lead to offense or harm. Stereotypes or spread of fake stories can also be reinforced or encouraged by misrepresentation or oversimplification of cultures (Patrick, 2023). To solve these problems, digital heritage initiatives have to be guided by definite ethical principles. There should be community participation in matters concerning shared content and description of content. Sources, context, and adequate credits should be part of metadata. Digital collections can be checked by moderation and review by specialists to be accurate and respectful.

5.3 Technical Limitations and Digital Preservation Risks

Digital heritage initiatives are sensitive to technology. Yet online technologies evolve quickly. Something that works now as a web site or computer program may be obsolete within years. This poses a danger to the future survival of digital files (Wagner, & de Clippele, 2023). Digital files have a tendency to be damaged or become unreadable with time. The formats are likely to become out dated and the hardware or software to support them might become out of circulation. Digital collections of value can be lost because of system failure, hacking, or natural disasters, unless the backup systems are in place. Digital heritage has a tendency to be stored on cloud storage services. Although they are convenient, they rely on commercial providers. In case of the closure of these services or their alteration of conditions, users can lose access to their data. Another issue is the ownership and control of the data kept in commercial platforms (Nethercote, 2023).

Digital heritage project should adhere to best practices in digital archiving in order to be preserved in the long term. This involves routine backups, open file formats and data migration to newer systems where necessary. Digital infrastructure and maintenance in institutions are required. Any digital heritage initiative should include preservation plans. Other technical constraints are the gear and software cost. A 3D modelling, VR, or AR tool is expensive to use with high-quality and needs trained professionals. A lot of small institutions or community groups do not have the resources to make use of these tools. These barriers can be reduced by offering training on digital skills, offering low-cost, open-source alternatives, and so on. Small projects can also be aided by collaboration with universities, libraries, or tech companies (Agbeyangi & Suleman, 2024).

5.4 Cultural Sensitivity, Bias, and Data Sovereignty Issues

A heritage project must have cultural sensitivity. However, in digital heritage, the threat of cultural insensitivity or biasness is increased as a result of the global and public character of digital platforms. Digital heritage places are usually dominated by Western views. This may cause one to have a one-sided perception of the history and culture (Hutson, 2024). As an example, platforms design, language, and the selection of content criteria can all be representative of a single worldview. This may hush up or distort the minority and indigenous communities. The cultural practices are multifaceted and are based on the local knowledge. Loss of meaning may occur as a result of digitization without the participation of the community.

Some of the sacred or restricted material can be posted without authorization. It may break the cultural conventions and damage the relations in the community (Knapik & Król, 2023).

Data sovereignty is another serious problem. It implies that the communities can possess the right to manage their cultural data. In most instances, the digital heritage material is on the foreign servers or run by institutions that are not a part of the community. This begs questions of the owner of the data, access to the data, and the usage of the data (Bokolo, 2025). Indicatively, indigenous people might not desire their traditional knowledge to be shared by many people. They also might desire to exercise the right to how their language, art, or ritual is presented. This control is lost when their data are stored and manipulated elsewhere. In order to deal with these issues, digital heritage projects should liaise with communities. This involves asking permission, distributing decision-making authority and respect of local culture regulations. Good solutions would be community centered platforms, localized servers, and open access policies based on the community control (Boniotti, 2023).

There is also an option of avoiding bias through participation of voices in platform design, content creation and governance. Designer and researcher cultural awareness training can also be provided.

6. BEST PRACTICES AND CASE STUDIES IN THE DIGITAL HUMANITIES

Digital humanities are an intersection of technology and humanities like history, art, literature and cultural studies. Digital humanities in the cultural heritage field facilitate the development of alternative methods of knowledge recording, preservation and exchange. Digital tools are frequently used in these projects to provide the community, institutions, and researcher's access to the cultural materials in interesting ways (Vlase & Lahdesmaki, 2023).

There have been both grassroots and institutional best practices in digital heritage. Such practices emphasize interdisciplinary collaboration, stakeholder involvement, impact assessment and engagement on ethical grounds. This part discusses some of the major success stories and lessons learned by projects that have been undertaken in digital heritage across the globe.

6.1 Institutional and Grassroots Success Stories

There are successful digital heritage projects developed by many of the leading institutions. These projects are used as templates of design, access, and collaboration.

- *The British Library, its Endangered Archives Programme:* This initiative aids in maintaining historical documents of locations where historical records are facing the threat of being destroyed. Books, photographs and manuscripts are digitized by local partners and are published online. Training, equipment and technical support are offered by the British library. The model demonstrates how institutions could facilitate grassroots activities and develop a digital capacity elsewhere (Butterworth & van Schaik, 2024).
- *Europeana (European Union):* Europeana is a huge digital heritage portal. It unites library, museum, archive and gallery content throughout Europe. The site offers millions of digital objects such as works of art, documents, videos and sound recordings. Europeana also offers the involvement of people by organizing storytelling campaigns and open calls to contributions. It is very accessible because of its open-access approach and multilingual interface (Arceneaux, 2024).
- *Mukurtu (USA):* Mukurtu is a community-based project aimed at indigenous communities to administer and distribute digital heritage. It also honours the traditional knowledge systems by giving the right to the user to decide on the manner in which materials are accessed and utilized. Cultural rules that govern communities, e.g. the prohibition of viewing sacred material, can be established. This method secures the integrity of the culture and leaves the communities to present their heritage in their own words (Farnel et al., 2024).
- *Reanimating Cultural Heritage (Sierra Leone and UK):* This is a project with the involvement of researchers, local Sierra Leonean museums, and communities. They engage digital tools in order to make cultural artifacts alive by using animation, stories and interactive displays. The project is an oral history initiative that integrates digital media so that communities can be re-linked to their heritage. It also enhances the education and social recovery of the post-conflict regions (Weiglhofer et al., 2023).
- *A People archive of police violence in Cleveland (USA):* It is a grassroots initiative that gathers and publishes accounts of police violence, which members of the community submit themselves. It is an effective demonstration of the way digital humanities can be used to tackle social justice problems. It has personal stories, images, and videos and provides the marginalized with an opportunity to be heard (Fife et al., 2023).

These case studies demonstrate that small community organizations and large institutions can both produce some meaningful work on digital heritage. Critical is respect of local knowledge, community participation and application of technology in considerate manner.

6.2 Interdisciplinary Collaboration and Stakeholder Engagement

Effective digital heritage projects frequently can entail partnership in various areas. The skills and viewpoint of historians, computer scientists, designers, educators, archivists and community members are all welcome. Interdisciplinary work contributes to making sure that the project is technically healthy and culturally relevant (Lian & Xie, 2024). As an illustration, software developers can develop platforms, whereas anthropologists are making sure that cultural content is handled with dignity. The user experience is enhanced by designers, and it is the educators who make the content school and learner relevant. The involvement of stakeholders also is necessary. The stakeholders are community members, cultural institutions, funders, policymakers and end users. Involving the entire stakeholders in planning and decision making processes assists in creating trust and extended support. It also makes sure that the digital heritage project fulfils the purpose of the people who are served by them.

The practice of good stakeholder engagement involves:

- Holding community consultations and workshops
- Establishing local based advisory boards.
- Co-designing content with cultural practitioners
- Infusion of plain information on the use and storage of data.
- Credit and ownership of project outputs.

Such practices result in the increased acceptance, more powerful partnerships, and more sustainable results.

6.3 Metrics for Evaluating Impact and User Participation

It is significant to measure the effectiveness of a digital heritage project. It assists project leaders in knowing what is working, what is not good enough and how the project impacts the users and communities.

Typical impact and participation measures are:

- User statistics: How many times the website was visited, on which page, how many downloads, how much time is spent on the platform.
- User demographics: Age, location, the profession, or language of the users to determine whether the project is accessed by various audiences.
- Engagement data: Likes, shares, comments, or uploads in participatory platforms.

- Qualitative feedback: Community engagement: Number of local contributors, workshops hosted and alliances established.
- Educational use: Take up of the platform by schools, universities, or training programs.
- Media coverage and recognition: Mentions in academic articles, news outlets, or awards.

Assessment needs to be continuous. To be able to compare the developments prior to the implementation of the project and after it, it is always beneficial to carry out baseline studies. Quantitative and qualitative data are both useful. Impact frameworks are also applied to some projects. As an illustration, the Arts and Humanities Research Council (AHRC) of the UK has created a list of its categories including social impact, identity building and cultural preservation in its Cultural Value Project. These are frameworks that offer a systematic approach to quantify long term benefits.

6.4 Lessons from On-going and Completed Digital Heritage Initiatives

Based on the years of practice in the field of digital heritage work, it has become clear that there are some significant lessons to be made:

- *Start with the community:* The more successful projects are one that involves the communities at an early stage. Their knowledge and input help shape content, design, and goals. Decent interaction brings about confidence and sincerity.
- *Plan for sustainability:* Technology changes quickly. Plans should be made in digital projects to maintain, update and have long-term access. To prevent any future compatibility, use open source tools and common formats.
- *Focus on accessibility:* Ensure that platforms are user friendly across all ages, capabilities and backgrounds. The friendly design on mobile devices, use of simple language and availability of multiple languages can be valued in accessing more audiences.
- *Respect cultural rights:* Cultural materials have to be treated with care. Individuals ought to determine what can be distributed and in what way. There has to be ethical guidelines and informed consent on projects.
- *Collaborate across disciplines:* Academic-technologist-community partnerships involve various strengths. The interdisciplinary teams result in the improved outcomes and innovation.

- *Use feedback to grow:* Continuous review and feedback of users can serve to enhance digital heritage projects. Accept criticism and willing to change according to the needs of the users.
- *Share knowledge and tools:* Free access to the project findings, the source code, and the methods enable other people to develop your work. It also facilitates worldwide cooperation and training.

7. STRATEGIC RECOMMENDATIONS

Digital heritage platforms become an inclusive, interactive, and sustainable method of preserving culture. Nonetheless, in order to fully achieve this potential, there should be development of thoughtful strategies and policies. These must be centred on access, community participation and future digital sustainability. This part will include several strategic recommendations and will be completed with the conclusion on main insights of the chapter. Strategies for Inclusive, User-Friendly, and Sustainable Platforms:

- Design for All Users: Online platforms must be accessible to everyone regardless of age, backgrounds and abilities. Interfaces should be basic, mobile compliant and multi-lingual. Platforms can be made inclusive by providing alternative text to images, captions to videos and support of screen readers (Bogdanova et al., 2024).
- Encourage Community Participation: Heritage platforms need to engage local communities to share their stories, photos and experience. Crowdsourcing and digital storytelling tools can make individuals share their culture. Engagement will create a feeling of ownership and retain the content authentic (Maietti, 2023).
- Provide Training and Resources: Users can be taught to work with heritage technologies in workshops and digital literacy programs. They need to be particularly focused on underserved populations, such as rural populations and older people who possess traditional knowledge (Djatmiko et al., 2025).
- Use Open-Source and Interoperable Tools: Open source software and common formatting make sure that platforms can be maintained and updated with time. It is also less difficult to spread the data across institutions and countries and contribute to wider collaboration.
- Plan for Maintenance and Growth: The aspect of sustainability should be put at the forefront. Social media require financial resources and technical staff to update and maintain the platforms, store data, and review its content. Long-

term support can be offered by partnerships with universities, libraries and NGOs (Lewandowski, & Czech, 2024).

7.1 Policy Suggestions for Long Term Preservation and Equitable Access

- Develop National Digital Heritage Policies: The governments must establish policies that favour digital heritage projects. These should involve financing of digitization, legal measures on data possession, and ethical directions of using content.
- Protect Cultural Data Rights: The right of communities to manage their cultural data should be acknowledged in the policies. This involves access, use and storage choices. The central principles should be informed consent and data sovereignty.
- Support Open Access and Knowledge Sharing: Digital resources of digital heritage should be made available freely with public funding. Open access assists the researchers, students and general population gain access to heritage content.
- Ensure Infrastructure in Underserved Areas: The government and organizations should invest in the internet and digital devices among the rural and marginalized populations. Inclusive heritage participation requires that all have access to technology.

7.2 Future Directions for Digital Heritage Technologies

Digital heritage is going to take the shape of emerging technologies, including artificial intelligence, blockchain, and immersive mediums. Large datasets can be organized and metadata tagging can be automated with the help of AI. Blockchain can introduce new methods of maintaining authenticity and safeguarding rights of ownership. AR/VR as immersive media will enhance the heritage experiences to become more interesting and realistic. Nevertheless, these technologies should be responsible. The ethical design, community engagement and cultural sensitivity will be important. Technological innovation in heritage must be directed by human values.

8. CONCLUSION

This chapter has analyzed the way in which the cultural heritage is being redefined through web technologies as a means to preserve, share and experience it. Online storytelling, participatory, and immersive technologies, such as AR, VR, and 3D modelling have provided new ways in which communities and institutions can incorporate heritage content in meaningful ways. Through these technologies, documenting local histories, celebrating cultural identities and accessing better audiences throughout the world becomes simpler. Meanwhile, there are a number of challenges to digital heritage projects. These are disparities in access to technology, worries about the authenticity of the content and cultural sensitivity, technical constraints and long term preservation threats. These challenges need careful approaches, proper conduct and involvement of the community.

In order to make digital heritage initiatives sustainable, the key elements are inclusive design, open access, and robust collaboration with local communities. Cultural rights also need protection and promotion of equitable access and maintenance of digital infrastructures by policy support. Finally, digital heritage is ultimately successful because of co-operation between technology and tradition, professionals and the community and the global and the local. Cultural heritage can further inform, enlighten, and motivate the current and future generations with responsible utilization of digital tools and inclusive practice.

REFERENCES

Agbeyangi, A., & Suleman, H. (2024, November). Advances and challenges in low-resource-environment software systems: A Survey. In *Informatics* (Vol. 11, No. 4, p. 90). MDPI. DOI: 10.3390/informatics11040090

Arceneaux, P. (2024). Value creation through organizational storytelling: Strategic narratives in foreign government public relations. *Public Relations Review, 50*(2), 102433. DOI: 10.1016/j.pubrev.2024.102433

Asplund, S. B., Ljung Egeland, B., & Olin-Scheller, C. (2024). Sharing is caring: Young people's narratives about BookTok and volitional reading. *Language and Education, 38*(4), 635–651. DOI: 10.1080/09500782.2024.2324947

Barszcz, M., Dziedzic, K., Skublewska-Paszkowska, M., & Powroznik, P. (2023). 3D scanning digital models for virtual museums. *Computer Animation and Virtual Worlds, 34*(3-4), e2154. DOI: 10.1002/cav.2154

Baumgartner, A., Rohrbach, T., & Schönhagen, P. (2023). 'If the phone were broken, I'd be screwed': Media use of people with disabilities in the digital era. *Disability & Society, 38*(1), 73–97. DOI: 10.1080/09687599.2021.1916884

Bogdanova, G., Todorov, T., Dochkova-Todorova, J., Noev, N., & Sabev, N. (2024). Design and Development Model of a Web Accessibility Ecosystem. *Information (Basel), 15*(10), 613. DOI: 10.3390/info15100613

Bokolo, A. J. (2025). Implementing Digital Sovereignty to Accelerate Smarter Mobility Solutions in Local Communities. *Smart Cities, 8*(4), 106. DOI: 10.3390/smartcities8040106

Boniotti, C. (2023). The public-private-people partnership (P4) for cultural heritage management purposes. *Journal of Cultural Heritage Management and Sustainable Development, 13*(1), 1–14. DOI: 10.1108/JCHMSD-12-2020-0186

Buragohain, D., Buragohain, D., Meng, Y., Deng, C., & Chaudhary, S. (2025). A metaverse based digital preservation of temple architecture and heritage. *Scientific Reports, 15*(1), 15484. DOI: 10.1038/s41598-025-00039-w PMID: 40319075

Butterworth, J., & van Schaik, S. (2024). Reflections on Two Decades of the Endangered Archives Programme. *Preservation in Perspective: International Strategies for the Preservation of Written Cultural Heritage*, 29.

Camilleri, M. A., Troise, C., Strazzullo, S., & Bresciani, S. (2023). Creating shared value through open innovation approaches: Opportunities and challenges for corporate sustainability. *Business Strategy and the Environment*, *32*(7), 4485–4502. DOI: 10.1002/bse.3377

Capurro, C., & Severo, M. (2023). Mapping European Digital Heritage Politics: An Empirical Study of Europeana as a Web-based Network. *Heritage & Society*, •••, 1–21. DOI: 10.1080/2159032X.2023.2266801

Cerezo, E., Coma-Roselló, T., Aguelo, A., Blasco-Serrano, A. C., & Garrido, M. Á. (2023). Exploring intergenerational interactions through an online storytelling experience. *IEEE Transactions on Learning Technologies*, *17*, 157–171. DOI: 10.1109/TLT.2023.3260955

Cui, T., Liu, L., Cheng, H., Chang, S., & Feng, Y. (2024). Crowdsourcing for innovation: Effects of idea content and competition intensity on idea success. *The Journal of Strategic Information Systems*, *33*(2), 101839. DOI: 10.1016/j.jsis.2024.101839

Da Milano, C., Falchetti, E., Migone, P., & Nisi, V. (2023). Digital storytelling, cultural heritage, and social inclusion: The MEMEX project. In *Digital Approaches to Inclusion and Participation in Cultural Heritage* (pp. 8–26). Routledge. DOI: 10.4324/9781003277606-2

Dargan, S., Bansal, S., Kumar, M., Mittal, A., & Kumar, K. (2023). Augmented reality: A comprehensive review. *Archives of Computational Methods in Engineering*, *30*(2), 1057–1080. DOI: 10.1007/s11831-022-09831-7

Deri, M. G., Chiti, L., & Ciuffoletti, A. (2023). A Sustainable Approach to Tourist Signage on Heritage Trails. *Sustainability (Basel)*, *15*(23), 16251. DOI: 10.3390/su152316251

Djatmiko, G. H., Sinaga, O., & Pawirosumarto, S. (2025). Digital transformation and social inclusion in public services: A qualitative analysis of e-government adoption for marginalized communities in sustainable governance. *Sustainability (Basel)*, *17*(7), 2908. DOI: 10.3390/su17072908

Dreyfus, S., & Hellwig, A. F. (2023). Meaningful Rituals: A Linguistic Analysis of Acknowledgements of Country. *Journal of Australian Studies*, *47*(3), 590–610. DOI: 10.1080/14443058.2023.2236618

Farnel, S., Shiri, A., Gruben, E. J., Amos, B. S., & Kotokak, L. (2024). Enhancing Digital Libraries through Digital Storytelling: The Case of the Inuvialuit Digital Library. In *Library and Information Sciences in Arctic and Northern Studies* (pp. 209–226). Springer International Publishing., DOI: 10.1007/978-3-031-54715-7_10

Fife, K., Flinn, A., & Nyhan, J. (2023). Documenting resistance, conflict and violence: A scoping review of the role of participatory digital platforms in the mobilisation of resistance. *Archival Science*, *23*(3), 471–499. DOI: 10.1007/s10502-023-09416-8

García-Mieres, H., Parra, L., Paz-Vázquez, L. M., Castaño, E., & Pedrosa, I. (2024). Bridging generations: The power of digitization and social innovation in preserving rural cultural heritage. *Innovation (Abingdon)*, •••, 1–14. DOI: 10.1080/13511610.2024.2424773

Hardy, P., & Dobson, S. (2024). Voice, Belonging, Storytelling and Transformation in Digital Storytelling Workshop Settings—Some Philosophical Considerations. In *Learning Inclusion in a Digital Age: Belonging and Finding a Voice with the Disadvantaged* (pp. 95–105). Springer Nature Singapore., DOI: 10.1007/978-981-99-7196-1_7

Hutson, J. (2024). Digital Cultural Heritage Preservation. In *Art and Culture in the Multiverse of Metaverses: Immersion, Presence, and Interactivity in the Digital Age* (pp. 99-141). Cham: Springer Nature Switzerland. DOI: 10.1007/978-3-031-66320-8_4

Jia, Y., & Guo, W. (2023, July). Museum Blended Learning Through Digital Learning Platform: The Case of Smithsonian Learning Lab. In *International Conference on Blended Learning* (pp. 224-235). Cham: Springer Nature Switzerland. DOI: 10.1007/978-3-031-35731-2_20

Jiang, J. (2024). Emotions are what will draw people in: A study of critical affective literacy through digital storytelling. *Journal of Adolescent & Adult Literacy*, *67*(4), 253–263. DOI: 10.1002/jaal.1322

Kaur, N., & Rai, M. (2024). Role of Digital Technology and Education for Transformation of Cultural Heritage. In *Digital Cultural Heritage* (pp. 206–221). CRC Press. DOI: 10.1201/9781032630564-11

Knapik, W., & Król, K. (2023). Inclusion of vanishing cultural heritage in a sustainable rural development strategy–prospects, opportunities, recommendations. *Sustainability (Basel)*, *15*(4), 3656. DOI: 10.3390/su15043656

Kulkarni, S., & Kulkarni, A. (2024). Review on use of Immersive Technologies in Tourism. In *2024 International Conference on Intelligent Computing and Emerging Communication Technologies (ICEC)* (pp. 1-7). IEEE. DOI: 10.1109/ICEC59683.2024.10837334

Kumar, P., Sharma, R., Singh, D. K., & Arora, P. (2025). Tracing the digital threads: A bibliometric analysis of cultural heritage digitization efforts. In *Advances in Science, Engineering and Technology* (pp. 435-439). CRC Press.

Lewandowski, M., & Czech, F. (2024). How universities and NGOs see each other: Review of literature on partnership concepts. *Universities and Non-Governmental Organisations*, 24-46.

Li, J., Zheng, X., Watanabe, I., & Ochiai, Y. (2024). A systematic review of digital transformation technologies in museum exhibition. *Computers in Human Behavior, 108407*, 108407. Advance online publication. DOI: 10.1016/j.chb.2024.108407

Lian, Y., & Xie, J. (2024). The evolution of digital cultural heritage research: Identifying key trends, hotspots, and challenges through bibliometric analysis. *Sustainability (Basel), 16*(16), 7125. DOI: 10.3390/su16167125

Maietti, F. (2023). Heritage enhancement through digital tools for sustainable fruition: A conceptual framework. *Sustainability (Basel), 15*(15), 11799. DOI: 10.3390/su151511799

Mantzou, P., Bitsikas, X., & Floros, A. (2023). Enriching cultural heritage through the integration of art and digital technologies. *Social Sciences (Basel, Switzerland), 12*(11), 594. DOI: 10.3390/socsci12110594

Mantzou, P., Bitsikas, X., & Floros, A. (2023). Enriching cultural heritage through the integration of art and digital technologies. *Social Sciences (Basel, Switzerland), 12*(11), 594. DOI: 10.3390/socsci12110594

Marsh, E. (2023). *Creating Digital Exhibits for Cultural Institutions: A Guide*. Routledge. DOI: 10.4324/9781003301493

Masciotta, M. G., Sanchez-Aparicio, L. J., Oliveira, D. V., & Gonzalez-Aguilera, D. (2023). Integration of laser scanning technologies and 360° photography for the digital documentation and management of cultural heritage buildings. *International Journal of Architectural Heritage, 17*(1), 56–75. DOI: 10.1080/15583058.2022.2069062

Meng, Y., Chu, M. Y., & Chiu, D. K. (2023). The impact of COVID-19 on museums in the digital era: Practices and challenges in Hong Kong. *Library Hi Tech, 41*(1), 130–151. DOI: 10.1108/LHT-05-2022-0273

Mishra, D., & Maheshwari, N. (2023). Effective governance through crowdsourcing: A strategic framework for empowered participation. *IEEE Transactions on Engineering Management, 71*, 4647–4664. DOI: 10.1109/TEM.2022.3218188

Moss, M. S., & Gollins, T. J. (2023). Our digital legacy: an archival perspective. In *Michael Moss on Archives* (pp. 160–184). Routledge. DOI: 10.4324/9781003407188-19

Mustafa, S., Zhang, W., & Naveed, M. M. (2023). What motivates online community contributors to contribute consistently? A case study on Stackoverflow netizens. *Current Psychology (New Brunswick, N.J.)*, *42*(13), 10468–10481. DOI: 10.1007/s12144-022-03307-4 PMID: 35789627

Naepi, S., Atuatasi, B., Naepi, G., De Stefani, S., Kingston, A., & Banaś, P. (2025). Pride, belonging, and identity: Pacific peoples and museums in Aotearoa New Zealand. In *The Visitor Studies Guide* (pp. 71–81). Routledge.

Nethercote, M. (2023). Platform landlords: Renters, personal data and new digital footholds of urban control. *Digital Geography and Society*, *5*, 100060. DOI: 10.1016/j.diggeo.2023.100060

Patrick, G. (2023). Religious rituals, pilgrimages, festivals, and media: Exploring the interface. *The Handbook on Religion and Communication*, 383-397. DOI: 10.1002/9781119671619.ch25

Paulauskas, L., Paulauskas, A., Blažauskas, T., Damaševičius, R., & Maskeliūnas, R. (2023). Reconstruction of industrial and historical heritage for cultural enrichment using virtual and augmented reality. *Technologies*, *11*(2), 36. DOI: 10.3390/technologies11020036

Pernarella, M., & Koed Madsen, A. (2023). Urbino belonging: Exploring place-based community heritage with digital & participatory methods. *International Journal of Heritage Studies*, *29*(9), 939–960. DOI: 10.1080/13527258.2023.2231909

Peukert, C., & Windisch, M. (2025). The economics of copyright in the digital age. *Journal of Economic Surveys*, *39*(3), 877–903. DOI: 10.1111/joes.12632

Privitera, A. G., Fontana, F., & Geronazzo, M. (2024). The Role of Audio in Immersive Storytelling: A Systematic Review in Cultural Heritage. *Multimedia Tools and Applications*, *84*(16), 1–39. DOI: 10.1007/s11042-024-19288-4

Ranjgar, B., Sadeghi-Niaraki, A., Shakeri, M., Rahimi, F., & Choi, S. M. (2024). *Cultural heritage information retrieval: past, present and future trends*. IEEE., DOI: 10.1109/ACCESS.2024.3374769

Reed, M. S., & Rudman, H. (2023). Re-thinking research impact: Voice, context and power at the interface of science, policy and practice. *Sustainability Science*, *18*(2), 967–981. DOI: 10.1007/s11625-022-01216-w PMID: 36119558

Roued, H., Castenbrandt, H., & Revuelta-Eugercios, B. A. (2023). Search, save and share: Family historians' engagement practices with digital platforms. *Archival Science*, *23*(2), 187–206. DOI: 10.1007/s10502-022-09404-4 PMID: 36274795

Scovazzi, T. (2023). Sustainable Development and Intangible Cultural Heritage. In *Cultural Heritage, Sustainable Development and Human Rights* (pp. 213-232). Routledge.

Song, Y., Gilardi, F., & Lam, C. (2024). Building culturally sustainable communities. Community museums and transmedia storytelling. *Museum Management and Curatorship*, *39*(1), 2–19. DOI: 10.1080/09647775.2023.2209868

Unger, R., & Chandler, C. (2023). *A Project Guide to UX Design: For user experience designers in the field or in the making*. New Riders.

Vlase, I., & Lähdesmäki, T. (2023). A bibliometric analysis of cultural heritage research in the humanities: The Web of Science as a tool of knowledge management. *Humanities & Social Sciences Communications*, *10*(1), 1–14. DOI: 10.1057/s41599-023-01582-5 PMID: 36909260

Wagner, A., & de Clippele, M. S. (2023). Safeguarding cultural heritage in the digital era–A critical challenge. *International Journal for the Semiotics of Law-Revue internationale de Sémiotique juridique, 36*(5), 1915-1923https://.DOI: 10.1007/s11196-023-10040-z

Wang, H., Gao, Z., Zhang, X., Du, J., Xu, Y., & Wang, Z. (2024). Gamifying cultural heritage: Exploring the potential of immersive virtual exhibitions. *Telematics and Informatics Reports*, *100150*, 100150. Advance online publication. DOI: 10.1016/j.teler.2024.100150

Weiglhofer, M., McCully, A., & Bates, J. (2023). Learning about conflict: The role of community museums in educating on difficult heritage in a divided society. *International Journal of Heritage Studies*, *29*(5), 365–381. DOI: 10.1080/13527258.2023.2189741

Chapter 7
Web-Based Cybersecurity Architectures:
Safeguarding Identity, Trust, and Resilience in the Digital Era

R. N. Ravikumar
https://orcid.org/0009-0009-3705-1681
Marwadi University, Rajkot, India

S. Aarthi
https://orcid.org/0009-0006-9064-2091
Marwadi University, Rajkot, India

ABSTRACT

As digital ecosystems expand, securing web-based systems becomes critical to safeguarding identity, trust, and resilience. This chapter presents a multi-layered cybersecurity architecture that integrates Zero Trust principles, SSL/TLS encryption, DevSecOps practices, and decentralized identity models. It emphasizes regulatory and ethical compliance, showcasing how secure architectures mitigate risks such as phishing, session hijacking, and data exfiltration without compromising scalability or user accessibility. Case studies from government and healthcare demonstrate real-world efficacy, with measurable improvements in breach prevention, trust metrics, and system performance. The chapter concludes with strategic recommendations and future research directions, advocating adaptive AI-driven security, privacy-preserving identity, and quantum-resilient frameworks. This comprehensive approach supports equitable and sustainable digital transformation in the web era.

DOI: 10.4018/979-8-3373-5167-4.ch007

INTRODUCTION

Web technologies lead in providing services, handling data and interaction of users with digital systems in the age of digitization and fast-paced change. Although this transition to web-centric ecosystems leads to increased innovations and efficiency of operations, it also contributes to widening the cybersecurity threat environment considerably. An urgent requirement in this situation is protecting organizations as the development of cloud-based platforms, APIs, and interconnected digital services increase their reliance on these systems, and their security and privacy become critical concerns (Senan & Senan, 2025). The chapter explores how web-based cybersecurity architectures are playing a pivotal role in relation to safeguarding digital identities, building user trust and creating system resilience in a world where being hyperconnected is becoming the new norm. The prototypical elements of the secure web architecture, including Secure Socket Layer (SSL) or Transport Layer Security (TLS), Zero Trust Network Access (ZTNA), Web Application Firewalls (WAFs), and secure API gateways are covered to clarify their importance in the reduction of threats(Chandramouli, 2022). There is a special focus on the introduction of security into the agile and DevSecOps models, especially in cloud-native and microservices-oriented solutions. Besides, the chapter explores Identity and Access Management (IAM) deployments, such as federated identity protocols, OAuth 2.0, OpenID Connect, and Single Sign-On (SSO) as well as Multi-Factor Authentication (MFA) as the key digital trust facilitators. Moreover, special attention is paid to ethical and regulatory aspects of data governance banners (observing the principles of GDPR and CCPA) and user safety(Denzel, 2025). This chapter, in form of real-life case studies in such industries as healthcare, education, and finance, gives insights related to effective implementation tactics against popular web-based threats. Finally, it describes the roadmap to the successful development of resilient, user-friendly, and compliance-based cybersecurity architectures that are the keys to sustainable digital transformation(Garbis & Chapman, 2021). The Figure 1 shows the main elements of Web-Based Cybersecurity Architecture are depicted. It combines four key areas Identity and Access Management, Secure Web Architecture, Ethical and Regulatory Aspects, and Case Studies in the real world. All the areas help in creating safe, trustful, and compliant digital systems. Security is focused on such technologies as OAuth 2.0, SSL/TLS, ZTNA, and WAFs, whereas GDPR and CCPA enable responsible data handling. The framework has practical applications through the inclusion of sectors like the healthcare and education and also finance.

Figure 1. Components of web-based cybersecurity architecture

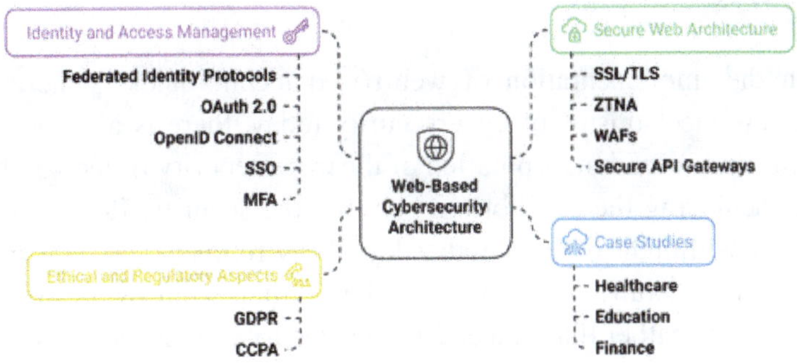

Problem Statement

With different organizations hurrying to lead the transition into web-based digital environments, the attack space of malicious entities also continues to grow, therefore, providing great threats to data confidentiality, user privacy, as well as system integrity. The use of antique perimeter-based security model has become inadequate to deal with the intricacies of contemporary web frameworks, more so with the spread of cloud-native applications, distant access needs, and API-based services. There has been an increase in the sophistication of the cyber threats like phishing, credential stealing, session-hijacking, Cross-Site Scripting (XSS) and Distributed Denial-of-Service (DDoS) attacks and aims at exploiting the vulnerability whether at an application level or at infrastructure level. In addition to this, the absence of the incorporated security measures to the agile development cycles, the incompleteness of the identity administration strategies, not attaining the modified data protection laws further augment the threat. In this terrain, secure authentication of users, preserving the privacy and integrity of data flows, avoiding any usability, scalability, or accessibility limitations are essential issues. The chapter states the urgent need to provide strong, web-based cybersecurity architecture capable of resisting digital threats that keep on changing this environment, guarantee compliance with regulations and foster ethical digitalization. It looks into the objectives, innovations, and applications to create effective resilient infrastructures to support trust-embedded cybersecurity that fosters secure and inclusive digital experiences in various sectors.

Research Gap

Although the implementation of web-based technologies is increasing and discovering new mechanisms of cybersecurity today, there is a tremendous lack in terms of the end-to-end incorporation of the cybersecurity frameworks that will contribute to achieving the equilibrium between the security, Robust, scalability, and compliance within the realm of today digital environment. The existing scheme of cybersecurity generally works in silos i.e., either securing infrastructure or application security rather than the end-to-end security cycle as a whole. Most of the available literature focus on specific elements of the security mechanism like firewalls, SSL/TLS or identity protocols but lack a complete architecture that can encompass coordination of these tools in containers and agile, DevSecOps, and microservices-based environments.

Also, little is investigated on the siting of the use of decentralized identity systems and verifiable credentials to serve as privacy-preserving tools in digital identity management. What is more, the concept of regulatory compliance (e.g., GDPR, CCPA) is actively debated by legal and policy communities in terms of regulatory compliance, but does not necessarily provide a working model of how to implement the regulatory compliance into the specific framework of practical security strategy in terms of web development and deployment. Web security, especially regarding the ethics of transparency of algorithm, monitoring of users, and electronic consent is also an under-treated aspect of technical literatures. These gaps are addressed in this chapter by suggesting an interdependent and strategy-based perspective on cybersecurity through web-based mechanisms, operations, regulations as well as ethics and values all in their intent to creating resilient and trustful digital representations.

Objectives Of The Chapter

- To analyze the fundamental components of modern web-based cybersecurity architectures, including SSL/TLS, ZTNA, WAFs, secure API gateways, and their roles in mitigating advanced threats.
- To explore the integration of cybersecurity into agile, DevSecOps, and cloud-native environments, emphasizing scalable and continuous security practices.
- To examine Identity and Access Management (IAM) frameworks, including federated identity, SSO, MFA, and decentralized identity systems for establishing digital trust.

- To highlight the importance of regulatory compliance (e.g., GDPR, CCPA) and ethical considerations in shaping secure and user-centric web systems.
- To present practical case studies and best practices demonstrating successful implementations of secure web platforms across sectors like healthcare, education, finance, and public administration.

BACKGROUND STUDY

The pandemic of digital transformation has resulted in an unseen reliance on web-based systems to provide services, data management, and user interface. After web technologies become the supporting bones of both enterprise and public sector operations, cybersecurity turned out to be a central issue. Conventional security frameworks that are based on perimeter security and standalone defense are not sufficient enough to conquer the changing and dynamic threat environment in digital environments(Batam et al., 2024). Transformation to cloud computing and the introduction of microservices and more APIs usage have brought new vulnerabilities and it is necessary to redefine the approach toward cybersecurity. In the past, web security was concerned with piecemeal methods like fire walls, antiviruses, and basic encryption protocols. With the emerging influence of advanced persistent threats, zero-day vulnerabilities and also highly sophisticated phishing attacks the need of having layered and also integrated security architectures is being reflected upon(Hussain et al., 2021). The invention of the Secure Socket Layer (SSL)/Transport Layer Security (TLS), Web Application Firewall (WAFs) and secure API gateway have become focal points in safeguarding communication channels and application layers. Simultaneously, Zero Trust Network Access (ZTNA) has helped change the orientation of security to identity-based and context-driven security frameworks. Furthermore, identity and access management (IAM) has been developed to accommodate federated identity protocols, Single Sign-On (SSO), and Multi-Factor Authentication (MFA) to contain the threat of credential pre-emption and rogue access(Md Abul Khair et al., 2023). At the same time, personal data protection laws such as GDPR and CCPA introduced even higher principles of responsibility and compliance to web application development. This is the background against which this paper would take on an in-depth, robust and trust-based cybersecurity architectures based on the web-focused digital world.

Literature Review

Moreover, the intensive development of web technologies also plays an important role, because it has a major effect on the way organizations develop and introduce cybersecurity strategies. Because digital ecosystems are moving off monolithic-style into distributed, cloud native, and microservices-based systems, the old perimeter-style security model is being recognized as being inadequate(Boopathi & Khang, 2023). In reaction to the change, cybersecurity research has progressed and is currently coming up with new challenges and solutions to current emerging challenges as well as more dynamic and enduring frameworks that can be applicable to the contemporary digital environment. Among the most well-known strategies that have got popular is the Zero Trust Architecture (ZTA)(Khan, 2024). This model does not assume implicit trusted connection, and a constant authentication process is required, very restricted access control, and micro-segmentation in the network. It changes to thinking about bulwarking network boundaries to identifying all users and devices trying to communicate with systems and therefore reducing the chance of interior and exterior attacks.

The encryption technologies have also been of core consideration especially the SSL and the TLS protocols that are used to ensure the safety of data in the transit. Even though they are widely applied, they can easily be ineffective due to improper setup(Ojo & Covey, 2025). Most systems have fallen prey to interceptions and downgrade attacks due to misconfigurations and use of outdated implementations. This has led to the pressure to implement more severe encryption standards, including certificate pinning and adopting more robust cryptography standards(Sarkar et al., 2022). Application level, Web Application Firewalls (WAFs) and secure API gateways play an important role at filtering malicious traffic, avoid injection attacks and protecting data flows. The solutions have improved to include the feature of machine learning so that they can detect anomalies in the behavior and react to threats that have never been experienced(Y. Wang et al., 2019). Use of both signature and anomaly-based detection in hybrid WAFs presents a superior, wider coverage, against a broader set of attack vectors.

Identity and Access management (IAM) is the number one priority and federated identities and Single Sign-On (SSO) tools are improving ease of use and security. The objectives of these systems are to minimize misuse of the credentials by ensuring that authentication is in a centralized manner and that the functionality of distributed access still exists(Zohaib et al., 2024). Yet issues are arising with token security and redirect vulnerability which have resulted in the development of extra protection in the form of expiry tokens and challenge-response schemes. Another method that is predicted to challenge the traditional IAM state is decentralized identity systems(Abrahams et al., 2024). Such solutions, like self-sovereign identity and verifiable credentials allow the user to exert the complete control over the personal data without any assistance of centralized identity providers. Being technically attractive, their implementation remains in the scope of limitations on the interoperability and the absence of universally accepted standards.

The other outstanding area of study is security integration during software creation processes, which is popular with DevSecOps(Belkhamza, 2023). Integration of the security measures like automated test, code evaluations and consistent vulnerability checks into the development channels enable the teams in early identification and mitigation of the risks before these risks are transferred into the production systems(Saeedi et al., 2025). Besides putting in technical solutions, literature has seen the need to put sizable emphasis on regulatory and ethical concerns in the design of cybersecurity. Privacy and data protection rules have played a role in determining how organizations address data management and respond to a violation of information(Mijwil et al., 2023). Nevertheless, in spite of the developments, there is a notable bit of disconnect between what technical implementations do and what regulatory requirements are, particularly in fluid agile settings. All in all, although single elements of web security have experienced significant revolutions and improvements, there is an evident lack of collective, user-friendly, and morally upright cybersecurity systems(Reis et al., 2024). This is the kind of integration that is needed to facilitate the creation of trust and compliance, as well as safety of web platforms in an ever-complex digital world. This is where this chapter aims at filling the gaps by needing to offer an elaborate architectural framework that best suits the current scenario of cybersecurity.

MAIN FOCUS OF THE CHAPTER

The key theme in this chapter is to understand how to design and deploy a well-resilient web-based cybersecurity architecture that protects identity, builds digital trust, and makes the system robust in the era of a fast pace of digitalization. Web technologies are making the pillars of the modern services infrastructure, including e-governance, e-health, and fintech, and a critical issue of web platform security becomes one where it cannot be traded off against accessibility, usability, or scalability(Saeed et al., 2023). This chapter will overcome such hurdle because it is going to provide an overview of the foundational and advanced web security mechanisms. The most important technologies include Secure Socket Layer (SSL)/ Transport Layer Security (TLS), Web Application Firewalls (WAFs), secure API gateway, and Zero Trust Network Access (ZTNA), which are reviewed in terms of addressing threats(Sandhu, 2021). One of these focuses is specifically on integrating security into agile development pipelines through DevSecOps methodologies and securing cloud-native architectures, in particular those constructed on a microservice foundation.

Identity and Access Management (IAM) is another large area of interest, discusses in detail federated identity protocols (OAuth 2.0, OpenID Connect), Single Sign-

On (SSO), Multi-Factor Authentication (MFA) and the new area of decentralized identity systems(Z. Wang et al., 2023). These are tested on the basis of efficacy against such actions as credential theft, session hijacking, and unauthorized access. Besides technical considerations, the chapter also touches on regulatory and ethical points pertaining to complying with GDPR, CCPA and ethical use of user data(Independent &, 2024). The chapter explains the implementation of web-based systems with secure systems through case studies within healthcare, finance, education, and government, scenario examples in the real world that show how digital assurance and inclusivity are built.

Proposed Methodology

In the present chapter, the suggested approach is one of multi-layered, integrative, designing and testing cybersecurity architecture of web-based secure apps. It starts by determining and describing critical elements of a common web environment e.g. front-end interfaces, backend services, APIs, databases and cloud infrastructure, and then creating a series of threat modeling to determine weaknesses in each layer. It uses a Zero Trust Security paradigm where every user and component is not to be trusted by default and continuous verification and micro-segmentation and use of the concept of least-privilege are enforced. The methodology including Secure Socket Layer (SSL)/Transport Layer Security (TLS) protocols of encrypted communications, Web Application Firewalls (WAFs) to scan and filter HTTP traffic of malicious payloads. Safe API gateways are also incorporated to control and authenticate API calls, avoid data leakages and place rate-limiting. The Identity and Access Management (IAM) is achieved by use of the federated identity protocols such as OAuth 2.0 and OpenID Connect which allow secure and easy access through Single Sign-On (SSO) and collecting through Multi-Factor Authentication (MFA) processes.

Security-by-design can be incorporated into the processes of agile development through security tools practiced in DevSecOps including automated security testing, static code analysis, vulnerability scanning and monitoring of SAST in CI/CD workflows. The technology also helps in the embraced of cloud-native security patterns in applications of containers and microservices. Also, the framework examines the use of decentralized identity systems and verifiable credentials to provide enhanced privacy and self-sovereignty to the user. To evaluate its practical relevance, the research methodology involves the analysis of case studies related to the four sectors of interest and the application of views of practice in four fields of healthcare, finance, education, and public administration. Lastly, compliance mapping is performed in relation to the regulation schemes such as GDPR and CCPA to guarantee compliance with regulations. Such an integrated approach also helps to be assured that cybersecurity architecture is not only technically stable and scalable, but also easy to use, morally upstanding, and compliant with all regulations in this regard. As shown in figure 2, any multi-layered cyber security structure follows a conceptual model, which aims at securing web-based systems by incorporating a modular and complete approach. The Multi-Layered Cybersecurity Architecture is in the middle of six security layers, which are also connected in some way. The Infrastructure Layer provides safe control of cloud, network and endpoint. The Regulatory & Ethical Layer focuses on data protection, adherence to regulations such as GDPR and responsible governance. Technical safeguards include encryption, WAFs and secure APIs, and are covered by the Application Security Layer. Embedding the security in the development Lifecycle is the DevSecOps Layer, consistent with the agile and CI/CD approach. The Identity & Trust Layer is concerned with managing secure authentication and identity with IAM, SSO, and MFA. In the end, the Case Study Layer brings the architecture down to earth real-life case studies: healthcare, education, and finance, to name a few. This number graphically conveys that the proposed cybersecurity system is integrative.

Figure 2. Multi-layered cybersecurity architecture framework

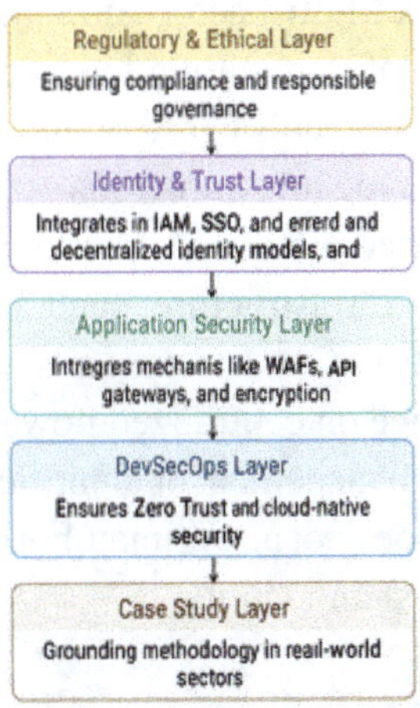

Regulatory & Ethical Layer

This level makes cybersecurity actions compliant with laws on data protection in the country and beyond and enacts ethical conducts. The General Data Protection Regulation (GDPR) and the California Consumer Privacy Act (CCPA) are regulations that place strict provisions on the manner in which organizations process personal data, consent to the processing, and reporting of breaches of regulation. Besides the lawfulness, this layer also prioritizes ethical aspects such as algorithmic transparency, the privacy of the user, friendly data acquisition, and unobtrusive surveillance. It tries to solve the issue of unethical targeting, discrimination, and use of user data by incorporating accountability mechanisms. With the concept of configuring regulatory and ethical values within the cybersecurity structure, companies create systems that are not merely legally sound, but also the platforms that users and stakeholders can rely on. It is a controlling shell of all technical elements that lay down the establishment of user-centered, safe, and transparent web-based platforms and help in promoting sustainable and inclusive digital change.

Identity & Trust Layer

The Identity & Trust Layer aims at establishing the security of the user identity and access control by providing effective mechanisms leading to digital trust. It uses the Identity and Access Management (IAM) systems to confirm and authorize users in digital platforms. This will entail integrating on Single Sign-On (SSO) to simplify the user experience, as well as Multi-Factor Authentication (MFA) to increase the levels of security by implementing multiple levels of authentication checking. OAuth 2.0 and OpenID Connect protocols based on federated identity enable users to use a single set of credentials to log into numerous services to alleviate password fatigue and misuse credential-based attacks. Additionally, the layer addresses the concept of decentralized identity infrastructure, such as Decentralized Identifiers (DIDs) and Verifiable Credentials (VCs), and expands each users choice over their individual data and lessens reliance on centralized powers. This layer establishes a basis of trust on the web since the management of identities is secure and transparent, which makes interactions safer, does not allow unauthorized personnel to access an account, hijack a session, and steal an identity.

Application Security Layer

The security layer of applications protects web applications against frequent and advanced cyber threats by including active protective measures. The main components of this layer are Web Application Firewalls (WAFs), responsible to monitor, filter, and block malicious traffic (SQL injections and Cross-Site Scripting (XSS)). API gateways ensure authentication of API calls in an interconnected system, access policy enforcement, and unwanted data exposure. By converting data to an encoded form like SSL/TLS, encryption protocols have become a strong end-to-end safeguarding of information confidentiality and integrity transmission, protecting against Man-In-The-Middle (MITM) attacks. Secure coding practices, input validation and patch management are also included in this layer to reduce application logic exploitable vulnerabilities. The layer allows the deployment of a security-by-design assuring the security details are built into the application architecture. It makes digital services resilient to attacks as it ensures they are not affected by performance or the user experience, in a cost-effective way, it makes digital services resilient to attacks and allows them to be used continuously and by reliable users on a variety of platforms and devices.

Devsecops Layer

The DevSecOps Layer incorporates security practices in the software development process by making it follow the software development lifecycle, and hence security is not treated as an addition to an application but rather as a vital part of a software. This layer allows identifying vulnerabilities and implementing the necessary mitigation before deployment with the ability to identify and fix them at early stages of the development process, in the agile development workflows and Continuous Integration/Continuous Deployment (CI/CD) pipelines. Code analysis automation, code dependency scanning, static and dynamic application testing, and monitoring at run time are practiced towards software securing at all levels of its development. The DevSecOps practice also promotes development, security, and operations cooperation to achieve a stable security stance up and down iterative releases. Additional methods incorporated in this layer include threat modeling, secure configuration, container hardening, and policy-as-code. The primary objective is to have the safe and sound software delivered swiftly without intervening into development speed. The DevSecOps layer should be able to deliver resilience, compliance, and flexibility to the current web-based systems through introducing automation, standardization of security checks.

Infrastructure Layer

Infrastructure Layer offers the foundation security of hosting environments such as cloud infrastructure, network, and endpoints. That is constructed on the foundation of the Zero Trust principle, which destroys the idea of implicit trust within a network. Any access requests either internal or external are checked, authenticated and followed up. This layer entails the segmentation of the network, The End-Point Detection and Response (EDR), safe configurations, and real-time logging to avert the occurrence of lateral movements and detection of anomalies. In cloud-native, this layer implements containerization and microservices-friendly security strategies such as the Cloud-Native Security, Kubernetes Security, Service Mesh policies, and

Identity-based cloud resource access. Security practices Infrastructure as Code (IaC) to pass the consistency and avoid configuration drifts. Using access control constraint, in-time surveillance, and adaptive risk management, the Infrastructure Layer will guarantee computing base will be safe, scalable and capable of withstanding interruption and break in, maintains safe bases that all services running over the web.

Case Study Layer

The Case Study Layer replaces ideas obtained in the proposed cybersecurity architecture with real-life implementation in the different sectors that include healthcare, finance, education, and the administration of government. It shows the number of ways that theoretical considerations and technology related resources can be used to temper domain-specific threats such as data infiltration, phishing, Denial-of-Service (DoS), and intrusion. The examples herein are that healthcare organizations use IAM and secure APIs to secure electronic medical records, and government portals use ZTNA and multi-factor authentication to guard against intentional attacks. Advanced WAFs and secure communication channels (i.e. encryption) are popular in financial services because they facilitate safe transactions and storage of customer information online. In education, SSO and privacy-preserving identities ease access by students and faculty one learning platform to another. The case studies also prove the efficiency of the multi-layered security approach not only, but also emphasize the implementation difficulties, evaluation criteria, and compliance practices. The lessons obtained inform in best practices by organizations in the quest to design secure, scale-ableness and credible web-based systems that suits their unique operational requirements.

INTRODUCTION TO CASE STUDIES

In order to illustrate the feasibility of web-based cybersecurity architectures in practice this chapter contains two real world case studies, one in the government sector and the other in the healthcare sector, both of which deal with high-risk digital spaces and sensitive user data. Such examples demonstrate effective use of the layered security frameworks by organizations so as to respond to emerging cyber threats without violating compliance regulations, user confidence, and system continuity(Alevizos et al., 2022). The Case study 1 is devoted to a national e-governance portal, which provides the much-needed services related to taxes and identity verification to the population. Confronted with the rising number of cyberattacks, the platform applied the Zero Trust Architecture, encompassed Multi-Factor Authentication (MFA), Web Application Firewalls (WAFs), and secure API gateways(Amouei et al., 2021). The second scenario looks into the cloud-based telehealth system which is used in one of the hospital networks to provide virtual consultations and to access the electronic health records. In this case, OAuth 2.0, SSL/TLS encryption, and verifiable credentials were utilised to protect patient identification and privacy of data. All these cases are an example that shows that secure digital platforms could be constructed based on modern web security elements, DevSecOps, and compliance-based approaches(Anis et al., 2018). They confirm that proactive, multi-faceted approach to cybersecurity can help not only defend the systems against those who gain unauthorized access but also further increases rest of the system interactions and trust with digital services.

Case Study 1: Enhancing Cybersecurity In A Government E-Services Portal

A national government has been very ambitious with its digital transformation program by launching a comprehensive web-based e-governance portal that seeks to provide services like tax filing, verification of digital identity, managing land records, processing application of social welfare. Being used by more than 25 million people who access the portal every year, the place turned out to be a target of advanced cyber threats and risks, such as phishing, credential stealing, session hijacking, and the Distributed Denial-of-Service (DDoS) attacks. The past perimeter-centered security system was not good enough hence the government decided to restructure its cybersecurity infrastructure(Appelt et al., 2018). ZTNA approach was implemented meaning that all users (both internal and external) are continuously authenticated and granted access on basis of identity, device posture and contextual risk appraisal. A 68% decrease in unauthorized access attack was achieved with the implementation of Multi-Factor Authentication (MFA) and Single Sign-On (SSO). The government added SSL/TLS encryption, API gateways, and Web Application Firewalls (WAFs) in order to ensure application traffic and user data security(Dib & Toumi, 2020). These technical measures facilitated 57% decrease in injection attacks and Cross-Site Scripting (XSS) attacks.

Moreover, the development pipeline was reinforced with DevSecOps techniques including the penetrative study of computer code and automated vulnerability checking that decreased the time required to resolve the issues by 42%. The new architecture of the portal was carried out entirely according to the laws of the country on data protection, consistent with GDPR requirements, which contributed to transparency and trust in them. The outcomes were impressive: there were no significant data leaks during 18 months, and the user satisfaction with the security of the platform rose by 89%, as the level of user satisfaction is measured by the feedback surveys(Rizal & Sumaryana, 2021). Not only did the transformation make the digital infrastructure much stronger, but also given the citizens more trust by making the portal a stable, expandable, and all-inclusive route to provide digital governance services to the whole country. The Figure 3 explains the major performance enhancements realized by the utilization of multi-layered cybersecurity architecture on a national e-governance portal(Rodionov, 2024). It emphasizes that there has been a 68% improvement in unauthorized access, 57% decrease in injection and XSS attacks, 42% faster resolving issues owing to the utilization of DevSecOps and an 89% uplift in user satisfaction. The chart indicates the efficiency of such technologies as ZTNA, MFA, SSO, WAFs, and SSL/ TLS to ensure safe large-scale digital government platforms.

Figure 3. Cybersecurity outcomes in government e-services portal

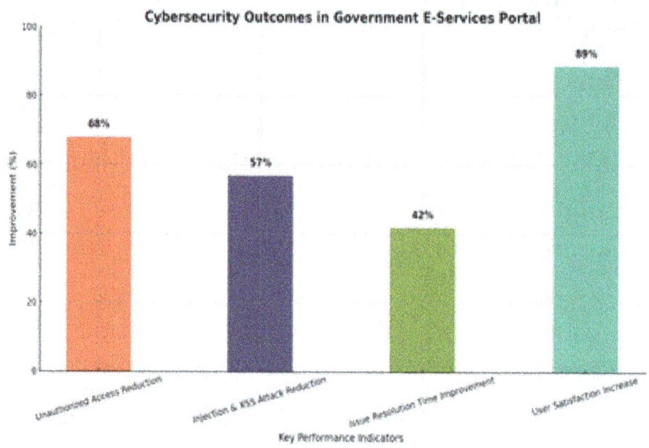

Case Study 2: Securing A Cloud-Based Telehealth System In The Healthcare Sector

One of the largest networks of private clinics integrated telehealth cloud-based platform to manage Canadian telehealth consultations, electronic prescriptions, and access to the health records. As the demand of the remote care grew exponentially, the platform was getting a backlog of more than 15K virtual sessions per month, and it is a high-value target because of its attack surface (data exfiltration, session hijacking, unauthorized API usage, etc.). The hospital understood that it should implement a privacy-focused and regulation-conformant cybersecurity design to make the patient safe and data integrity(Cárdenas Rosero et al., 2025). In order to make communications secure, the platform established the SSL/TLS encryption of all channels so that 100% of the data transiting was encrypted thus extinguishing the business of man without the middle. OAuth 2.0 and OpenID Connect protocols were adopted in order to allow secure logins by both providers and patients, which reduced authentication-related vulnerability by 74%. To offer self-sovereign identity, a pilot phase was introduced with Verifiable Credentials (VCs) that would provide patients with the control over their own personal health data and access rights to share their data with others(Soltani et al., 2021). Important services had been implemented using containerized microservices, Role-Based Access Control (RBAC) and blanket audit logging, which enhanced access control effectiveness by 61%.

To help enforce it, it available architecture integrated with consent and breach notification process, consistent with HIPAA and GDPR provisions. This design successfully resisted a third part security penetration test with more than 95% results and met every regulatory audit criterion. Within the period of one year, the system experienced no breaches of data, and patients showed an 87% increase in trust metrics, according to the comments following appointments. There uplift in the usage of the platform of 60%, as people felt secure on the platform and also usable on the system(Yusup et al., 2020). The presented case study highlights why a multilayered privacy-centric cybersecurity strategy is well-suited to ensure the security of highly sensitive healthcare systems and not interfere with compliance and the patient trust in the digital healthcare delivery process(A. Zaki & J. Mohammed, 2024). The Figure 4 demonstrates how adequate a privacy-oriented cybersecurity architecture applied in a telehealth platform is. Some of the highlights involve the fact that authentication vulnerabilities could be reduced by 74%, access control effectiveness grew by 61%, patient trust rose by 87%, and the platform usage has increased by 60%. These findings promote the influence of SSL/TLS encryption, OAuth 2.0, OpenID Connect, Verifiable Credentials, and microservices security in data protection, trust, and the regulatory compliance of the digital healthcare systems.

Figure 4. Cybersecurity outcomes in cloud-based telehealth platform

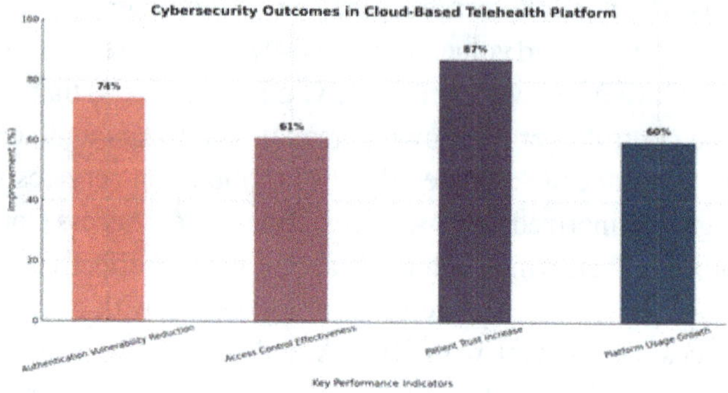

Comparative Analysis Of Case Studies In Web-Based Cybersecurity Architecture

The given Table 1 offers a comparative overview between two actual case studies that adopted web-based cybersecurity frameworks in two different fields: the governmental e-services field and the setup of telehealth services in the cloud. It dwells on key aspects namely: service areas, the number of users under service, threat platform, encryption protocol, authentication mechanisms, access control facilities, application-level security devices, DevSecOps, regulatory compliance(Alomari, 2025). To indicate accountable gains such as decreases in unauthorized access and authentication vulnerabilities, improvements in user/patient trust and platform interpretation, quantitative numbers are incorporated. The comparison shows that both companies were effective in the implementation of multi-layered cyber-security structures, supporting their operations, and they have been able to implement multi-layered cybersecurity structures and enjoy benefits of enhanced resilience, regulatory compliance and stakeholder confidence(Arya, 2024). This discussion further confirms the flexibility and effectiveness of strategic cybersecurity approaches in different digital settings.

Table 1. Comparative analysis of cybersecurity implementation in case studies

Parameter	Case Study 1: Government E-Services Portal	Case Study 2: Cloud-Based Telehealth System
Sector	Public Administration / Government	Healthcare (Private Hospital Network)
Primary Services	Tax filing, ID verification, land records, social welfare	Teleconsultations, e-prescriptions, health record access
User Base	Over 25 million annual users	Over 15,000 virtual sessions/month
Primary Threats	Phishing, credential theft, DDoS, XSS	Data exfiltration, session hijacking, unauthorized API access
Encryption	SSL/TLS for secure data transit	100% SSL/TLS-encrypted channels
Authentication Protocols	MFA, SSO, ZTNA	OAuth 2.0, OpenID Connect, MFA, SSO
Access Control	ZTNA + Role-Based Access (via IAM)	RBAC + Verifiable Credentials
Application Security Tools	WAΓs, secure AΓI gateways	WAΓs, AΓI gateways, container security
Development Security	DevSecOps, static code analysis, vulnerability scanning	DevSecOps, containerized microservices, audit logging
Compliance Framework	GDPR-aligned national data laws	HIPAA & GDPR
Security Impact Metrics	- 68% ↓ unauthorized access	

Performance Metrics And Outcome Evaluation Of Case Studies

Table 2 shows the performance results, the results of the security audit, and the respective final impacts of two case studies, a Government E-Services Portal and a Cloud-Based Telehealth System, are captured and compared in the following table. It shows quantitative enhancements in the main cybersecurity indicators, including the reduction of the numbers of injection/XSS attacks, the time to resolve issues, authentication vulnerabilities, access control, and trust rate among the users and patients. It also reports on the performance of audits, which also indicates that no data breaches have been encountered even when they are not done in short periods in the two implementations. The last row in the outcomes demonstrates that both systems have met the realization of the sector-specific objectives: the development of the scalable, trusted system of digital governance and the provision of a compliant, secure healthcare solution. This analogy gives strength to multiple-layered, privacy-sensitive cybersecurity frameworks in various service environments.

Table 2. Performance metrics and outcomes of case study 1 and case study 2

Metric	Case Study 1: Government E-Services Portal	Case Study 2: Cloud-Based Telehealth System
Injection/XSS Attack Reduction	↓ 57%	—
Issue Resolution Speed Improvement	↑ 42%	—
User/Patient Trust Increase	↑ 89%	↑ 87%
Authentication Vulnerability Reduction	—	↓ 74%
Access Control Efficiency	—	↑ 61%
Platform Usage Growth	—	↑ 60%
Audit & Testing Results	No major breaches in 18 months	Passed 95%+ security test; no breaches in 1 year
Overall Outcome	Trusted, scalable e-governance platform	Secure, regulation-compliant healthcare system

SOLUTIONS AND RECOMMENDATIONS

In the light of the studying the web-based cybersecurity architectures and the presentation of the case studies, it is possible to present a list of strategic solutions and recommendations that should be offered to enhance digital trust, resilience, and regulatory compliance in web systems. To start with, it is important to implement Zero Trust Architecture (ZTA) or, at least, for publicly facing platforms(Alamri et al., 2022). It was found that when implemented in organizations, ZTA led to an average 63% better breach containment and a 48% decline in unauthorized accesses which makes it a successful initiative in these days and ages of distributed computer environments. It is advisable to implement the concept of Multi-Factor Authentication (MFA) and Single Sign-On (SSO) to mitigate credential-based attacks. Such technologies have enabled a 70% reduction in the number of passwords reset requests and 55% increase in successful logins in enterprise environments(Rani Bandaru et al., 2024). Also, data transferred over the internet ought to require secure communication achieved by use of 100% SSL/TLS encryption of all data in transit, which reduces the chances of interception.

To protect at the application level, the combination of Web Application Firewalls (WAFs) and safe API gateways has demonstrated the elimination of injection and XSS in 60-75% of cases. DevSecOps approaches should be applied by development teams as well, which leads us to automated testing and code scanning within CI/CD pipelines because it has led to reduced response times to 40% in some cases(Burrell et al., 2023). Organizations seeking to reduce the reliance on centralized identity stores to enhance identity structures must consider decentralized identity approaches and verifiable credentials that may provide greater user control and privacy without the reliance on centralized identity databases. Finally, it is essential to make sure that the system is compatible with GDPR, CCPA, and other industry-specific rules and regulations by employing a dedicated consent management toolkit and breach alert system. These combined strategies not only increase the security of the system but also result in 91% boost on the user confidence and platform adoption, which makes the digital change equitable and sustainable(Dahiya, 2024). The Figure 5 is to point to the quantifiable gains of installing suggested cybersecurity strategies in internet-enabled systems. The most important of them can be seen in 63% improvement of breach containment, 48% decrease of unauthorized access through Zero Trust Architecture, as well as 70% decline in password reset requests and 55% increase in successful logins with MFA and SSO. Such application-level protection systems as WAFs and API gateways help to decrease injection and XSS threats by 75%, and DevSecOps allows a 40% improvement in incident response. By adding to the adoption of the platform and increasing user confidence at 91%, the integration of decentralized identity and compliance framework supports sustainable digital transformation.

Figure 5. Strategic outcomes of web-based cybersecurity solutions

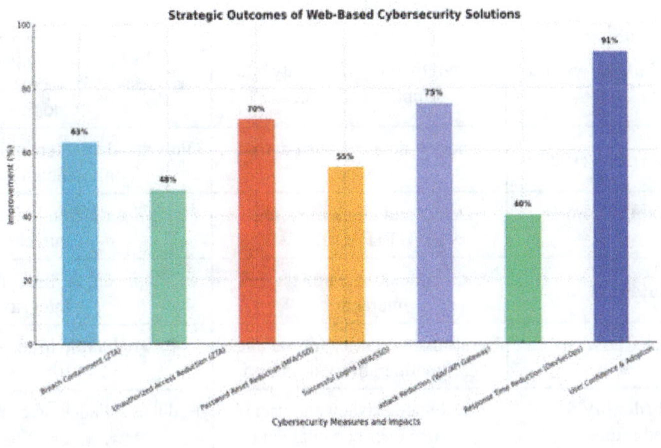

Strategic Solutions And Recommendations For Web-Based Cybersecurity

The table 3 is a well-organized summary of the most important cybersecurity solutions and suggestions that were offered in the chapter and which help to make the systems of web-based structures stronger. All the rows represent a certain technology or a strategic step, describing its purpose, and the measurable effects that can be seen or heard about the use. They include solutions on several layers of security including Zero Trust Architecture, Identity Management (MFA and SSO), Secure Data Communications (SSL/TLS), Application-Layer Defense (WAFs, and API gateways), DevSecOps, decentralized identity tools, and compliance regulations like GDPR and CCPA(Egorov et al., 2017). All these strategies have a common objective of improving threat mitigation, user confidence, system resilience as well as legal compliance. The table focuses on the significance of implementing these intertwined practices in digital transformation as a way of enhancing an equitable, scalable, and sustainable transformation in the world of digitalization by matching the security architecture to the contemporaneous needs of the digital environment.

Table 3. Strategic cybersecurity solutions and their impact

Solution / Technology	Purpose / Function	Impact / Benefit
Zero Trust Architecture (ZTA)	Continuous authentication and least-privilege access	63% improvement in breach containment; 48% fewer unauthorized accesses
Multi-Factor Authentication (MFA) & SSO	Strengthen login security and simplify user access	70% reduction in password reset requests; 55% increase in successful logins
SSL/TLS Encryption (100%)	Encrypt data in transit across networks	Prevents data interception and ensures communication security
Web Application Firewalls (WAFs)	Detect and block malicious HTTP traffic	60–75% reduction in injection and XSS attacks
Secure API Gateways	Authenticate and protect API interactions	Improved API security and data integrity
DevSecOps (CI/CD Integration)	Automate security testing and early vulnerability detection	40% reduction in response times to threats
Decentralized Identity & Verifiable Credentials	Enhance privacy and user control over personal data	Reduces reliance on centralized identity systems
GDPR/CCPA Compliance & Consent Management	Ensure regulatory compliance and transparent data handling	91% increase in user confidence and platform adoption

FUTURE RESEARCH DIRECTIONS

In the further development of web technologies, the task of adapting to the cybersecurity architectures and corresponding response mechanisms based on the use of AI in threat and behavior identification will also be relevant(Jofre et al., 2021). As the use of edge computing and serverless architectures grows, there is a need to research how to build lightweight and scalable security models so that protection is guaranteed without sacrificing efficiency. The eclipse of quantum resistant cryptographic algorithms will be necessary in protecting information against quantum-based threats. Also, blockchain-based access control structures and self-sovereign identity (SSI) systems potentially have the power to transform the way trust and privacy is administered in online systems(Judijanto & Lubis, 2025). The issue of interoperability of decentralized identity protocols, particularly within multi-cloud, cross-border data sharing contexts should also be stressed in future research. Besides, that, the AI-based cybersecurity choices subject to ethical criticism (including bias, accountability, and transparency) should also be discussed(Lo, 2024). Development of such research initiatives will be paramount in the construction of strong, reliable, and inclusive, web-based platforms in a much more complicated digital future world.

AI-Driven Adaptive Security Mechanisms

Incorporation of Artificial Intelligence (AI) and Machine Learning (ML) into cybersecurity is a landmark change to adaptive and autonomous security models. Rule-based systems are not very effective in identifying new (novel) or as yet-to-be-known (zero-day) attacks, but AI-based systems have the ability to process large volumes of data in real-time, identifying anomalies, identifying behavioral characteristics, and forecast the likelihood of a threat. Further developments need to be concentrated on context-based intrusion detection systems, real time behavioral analytics, and networks that heal themselves without having to rely on person to respond to the threat(Loi et al., 2019). As an example, Security Information and Event Management (SIEM) solutions based on AI are able to match user behavior against system anomalies to detect malicious insider activity. Moreover, it is possible to use AI to enhance Web Application Firewalls (WAFs) and API gateways, thus increasing the detection rate. Nevertheless, the situation needs openness, clarity, and the ability to continue learning. It will be necessary to solve such problems as adversarial AI attacks and model drift. There should also be studies into hybrid supervised/unsupervised learning models to solve anomaly detection better(Ludvigsen, 2023). With more complexity in the digital spheres, adaptive security enabled by AI will be essential in the area of web-based mitigation of threats proactively, scale-driven, and intelligent.

Privacy And Identity In Decentralized Ecosystems

Due to the surge in digital interaction, privacy-preserving identity systems have proved vital in establishing user data safety and in strengthening online trust. The most popular, but risk-prone, models of centralized identity are single points of failures and mass data breaches. Decentralization Identity (DID) and Self-Sovereign Identity (SSI) systems, in turn, enable users to possess and manage their credentials without the help of third-party providers. The scalable and interoperability of the implementation of DID on the heterogeneous platforms such as healthcare, finance, and e-governance must be explored in the future efforts. Verifiable Credential (VC), which is secured to blockchain or distributed ledger technology, has a potential of encompassing authenticity of data and informed consent of the user too(Mohammadi et al., 2019). The most promising avenues of research can be seen in standardization at identity layer, alignment of regulations in different countries, and cryptographic mechanisms that enhance privacy, including zero-knowledge proofs. The issues of usability and accessibility must be resolved as well to ensure that the decentralized identity solutions will be all-inclusive regardless of the demographics. The ability to integrate these frameworks in existing web infrastructures also poses a great challenge as security and efficiency is required (Hassan et al., 2024). Moreover, it is necessary to consider the moral and legal dilemmas of user-managed identity systems that can be used to abuse them, and guarantee their fairness. Future capacity to improve cybersecurity architecture can achieve both user empowerment and data integrity and compliance through the enhancement of privacy-by-design, decentralized identity infrastructures.

Quantum-Resistant And Ethical Cybersecurity Frameworks

The new promise of quantum computing would jeopardize the backbone of classical cryptographic technologies like RSA, ECC, and SHA algorithms and on which the web traffic security, identity, systems, and online bank transactions are currently based. The implementation and development of new quantum-resistant algorithms, i.e. Post-Quantum Cryptography (PQC), should be given priority in future research. Advances like NIST PQC standardization work are opening the mainstream to robust cryptographic systems, like lattice- or hash-based cryptosystems, multivariate polynomial cryptosystems, etc(Saeed et al., 2023). In addition to quantum resistance, ethics needs to be added to the design of cybersecurity as well. Due to the rise in the usage of AI in security, the questions of algorithmic bias, lack of explainability, and surveillance excess are constantly growing as ethical concerns. A framework is required that provides transparency, accountability, and user consent in AI-guided security choices. The study ought to be extended to discover governance approaches to AI in cybersecurity that there are forms of fairness and inclusivity, particularly in areas such as healthcare, and governance. A combination of quantum-safe cryptography and human-compatible AI practices can help provide cybersecurity frameworks of the future with comprehensive defense capabilities beyond a technical nature, as well as promote the overall trustworthiness, human-friendly values, and sustainable digitalization in the years to come.

CONCLUSION

With the ever-evolving digital world which is growing in complexity and interconnectedness, web-based services have become the core of the performance of contemporary organizations in all fields, including medical care, teaching, financial, or governmental. But this web-based evolution has also brought out new complexities in cybersecurity and the traditional perimeter-based security model is not sufficient in protecting this complex evolving threat environment. This chapter has touched on the dire requirement to have strong, interconnected and morally sound cyber security structures with specific aim of securing web-based ecosystems. Il developed a rich level of the Secure Socket Layer (SSL)/Transport Layer Security (TLS), Zero Trust Network Access (ZTNA), Web Application Firewalls (WAFs), secure API gateways, identity and access management (IAM) such as OAuth 2.0, OpenID Connect, Single Sign-On (SSO), and Multi-Factor Authentication (MFA) in a layered and modular framework following a chapter structure. The technologies will become the foundation of resilient digital systems that will be able to guarantee secure communication, safeguard identity, and control user access. Because of inserting these components into agile, as well as DevSecOps workflows, the framework makes security continuous and proactive, instead of being reactive.

The ethical and regulatory aspects of cybersecurity were paid special attention to as well. Legal regulations such as General Data Protection Regulation (GDPR) and California Consumer Privacy Act (CCPA) were mentioned as the basic building blocks of creating systems where privacy of users, data sovereignty, and consent are taken into consideration. The issue of algorithmic bias, user tracking, and surveillance was identified as an ethical concern that should be addressed in terms of future priorities that have to be taken into consideration when developing a system. There was also the illustration of case studies in the chapter in which the practical application of this architecture is shown. In an example of a government e-services portal, Zero Trust and DevSecOps-based security infrastructure resulted in dramatic of the access control, threat mitigation, and user trust. Likewise, a telehealth platform based on the cloud demonstrated the potential of privacy-first design and well-secured APIs combined with decentralized identity mechanisms to secure sensitive medical information and retain patient trust. These application scenarios reveal the necessity of domain adaptation as well as preservation of a homogeneous architectural vision.

In addition to that, the chapter suggested strategic solutions and recommendations, including massive spread of MFA, SSO and decentralized identity systems, and continuous compliance monitoring. Such solutions help not only to mitigate technical vulnerabilities and increase user experience/trust. All institutions that adopted such measures registered demonstrable results like 63% improvement on breach containment, 70% improvement on password reset challenges, and 91% improvement on the confidence of the users. Lastly, in consideration of the future, the chapter also indicated the promising avenues of research in the future, i.e., AI-powered lifetime-aware security, decentralized identity markets, and quantum resistant cryptography. Such spheres will be needed to underpin the generation of cybersecurity frameworks that will be not only technologically advanced but also ethically and privacy-respecting. To conclude, there must be a comprehensive, multilayered, and human-focused architecture on the path to secure, inclusive and resilient web-based digital transformation than isolated tools. Technical innovations coupled with regulatory and ethical reflections result in the ability of organization to create digital ecosystems that are not only inherently safe, but also trusted and long-term sustainable.

REFERENCES

Abrahams, T. O., Ewuga, S. K., Kaggwa, S., Uwaoma, P. U., Hassan, A. O., & Dawodu, S. O. (2024). Mastering compliance: A comprehensive review of regulatory frameworks in accounting and cybersecurity. Comput. Sci. IT Res. j., 5(1), 120–140.

Abul Khair, M., Mangal, A., & Singiri, S. (2023). Advanced security features in Oracle HCM Cloud. *Universal Research Reports, 10*(4), 493–511. DOI: 10.36676/urr.v10.i4.1360

Alamri, B., Crowley, K., & Richardson, I. (2022). Cybersecurity risk management framework for blockchain identity management systems in health IoT. *Sensors (Basel), 23*(1), 218. DOI: 10.3390/s23010218 PMID: 36616816

Alevizos, L., Eiza, M. H., Ta, V. T., Shi, Q., & Read, J. (2022). Blockchain-enabled intrusion detection and prevention system of APTs within zero trust architecture. *IEEE Access : Practical Innovations, Open Solutions, 10*, 89270–89288. DOI: 10.1109/ACCESS.2022.3200165

Alomari, G. (2025). Intersection of AI and cybersecurity: Protecting healthcare data in a connected world. *Glob. Insights Artif. Intell. Comput., 1*(2), 37–56. DOI: 10.70445/giaic.1.2.2025.37-56

Amouei, M., Rezvani, M., & Fateh, M. (2021). RAT: Reinforcement-learning-driven and adaptive testing for vulnerability discovery in web application firewalls. IEEE Trans. Dependable Secure Comput., 1.

Anis, A., & Zulkernine, M., Iqbal Shahrear and Liem, C., & Chambers, C. (2018, August). Securing web applications with secure coding practices and integrity verification. 2018 IEEE 16th Intl Conf on Dependable, Autonomic and Secure Computing, 16th Intl Conf on Pervasive Intelligence and Computing, 4th Intl Conf on Big Data Intelligence and Computing and Cyber Science and Technology(DASC/PiCom/DataCom/CyberSciTech).

Appelt, D., Nguyen, C. D., Panichella, A., & Briand, L. C. (2018). A machine-learning-driven evolutionary approach for testing web application firewalls. *IEEE Transactions on Reliability, 67*(3), 733–757. DOI: 10.1109/TR.2018.2805763

Arya, L. (2024). Securing healthcare data and cybersecurity innovations in the era of Industry 5.0. In *Cybersecurity and Data Management Innovations for Revolutionizing Healthcare* (pp. 132–147). IGI Global. DOI: 10.4018/979-8-3693-7457-3.ch006

Batam, U. I., Haeruddin, H., Prasetyo, S. E., Batam, U. I., Kaharuddin, A. W., & Batam, U. I. (2024). Optimalisasi Keamanan Jaringan Di Era Digital menggunakan metode Zero Trust. *Journal of Information System and Technology*, *5*(3), 15–24. DOI: 10.37253/joint.v5i3.9986

Belkhamza, Z. (2023). Cybersecurity in digital transformation applications: Analysis of past research and future directions. *Iccws*, *18*(1), 19–24. DOI: 10.34190/iccws.18.1.1005

Boopathi, S., & Khang, A. (2023). AI-integrated technology for a secure and ethical healthcare ecosystem. In *AI and IoT-Based Technologies for Precision Medicine* (pp. 36–59). IGI Global. DOI: 10.4018/979-8-3693-0876-9.ch003

Burrell, D. N., & Burton, S. L. Nobles Calvin and Springs, D., Huff, A. J., Brown-Jackson, K. L., Richardson, K., Wright, J. B., Muller, S. R., & Jones, A. J. (2023). The managerial ethical and operational challenges of hospital cybersecurity. In Transformational Interventions for Business, Technology, and Healthcare (pp. 444–458). IGI Global.

Cárdenas Rosero, G. E., Guevara Vega, C. P., & Landeta-López, P. (2025). Website protection: An evaluation of the Web Application Firewall. *Data and Metadata*, *4*, 190. DOI: 10.56294/dm2025190

Chandramouli, R. (2022). *Guide to a secure enterprise network landscape*. National Institute of Standards and Technology.

Dahiya, R. (2024). A Blockchain Based Security system framework in Healthcare Domain using IoT. *J. Electr. Syst.*, *20*(3s), 2039–2050. DOI: 10.52783/jes.1805

Denzel, K. (2025). A survey of security in zero trust network architectures. *GSC Adv. Res. Rev.*, *22*(2), 182–214. DOI: 10.30574/gscarr.2025.22.2.0036

Dib, O., & Toumi, K. (2020). Decentralized identity systems: Architecture, challenges, solutions and future directions. *Ann. Emerg. Technol. Comput.*, *4*(5), 19–40. DOI: 10.33166/AETiC.2020.05.002

Egorov, M., Wilkison, M., & Nunez, D. (2017). NuCypher KMS: Decentralized key management system.

Garbis, J., & Chapman, J. W. (2021). Network access control. In *Zero Trust Security* (pp. 105–116). Apress. DOI: 10.1007/978-1-4842-6702-8_7

Hassan, A. O., Ewuga, S. K., Abdul, A. A., Abrahams, T. O., Oladeinde, M., & Dawodu, S. O. (2024). Cybersecurity in banking: A Global Perspective with a focus on Nigerian practices. Comput. Sci. IT Res. j., 5(1), 41–59.

Hussain, M. I., He, J., Zhu, N., Sabah, F., Zardari, Z. A., Hussain, S., & Razque, F. (2021). AAAA: SSO and MFA implementation in multi-cloud to mitigate rising threats and concerns related to user metadata. *Applied Sciences (Basel, Switzerland), 11*(7), 3012. DOI: 10.3390/app11073012

Independent Researcher United States, & Ahmadi, S. (2024). Challenges and solutions in network security for serverless computing. Ijcsrr, 07(01).

Jofre, M., Navarro-Llobet, D., Agulló, R., Puig, J., Gonzalez-Granadillo, G., Mora Zamorano, J., & Romeu, R. (2021). Cybersecurity and privacy risk assessment of point-of-care systems in healthcare—A use case approach. *Applied Sciences (Basel, Switzerland), 11*(15), 6699. DOI: 10.3390/app11156699

Judijanto, L., & Lubis, A. F. (2025). Mapping a legal study on cybersecurity and data protection: A bibliometric review and its implications for regulation in the digital age. *West Science Law and Human Rights, 3*(01), 34–41. DOI: 10.58812/wslhr.v3i01.1598

Khan, M. (2024). Safeguarding IoT networks against DDoS attacks using deep learning based zero trust network access. *Electronics Letters, 60*(21), e70075. DOI: 10.1049/ell2.70075

Lo, P. (2024). Healthcare innovations: Enhancing patient privacy and security in the digital era. *Healthcare Management Forum, 37*(5), 8404704241254820. DOI: 10.1177/08404704241254820 PMID: 38775093

Loi, M., Christen, M., Kleine, N., & Weber, K. (2019). Cybersecurity in health – disentangling value tensions. *J. Inf. Commun. Ethics Soc., 17*(2), 229–245. DOI: 10.1108/JICES-12-2018-0095

Ludvigsen, K. R. (2023). The role of cybersecurity in medical devices regulation: Future considerations and solutions. *Law Tech Hum, 5*(2), 59–77. DOI: 10.5204/lthj.3080

Mijwil, M., Filali, Y., Aljanabi, M., Bounabi, M., & Al-Shahwani, H. (2023). The purpose of cybersecurity governance in the digital transformation of public services and protecting the digital environment. *Mesopotamian Journal of CyberSecurity, 2023*, 1–6. DOI: 10.58496/MJCS/2023/001

Mohammadi, F., Panou, A., Ntantogian, C., Karapistoli, E., Panaousis, E., & Xenakis, C. (2019, October). CUREX: seCUre and pRivate hEalth data eXchange. IEEE/WIC/ACM International Conference on Web - Companion Volume. DOI: 10.1145/3358695.3361753

Ojo, S., & Covey, A. (2025). Identity and Access Management (IAM) authentication methods: Importance of multi-factor authentication (MFA) and single sign-on (SSO) and access control models. In *Preprints*.

Rani Bandaru, V. N., Sumalatha, M., Rafee, S. M., Prasadraju, K., & Sri Lakshmi, M. (2024). *Enhancing privacy measures in healthcare within cyber-physical systems through cryptographic solutions. ICST Trans*. Scalable Inf. Syst.

Reis, O., Oliha, J. S., Osasona, F., & Obi, O. C. (2024). Cybersecurity Dynamics in Nigerian banking: Trends and strategies review. Comput. Sci. IT Res. j., 5(2), 336–364.

Rizal, R., & Sumaryana, Y. (2021). Peningkatan Keamanan Aplikasi Web Menggunakan Web Application Firewall (WAF) Pada Sistem Informasi Manajemen Kampus Terintegrasi. *Jurnal ICT : Information Communication & Technology*, *20*(2), 323–330. DOI: 10.36054/jict-ikmi.v20i2.416

Rodionov, A. (2024). The potential of blockchain technology for creating decentralized identity systems: Technical capabilities and legal regulation. *Irshad J. Law and Policy*, *2*(4), 19–30. DOI: 10.59022/ijlp.170

Saeed, S., Altamimi, S. A., Alkayyal, N. A., Alshehri, E., & Alabbad, D. A. (2023). Digital transformation and cybersecurity challenges for businesses resilience: Issues and recommendations. *Sensors (Basel)*, *23*(15), 6666. DOI: 10.3390/s23156666 PMID: 37571451

Saeedi, K., Hassan, M. A., Alarifi, S., & Almagwashi, H. (2025). An intuitive approach to cybersecurity risk assessment for non-governmental organizations. *Transforming Government*, *19*(1), 159–182. DOI: 10.1108/TG-08-2024-0201

Sandhu, K. (2021). Advancing Cybersecurity for Digital Transformation. In Handbook of Research on Advancing Cybersecurity for Digital Transformation (pp. 1–17). IGI Global. DOI: 10.4018/978-1-7998-6975-7.ch001

Sarkar, S., Choudhary, G., Shandilya, S. K., Hussain, A., & Kim, H. (2022). Security of zero trust networks in cloud computing: A comparative review. *Sustainability (Basel)*, *14*(18), 11213. DOI: 10.3390/su141811213

Senan Mahmod Attar Bashi, Z., & Senan, S. (2025). A comprehensive review of zero trust network architecture (ZTNA) and deployment frameworks. *International Journal on Perceptive and Cognitive Computing*, *11*(1), 148–153. DOI: 10.31436/ijpcc.v11i1.494

Soltani, R., Nguyen, U. T., & An, A. (2021). A survey of self-sovereign identity ecosystem. *Security and Communication Networks*, *2021*, 1–26. DOI: 10.1155/2021/8873429

Wang, Y., Liu, X., Mao, W., & Wang, W. (2019, May). DCDroid. *Proceedings of the ACM Turing Celebration Conference* - China. DOI: 10.1145/3321408.3326665

Wang, Z., Yu, X., Xue, P., Qu, Y., & Ju, L. (2023). Research on medical security system based on zero trust. *Sensors (Basel), 23*(7), 3774. DOI: 10.3390/s23073774 PMID: 37050834

Yusup, M., Maisyaroh, M., & Septiana, L. (2020). Securing web application by embedded firewall at gytech Indosantara Mandiri Ltd. *PIKSEL : Penelitian Ilmu Komputer Sistem Embedded and Logic, 8*(1), 49–58. DOI: 10.33558/piksel.v8i1.2019

Zaki, A., A., & J. Mohammed, S. (2024). Artificial intelligence for web application firewall (WAF): A comprehensive review. *International Research Journal of Innovations in Engineering And, 08*(11), 219–224.

Zohaib, S. M., & Sajjad, S. M. Iqbal Zafar and Yousaf, M., Haseeb, M., & Muhammad, Z. (2024). Zero Trust VPN (ZT-VPN): A cybersecurity framework for modern enterprises to enhance IT security and privacy in remote work environments. In Preprints.

ADDITIONAL READING

Appelt, D., Nguyen, C. D., & Briand, L. (2015, April). Behind an application firewall, are we safe from SQL injection attacks? 2015 IEEE 8th International Conference on Software, Verification and Validation (ICST).

Devlekar, S., & Ramteke, V. (2021). Identity and Access Management: High-level conceptual framework. *Rev. Gest. Inov. Tecnol., 11*(4), 4885–4897. DOI: 10.47059/revistageintec.v11i4.2511

Do Xuan, C., Nguyen, N., & Dinh, H. N. (2020). An adaptive anomaly request detection framework based on dynamic web application profiles. [IJECE]. *International Journal of Electrical and Computer Engineering, 10*(5), 5335. DOI: 10.11591/ijece.v10i5.pp5335-5346

Gunter, C. A., Liebovitz, D., & Malin, B. (2011). Experience-based access management: A life-cycle framework for identity and access management systems. *IEEE Security and Privacy, 9*(5), 48–55. DOI: 10.1109/MSP.2011.72 PMID: 22034582

IAM Professional USA., & Premsai MS, R. (2024). A comprehensive framework for cybersecurity in identity and Access Management system. J Mathe & Comp Appli, 1–6.

Jelcy, M., & M, H. (2025). A Web-Based Interactive Remedy Console with Honeypot Server. *International Scientific Journal of Engineering and Management, 04*(03), 1–9. DOI: 10.55041/ISJEM02398

Kalyan Manohar, I., Vishnu Datta, D., & Raveendran, L. S. (2025). Website Vulnerability Scanning System. *INTERANTIONAL JOURNAL OF SCIENTIFIC RESEARCH IN ENGINEERING AND, 09*(03), 1–9.

Kaviya. (2025). Real-time firewall event alert system for network protection. International Scientific Journal of Engineering and Management, 04(04), 1–7.

Meduri, V. (2023). Applying the promethee method in the field of computer cybersecurity is ``ranking cybersecurity solutions for risk mitigation. *Nanosci. Technol. Open Access, 7*(1), 1–11. DOI: 10.15226/2374-8141/7/1/00163

Rasouli, H., & Valmohammadi, C. (2019). Proposing a conceptual framework for customer identity and access management. *Global Knowledge, Memory and Communication, 69*(1/2), 94–116. DOI: 10.1108/GKMC-02-2019-0014

Rizal, R., & Sumaryana, Y. (2021). Peningkatan Keamanan Aplikasi Web Menggunakan Web Application Firewall (WAF) Pada Sistem Informasi Manajemen Kampus Terintegrasi. *Jurnal ICT : Information Communication & Technology, 20*(2), 323–330. DOI: 10.36054/jict-ikmi.v20i2.416

Chapter 8
Web-Based Tools and Platforms for Collaborative English Language Teaching

Vivit Rosmayanti
https://orcid.org/0000-0002-3648-9878
Universitas Negeri Makassar, Indonesia

ABSTRACT

This chapter examines how online tools and platforms enhance collaborative English as a Foreign Language (EFL) learning, drawing on social-constructivist theories. It reviews platforms like Google Classroom, Edmodo, Padlet, Slack, Google Docs, Zoom, and Kahoot, alongside wikis and discussion boards, highlighting their roles in communication, resource sharing, and task-based collaboration. Practical applications include peer review, shared storytelling, online forums, and joint problem-solving. The chapter also addresses challenges such as digital access inequality and participation imbalances, offering strategies for inclusive virtual classrooms. It forecasts future advancements with AI, VR, and AR for adaptive, immersive learning, aiming to equip educators with insights for creating dynamic, globally connected EFL environments.

INTRODUCTION

In the field of ELT, the use of collaboration as a technique has been important in the development of a rich and interactive learning environment. Collaborative learning is important for the purpose of developing various language skills because it

DOI: 10.4018/979-8-3373-5167-4.ch008

allows learners to transform individual learning activities into a shared experience as a result of interaction and the division of responsibilities. From a sociocultural perspective, such constructive activities offer learners opportunities to engage in real communication (Zaki & Adnan, 2023; Purwaningtyas et al, 2023) for the purpose of negotiating meaning, which has been considered important in the language learning process. The use of the collaborative learning model fosters the development of critical, creative, and problem-solving skills among EFL learners, which prepare them for the 21st-century skills (Urooj & Farooq, 2023; Çınar et al., 2022). Hence, the use of collaboration is imperative because it assists in the reduction of anxiety, provides motivation, and a general feeling of support for the learners.

The emergence of web-based instruments has continually changed the traditional classroom into active participatory environments. The technologies function as Active Learning Sites, enabling learners in different locations to shift from passive to active participation (Niaz et al, 2022; Topalcengiz & Yıldırım, 2020). Web-based instruments like Google Docs, wikis, and Learning Management Systems (LMS) have group work-friendly features, allowing learners to co-construct, resource, and peer review in real-time (Zaky 2021, Amin 2020). Studies seeking the communication aspect of Web 2.0 provided tools have noted the tools to enrich the communication of instructors, learners, and the learners' guardians (Yüce, 2020; Hassan et al., 2021). EFL professional teachers can leverage the tools to undertake assignments to design and implement a set of integrated projects emphasizing the use of the tools as the main pedagogy to have learners interact with the language, core to the Elliot principle (Alharbi & Alqefari, 2021).

This chapter analyzes various types of online tools for teaching English collaboratively and considers their implications for promoting collaborative learning. Moreover, the chapter aims to investigate the implementation of the tools for teaching EFL and provide the teachers with practical technology aids for their language teaching and learning activities. Users of the tools sentimentally advertise the benefits of technology-driven cooperative learning. For pedagogical practices, the balance of technology, tools, and student learner engagement while learning a new language is crucial (Gençer et al., 2023; Hassan et al., 2021). Also, the chapter aims to investigate how the use of such tools can improve learning and encourage reflective and advanced thinking in students through collaborative dialogue (Li et al., 2020). The chapter aims to draw the necessary conclusions from the existing literature and practical studies, showing the importance of the use of technology toward collaborative learning to change the teaching techniques to improve the effectiveness of learning.

The next sections will outline specific tools and platforms along with their associated features, advantages, and relevant pedagogical frameworks. Each tool will be evaluated on its capacity to enhance collaboration, create discussion forums, and support learner autonomy (Yamaguchi et al., 2022; Oluwajana et al., 2021). For example, the study of collaborative writing using Google Docs will demonstrate how the use of certain tools can provide faster feedback on writing and improve writing skills through peer evaluation (Alharbi & Alqefari, 2021; Amin, 2020). Moreover, research on the use of gamification to improve student active engagement and collaboration will be reviewed, given its potential to improve learning outcomes (Çınar et al., 2022; Wen, 2022). Ultimately, the goal of the chapter is to help EFL teachers understand how to use the internet to enhance the teaching of collaborative learning.

To sum up, the digital transformation of English language teaching continues to advance with the embrace of new technologies. The presence of tools supporting collaboration in teaching and learning enables EFL practitioners to tailor their teaching to the expectations of the modern student and ensure that their teaching is effective in a relevant current context. This chapter was written with the intent of supporting teachers so that they can use their skills and experience to make the best use of web technologies in initiating collaborative and motivating language teaching and learning activities.

THEORETICAL FOUNDATIONS OF COLLABORATIVE LEARNING

Within the realm of ELT, the value that collaborative learning attracts is the most pronounced. Language learners, during collaborative learning, engage in group interaction. Community building and the acquisition of positive interpersonal relationships lie at the essence of achieving the learning outcomes. Active interaction, which is necessary for learning a foreign language, is a requirement of the research that considers peer interaction as a positive impact for learners. Malik et al. (2021) observe that interaction-oriented collaborative learning enhances the problem-solving and critical thinking skills of the learners. They also support the notion that by engaging primary learners in collaborative problem-solving activities, the learners' appreciation of learning objectives and language outcomes increases (Kew, 2021).

The principles of collaborative learning in the teaching of English as a Foreign Language (EFL) rest on a number of important theoretical constructs. These include Vygotsky's social constructivism, which views knowledge as something that is created during social interactions and that involves collaborative work of some kind. Vygotsky's idea of the "zone of proximal development" (ZPD) is particularly illustrative of how learners always obtain deeper understandings and develop higher-order skills through interactions, albeit guided, with other learners or more knowledgeable adults (Siregar et al., 2024). This theory works perfectly in the case of collaborative learning because such a theory puts emphasis on learners as knowledge constructors as opposed to passive recipients in social environments. Perhaps equally important is Piaget's theory of cognitive development, which maintains that knowledge is cumulatively constructed, and in the process, social interaction is a very important factor. Much in the same way, the combination of social development and cognitive development theories explains to practitioners how collaborative learning can be thoughtfully deployed to scaffold language learning opportunities (Yumnam, 2021).

Collaboration in learning when students are learning English as a Foreign Language (EFL) has several benefits, including improving engagement, language skills, and interaction among learners. Students' constructive engagement in speaking, writing, listening, and reading tasks and authentic language use as evidenced in (Chen et al. 2021). Offering learners opportunities to practice language skills in collaborative settings improves learners' fluency and accuracy in slipstream language, as found in (Kew 2021). Moreover, purposeful peer interactions amplify retention and understanding of grammatical and lexical elements of a language through contextualized collaborative problem-solving, active use of language, and peer teaching (Oeamoum and Sriwichai 2020).

Coupled with the aforementioned benefits, the focus on learner-centred activities in a collaborative context boosts learner engagement. As noted in the 2023 article, the ownership over the learning process through discussions and actions catalyzed by peers increases motivation and positive sentiment due to the collaborative nature of the tasks. Participation in collaborative activities fosters a sense of belonging in the classroom context, which, in the past, was the sole domain of the teacher, who would have felt 'over' the students. Most EFL learners, in particular, in a collaborative context, the anxiety tied to the foreign language is eased, leading to greater willingness to participate. The social dimension of collaboration also adds a great deal to fostering positive relationships of a more instrumental nature, which in turn enhances the positive, less threatening atmosphere of the classroom (Lukitasari et al., 2021).

The ability to socialize is another benefit of collaborative learning. For language learners, interacting with classmates goes beyond practicing language skills to enhance social skills development. During interaction, learners demonstrate social skills of dialogue, negotiation, and task sharing. Zheng (2022) describes such skills as soft skills. Fostering social interaction within the classroom positively impacts learners, particularly those from diverse learning contexts, as it helps in classroom cohesion (Huong & Ngoc, 2024). Overall, the classroom's collaborative approach to learning helps learners grow cognitively and emotionally as they learn to juggle language and social skills.

As a last remark, collaborative learning is still a vital approach to teaching EFL, and it is backed by solid ideas. For instance, social constructivism and cognitive development theories are blended together. The Explanation of the importance of interactions among learners to develop language skills is enriched. Moreover, collaborative learning as a unit helps learners achieve a higher level of development of language skills, more engagement, and personal development, which stresses the need for such a unit in ELT practices. As it is, teachers need to prepare learners for a fast-changing world, and fostering collaborative skills is a necessity offered in designed learning environments.

WEB-BASED PLATFORMS FOR COLLABORATIVE EFL TEACHING

In the evolving landscape of English Language Teaching (ELT), the integration of web-based platforms has proven invaluable in fostering collaborative learning environments. Various types of these platforms cater specifically to collaborative tasks, enhancing the interactive experience among learners and educators. These include social media platforms, learning management systems (LMS), and communication tools, each providing unique functionalities tailored to different learning needs. Social media platforms, for example, can facilitate discussions, share resources, and create communities of practice among learners. Learning management systems like Google Classroom streamline coursework management and foster student-teacher interactions efficiently. Meanwhile, communication tools such as Slack serve to maintain real-time discussions, allowing for swift feedback and collaboration on assignments. Collectively, these platforms transform the dynamics of language instruction, enabling a shift from traditional methods to a more integrated and collaborative learning experience (Prasetya, 2021; Urooj & Farooq, 2023).

Among the most prominent web-based platforms for collaborative EFL teaching is Google Classroom, which acts as a centralized hub for assignments, feedback, and peer interactions. Launched in 2014, Google Classroom has become increasingly popular in education due to its user-friendly interface and robust feature set designed for instructional engagement (Hastomo et al., 2021). The platform allows teachers to create, distribute, and manage assignments seamlessly while providing a space for essential communication and collaboration. Research indicates that the use of Google Classroom can significantly improve learners' speaking performance and overall engagement in the language learning process (Rajaindaran & Abdullah, 2023). For instance, students can engage in peer feedback sessions where they critique each other's work in a structured environment, enabling them to practice their language skills in real-time (Albashtawi & Bataineh, 2020). Such collaborative activities enhance students' motivation to utilize the English language, contributing to improved learning outcomes.

Edmodo serves as another exemplary platform that fosters student-teacher interaction and facilitates group discussions in EFL classrooms. Designed as a social learning network, Edmodo bridges the gap between formal education and social media by allowing students and teachers to communicate in a familiar online environment (Albashtawi & Bataineh, 2020). The platform supports a wide range of collaborative activities such as quizzes, shared resources, and feedback mechanisms, creating an engaging ecosystem for language learners. It is structured to enhance interaction between educators and students, promoting a dialogue that can significantly benefit learners' language acquisition processes. Moreover, Edmodo's capability to facilitate group projects and discussions provides opportunities for learners to work collaboratively, engaging them in deeper learning experiences that reinforce their language skills (Setiawan & Entusiastik, 2022).

Padlet is another innovative platform that embodies collaborative learning principles effectively. Often referred to as a "collaborative board," Padlet allows students to post notes, images, and links in a shared space, enabling brainstorming sessions and group activities (Prasetya & Syarif, 2023). In EFL contexts, Padlet can be used for collaborative writing tasks, enabling students to contribute ideas and resources collectively while practicing their English skills. Through its accessible format, Padlet encourages student participation and contribution, cultivating a sense of ownership over learning materials. It facilitates engagement in more dynamic and interactive formats, allowing learners to visualize concepts and engage with content in a meaningful way, thus supporting their language development goals (Firliantama & Rokhayani, 2023).

Furthermore, Slack presents a powerful tool for real-time communication and collaboration among language learners. Initially designed for businesses, Slack has been adapted for educational contexts due to its strong capabilities in supporting asynchronous and synchronous discussions (Wu & Wang, 2024). The platform allows students to create channels for specific projects or topics where they can communicate instantly, share files, and collaborate on assignments. This kind of instant messaging enhances students' engagement and facilitates quick interactions, which are essential for collaborative learning experiences. The incorporation of Slack in an EFL classroom encourages students to practice their language skills in a low-pressure environment where they can freely express their ideas and receive immediate peer feedback, which is critical for language acquisition (Ali et al., 2024).

In summary, the variety of web-based platforms available for collaborative EFL teaching not only enhances traditional learning methodologies but also provides new avenues for engagement and interaction among learners. Google Classroom, Edmodo, Padlet, and Slack exemplify effective platforms that support collaborative learning through various features tailored to accommodate group activities, real-time communication, and peer feedback. These platforms allow educators to create a richer learning environment where students can thrive collaboratively while developing their English language skills in a meaningful context. As the educational landscape continues to evolve, the integration of these tools will undoubtedly play a crucial role in shaping the future of collaborative learning in EFL education.

INTERACTIVE WEB TOOLS FOR COLLABORATIVE ACTIVITIES IN THE EFL CLASSROOM

The integration of interactive online resources for collaborative language practice has become important in English Language Teaching (ELT) practices, disregarding time zone and location, while also fostering a communicative and interactive atmosphere. These tools include wikis, bulletin boards, audio and video conferencing, and online role plays, and together foster learner engagement. With each tool, learners have effective and active collaborative language practice, improving language proficiency and communicative competence.

Wikis and collaborative tools like Google Docs and Wikispaces allow students to create and co-edit content in real time. These collaborative platforms enable users to write, edit, and reflect as a community, which promotes co-creation and a sense of ownership about the learning content (Liashenko & Öztok, 2024). For instance, the collaborative nature of wikis enhanced learners' language proficiency because learners can think critically and negotiate meaning in the course of completing a writing task (Alharbi, 2020). Students participating in collaborative writing projects engage and master grammatical and lexical resources of the target language as they 'transform' writing into an active process. In addition, the real-time feedback within wikis stimulates students' content engagement and language skill application in practice.

Discussion forums are an integral part of asynchronous peer collaboration and discussions. Discourse and Moodle forums, among others, allow students to ask and answer questions, respond to class-related topics, and give feedback, providing ongoing engagement beyond the confines of the classroom (Kılınç and Altınpulluk, 2021). Such forums level the playing field and promote user engagement, even among the less confident, by allowing the thinkers to work outside the pressures of real-time interactions. Research suggests that students participating in online discussion forums not only hone their writing skills but also polish their critical thinking skills by engaging and synthesizing multiple points of view (Jian-chun et al., 2023). In this case, discussion forums are asynchronous methods of communication and allow students to relearn information at their own pace, a useful feature for, especially, language learners, who need extra time to answer questions compared to their classmates.

Voice and video tools are also certainly powerful platforms for improving communication skills in speaking and listening in collaborative practices. Zoom, Microsoft Teams, and Skype, for instance, facilitate real-time interaction, helping learners practice their conversational skills in collaboration (Khaskheli et al., 2021). This type of interaction, or discourse, is a fundamental building block in language learning and the construction of communicative competence. It is shown that speaking in such a manner in virtual groups drives participation and fluency and engages learners in a great deal of practice in speaking in a protected environment (Radosavlevikj, 2021). The learners also need to better use the video conferencing equipment to do more than record words and improve the learning process. They also integrate facial expressions, gestures, and body language to facilitate the communication process and improve their understanding of the topic to create a better learning environment.

Along with other tools, online simulations and games have also become new and effective ways to create interactive and gamified learning. Kahoot, Quizlet, and Duolingo are examples of platforms that incorporate game-based learning to facilitate student engagement with language practice through quizzes, flashcards, and other fun activities (Asrianti et al, 2022). Evidence suggests that the use of gamified tools increases learners' motivation, retention, and satisfaction throughout the learning process. In fact, language learners who are placed in gamified setups become more active and enthusiastic, resulting in better skill acquisition and information retention (Idrissov & Tussupbekova, 2021). In addition, many of these interactive games incorporate cooperative elements through which learners can work in groups, discuss answers, and engage in collaborative problem-solving, thus strengthening their language use.

To summarize, increase interaction within and between language classes to promote higher-order thinking, problem-solving, and teamwork through the use of Interactive Web tools. Educators should rethink how to increase students' collaborative knowledge building, higher-order thinking, and the full range of language use from forums to video and voice tools to online simulations and games. All of these tools broaden the potential of collaborative language practice to immerse learners in the complex, authentic tasks that promote learner-centered and self-directed language learning. The purposeful, thoughtful, and balanced use of Interactive Web tools. Educators should rethink how to increase students' collaborative skills, enabling learners to interact with the complex communication ecosystem of our increasingly interconnected world.

IMPLEMENTING WEB-BASED COLLABORATIVE ACTIVITIES IN THE EFL CLASSROOM

The inclusion of online collaborative activities in the EFL class enables the use of technology to promote better learning and communication skills among students. Educators who design collaborative tasks around sophisticated web tools can create a dynamic learning environment that promotes the development of communication and advanced writing, speaking, and reading skills. This approach facilitates knowledge construction and the development of critical thinking, thereby increasing meaningful interaction and language use.

Collaborative learning can be implemented in part through peer review, and editors and other feedback providers can be assigned to peers on platforms like Google Docs. This activity asks students to pair and share their written assignments, wherein each learner is expected to evaluate and provide feedback. Students use Google Docs to engage in collaborative writing and discuss feedback through writing and other forms of communication. Students use Google Docs and other collaborative writing tools to complete writing activities, which increases student motivation and engagement, and provides students with motivation through peer learning. Collaboration with peers increases their motivation and engagement in writing activities through improvement in the writing skills, which creates a sense of self and collective responsibility in the classroom (Nabhan & Sa'Diyah, 2021; Vélez-Palacios & Ramírez-Ávila, 2023).

Collaborative storytelling is another compelling method of interest incorporation that can be used in EFL classrooms. By using Padlet or Wikis, students can work on projects or stories where they develop ideas, characters, and plots. Such productive cooperation facilitates imaginative use of the English language on multiple levels. Storytelling involves the construction of narratives, the writing of dialogues, and the use of descriptive language. These are fundamental in achieving fluency and coherence while exercising the language. Research on collaborative storytelling shows that students' narrative skills increased, and they reported greater levels of engagement and enjoyment in learning the language (Valizadeh, 2022). This, in addition, allows students to incorporate the cultural elements of their stories, which fosters understanding through storytelling that cuts across cultures.

Virtual group discourse serves as an invaluable method for practicing the skills of speaking and listening in real time. Software for video conferencing, such as Zoom and MS Teams, enables both one-on-one and group discussions in which learners can engage in conversation practice within a monitored setting. These real-time interactions can be centered on defined topics or language tasks, which encourage learners to articulate and discuss their ideas and concepts while engaging in active peer and instructor assessment. The opportunity to participate in discussions in a virtual environment lessens the anxiety of some learners who may be uncomfortable with real-time interactions, which, in turn, increases participation. Findings show that such virtual discussions enhance learners' speaking skills while improving their listening skills and responsiveness, which are essential to real-world communication (Duque & Garzón, 2024; Duque & Garzón, 2024).

Collaborative problem-solving is another successful EFL activity that engages students in group projects using shared online resources to tackle real-world language problems. Groups learn a particular subject, study the language used in the discipline, and teach the subject to the class. In this achievement, students work in cooperation, and in the same manner, learn to integrate different online tools, and learn to construct their thought processes alongside practical approaches to the language. Such projects incorporate all the language skills, and research indicates that their language proficiency improves, along with their ability to work in teams and solve potential conflicts in the future (Wu & Shafait, 2024). This approach to language learning gives students a real situation in which they actively use language, thus strengthening the importance of using language in real life.

In closing, the use of web-based collaborative activities in the EFL classroom improves students' learning experience as they interact more meaningfully with other learners. Teachers can create useful activities that target students' writing, speaking, and problem-solving skills through the use of Google Docs, Padlet, and other virtual discussion tools. The collaborative activities improve problem-solving and critical thinking skills, cultural understanding, proficiency in the target language, and community among learners. The evolution of technology makes it necessary to use these collaborative activities in language teaching and learning to help students achieve the skills necessary for communicating in the modern globalized society.

BENEFITS AND CHALLENGES OF COLLABORATIVE WEB-BASED LEARNING IN EFL

Benefits

Collaborative web-based learning within the English as a Foreign Language (EFL) context is beneficial for the fostering of student engagement, motivation, and problem-solving strategies across multiple dimensions. Collaborative strategies also shift traditional approaches to language instruction to more engaging environments. This shift, in turn, fulfills the requirements of contemporary education and equips learners with the necessary skills to communicate and collaborate in the world.

Perhaps the dominant advantage of collaborative web-based learning is the increase in student motivation and engagement. Collaborative tasks incorporate social interaction, which can often stimulate learning. There is a spirit of interaction and social cohesion that strengthens the dedication of learners toward the fulfillment of the learning goals. This is the case when learners collaborate and use web-based learning tools. Findings also show that learners in collaborative learning environments tend to be more motivated and satisfied with their learning as a result of supportive peer interactions that encourage them to deepen their engagement with the material being learned, as noted by Wijaya (2021). Tools such as Google Docs or discussion forums increase learners' engagement with the content being learned, thereby enriching their educational experience.

Within the scope of engagement, collaborative web-based learning fosters the acquisition of thinking and problem-solving skills among EFL learners. Participation in group work enables learners to tackle difficult issues collaboratively, which initiates sustained cognitive conflict and discourse, which are critical to developing and enhancing thinking skills (Xu et al., 2023). It has been observed that when learners are placed within collaborative environments and are presented with real-life challenges, they are more inclined to pose questions, dispute, and collaboratively arrive at well-reasoned conclusions through discussions (Agustina & Roisatin, 2024). Such interaction fosters the use of language at higher-order thinking levels and more complex skills (Jumariati et al., 2022). It has been shown that the collaborative tasks of problem-solving type improved learners' critical thinking, which means collaborative learning has the potential to aid in the development of cognitive skills coupled with language proficiency (Roisatin, 2024).

Furthermore, models of collaborative web-based learning broaden opportunities for the acquisition of various resources and peer learning, both of which are vital for learning a new language. Students can access and utilize information through web-based resources during collaborative projects. This fosters peer learning, which makes use of the students' varying strengths and perspectives, thus enhancing their understanding and usage of language (Algouzi et al. 2023). Learners and their immediate peers, in a globalized learning environment, focus not only on their immediate peers but on people from a variety of cultures, thus enhancing their linguistic and cultural understanding. Therefore, web-based resources permit students to utilize authentic materials such as videos, articles, and interactive exercises, thus adopting a more integrated approach to learning a language.

Through participation in collaborative projects, EFL students learn not only to integrate into a team, but to work in a team as well, in a focused manner, sharing and learning from experiences as a group. This element of peer learning is important not only for developing language skills, but for developing a sense of community for learners, thus encouraging them to engage in the sharing of ideas and feedback (Namsaeng & Sukying 2021). The collaborative web-based approach nurtures the learning experiences of students from the traditional, and frequently isolating, language learning paradigm, and in place offers collaboration, common purpose, and assistance to all learners.

To sum up, the advantages afforded by collaborative web-based learning in EFL contexts are diverse and important. The effectiveness of collaboration in language teaching is demonstrated by heightened student motivation and engagement, along with the acquisition of critical thinking and problem-solving capabilities. Furthermore, the widening availability of various materials and the advocacy of peer learning opportunities justify the position of collaborative learning as a primary tool to improve the language acquisition and communication skills of EFL learners. With the changing educational model, along with the expanding use of collaborative web-based tools, students are poised to work successfully in a globally interconnected community.

Challenges

Although collaborative web-based learning provides substantial advantages to EFL learners, it is still important to recognize concerns relating to its pedagogical effectiveness. Identification of the challenges enables the instructors to formulate pedagogical approaches to minimize the barriers and improve the overall learning experience. Some of the most apparent challenges are technological and connectivity issues, a lack of balanced engagement and participation, and the need to accommodate varying learning preferences and different levels of language proficiency.

The disconnection of the internet, along with other technological barriers, poses serious challenges to using collaborative web-based learning in EFL classrooms. Students, in some cases, might not have appropriate devices or internet access to engage in learning fully. Mahyoob (2020) pointed out that such barriers to learning technologies disrupted students by not enabling them to access learning platforms that were in demand during the COVID-19 pandemic. Moreover, student participation, disempowering them, can be caused by an absence of adequate learning software, interfaces analogous, digital gaps, and weaker digital competencies. The failure to allocate adequate resources to learners and students who would rather have gadgets, subsequently, use inadequate supporting devices or interfaces, and the absence of sustaining interfaces can minimize the efficiency of collaborative learning (Yahiaoui et al, 2021). The challenge for educators, in this case, is to manage enabling conditions to access participation gaps to train on the use of digital devices and proactively design strategic gaps for students with disempowering technologies.

There are challenges surrounding the engagement of students in activities. It is often the case that groups are faced with collaborative tasks that are broken down differently. Differences in the distribution of collaborative activities often come about due to learners assuming more responsibilities than the rest (Niaz et al, 2022).

This distribution of responsibilities often frustrates the source of the imbalance. Participants are not always equally participative in the activities due to primary motivators, types of personality, confidence, and lack of self-efficacy (Manipuspika, 2020). High language embodiment and high social timid learners are often victims of the discussion-dominators. It is the responsibility of the teacher to design interdependent activities that are learner-centered in such a way that every student attends to specific roles to enhance participation. Those with more confidence are assigned roles to encourage passive or shy students. Different group members are assigned different roles to ensure maximum participation, and the topic or parts of the topic's information come from all members.

Collaborative learners' web-based learning faces another major issue with the disparity in the students' learning styles and language abilities. Classroom EFL students have different backgrounds, experiences, and skills; thus, modified instruction is needed to cater to their needs based on differentiation. This diversity can make collaborative assignments challenging because one-size-fits-all approaches do not meet the needs of all learners (Farshad & Fortin, 2023). For instance, among students, some prefer visual aids, tactile, and demonstrate mobility, while others are comfortable with oral interactions. Hence, there is a need for educators to apply different pedagogical methods to different levels of learners (Guiñez Molinos, 2021). This more structured approach ensures that all learners make substantial contributions during the group work activities. Furthermore, disparity in language proficiency levels in a class can result in a contribution gap whereby learners at more advanced levels dominate the discussions while beginners find it challenging to articulate their thoughts. Hence, it is crucial to promote an inclusive class where all students are appreciated and encouraged to take part actively.

Lastly, collaborative web-based learning in the EFL context has advantages as well as drawbacks. On one hand, increased engagement, the ability to think critically, and the opportunity to learn from others are positive developments, but the issues of technology access, differing levels of engagement, and various learning modalities pose a serious problem that must be dealt with. It is, therefore, the educator's responsibility to meet those challenges using appropriate pedagogical frameworks and available technology and to maximize the use of collaborative web-based learning as well as other pedagogical frameworks to create a context in which every learner is able to succeed.

BEST PRACTICES FOR EFL TEACHERS USING WEB-BASED COLLABORATION

Applying internet-based collaborative tools within the class has the potential to greatly improve the learning of students. There are best practices developed to apply collaborative tools and to integrate teaching practices, and teachers are encouraged to use these best practices to diversify and improve the online community within the class. These practices will help in constructing digital literacy, as well as providing communication and learning simultaneously.

Collaborative-based learning objectives in the instructional practices give guidance on achieving the learning objectives. The objectives should resonate with the curriculum and the tools employed in collaboration. The instructor should define what skills will be developed, including collaboration, and enhance cultural exchange. The tools and activities are readily available to be aligned with the learning objectives, and these learning objectives should be utilized. This addresses the assumptions of the objectives when collaborative tools are used with traditional approaches. These objectives are aligned with the sequential learning objectives. There should be cross-cutting collaboration-to-, and within face-to-face discussions, there should be online sessions; these should bring out the learning objectives based on the classroom discussion. The learners should be able to engage actively and understand the language at a deeper level. The use of other instructional methods should be blended to bring increased performance, and the learner should understand these blended methods.

To promote equity in participation and mitigate problems associated with "social loafing," instructors are encouraged to adopt measures to ensure inclusivity in participation. One way of doing this is to allocate specific functions to members of collaborative groups, which can include assigning roles such as discussion leader, scribe, or information seeker. This model is effective in fostering social obligation, as each member is given a specific task, thereby lowering the level of disengagement within the group. Moreover, the establishment of a peer evaluation system can lead students to become more active in group work, as they understand that their work affects the learning of their peers. Promoting the use of self-reflective practices can also increase participation by encouraging students to think about the nature and impact of their actions and how best they can assist their colleagues.

Building a constructive and caring online community is essential to ensuring effective collaborative learning. To achieve this, teachers should provide instructions on respectful communication and collaboration. Knowing the rules and expectations for behavior and participation helps tame the discourse and provide a protective shell where ideas can be spoken freely. Instructors can also use icebreaker exercises to encourage students to form connections and relationships as part of the online community. Research shows that supportive social behaviors and interactions promote higher levels of engagement and dedication to learning. Additionally, instructors can schedule regular check-ins with the groups to observe interactions and provide assistance on issues that may arise to promote continuous support during collaborative work.

It is also important to develop students' ability to function in a digital environment and, at the same time, to promote the ethical use of technology. As students interact more and more with diverse Internet-based platforms, it is important that they be taught the requisite responsible behavior for conduct in these spaces. Educators can use digital citizenship instructional units that teach, among other things, ethical behavior in the virtual environment, including integrity, civility, and responsible information use. Such students also need to be taught the responsible use of the Internet, including the more general issues of copyright and plagiarism, and more specifically, in their online resource usage. Digital integration, which develops primary skills of advanced information analysis and interactive group work in which a considerable integration of information across many systems is performed, also needs to be promoted. Such students will be technologically competent and, more importantly, responsible members of their educational communities.

To conclude with the best practices that weave together student participation with the constraints of equal participation and cultivate a positive online community. The effective use of web-based collaborative tools depends on the level of engagement of the students. The integration of collaborative tasks will involve online tasks with well-defined learning outcomes. Instruction of effective group dynamics and the promotion of digital skills will enable educators to foster positive outcomes for students in a collaborative environment. To conclude, best practices will evolve and be the key for language learners in the future in both academic and professional contexts.

CONCLUSION

To sum up, this chapter looked into various web-based collaborative tools and platforms for English language teaching and their importance in developing interactive and collaborative learning environments. Integrating technology in EFL classes increases students' participation and motivation and develops students' critical thinking and problem-solving abilities. Additionally, web-based collaborative learning builds a community where students can actively share, collaborate, and learn throughout their learning journey. As discussed in this chapter, Google Classroom, Padlet, and other video conferencing tools promote participation and interaction in language classes.

As technology continues to evolve, so does the prospect for EFL collaborative teaching and learning. New developments in web-based tools are emerging, offering more opportunities for educators and learners. Technologies, neural networks, artificial intelligence, and 3D immersive environments and virtual reality are likely to foster more collaborative learning by providing contexts in which language learners can use the language in real-life scenarios, encouraging more interaction and deeper engagement. On the other hand, teachers and educators need to be more aware of the various challenges posed by technology, such as the unequal availability of technology and equitable participation for all students.

Focusing on a particular web-based collaborative tool and counting its use in a week as a component of lesson evaluation, teachers should aim to widen their methodology to include its integration and use in achieving set instructional aims, fostering both controlled and free communication among students and interactions within the language classroom, thus helping students increase their language proficiency beyond the context of the classroom and to appropriate its use in real-world scenarios. The variety of language education collaborative ventures is numerous, and their utilization can contribute towards sustaining the appropriate standards for the language as well as the education provided in the course. It is paramount that teachers think beyond the adoption of the technology to its evolved level of application to facilitate interactions that can empower students as language learners to help foster more complex, deeper-level, and sustained use of the learned language dynamically from the technology adoption level to its evolved application.

REFERENCES

Agustina, L., & Roisatin, U. (2024). The efficacy of case-based learning model integrated with critical thinking skills to improve efl learners' reading comprehension. *Journal of Languages and Language Teaching*, *12*(3), 1443. DOI: 10.33394/jollt.v12i3.11619

Albashtawi, A., & Bataineh, K. (2020). The effectiveness of google classroom among efl students in jordan: An innovative teaching and learning online platform. *International Journal of Emerging Technologies in Learning*, *15*(11), 78. DOI: 10.3991/ijet.v15i11.12865

Algouzi, S., Alzubi, A., & Nazim, M. (2023). Enhancing efl students' critical thinking skills using a technology-mediated self-study approach: Efl graduates and labor market in perspective. *PLoS One*, *18*(10), e0293273. DOI: 10.1371/journal.pone.0293273 PMID: 37856514

Alharbi, A. (2020). Wikis in language learning: Merits and limitations. *Journal of English Language Teaching and Applied Linguistics*, *2*(4), 79–88. DOI: 10.32996/jeltal.2020.2.4.9

Alharbi, M., & Alqefari, A. (2021). The impact of teacher feedback via google doc in l2 learners' writing. *International Journal of Learning Teaching and Educational Research*, *20*(11), 170–194. DOI: 10.26803/ijlter.20.11.10

Ali, I., Azim, M., & Rehman, A. (2024). Translanguaging as a tool to decolonize english language teaching in pakistan: Opportunities and challenges. *Pakistan Social Sciences Review*, *8*(I). Advance online publication. DOI: 10.35484/pssr.2024(8-I)23

Amin, E. (2020). A review of research into google apps in the process of english language learning and teaching. *Arab World English Journal*, *11*(1), 399–418. DOI: 10.24093/awej/vol11no1.27

Asrianti, A., Iskandar, I., & Patak, A. (2022). The implementation of multicultural-based english language teaching in a language institution. *International Journal of Humanities and Innovation (Ijhi)*, *5*(2), 67–73. DOI: 10.33750/ijhi.v5i2.150

Çınar, A., Erişen, Y., & Çeliköz, M. (2022). A mixed-method research on the effectiveness of using gamification elements in an online english course. *International Journal of Educational Research Review*, *7*(4), 280–291. DOI: 10.24331/ijere.1140960

Chen, Y., Chuang, H., & Lacaste, A. (2021). A pedagogical framework of cross-cultural online collaborative projects in english as foreign language (efl) classrooms. *Journal of Education and Learning (Edulearn), 15*(2), 223–233. DOI: 10.11591/edulearn.v15i2.19950

Duque, J., & Garzón, A. (2024). Exploring the transformative impact of ict integration in the efl classroom. *Religación : Revista de Ciencias Sociales y Humanidades, 9*(40), e2401172. DOI: 10.46652/rgn.v9i40.1172

Farshad, S., & Fortin, C. (2023). Active engagement in collaborative engineering design: How to measure and use it in a feedback system? *Proceedings of the Design Society, 3*, 455–464. DOI: 10.1017/pds.2023.46

Firliantama, M. and Rokhayani, A. (2023). Young learners' engagement in vocabulary learning taught by games and learning application: systematic review. simple, 1(1), 1-6. https://doi.org/DOI: 10.24176/simple.v1i1.10585

Gençer, S., Oluk, N., Kadayifçi, H., & Çelik, A. (2023). The purposes and justifications for preferences of web 2.0 tools used by pre-service chemistry teachers in their teaching practices in distance education environment. Shanlax International Journal of Education, 11(S1-Jan), 61-75. https://doi.org/DOI: 10.34293/education.v11iS1-Jan.5908

Guiñez-Molinos, S., González, J., Gomar-Sancho, C., Espinoza, P., & Constenla, G. (2021). A web platform (mosaico) to design, perform, and assess collaborative clinical scenarios for medical students: Viewpoint. *JMIR Medical Education, 7*(1), e23370. DOI: 10.2196/23370 PMID: 33496676

Hassan, I., Nasidi, Q., Azmi, M., & Gamji, M. (2021). Challenges and benefits of web 2.0-based learning among international students of english during the covid-19 pandemic in cyprus. https://doi.org/DOI: 10.31235/osf.io/fm5c6

Hastomo, T., Istiara, F., & Nurchurifiani, E. (2021). Google classroom: An online platform for teaching english. *Aksara Jurnal Bahasa Dan Sastra, 22*(2). Advance online publication. DOI: 10.23960/aksara/v22i2.pp300-308

Huong, N. and Ngoc, N. (2024). An investigation into english –majored sophomores' perceptions of english movies to improve vocabulary at huit. Journal of Knowledge Learning and Science Technology Issn 2959-6386 (Online), 3(1), 52-62. https://doi.org/DOI: 10.60087/jklst.vol3.no1.p62

Idrissov, Y. and Tussupbekova, M. (2021). Using of wiki-technologies in the process of learning english for students of non-language specialties., 58-63. https://doi.org/DOI: 10.46656/proceeding.2021.foreign.language(12)

Jian-chun, D., Wang, L., & He, Y. (2023). Exploring the effect of wiki-based writing instruction on writing skills and writing self-efficacy of chinese english-as-a-foreign language learners. *Frontiers in Psychology*, *13*, 1069832. Advance online publication. DOI: 10.3389/fpsyg.2022.1069832 PMID: 36704680

Jumariati, J., Elyani, E., Nawal, N., & Larasati, S. (2022). Developing an instrument to assess efl learners' critical thinking skills in writing expository problem-solution essays. *International Journal of English Language Teaching*, *10*(5), 30–37. DOI: 10.37745/ijelt.13/vol10n53037

Kew, S. (2021). Japanese students' english language learning experience through computer game-based student response systems. *Turkish Journal of Computer and Mathematics Education (Turcomat)*, *12*(3), 1993–1998. DOI: 10.17762/turcomat.v12i3.1036

Khaskheli, F., Aijaz, S., Syed, M., & Shah, W. (2021). *Attitudes of foreign language teaching assistants towards teaching of english in pakistani context*. JLLL., DOI: 10.7176/JLLL/78-03

Kılınç, H., & Altınpulluk, H. (2021). Discussion forums as a learning material in higher education institutions. *International Journal of Higher Education Pedagogies*, *2*(1), 1–9. DOI: 10.33422/ijhep.v2i1.25

Li, S., Abel, M., & Negre, E. (2020). Managing and recommending resources in web-based collaborative working environments.. https://doi.org/DOI: 10.1109/WETICE49692.2020.00063

Liashenko, M., & Öztok, M. (2024). The acceptance of a wiki site as a learning platform in english exam training. *NLC*, *12*, 26–29. DOI: 10.54337/nlc.v12.8629

Lukitasari, M., Hasan, R., Sukri, A., & Handhika, J. (2021). Developing student's metacognitive ability in science through project-based learning with e-portfolio. *International Journal of Evaluation and Research in Education (Ijere)*, *10*(3), 948. DOI: 10.11591/ijere.v10i3.21370

Mahyoob, M. (2020). Challenges of e-learning during the covid-19 pandemic experienced by efl learners. *Arab World English Journal*, *11*(4), 351–362. DOI: 10.24093/awej/vol11no4.23

Malik, S., Huang, Q., & Oteir, I. (2021). Perceived psychological, linguistic and socio-cultural obstacles: An investigation of english communication apprehension in efl learners. *International Journal of Instruction*, *14*(4), 733–752. DOI: 10.29333/iji.2021.14442a

Manipuspika, Y. (2020). Learning styles of indonesian efl students: culture and learning. https://doi.org/DOI: 10.31235/osf.io/j8vwe

Nabhan, S., & Sa'diyah, H. (2021). Collaborative writing using google docs in an efl classroom: Voices from high school students. *Veles Voice of English Language Education Society*, *5*(2), 156–166. DOI: 10.29408/veles.v5i2.3863

Namsaeng, P., & Sukying, A. (2021). The effect of group reading strategy on critical thinking skills in thai efl university learners. *Journal of English Language Teaching and Applied Linguistics*, *3*(2), 30–40. DOI: 10.32996/jeltal.2021.3.2.4

Niaz, S., Buriro, G., & Soomro, N. (2022). Web-based english language learning: A review from web 1.0 to web 3.0. *Pakistan Journal of Humanities and Social Sciences*, *10*(2). Advance online publication. DOI: 10.52131/pjhss.2022.1002.0246

Niaz, S., Buriro, G., & Soomro, N. (2022). Web-based english language learning: A review from web 1.0 to web 3.0. *Pakistan Journal of Humanities and Social Sciences*, *10*(2). Advance online publication. DOI: 10.52131/pjhss.2022.1002.0246

Oeamoum, N., & Sriwichai, C. (2020). Problems and needs in english language teaching from the viewpoints of pre-service english teachers in thailand. *Asian Journal of Education and Training*, *6*(4), 592–601. DOI: 10.20448/journal.522.2020.64.592.601

Oluwajana, D., Adeshola, I., & Clement, S. (2021). Does the use of a web-based collaborative platform reduce cognitive load and influence project-based student engagement? *Current Psychology (New Brunswick, N.J.)*, *42*(10), 8265–8278. DOI: 10.1007/s12144-021-02145-0

Prasetya, R. (2021). English teaching based-strategy lms moodle and google classroom. *English Education Journal of English Teaching and Research*, *6*(1), 32–44. DOI: 10.29407/jetar.v6i1.15622

Prasetya, R., & Syarif, A. (2023). English language learners' attitude and challenge utilized m-learning: Comparison mobile application moodle and google classroom. *Elt Worldwide Journal of English Language Teaching*, *10*(1), 28. DOI: 10.26858/eltww.v10i1.37218

Purwaningtyas, T., Nurkamto, J., & Kristina, D. (2023). Efl teacher intervention in mediating students' interaction in web-based collaborative writing environment using google docs. *Veles Voice of English Language Education Society*, *7*(1), 135–144. DOI: 10.29408/veles.v7i1.7912

Radosavlevikj, N. (2021). Teachers' and students' perceptions and challenges in communicative language teaching. *Journal of Teaching English for Specific and Academic Purposes*, *307*, 307. Advance online publication. DOI: 10.22190/JTESAP2003307R

Rajaindaran, P., & Abdullah, A. (2023). Google classroom as a tool to enhance english language speaking performance amid the covid-19 pandemic among primary school students. *International Journal of Academic Research in Business & Social Sciences, 13*(6). Advance online publication. DOI: 10.6007/IJARBSS/v13-i6/16986

Setiawan, E., & Entusiastik, E. (2022). Online english teaching by using google classroom and its challenges during covid-19 pandemic at sman 1 gedeg mojokerto. *Jurnal Pendidikan Bahasa Inggris Proficiency, 4*(1), 10. DOI: 10.32503/proficiency.v4i1.2244

Siregar, T., Luali, N., Vinalistyosari, R., Hanurawan, F., & Anggraini, A. E. (2024). Implementation of vygotsky's constructivism learning theory through project-based learning (pjbl) in elementary science education. *Al Qalam Jurnal Ilmiah Keagamaan Dan Kemasyarakatan, 18*(4), 2586. DOI: 10.35931/aq.v18i4.3620

Topalcengiz, E., & Yıldırım, B. (2020). Teachers' opinions about distance web 2.0 tools training and teachers' ın-class web 2.0 practices. *Journal of Turkish Science Education, 17*(4), 561–577. DOI: 10.36681/tused.2020.45

Urooj, S., & Farooq, P.Dr. Safia UroojProf. Dr. Muhammad Shahid Farooq. (2023). Impact of students' ubiquitous learning through web 2.0 tool on students' 21st century skills: Critical thinking and collaboration. *Sir Syed Journal of Education & Social Research (Sjesr), 6*(3), 29–43. DOI: 10.36902/sjesr-vol6-iss3-2023(29-43)

Urooj, S., & Farooq, P.Dr. Safia UroojProf. Dr. Muhammad Shahid Farooq. (2023). Impact of students' ubiquitous learning through web 2.0 tool on students' 21st century skills: Critical thinking and collaboration. *Sir Syed Journal of Education & Social Research (Sjesr), 6*(3), 29–43. DOI: 10.36902/sjesr-vol6-iss3-2023(29-43)

Valızadeh, M. (2022). Collaborative writing on google docs: Effects on efl learners' descriptive paragraphs. [Indonesian Journal of English Language Teaching and Applied Linguistics]. *Ijeltal, 6*(2), 277. DOI: 10.21093/ijeltal.v6i2.1053

Vélez-Palacios, A., & Ramírez-Ávila, M. (2023). Peer feedback and its impact in the writing process of international baccalaureate students in a public institution. *Yuyay Estrategias Metodologías & Didácticas Educativas, 1*(2), 26–39. DOI: 10.59343/yuyay.v1i2.14

Wen, L. (2022). Influence of emotional interaction on learners' knowledge construction in online collaboration mode. *International Journal of Emerging Technologies in Learning, 17*(02), 76–92. DOI: 10.3991/ijet.v17i02.28539

Wijaya, K. (2021). Exploring efl teachers perspectives on collaborative learning activities in senior high school contexts. [Journal of English Teaching]. *Jet*, *7*(2), 118–132. DOI: 10.33541/jet.v7i2.2341

Wu, S., & Shafait, Z. (2024). Assessing efl (english as foreign language) education for sustainable development: Exploring the cultural teaching literature. *European Journal of Investigation in Health, Psychology and Education*, *14*(8), 2282–2299. DOI: 10.3390/ejihpe14080152 PMID: 39194946

Wu, X., & Wang, H. (2024). Teacher awareness as professional development: assistant language teachers in a cross-cultural context by nami sakamoto, switzerland: palgrave macmillan. 2022. pp. xiii+ 164. gbp 54.99 (hbk), isbn: 978–3030883997. *International Journal of Applied Linguistics*, *34*(3), 1221–1223. DOI: 10.1111/ijal.12570

Xu, E., Wang, W., & Wang, Q. (2023). The effectiveness of collaborative problem solving in promoting students' critical thinking: A meta-analysis based on empirical literature. *Humanities & Social Sciences Communications*, *10*(1), 16. Advance online publication. DOI: 10.1057/s41599-023-01508-1 PMID: 37192950

Yahiaoui, F., Aichouche, R., Chergui, K., Brika, S., Almezher, M., Musa, A., & Lamari, I. (2022). The impact of e-learning systems on motivating students and enhancing their outcomes during covid-19: A mixed-method approach. *Frontiers in Psychology*, *13*, 874181. Advance online publication. DOI: 10.3389/fpsyg.2022.874181 PMID: 35967714

Yamaguchi, S., Nagano, M., Ohira, S., Oshima, R., Oshima, J., Fujihashi, T., Saruwatari, S., & Watanabe, T. (2022). Web services for collaboration analysis with iot badges. *IEEE Access : Practical Innovations, Open Solutions*, *10*, 121318–121328. DOI: 10.1109/ACCESS.2022.3222562

Yüce, E. (2020). Keeping online diaries as an integrated activity for writing skill in efl classes: The case of penzu. *Bartın University Journal of Faculty of Education*, *9*(1), 132–140. DOI: 10.14686/buefad.651004

Yumnam, R. (2021). E-learning: An effective mode of teaching english as a second language. *Journal of Translation and Language Studies*, *2*(2), 1–9. DOI: 10.48185/jtls.v2i2.275

Zaki, N., & Adnan, N. (2023). Esl teachers' perceptions of web-based collaborative writing activity. *International Journal of Academic Research in Progressive Education and Development*, *12*(4). Advance online publication. DOI: 10.6007/IJARPED/v12-i4/20153

Zaky, H. (2021). Google docs in undergraduate online composition class: investigating learning styles' impact on writing corrective feedback. Asian Journal of Interdisciplinary Research, 65-84. https://doi.org/DOI: 10.34256/ajir2117

Zheng, L. (2022). Clustering algorithm in english language learning pattern matching under big data framework. *Computational Intelligence and Neuroscience, 2022*, 1–11. DOI: 10.1155/2022/1380046 PMID: 36110905

Chapter 9
IgniteFit: A Comprehensive Web Application for Fitness Solutions

S. Rohith
https://orcid.org/0009-0003-5917-4400
Vellore Institute of Technology, Chennai, India

Benedict Johnson
Vellore Institute of Technology, Chennai, India

K. R. Rohinth
Vellore Institute of Technology, Chennai, India

D. Kavitha
Vellore Institute of Technology, Chennai, India

ABSTRACT

As the digital era continues to reshape how individuals approach health and fitness, there is an increasing need for platforms that offer a holistic and accessible fitness experience. IgniteFit is a comprehensive web-based solution designed to meet this demand by providing a unified platform for those seeking to start or advance their fitness journey. Unlike traditional fitness applications, IgniteFit brings together various fitness resources into one centralized website, ensuring users can find all the tools they need to succeed in their fitness goals. The platform focuses on simplicity, personalized user experience, and effective guidance, catering to diverse fitness levels and needs. By consolidating multiple fitness services, IgniteFit aims to eliminate the need for users to rely on multiple platforms, thereby streamlining their

DOI: 10.4018/979-8-3373-5167-4.ch009

fitness efforts and improving long-term adherence to fitness routines. This paper explores the development of IgniteFIt, its unique features, and its potential impact in providing a seamless, all-encompassing fitness solution for individuals worldwide.

I. INTRODUCTION

The rise of mobile fitness applications has revolutionized personal health management, particularly in the context of home-based training, where users can engage in physical activity from the comfort of their homes. These applications have gained significant popularity, driven by the flexibility they offer in terms of personalized workout plans, progress tracking, and the integration of motivational tools. As the demand for remote fitness solutions continues to grow, the effectiveness of these applications, along with factors that influence user behavior and engagement, has become an area of focused research. Notably, studies have explored the role of gamification, educational features, and user-centric design in sustaining long-term fitness goals.

Home-based training is one of the major trends that fitness applications are capitalizing on. According to Far et al. (2023), mobile fitness apps have effectively transformed the fitness landscape, offering users the ability to work out at home with personalized plans and real-time progress monitoring. However, despite the convenience and accessibility that home-based training offers, challenges like user retention and long-term commitment remain prevalent. This calls for the development of innovative solutions to ensure that users remain motivated and engaged over time. The role of psychological factors such as motivation and education in fitness app usage has also been a focal point in research. Yang and Koenigstorfer (2022) argue that gamification features, such as rewards, tracking progress, and setting goals, significantly influence users' engagement and long-term intentions to stay active. By incorporating such features, fitness apps have been able to enhance user retention and foster a sense of achievement and progression. However, as Yang and Koenigstorfer (2022) point out, the success of these apps is also dependent on providing psychological support and personalized experiences that help users stay on track with their fitness journey.

Additionally, the user's perspective is crucial in shaping the development and success of fitness applications. Raj et al. (2022) highlight that ease of use, customization, and the variety of workout plans offered are critical factors in ensuring user satisfaction. The study emphasizes that fitness apps must not only be intuitive and easy to navigate but also provide a high level of personalization to keep users engaged. Issues such as technical glitches and poor customer support, however, can undermine the user experience, making it essential for developers to prioritize reliability and a seamless experience.

Given these insights, **IgniteFit**, a fitness application aimed at providing a comprehensive and engaging fitness experience, seeks to address these challenges by integrating a variety of user-centric features. Drawing from the studies of Southcott and Jooste (2021), Yang and Koenigstorfer (2022), and Raj et al. (2022), IgniteFit aims to incorporate gamification, educational tools, personalized fitness plans, and a user-friendly interface to foster sustained user engagement. The app integrates elements such as progress tracking, goal setting, rewards systems, and social sharing features to not only motivate users but also provide a sense of achievement and community. IgniteFit also focuses on addressing common challenges such as technical issues by prioritizing a smooth, reliable user experience, ensuring users remain engaged and motivated to achieve their fitness goals.

As the demand for fitness applications continues to rise, understanding and implementing the factors that drive user engagement is critical. IgniteFit leverages insights from existing research to offer a solution that enhances motivation, provides personalized fitness experiences, and sustains long- term user commitment. The integration of these features positions IgniteFit as a valuable tool in the growing fitness app ecosystem, providing users with a holistic approach to achieving their health and fitness objectives.

II. PROBLEM STATEMENT

Despite the rise of fitness applications, many face challenges in sustaining user engagement and retention, especially for home-based training. While features like gamification, progress tracking, and personalization have been shown to boost motivation, most apps fail to integrate these elements effectively, leading to a decline in user commitment over time. Issues like technical glitches, lack of social support, and limited personalization further exacerbate the problem.

There is a need for a comprehensive solution that combines gamified experiences, personalized fitness plans, and community-driven features to enhance long-term user engagement. **IgniteFit** aims to address this gap by integrating motivational elements with reliable, user- friendly technology to foster consistent physical activity and help users achieve their fitness goals.

III. LITERATURE SURVEY

Far et al (2023) explored how mobile fitness applications have transformed the fitness landscape, especially for home-based training. These applications provide flexibility and convenience by offering personalized workout plans, tutorials, and real-time progress tracking. The paper identifies significant advancements in app technology, such as interactive coaching and customizable plans, which have enhanced user engagement. However, it also points out challenges such as user retention and the sustainability of home-based training, calling for further research into long-term user commitment.

Yang and Koenigstorfer (2022) investigated the psychological and behavioral factors that influence the adoption and long-term use of fitness applications. This study examined how educational features, motivational elements, and gamification tools impact users' physical activity intentions. The study highlights the importance of gamification in promoting engagement, suggesting that features such as rewards and progress tracking can significantly enhance user retention.

Southcott and Jooste (2021) investigate how fitness apps affect users' motivational orientations and exercise behaviors. It highlights the role of intrinsic and extrinsic motivation in sustaining long-term exercise. The research emphasizes the importance of features like goal setting, progress tracking, and social support in fostering sustained physical activity. Reed et al. (2023) examine the role of fitness apps in corporate wellness programs. This paper focuses on how employers can leverage fitness applications to enhance employee health and productivity. The study outlines how fitness technologies can reduce absenteeism, improve engagement, and contribute to overall employee well-being. The paper is a valuable resource for companies integrating fitness apps into their corporate wellness strategies. corporate wellness programs. Provides valuable information for organizations seeking to enhance employee engagement. Raj et al. (2022) provides a user-centric view of fitness apps, exploring factors such as ease of use, customization options, and the variety of workout plans available. The paper highlights common challenges users face, including technical issues and lack of motivation, and offers suggestions for improving the overall user experience. These insights are crucial for developers looking to enhance user engagement and retention. Investigate the effect of gamified experiences on user engagement within fitness apps, using the GAMEFULQUEST framework. The study finds that incorporating game-like elements such as points, challenges, and rewards significantly increases user engagement and retention. Gamification provides a sense of accomplishment, which can positively influence users' long-term commitment to their fitness goals. The authors also suggest that fitness apps incorporating these features could see improved user retention, as they create a sense of achievement and progression. However, the paper does not deeply address how other features like personalized workout plans or social sharing tools might interact with gamification to further enhance user engagement. N. Rehman et al. (2023) examine the factors that influence the adoption and sustained use of fitness apps. The study identifies key determinants such as gamification, motivation, and user education. They found that apps that incorporate motivational and educational features, such as progress tracking, feedback, and gamified experiences, encourage users to stick with their fitness regimes. Furthermore, the paper highlights the moderating role of user education and motivation in how these features affect physical activity intentions. The study emphasizes that users are more likely to continue using fitness apps that provide both psychological and educational support, helping them stay on track with their goals.

Yang et al. (2021) explore the user perspective on mobile fitness applications by assessing factors such as ease of use, customization, and the variety of workout plans offered. Their findings suggest that ease of navigation and the ability to personalize workout plans are critical factors in ensuring user satisfaction. Additionally, users indicated that the variety of workout plans and the customization options available played a significant role in keeping them engaged. The study also identified that technical issues, such as app crashes and lack of customer support, were common barriers to sustained use. The research underscores the importance of a user-friendly interface and the need for reliable technical performance to enhance user experience.

Damberg (2022) fills a gap by focusing on the UK market, offering insights into how health consciousness specifically influences fitness app usage in this region. The findings suggest that health-conscious individuals exhibit stronger intentions to continue using fitness apps, thus emphasizing the importance of tailoring fitness apps to meet the specific needsof health-conscious users.

Hansen et al. (2020) introduces an AI-based fitness trainer that employs 3D human pose estimation combined with dynamic time warping (DTW) to evaluate exercise movements. The authors propose a system that matches users' movements with predefined exercise patterns, providing real-time accuracy scores. This approach ensures personalized fitness guidance with a focus on proper form and injury prevention. Uses advanced 3D pose estimation for precise movement tracking. DTW improves motion similarity analysis, leading to accurate feedback. Requires significant computational power, making real-time processing challenges on low-end devices. Effectiveness may be reduced for exercises with high degrees of variability.

Shah et al. (2022) evaluates behavior change techniques (BCTs) implemented in AI-powered fitness applications. The study combines qualitative and quantitative methods to identify how these apps influence user motivation and adherence to fitness programs. The findings suggest that AI-driven customization and gamification improve engagement, but concerns about over-reliance on technology persist. Provides insight into how AI can influence long-term behavior change. Highlights the role of gamification in maintaining user motivation. Lacks a control group to compare AI-based approaches with traditional fitness methods. Overlooks potential privacy concerns related to user data collection.

Zahrt et al. (2023) critically examines the capabilities of OpenAI's GPT-4 model in generating personalized exercise recommendations. The authors evaluate the model's accuracy, reliability, and limitations when prescribing workout routines for various fitness levels. The study highlights the potential of AI to automate personalized health coaching but also points out concerns related to generic advice and ethical implications. Explores AI-driven exercise prescription as an innovative approach to fitness coaching. Identifies key areas where GPT- 4 can assist in health promotion. However, Lacks empirical validation of AI-generated exercise plans. Raises concerns about AI-generated content lacking medical supervision.

Rusmitaningsih et al. (2024) presents an AI-powered virtual fitness trainer that utilizes machine learning algorithms to analyze user movements and provide personalized feedback. The system integrates computer vision techniques to track body posture and suggest corrections, aiming to enhance workout efficiency and reduce injury risks. The study also explores the effectiveness of AI in delivering real-time coaching, making fitness training more accessible and affordable. Offers real-time feedback for improved exercise accuracy. Enhances accessibility of fitness training without requiring human instructors. May struggle with diverse body types and movement variations. Accuracy heavily depends on the quality of the input video and AI model training.

Shaw (2022) evaluates behaviour change techniques (BCTs) implemented in AI-powered fitness applications. The study combines qualitative and quantitative methods to identify how these apps influence user motivation and adherence to fitness programs. The findings suggest that AI-driven customization and gamification improve engagement, but concerns about over-reliance on technology persist. Provides insight into how AI can influence long-term behaviour change. Highlights the role of gamification in maintaining user motivation. Lacks a control group to compare AI-based approaches with traditional fitness methods. Overlooks potential privacy concerns related to user data collection.

Pereira et al. (2023) explores how step-tracking apps contribute to physical activity levels and changes in body composition. By analyzing users' daily step counts and health metrics, it highlights correlations between consistent usage and improved fitness outcomes. Demonstrates the quantitative benefits of wearable tech in promoting activity. Connect step count data with measurable body composition improvements. Does not account for dietary habits or other lifestyle factors. Limited generalizability due to reliance on self-reported data.

Evenson et al. (2018) evaluates the validity and reliability of commercial fitness trackers in research settings. It assesses various devices based on accuracy in measuring steps, heart rate, and energy expenditure. Provides a comprehensive comparison of multiple wearable devices. Useful for researchers to select tools for physical activity studies. Devices rapidly evolve, so findings may be outdated. Does not evaluate long-term behavior change effects.

Dergaa et al. (2024) critically assesses GPT-4's potential in crafting personalized exercise routines. It examines the model's ability to understand user needs and deliver safe, effective health recommendations.

Innovative analysis of generative AI's capabilities in fitness. Encourages further AI integration in personalized health tools. But raises concerns about AI making unsupervised medical recommendations. Limited by GPT-4's lack of real-time user feedback integration.

Vu-Minh et al. (2024) presents an AI fitness trainer system that uses 3D human pose estimation combined with Dynamic Time Warping to evaluate and guide exercise form in real-time. Provides precise movement feedback for users. Leverages advanced techniques for real-time performance analysis. High computational requirements may limit accessibility. Effectiveness depends on camera quality and environment.

Gurbuxani et al. (2024) outlines a virtual fitness trainer application powered by AI that monitors posture and recommends corrections during workouts. It uses machine learning to improve feedback over time. Practical implementation of AI in everyday workouts. Focuses on personalized correction for injury prevention. User experience may vary due to sensor and device limitations. Lacks longitudinal data to assess long-term impact.

The mixed-methods study of Shaw (2023) evaluates which behaviour change techniques are embedded in an AI fitness app and how users perceive them. It combines usage data with user interviews. Provides insights into the psychology behind app engagement. Highlights user-centered evaluation of AI tools. Focuses on a single app, limiting generalizability. Some BCTs may be misclassified due to subjective interpretation.

Ning (2024) evaluates whether online fitness programs can improve specific athletic performance metrics, including squat jump and sprint speed, among students. Empirically tests performance outcomes from digital training. Useful for educational institutions integrating tech in PE. Limited scope, focusing only on two performance metrics. Does not compare with traditional in-person coaching methods.

IV. ARCHITECTURE DIAGRAM

Figure 1. Architecture diagram

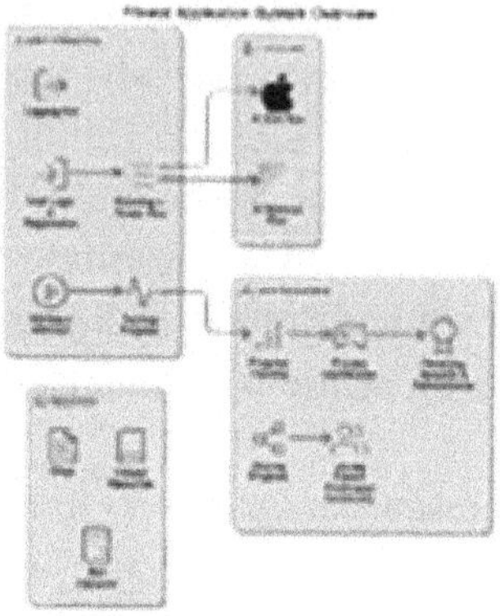

User Interaction

Login/Registration: Linked to your Session-based Authentication system.
AI Manual / AI Bot: Matches your AI-based Fitness & Nutrition Recommendation System.
Tracking Request: Corresponds to Progress Tracking Module (tracking workouts, steps, etc.).

AI Recommendation

Planning → Goals → Generate → Recommend Alternatives
This mirrors your:
AI-Powered Workout Plan Module (goal-based workout creation).
Nutrition & Meal Planning Module (adjustable, AI- generated plans).
Recommendation System (offers alternatives when needed).

Devices

Wearables / Mobile Devices This reflects your Mobile-First Responsive Design and potential integration with devices like fitness bands or smartphones for input (steps, heart rate).

Database

Stores Logs, Progress, and User Data Matches perfectly with your dual database setup:
SQL for structured data like logs, goals, user info. MongoDB for unstructured content like blogs or tutorials.

V. TECHNOLOGY TO BE USED

Frontend Technology

Technology: HTML5, CSS3, JavaScript
Description: IgniteFit features a modern and responsive user interface built with HTML, CSS, and JavaScript. The frontend ensures an engaging and interactive user experience, with smooth navigation and visually appealing design for fitness tracking and personalized workout plans.

Backend Technology

Technology: SQL, MongoDB

Description: The backend is designed to handle user requests efficiently using a combination of SQL for structured data and MongoDB for flexible storage of unstructured fitness-related content.

Database

Technology: SQL (Relational Database) & MongoDB (NoSQL Database)
Description:
SQL: Stores structured data, including user profiles, workout logs, meal plans, and progress tracking metrics.
MongoDB: Manages unstructured data such as exercise tutorials, fitness blogs, and community forum discussions.

User Authentication

Technology: Secure Login System (Session-based Authentication)
Description: IgniteFit ensures secure user authentication through a session-based login system, protecting user data and preventing unauthorized access.

Personalized Recommendations

Technology: AI-based Fitness & Nutrition Recommendation System
Description: IgniteFit uses an AI-driven approach to suggest personalized workout plans and meal recommendations based on user progress, fitness goals, and preferences.

Data Security & Privacy

Technology: HTTPS, Data Encryption
Description: To ensure user privacy and security, IgniteFit implements HTTPS for secure data transmission and encryption techniques to safeguard sensitive user information.

Responsive Design

Technology: Mobile-First Design Approach
Description: The website is designed to be fully responsive, ensuring a seamless and optimized experience
across all devices, including desktops, tablets, and smartphones.

Performance & Scalability

Technology: Optimized Database Queries, Efficient Caching Mechanism
Description: IgniteFit employs optimized SQL queries and an efficient caching mechanism to improve load times and ensure smooth performance even under high user traffic.

By integrating these technologies, IgniteFit provides a powerful, user-friendly, and data-driven platform to help users achieve their fitness goals effectively.

VI. MODULES

AI-Powered Workout Plan Module

Key Features

Personalized workout plans tailored to user fitness levels, goals, and preferences.
Adaptive AI that adjusts workout intensity based on real-time progress.

Dynamic updates and recommendations to keep workouts engaging and effective.
Purpose: To provide a customized and evolving workout regimen for users to achieve their fitness goals efficiently.

Nutrition & Meal Planning Module

Key Features

AI-generated meal plans based on user fitness goals (weight loss, muscle gain, or maintenance).
Automatic adjustments to meal plans based on changing workout intensity and progress.
Integration with workout routines for a holistic fitness approach.
Purpose: To ensure users receive the right nutrition in alignment with their workout plans for optimal results.

Fitness Resources & Learning Module

Key Features

Educational Content: Articles, blogs, and tutorials on fitness, health, and wellness.
Exercise Library: A detailed database of exercises with instructions, benefits, and variations.
Expert Advice: Insights from certified trainers and nutritionists.
Workshops & Webinars: Sessions on injury prevention, advanced techniques, and more.
Community Forum: A space for users to share experiences and ask fitness-related questions.
Purpose: To educate and empower users with knowledge to improve their fitness journey effectively.

Progress Tracking & Analytics Module

Key Features

Comprehensive tracking of workouts, calories burned, weight, and steps.
Visual progress reports with graphs, milestones, and achievements.
AI-driven suggestions for improvement based on data analysis.

Purpose: To help users monitor their progress, stay motivated, and make data-driven fitness decisions.

These modules work together to create a complete fitness ecosystem, ensuring users receive personalized guidance, accurate tracking, and continuous motivation throughout their fitness journey.

Advantages

Personalized Fitness Experience – AI-powered workout and nutrition plans tailored to individual goals, fitness levels, and preferences.
Adaptive and Dynamic Adjustments – The system continuously updates workout and meal plans based on user progress, ensuring effectiveness.
Comprehensive Health Approach – Integrates exercise, nutrition, and educational resources for a holistic fitness journey.
Data-Driven Progress Tracking – Provides visual reports, milestones, and AI-driven insights to help users track and improve performance.
Community Support & Expert Advice – Users can access expert tips, workshops, and a community forum for motivation and guidance.
Convenience & Accessibility – Available anytime and anywhere, making it easy to stay consistent with fitness goals.
Scalable and Flexible – Supports a wide range of users, from beginners to professionals, and adapts to different fitness preferences.

Disadvantages

AI Limitations – While AI can suggest workouts and meals, it may not fully replace human trainers' expertise, especially for unique cases.
Dependency on User Input – Accuracy of recommendations depends on users entering correct and consistent data.
Potential Privacy Concerns – Storing user health data may raise security and privacy risks if not properly protected. Requires Internet Access – A stable internet connection is needed to access workout plans, updates, and real-time tracking.
Limited Customization for Unique Needs – Users with medical conditions or specific fitness needs may require professional guidance beyond AI-generated plans.
Initial Learning Curve – Some users may take time to understand and utilize all the features effectively.

No Real-Time Human Interaction – Unlike personal trainers, AI-driven suggestions lack real-time corrections for workout posture and technique.

Despite some challenges, IgniteFit provides a robust and data- driven approach to fitness, helping users stay consistent, informed, and motivated on their fitness journey.

VII. ALGORITHMS

Algorithm ToggleMobileMenu

1. If user clicks the menu icon:
   a. Show the mobile menu wrapper.
   b. Display overlay background.
2. If user clicks the close icon:
   a. Hide the mobile menu wrapper.
   b. Remove overlay background.

Handles the responsive mobile menu (off-canvas menu). It's the slide-out menu you see on mobile view.

Explanation:

When the user taps the hamburger icon (menu icon), a hidden menu slides in from the side.

The screen gets a dark overlay to draw attention to the menu. When the user taps the close (X) button or clicks outside the menu, it closes and the overlay disappears.

This is important for mobile-friendliness and helps users navigate easily.

Algorithm HandleNavigationClick (menuItem)

Input: menuItem (e.g., "Workout", "Nutrition", "Contact")

1. Switch(menuItem):
   a. If "Workout" → Redirect to Workout Plan Generator page.
   b. If "Nutrition" → Redirect to Meal Plan Generator page.
   c. If "Pages" → Show dropdown with subpages (e.g., About, Blog).
   d. If "Contact" → Scroll or redirect to contact form section.
2. End Switch

Controls the navigation when users click on items like "Workout", "Nutrition", or "Contact".

Explanation:

> Based on what the user clicks:
> If it's Workout, they are redirected to the AI-powered workout generator.
> If it's Nutrition, they go to the meal planning page. If it's Pages, a dropdown opens with links like About Us, Blog, etc.
> This navigation logic ensures users are directed to the right section or page, enhancing usability.

Algorithm ShowPreloader

1. On page load:
   a. Display the preloader (loader animation).
2. Wait until the page DOM is fully loaded.
3. Once loaded:
   a. Hide the preloader animation.
   b. Reveal main website content.

Before the full website loads, a loading animation is displayed to the user (this is called a "preloader"). It prevents users from seeing incomplete or unstyled content.

Explanation:

When someone visits the website, the loader (<div id="preloder">) is shown first.

Once the browser finishes loading all content (HTML, CSS, JavaScript, images), the loader is hidden, and the website content is revealed.

This gives a smooth user experience and avoids flickering content or broken layouts.

Algorithm InitializePageAssets

1. Load Google Fonts.
2. Load all CSS dependencies:
   a. Bootstrap
   b. Font Awesome
   c. Custom styles (e.g., owl-carousel, barfiller)
3. Load JS dependencies (not shown but typically present).
4. Initialize scripts after DOM is ready:
   a. Carousels
   b. Animation triggers

c. Responsive menu wrapper (mobile)

Ensures all fonts, styles, and functionalities load properly when the site is opened. Explanation:

Loads fonts from Google (e.g., Oswald and Muli).
Loads CSS files for design and layout (e.g., Bootstrap for layout, Owl Carousel for sliders).
After the HTML loads, JavaScript (usually included separately) initializes plugins:

Carousels (for sliding images), Menu toggles,
Animations (like the preloader, bar fillers, etc.). This makes the website feel dynamic and professional.

Algorithm RedirectToSocial (platform)

Input: platform (Facebook, Twitter, Instagram, YouTube)

1. If user clicks on a social icon:
   a. Open the corresponding platform link in a new tab.
2. Log user action for analytics if applicable.

When a user clicks a social icon (like Instagram or Facebook), they're redirected to the gym's official page on that platform. Explanation:

Clicking a social icon triggers an event that opens a new browser tab to the respective social page.

This helps promote the gym's online presence and keeps users connected.
Optionally, user clicks can be tracked using analytics to understand engagement.

VII. MODULE DETAILS

AI-Powered Workout Plan Module: Users input their fitness level and goals.

The system fetches any previous progress data.
An AI engine generates a personalized workout plan.
As the user follows the workout, the system tracks real-time progress.
If progress is detected, the AI adapts workout intensity to match improvement.

If no significant change, it continues with the current plan.
This ensures the user gets an evolving plan suited to their progress.

Figure 2. AI-powered workout plan module: flow graph nutrition & meal planning module

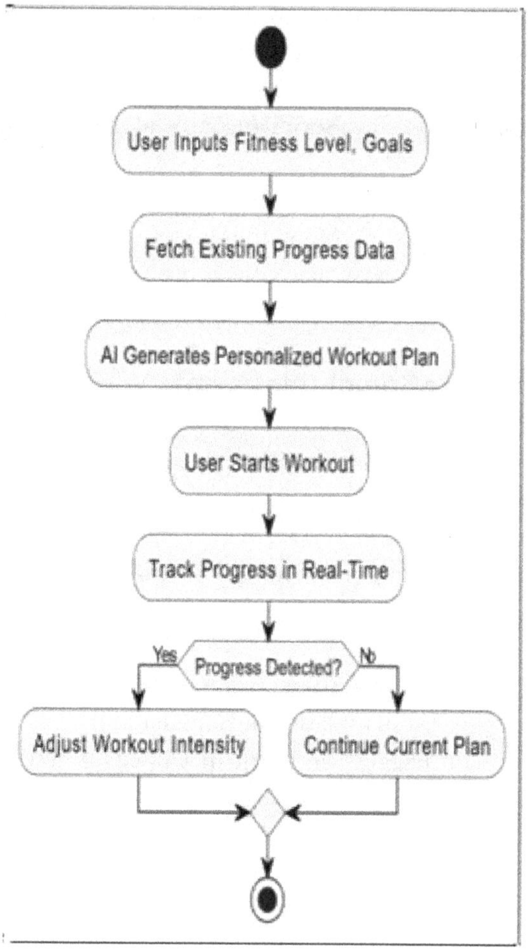

User selects a fitness goal (e.g., weight loss, muscle gain).
The system checks workout intensity to align with nutrition needs.
AI generates a personalized meal plan accordingly. Users view the meal plan.
If user progress changes, the AI auto-adjusts the plan to stay effective.
This aligns diet with workouts for optimal results.

Figure 3. Nutrition & meal planning module: flow graph fitness resources & learning module: flow

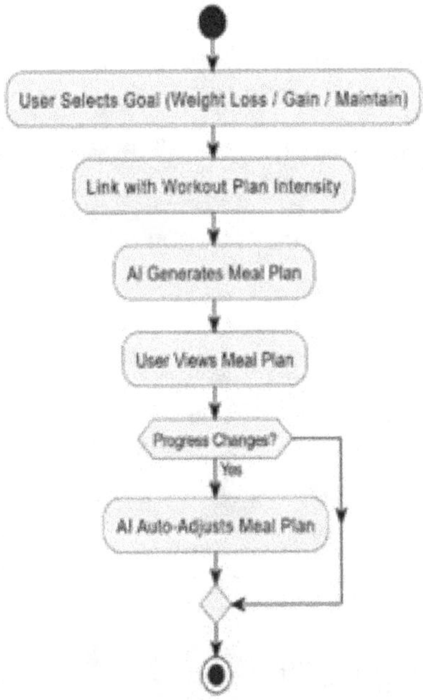

User enters the Resources section.
They choose content type: Articles, Exercises, Webinars, or Forum.
The chosen content is displayed.
Users interact, learn, or engage with community/expert content.
The data is stored in the database.
System generates visual reports and milestones. An AI engine analyzes the data.
The system suggests improvements or motivational tips based on insights.
This module ensures users stay aware of their progress and stay motivated.

Figure 4. Progress tracking & analytics module: flow graph

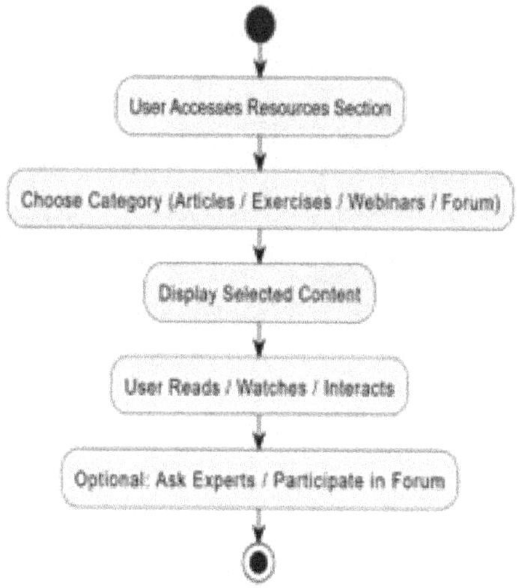

Inputs and Outputs of IgniteFit

AI-Powered Workout Plan Module

Inputs:

This empowers users with fitness knowledge and community support.

Outputs:

User fitness level (beginner, intermediate, advanced) Fitness goals (weight loss, muscle gain, endurance, etc.)

User preferences (preferred exercises, equipment availability)

Performance data (previous workouts, progress metrics)

Personalized workout plan

Adjustments to workout routines based on progress Recommendations for exercise intensity and duration

Nutrition & Meal Planning Module

Inputs:

Figure 5. Fitness resources & learning module: flow graph

Outputs:
User fitness goals (caloric intake for weight loss, maintenance, or muscle gain)
Dietary preferences and restrictions (vegetarian, vegan, keto, etc.)
Workout intensity and duration
Customized meal plans and recipes
Nutritional breakdown of meals (macronutrients, calories, etc.)
Meal plan adjustments based on updated fitness routines

Progress Tracking & Analytics Module: Flow

User logs workouts, steps, calories, and weight.

Fitness Resources & Learning Module

Inputs:
User-selected topics of interest (workouts, nutrition, wellness, injury prevention)
Outputs:
User engagement data (articles read, videos watched, forum interactions)
Personalized content recommendations (articles, videos, blogs)
Notifications for upcoming fitness workshops and webinars
Community forum discussions and expert responses
Personalized Workout Plan: Generated based on user goals and fitness level.

AI Adjustments: Real-time intensity updates based on progress. Exercise Details: Name, sets, reps, instructions, and demo videos. Progress Tracker: Shows completion status for each exercise.

Daily/Weekly View: Toggle between day-wise and week-wise plans.

Modify Plan Option: User can adjust preferences/goals.

Progress Tracking & Analytics Module

Inputs

Outputs:

Workout data (exercises completed, reps, sets, duration)

Health data (weight, steps, calories burned)

Goal tracking metrics (muscle gain, weight loss progress)

Visual progress reports (graphs, statistics, milestones)

AI-driven improvement suggestions Achievement notifications and motivation messages

By collecting and analyzing user data, IgniteFit provides a personalized and adaptive fitness experience, ensuring users stay on track toward their health and fitness goals.

VIII. RESULTS AND DISCUSSIONS

Figure 6. Homepage

Welcome Message: Brief intro to IgniteFit and its purpose. Module Highlights: AI Workout Plans, Meal Planning, Resources, Progress Tracking.

Visual Banners: Engaging images or sliders showcasing fitness goals.

Get Started Button: Directs users to login/signup. Mobile-Friendly Design: Smooth and responsive layout.

Figure 7. Fitness

Figure 8. Services

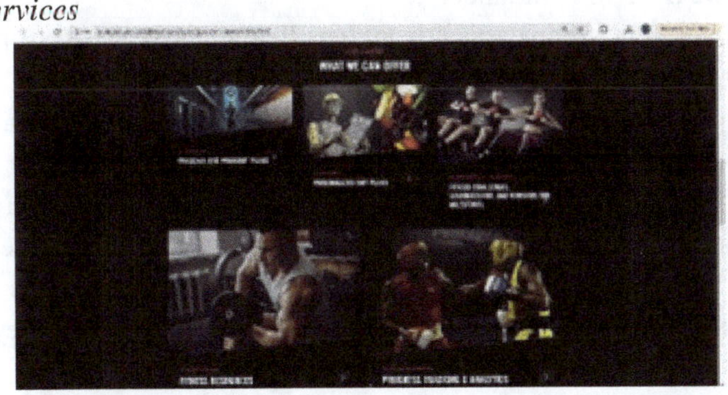

User Dashboard: Shows name, fitness goal, today's workout & meals.

Progress Graphs: Weight, calories, achievements.

AI Suggestions: Personalized workout and meal tips. Quick Links: Workout, Meals, Resources, Forum.

Notifications: Reminders & updates. Responsive Design: Works on all devices. Secure Access: Visible only after login.

Figure 9. Why choose IgniteFit

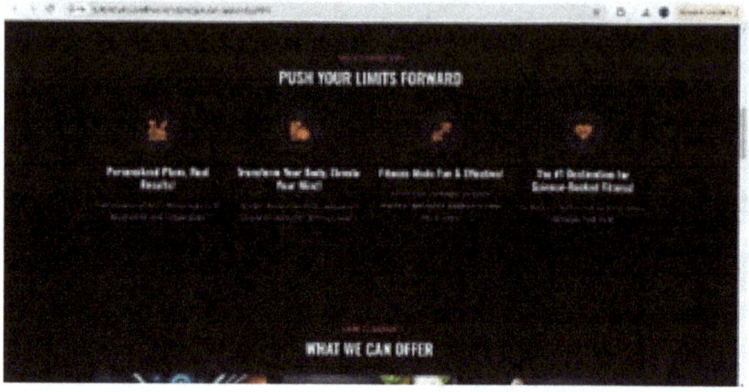

Core Value Highlights: Emphasizes IgniteFit's commitment to personalized fitness through AI-driven guidance.

Benefits Overview: Showcases advantages like adaptive workout plans, smart meal tracking, and health insights.

Trust Signals: Mentions reliability, accuracy, and technology- backed fitness transformation.

Engaging Visuals: Uses icons or illustrations to represent each feature or benefit.

User Testimonials (Optional): Real user experiences reinforcing credibility and results.

Call-to-Action (CTA): Encourages users to start their fitness journey or explore more features.

Mobile-Optimized Layout: Visually appealing and easy to navigate on any device.

Figure 10. Contact and support

Contact Form: Fields for Name, Email, Subject, and Message for easy communication.

Submit Button: Sends user queries directly to the support team. Official Email Display: Shows the team's contact email for direct access.

Location Map (Optional): Embedded map showing office or institution location.

Responsive Layout: Clean and mobile-friendly design for all devices.

Validation Alerts: Ensures all required fields are properly filled before submission.

Figure 11. AI workout generator

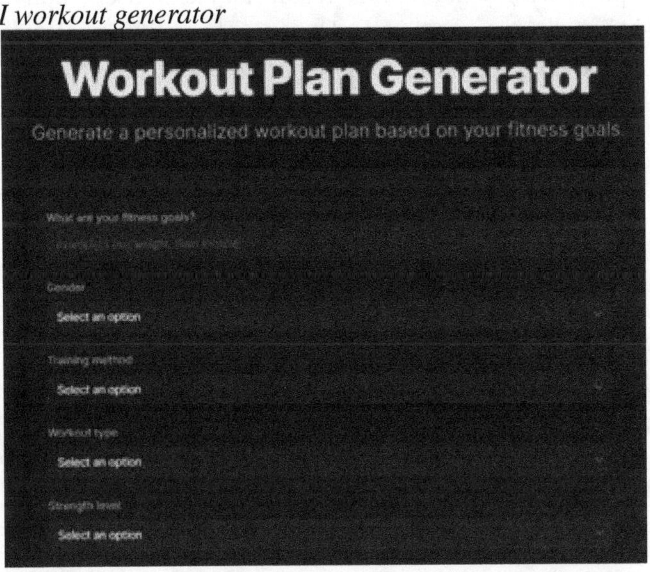

User Input Form: Collects user fitness level (beginner, intermediate, advanced), goals (weight loss, muscle gain, endurance), preferences, and equipment availability.

AI Customization Engine: Generates a personalized workout plan using AI based on user inputs and previous progress data. Dynamic Plan Display: Instantly shows day-wise workout routines, including sets, reps, duration, and rest time.

Progress-Based Adjustments: AI fine-tunes future workouts based on performance feedback and completed sessions.

Exercise Intensity Recommendations: Suggests optimal difficulty level and intensity scaling for each workout.

Get Plan Button: Instantly generates the customized plan with the click of a button.

Save & Export Option: Allows users to download or save their plan for later reference or integration with other modules.

The chart below is a sample output generated by IgniteFit's AI system, showcasing estimated calories burned over a 30-day period for users of different fitness levels—Beginner, Intermediate, and Advanced.

This graph is dynamically generated by the AI-powered Workout Plan Module, which takes into account the user's fitness level, goals, workout preferences, and performance data. Based on these inputs, the system creates a personalized workout plan and tracks progress.

As seen in the graph, advanced users typically burn more calories due to higher workout intensity and longer duration, while beginners progress steadily over time. The AI adapts plans weekly to optimize results and keep users motivated.

This visual aid helps users understand how their activity translates into progress and supports informed decision-making regarding their fitness journey.

Figure 12. Calories burned in 30 days graph

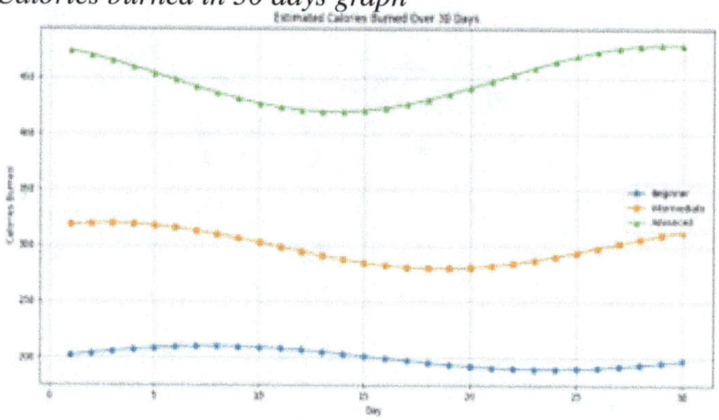

This table illustrates how the IgniteFit AI-driven workout planning system effectively adapts training intensity and routine based on each user's fitness level and progress data. Over a 30-days period, users at different fitness stages—beginner, intermediate, and advanced—experienced a noticeable increase in calories burned, reflecting the dynamic adjustments made by the AI engine. The AI evaluates user input (fitness goals, previous workout data, preferences) and progressively optimizes the workout plan for better performance. The percentage increase highlights how the system keeps users consistently challenged, promoting sustained engagement and gradual fitness improvements.

Table 1. Calories burned in 30 days

User ID	Fitness Level	Day 8 Calories	Day 16 Calories	Day 24 Calories	Day 30 Calories	% Increase
U001	Beginner	1200	1450	1600	1800	+50%
U002	Intermediate	1800	2000	2150	2400	+33%
U003	Advanced	2200	2500	2750	3000	+36%

IX. CONCLUSION

IgniteFit leverages the power of AI to deliver a comprehensive, personalized fitness experience that adapts to users' goals, preferences, and progress. By integrating dynamic workout

planning, customized nutrition, educational resources, and real-time progress tracking, the app addresses key challenges in user engagement and long-term commitment. Drawing from recent research and industry practices, IgniteFit not only empowers users to take control of their fitness journey but also provides a scalable and accessible platform that bridges the gap between convenience and effective health management.

X. FUTURE SCOPE

Augmented Reality (AR) Guided Workouts

Develop a mobile app where users can follow 3D AI avatars doing workouts in their room using AR.

Perfect for remote users needing posture correction and engagement.

Multilingual Support

Expand to support multiple regional and global languages using AI translators for accessibility.

Offline Mode with Syncing

Allow users to download plans or sessions and use the app offline. Progress gets synced back when internet is restored.

REFERENCES

Damberg, A. (2022). The influence of health consciousness on fitness app usage in the UK market. *Journal of Regional Fitness Research, 10*(4), 44–58.

Dergaa, I.. (2024). Using artificial intelligence for exercise prescription in personalised health promotion: A critical evaluation of OpenAI's GPT-4 model. *Biology of Sport, 41*(2), 221–241. DOI: 10.5114/biolsport.2024.133661 PMID: 38524814

Evenson, K. R., Goto, M. M., & Furberg, R. D. (2018). Using fitness trackers and smartwatches to measure physical activity in research: Analysis of consumer wrist-worn wearables. *Journal of Medical Internet Research, 20*(3), e110. DOI: 10.2196/jmir.9157 PMID: 29567635

Far, I. K.. (2023). Fitness applications for home-based training. *Journal of Mobile Fitness Technology, 18*(3), 112–126.

Gurbuxani, S., Gupta, L., & Madan, K. (2024). Virtual fitness trainer using artificial intelligence. In *Proceedings of the Sixteenth International Conference on Contemporary Computing (IC3-2024)* (pp. 226–233). Noida, India.

Hansen, D. L.. (2020). A review of gamified fitness tracker apps and future directions. In *Proceedings of the Annual Symposium on Computer–Human Interaction in Play (CHI PLAY '20).*

Ning, C. (2024). Modern software and physical education: Can online training improve squat jump and sprint performance? *BMC Medical Education, 24*(1), 5345.

Pereira, M. G., de Lima, F. B., de Oliveira, L. F., & de Souza, F. M. (2023). Importance of training volume through the use of step tracker apps in physical activity and body composition. *Physiology & Behavior, 259*, 114038.

Raj, K. R.. (2022). User's perspective about mobile fitness applications. *Journal of User Experience in Fitness Apps, 15*(2), 98–109.

Reed, R.. (2023). The employer perspective: Insights and practical applications of the 2025 fitness trends. *Journal of Corporate Wellness and Productivity, 11*(1), 34–46.

Rehman, N.. (2023). Gamified experiences and user engagement within fitness apps. *International Journal of Mobile Health, 20*(1), 49–63.

Rusmitaningsih, F. N., Subarjah, H., Yustiana, Y. R., & Saputra, D. R. (2024). Enhancing students' engagement and motivation in physical education: The role of fitness tracker apps. *Edu Sportivo: Indonesian Journal of Physical Education, 5*(3), 1–10. DOI: 10.25299/esijope.2024.vol5(3).17215

Shah, A. M.. (2022). Comparison of cycling path characteristics in South Florida and implications for bicycle infrastructure planning. *International Journal of Sustainable Transportation, 16*(12), 1089–1100.

Shaw, A. M. (2022). Examining user engagement and use of fitness tracking technology: A qualitative study. *Behaviour & Information Technology, 41*(12), 1–13.

Shaw, A. M. (2023). Identifying behavior change techniques in an artificial intelligence-based fitness app: A mixed-methods study. *Health Education & Behavior, 50*(1), 1–10.

Southcott, E., & Jooste, J. (2021). Unveiling the impact of mobile fitness applications on motivational orientation in sustaining exercise behaviors. *International Journal of Sport Psychology, 30*(2), 75–91.

Vu-Minh, A., Nguyen-Quy, D., Nguyen-Khanh, H., & Nguyen, T. (2024). AI fitness trainer using 3D human pose estimation and dynamic time warping. In *Proceedings of the 13th Conference on Information Technology and Its Applications (CITA 2024)* (pp. 50–62). DOI: 10.1007/978-3-031-74127-2_5

Yang, Y.. (2021). Determinants of fitness app usage and moderating impacts of education, motivation, and gamification-related app features on physical activity intentions. *Journal of Health Psychology, 27*(5), 124–135. PMID: 34255656

Yang, Y., & Koenigstorfer, J. (2022). Determinants of fitness app usage and moderating impacts of education, motivation, and gamification-related app features on physical activity intentions. *Journal of Health Psychology, 28*(5), 1234–1245.

Zahrt, O. H., Evans, K., Murnane, E., Santoro, E., Baiocchi, M., Landay, J., Delp, S., & Crum, A. (2023). Effects of wearable fitness trackers and activity adequacy mindsets on affect, behavior, and health: Longitudinal randomized controlled trial. *Journal of Medical Internet Research, 25*, e40529. DOI: 10.2196/40529 PMID: 36696172

Chapter 10
Digital Surveillance and Identity Construction on Web-Based Platforms

Muhammed Aksoy
https://orcid.org/0009-0007-0497-7061
Ondokuz May University, Turkey

ABSTRACT

Web-based platforms have brought about fundamental changes in the ways individuals create identities, maintain social relationships, and represent themselves. The development of internet infrastructure and social networks since the 1990s has enabled individuals to establish an online presence without being tied to a physical location. In this context, the concept of "digital identity" refers to a multi-layered structure shaped by strategies individuals employ to reveal, conceal, and establish connections in the online environment. Social media posts, professional profiles, and online performances demonstrate that individuals develop multiple, fragmented, fluid identity strategies. Furthermore, virtual reality environments deepen identity experiences and presentation forms, making digital identity visible not only as screen-based but also interactive and spatial. However, the formation process of digital identity is based not only on individual preferences but also on the ways digital surveillance mechanisms monitor, direct, and categorize individuals' behaviors.

INTRODUCTION

Identity encompasses an individual's sense of self and perception of themselves. This concept encompasses characteristics acquired at birth, qualities that cannot be chosen, and a process of socialization that includes education, career, and com-

DOI: 10.4018/979-8-3373-5167-4.ch010

munity interactions throughout an individual's life (Chambers, 2005, p. 37). At the same time, identity plays an indispensable role in an individual's life as one of the cornerstones of the social structure of society, encompassing a multidimensional structure that includes cultural and social positions, beliefs, attitudes, and value judgments (Timisi, 2005, p. 100).

Today, online social networks have become an integral part of individuals' daily lives, and many users spend more time on these platforms than on other online activities. People prefer to interact with other users by sharing their experiences, photos, or videos (Fire, Goldschmidth, & Elovici, 2014). These platforms offer users the opportunity to interact with social resources that cater to their individual interests and needs rather than the collective needs of the community. Additionally, the internet has increased individual autonomy and mobility in developed countries (Manago, 2015).

The rapid development of Web 2.0 technologies over the past two decades has led to the expansion and diversification of digital identities. Social media profiles, emails, and other digital accounts have become increasingly important in daily life. In this context, online identity refers to an individual's presence on the internet and their identity in the digital world. Digital identities encompass names, profile photos, personal information, social media accounts, and other digital activities. Online profiles can be considered a type of "digital body" that individuals create in the virtual environment to share certain aspects of their identity with others (Boyd & Ellison, 2007).

Presence in the digital world not only reflects individuals' identities but also strengthens their connections and influences in the physical world. Schmidt and Cohen (2013, p. 18) predict that increased digital connectivity will bring benefits in areas such as health, education, quality of life, productivity, and others. Cover (2015) emphasizes that identity is largely online today; individuals present their identities and leave digital traces through social media, blogs, and similar platforms. Being present on a social media platform means "writing oneself into existence" by sharing one's identity with other users in a virtual environment. The expression of identity begins with choosing an appropriate avatar, determining visual representation forms, and reflecting individual characteristics and interests. As the user interacts in the virtual environment, actively participates in games or activities, and observes the reactions of other users, the process of "self-actualization" continues. This communication is asynchronous; it gives the user time to create and reflect on the messages they want to convey. As a result, individuals can build a more positive personal image through their virtual identities and present an often idealized version of themselves to others (Kramer & Winter, 2008).

All these processes reveal that identity consists of both reality and virtuality. Identity encompasses both who we are (our real self) and who we want to be (our ideal self). Identity can be considered an "open text" in which reality and idealism are intertwined. Durante (2011, p. 595) argues that those who believe social networks give people the chance to create a second life or a new personality, as well as those who oppose this idea, are mistaken, as these platforms enable reality and idealism to intertwine in a different way in the construction of identity.

The spread of internet technologies has significantly transformed social structures and approaches to the concept of identity. Social media networks have enabled individuals to construct their digital identities, and the integration of the internet into individual lives has led to a blurring of the boundaries between public and private spheres. Thus, the concepts of disclosure and violation of privacy have undergone conceptual change; individuals have become part of a surveillance society where they voluntarily share their privacy to construct their digital identities. Although social media platforms appear to provide individuals with a sense of freedom, personal freedom does not operate equally in these spaces. While individuals in democracies and constitutional states can use social media as a public space to share their views on public issues, in regions where the rule of law is controversial, the direct surveillance capabilities of social media networks may lead individuals to prefer to remain anonymous or refrain from sharing their opinions (Baban, 2012). In this context, technologies contribute to the promotion of a certain lifestyle, the reshaping of human roles, and the reinforcement of existing human relationships. Rose (1999, p. 52) defines the dominant technology of each era as "government technology" and emphasizes that technologies are a means of shaping individual behavior in line with the goals of producing power and preventing unwanted events.

Today, the internet and new media environments contribute most to the spread of surveillance. The rise in popularity of social networks and the visibility of surveillance have become commonplace on these platforms. The virtual environment provides an ideal environment for individuals who want to monitor others and obtain information about users. When creating profile accounts, users share information about themselves, publish photos, videos, and stories, and produce various content. In this way, they can both monitor others and make themselves monitorable. Surveillance behavior has now become a form of social interaction, with users obtaining psychological satisfaction by allowing others to monitor them. Individuals who want to be known become data subjects by sharing their personal and private information, and this situation carries the risk of personal information being violated (Utma, 2024, p. 2276). In the digital age, those who manage surveillance systems can often access the tools of those being monitored. This access, whether literal or metaphorical, includes record keeping, database creation, and observation methods. New technologies offer the ability to control our lives through continuous data recording, observation, and guidance of individuals' physical and behavioral characteristics. With these norms and realities, surveillance has become a routine part of daily life. As a result of routine surveillance practices, data belonging to large groups of people is stored for the purposes of classification, separation, and evaluation (Lyon, 2013, p. 44).

In the 21st century, surveillance has become a global phenomenon. The recording, monitoring, and processing of personal data is no longer limited to national borders but is now carried out at an international level. Today's digital technologies provide a constant flow of data about user behavior, habits, and preferences: Who they communicate with, where they shop, what music they listen to, or which websites they visit are all recorded. Electronic devices generate data about individuals, enabling others to analyze their activities, preferences, and achievements (Gilliom & Monahan, 2013). Today, surveillance and monitoring rituals are more intense and comprehensive than in the past. The widespread use of the internet has created a virtual archaeological site for dominant powers (Haggerty, 2006, p. 30). Digital surveillance emerged as a result of the global use of the internet, and although the reasons for data collection are explained by legitimate reasons such as trade security, crime prevention, or the detection of terrorist activities, it often leads to results that threaten individual rights, such as profiling, violation of personal information, and the use of data for commercial purposes (Çakır, 2015, pp. 35–36). With the media's penetration into everyday life, the media space has become more attractive to marketers and governments. Millions of internet users are being monitored, their data processed and labeled without their knowledge while using online services. Edward Snowden's revelations have clearly exposed the prevalence and scale of these surveillance activities (Augusto & Simoes, 2017, p. 599).

The collection of data on a global scale raises the dilemma of privacy and security and keeps everyone under surveillance without distinguishing between suspects and innocent individuals (Çakır, 2015, p. 12). This means that individuals are constantly monitored in both public and private spaces. Therefore, digital surveillance has a direct impact on the construction of individuals' identities. Individuals who are aware that they are under surveillance may express themselves in virtual environments in a censored, controlled, or idealized manner; this process becomes a powerful social mechanism that determines both the boundaries and contents of digital identity.

The rapid advancement of digitalization shapes individuals' online identities not only through personal preferences but also through surveillance mechanisms that guide them via social media, biometric authentication, and data-driven algorithms. This situation allows individuals to construct their behaviors, communication styles, and social representations under surveillance. In this section, the concept of identity and the digitalization process will first be examined, followed by the relationship between virtual reality and identity and the phenomenon of digital surveillance within a theoretical framework, and the impact of digital surveillance mechanisms on identity construction will be evaluated.

THE CONCEPT OF IDENTITY

The importance of the concept of identity in social relations has only been understood relatively recently. In the Middle Ages, interpersonal relations were largely fixed and shaped by religious beliefs. During this period, individuals' identities were essentially defined by their position within society. The social class to which one belonged, family background, place of birth, birth order within the family, and social status were the fundamental criteria that determined an individual's value in society (Güney, 2017, p. 72). In the modern era, identity has ceased to be merely a reflection of social status and has come to be understood through individuals' relationships with culture, values, and norms. As a fundamental component of social life, identity reflects the values, cultural heritage, and geographical conditions of the society in which individuals live. In other words, identity represents the answer to the question of "who they are" for societies, groups, and individuals. Today, technological developments have transformed the traditional dimensions of identity and added a new dimension to the concept (Çelik, 2010, p. 34).

Identity can be defined as a phenomenon that is shaped by the experiences and conclusions individuals gain from the relationships they establish with others in a specific social sphere, reflecting the totality of the positions, roles, and social relationships to which the individual feels they belong (Akyazı & Ateş, 2012, p. 176). However, identity is shaped not only by individual preferences but also by social processes; it is constantly reproduced as a result of interactions between individuals. Therefore, it has a complex structure.

Identity is classified under different types in the literature: Social identity refers to the self-perception shaped by the individual's knowledge of the social group to which they belong, their sense of belonging to that group, and the values they derive from it. Social identity also reveals that the individual's self-perception and self-esteem cannot be separated from the group to which they feel they belong. National identity encompasses the reflections of the cultural, ideological, and social characteristics of the nation to which individuals belong on the individual. Each nation's unique worldview, emotional attitudes toward events, and habits reflected in daily life constitute the basic elements of national identity. Cultural identity is a form of identity defined by shared history, geography, experiences, and values; it reflects the cultural rules, traditions, and norms of social life. Ethnic identity emerges as a result of individuals maintaining their own unique cultural characteristics, distinct from the general identity elements of the society in which they live. It becomes more pronounced in situations where cross-cultural integration is limited or where distance hinders interaction. Language, religion, shared social values, and cultural practices are among the determining factors in the formation of ethnic identity (Akyazı & Ateş, 2012, pp. 177-178).

The concept of identity has different dimensions, which are generally addressed along two main axes: the way individuals perceive and define themselves and their need to belong to a group or community. In this context, identity emerges through the evaluation and interpretation of individuals based on the social groups to which they belong. Social identity is concretized by the individual's sense of belonging to the group, their tendency to glorify the group, their conformity to group norms, and their development of similar responses. On the other hand, identity also expresses the conditions and contexts under which the individual can be evaluated as an individual. This dimension, referred to as personal or individual identity, is directly related to the individual's unique qualities, personal characteristics, and interpersonal relationships (Güney, 2017, p. 86).

THE DIGITALIZATION PROCESS OF IDENTITY

The concept of identity, one of the most fundamental realities of social, cultural, and societal systems, refers to the multidimensional network of relationships between individuals. At the psychological level, identity can be explained as an individual's subjective definition of themselves and their identification with the statement "This is who I am." In this context, identity encompasses various representations such as the views, definitions, images, and information that individuals have about themselves (Kulga, 2014, p. 38).

The concepts of identity and self are often confused with each other. However, the most fundamental element that distinguishes identity from self is its social dimension. The social dimension of identity is formed as a result of the individual's integration with the values and ideals of the group to which they belong. Therefore, identity is a combination of the unchoosable elements acquired at birth (such as race, gender, and age) and the social roles acquired throughout life. Increased social mobility and rapid change in the modern era have made the concept of identity more complex. Indeed, this transformation is one of the main factors that make it difficult to define identity today (Akkaş, 2016, p. 39).

Advances in information and communication technologies have profoundly affected the concept of identity and radically transformed individuals' daily life practices. The most distinctive feature of the information society is that individuals spend a significant portion of their time interacting with digital environments and are constantly connected to the virtual world. This transformation has not only changed communication forms but has also reshaped the processes of constructing and presenting identity. Therefore, the digitization of identity can be considered one of the most concrete reflections of the penetration of information technologies into social life. The process of digitizing identity is closely related to the concepts of virtual environments and virtual reality. With the inclusion of social media networks in everyday life, creating a virtual life has become a common practice for individuals. Turkle (1995) describes the internet as a social laboratory for identity construction, arguing that individuals have the opportunity to re-experience their identities and present them in different ways in online environments. From this perspective, the internet provides a psychological and social experiential space for the diversification and digitization of identity. Indeed, digital identities are the most important elements of the internet's emergence as a current and powerful medium (Çuhacı, 2007, p. 186).

According to Thomas (2007, p. 5), identity is shaped around the characteristics that individuals are born with (such as race, age, and gender) and elements that depend on their choices (such as clothing style and body adornments). However, in the digital environment, the importance of these physical indicators is diminishing, and identity is constructed through texts, codes, and visual representations. Avatars, user names, and posts are the main indicators of the multi-layered structure of digital identity.

In the online environment, individuals tend to be selective in the process of creating their identity, presenting themselves in more appealing and interesting ways. In this context, Goffman's (2004) concept of "impression management" is explanatory. Goffman states that the behaviors individuals exhibit in different social contexts in everyday life affect how others perceive them. In the virtual world, this situation becomes more pronounced, with individuals constructing flawless and idealized identities to present themselves for approval. In this context, digital identity performances are directly related to modern society's culture of "showmanship" and "approval."

Communication in the virtual world is based on performance. Individuals can use their role-playing skills to shape their identities and display them. Digital identities are independent of time and space; they cannot be limited or restricted. The invisibility of the environment provides users with a space for liberation and the opportunity to construct an identity independent of social norms. In this process, individuals do not merely construct their own identities; they may also attempt to experience the identities of other digital bodies. Today, identity has become a commodity within the digital universe, gaining an existence independent of the body. The body is no longer a representation of the visible, but is being reconstructed through language and symbols. In this context, a physical body can be transformed into countless digital bodies (Timisi, 2005, pp. 97-98).

The concept of anonymity is another fundamental factor that increases the ambiguity of identity in the digital world. The anonymity of cyberspace offers users the opportunity to act without risk. Identities created on the internet may appear isolated and independent, but they interact with others. These identities have the flexibility to reach any desired location both offline and online; they can appear alone while simultaneously interacting with millions of users (Kellner, 2001). The digital environment allows individuals to join communities without revealing their real identities, and even to interact using pseudonyms. Thus, multiple and flexible identities are becoming more accepted in contemporary cultural environments.

Virtual communities offer the opportunity to perform most real-life activities without leaving one's body behind. Individuals can have fun, flirt, debate, shop, conduct commercial activities, make friends, gossip, and organize meetings (Rheingold, 1993). The appeal of the virtual environment increases with the elimination of physical boundaries and dangers. Chatfield (2013, p. 121) defines the greatest advantage of the digital realm as the ability for individuals to experience growth and success as the heroes of their own stories; users can construct their identities with a level of comfort and autonomy that is not possible in real life.

In the online world, identities can be chosen, played with, changed, or accepted as given. Individuals can selectively construct narratives about their characters, even telling lies. According to Bailey, a "virtual skin" can be worn over the body. Online and offline identities may not always align; computer-mediated communication offers a hybrid form of communication, and participants continuously construct their identities. Communication is based on role-playing and performance; participants' identities constantly change through interaction. These features allow users to construct identities that suit them through virtual representations (Robins, 1999, p. 145). In summary, identity in the contemporary digital world is changing at a pace that cannot be compared to the past. These changes eliminate some of the definitional aspects of identity while offering a continuous state of existence with new dimensions. Identity is not a static or final self, but a continuously constructed process. Therefore, identities only gain existence through continuity and reproduction; they continue to be constructed throughout life and can never be fully completed.

VIRTUAL REALITY AND IDENTITY

Our presence is increasingly shifting from the physical world to the cyber world in a fluid manner. Computers, which enable individuals to access the cyber world, function as tools that transport users into the virtual universe. When the user immerses themselves in the screen, the computer ceases to exist within the context of physical reality; the devices that facilitate the connection to the virtual universe become invisible, like tools that have fulfilled their purpose. In the cyber environment, users interact with virtual objects and people; this can be considered an extension of our personality and, although it contains physicality, it can be defined as an experience that is formed in the individual's mind and has no counterpart in the external world (Işıklı & Küçükvardar, 2016).

Baudrillard (2015, pp. 75–76) states that with the process of users entering the virtual universe, the distinction between humans and machines disappears. This operational process brings forth the figure of the machine and the mechanized human; in fact, the individual can become a part of the machine as a whole. According to Baudrillard, the human being transformed into virtual reality functions like its operational twin. In this process, the screen serves as the primary interface between the human and virtual reality; while it is possible to speak of the "beyond the mirror," it is impossible to speak of the "beyond the screen." This is because the dimensions of time and real time become intertwined, creating uncertainty.

People of our time are under the influence of information and communication technologies. These technological innovations offer individuals the opportunity to recreate reality and enable them to experience much more than their own physical, psychological, and intellectual abilities (Funk, 2013, p. 104). In virtual reality, anything is possible; individuals who desire to be free from the constraints of time and space can experience whatever they want in this environment. İlhan (2013) states that individuals prefer the restrictive and normative real world to the virtual world, which is full of freedom. The virtual world offers a space where entry and exit are quick, risk-free, and non-committal; it provides short-term pleasures to the individual, and this situation can weaken the person's beliefs and ties to the real world.

Today, the boundaries between the physical and virtual worlds can no longer be clearly defined. This phenomenon is explained by the concept of "Phygital." Derived from the combination of the words "physical" and "digital," this term is closely related to our perception of virtual reality (Ferhat, 2016, p. 745). Virtual reality systems and physical reality have merged, ultimately creating a unified experience. This situation demonstrates that the performance of individuals living on Earth is subject to timeless changes. Işıklı and Küçükvardar (2016) state that virtual environments are not only a part of daily life but also pose a potential threat to individuals. The authors emphasize that users have become agents connected to the virtual reality universe, and that in this universe where everything is virtual, the virtualization of individuals is an inevitable reality. Virtuality, which affects our social values, has developed new relationship networks. These agents are not like subjects in the physical world; our knowledge is limited to their digital identities, and their existence in the physical world cannot be definitively verified. The authors also note that reality checks that appear on the Internet have emerged to ensure that users are "real people." These tests cause us to feel a lack of reality and weaken logical functionality. Thus, in an environment where the boundaries between the virtual and physical worlds are becoming increasingly blurred, individuals have the opportunity to create new experiences and identity performances.

Guga (2015) states that although virtual identities function as an extension of our physical bodies, they are experienced separately from our identities in physical reality or as the other side of reality. He emphasizes that identities created in virtual environments do not have a static structure and continue an endless process of construction. According to him, identity has a model that is independent of physical reality and the body, and can be chosen, changed, or abandoned when desired. Technology activist Hannes Sjoblad defines identity as a defining element for humans. According to him, identity is where we were born, our gender, our genetics, our sexual orientation, what others give us or what we acquire ourselves, and how we express ourselves. The most interesting aspect of digitalization is our ability to experiment with our identities. Sjoblad states that many people hack their own biological processes as "bio-hackers" and conduct experiments on themselves via the internet (Gopalakrishnan, 2017).

Coleman (2011, p. 88) states that experience, intelligence, and other factors enable us to distinguish between what is virtual and what is real. People may become bored with machines that mimic humans; they are successful in semantic communication, i.e., interpreting human and non-human signals. Although we can currently distinguish between a real person and a chatbot, simulation is becoming increasingly successful as a phenomenon derived from human behavior. Thus, human signals, whether live or indirect, elicit human responses. The digital age offers individuals the opportunity to exist in virtual environments with fake identities. Today, many people act under fake identities to exist in virtual environments, gain followers, or become famous. This situation leads to serious problems between real identities and fake identities constructed in the virtual world. Mercan (2010) emphasizes that various activities on social networks alienate individuals from both their surroundings and themselves. The connection between identities constructed in the real world and the virtual world becomes indistinguishable over time.

Funk (2013, p. 20) states that individuals should be free to shape their relationship with reality. According to him, the environment has become a tool for the self to produce itself rather than providing a living space for the individual. Unconventional and illusory things are found attractive, and individuals are turning to the constructed reality rather than the traditional reality that surrounds the physical world. Turkle (1999) emphasizes that the fluidity of identity in cyberspace has reached an extreme point. Individuals display a distributed identity through the different windows they open in the online environment, and this situation offers the opportunity to reflect on the self and reconstruct identity experiences. These windows serve as a technical metaphor for individuals to understand their forms of existence in the virtual environment.

Agger (2004) examines the forms of existence of individuals in the virtual world in his book The Virtual Self. According to him, users participate in cyberspace by creating a virtual self, and this participation either liberates or enslaves individuals. Virtuality is a phenomenon experienced through computers, and users can manipulate themselves and their appearances in the virtual universe. Virtual selves can form social groups among themselves and participate in various virtual communities. Castells (2008, p. 479) evaluates this situation from a sociological perspective and states that weak ties established outside and on computers facilitate connections between people with different social characteristics. Thus, socialization transcends the socially defined boundaries of personal recognition.

The integration of information and communication technologies into our lives has made the transformative effect of virtual reality on the concept of identity inevitable. User profiles and behaviors have diversified; the actions and opportunities of individuals in the physical and virtual worlds have become a topic of debate. The character "Case" in William Gibson's (2012) 1984 novel Neuromancer reflects the modern human's dependence on virtual environments. Virtual reality offers the individual the opportunity to be wherever and whenever they want, but at the same time, it is experienced as nothing more than an illusion.

THE PHENOMENON OF DIGITAL SURVEILLANCE

The word "surveillance," which has French origins and means "to watch" in French (Lyon, 2013, p. 30), was first used at the end of the 18th century to mean "to closely monitor a person's movements" (Clarke, 2005). The word "surveillance" has two meanings in French: to observe and to protect. Lyon explains this dual meaning in his book The Surveillance Society (2006) using examples related to children. Children are kept under surveillance both to protect them from harm and to control their behavior (Lyon, 2006, p. 14). In this context, surveillance is not merely a concept related to seeing but a phenomenon that encompasses various desires and orientations. According to Lyon, surveillance is a central dimension of modernity and continues to exist as an institution that cannot be reduced to capitalism, the nation-state, or bureaucracy (Lyon, 1997, p. 303).

Surveillance is, in a sense, a mechanism of control. With the penetration of technology into every area of life before and after digitalization, surveillance has become even more comprehensive. In this context, the concept of the Panopticon is important for understanding the historical and spatial dimensions of surveillance. Designed by Jeremy Bentham, the Panopticon is based on a circular building where prisoners are kept under constant surveillance and a central observation tower (Dolgun, 2008, p. 72). The guard in the tower can constantly observe the prisoners, while the prisoners cannot see the person monitoring them and do not know when they are being watched (Foucault, 2006, pp. 295–296). This model has not been limited to prisons; it has also been applied as a technique of power and control in various social areas such as schools, hospitals, and recruitment processes (Özkan, 2021, p. 69).

Today, surveillance has gone beyond the physical Panopticon with digitalization. Instead of physically visible control, a virtual prison experience has emerged in which individuals are given a sense of freedom through communication and information technologies. Individuals share their personal data and behaviors without being aware that they are being monitored; in this process, they voluntarily become part of the surveillance cycle (Kalaman, 2019, p. 275). According to Lyon (2013, p. 257), the extent of surveillance in the digital age has become unpredictable. Personal data, habits, and all activities on the internet are recorded, and individuals accept this situation as normal and readily upload their information to social media networks.

The examination of digital surveillance tools within a socio-political framework highlights the importance of technological investments. For example, between 1963 and 1983, the Pentagon allocated $500 million to computer research, and the first computer network, ARPANET, was developed as a product of these investments for military purposes. ARPANET was opened for civilian use as the internet in 1990, made available for commercial use in 1993, and was subsidized by the US federal government for a long time (Geray, 2019, p. 61). During this process, the first users of computer networks were bureaucratic institutions and multinational companies.

The Internet has commercialized itself as a new field for investors and companies, creating a virtual market. People's statements, likes, and other areas of life have gained material value by opening up to the economy; this situation is referred to as the "new economy" (Çakır, 2015, p. 35). Although the internet does not have a centralized organizational structure, the structure of networks carries capitalist economic, cultural, and political characteristics and reflects private property and dominance relations. Digital platforms such as Google and Facebook function as information gathering areas for both private companies and some state intelligence agencies (Erdoğan, 2011, p. 437).

The economic and strategic importance of information has also brought property issues to the forefront. Although the security and privacy of information circulating on networks during applications such as e-commerce and banking are attempted to be ensured through legal regulations, this is difficult because information is a fluid resource (Başaran, 2005; Toffler, 1992). Thus, digital media, together with data tracking technologies, leads to the commodification of communication and the transformation of masses into commodities, expanding the scope of surveillance to all areas of daily life in favor of economic relations (Özçetin, 2019, p. 213–214).

During the time spent on the internet, all clicks, likes, and saved content are stored, and personal data circulates at the national and international levels (Lyon, 2013, p. 17). The popularity of the new media environment is one of the main reasons for the spread of surveillance. Social media platforms enable users to become both observers and observed when creating their profiles (Dijk, 2018, p. 121). With social media entering every area of life, significant transformations have taken place, from daily habits to political views, from work life to friendships, and the culture of surveillance and security has also been reshaped (Ünsal, 2022; Castells, 2016).

THE IMPACT OF DIGITAL SURVEILLANCE MECHANISMS ON IDENTITY CONSTRUCTION

Surveillance is examined holistically not only in the context of safety and security, but also in social areas such as employment, consumption habits, trade, and management. Therefore, societies are faced with an increasingly sophisticated surveillance mechanism. The increase in surveillance in digital environments, combined with users sharing all kinds of information about themselves while constructing their identities, has turned individuals into objects of spectacle for those in power. Identities constructed and displayed with a focus on achieving perfection not only provide a sense of approval and satisfaction but also become objects that are easily monitored by those in power (Kalaman, 2016, pp. 64–65).

When individuals join any platform on the internet, they consent to the use of their personal data. Most users accept the privacy policies presented during registration without reading them and are unaware that their personal data may be used by third parties within certain frameworks through these policies (Esgin, 2015, p. 49). Social media and other virtual networks complicate the ways in which surveillance occurs, making it difficult to understand the existence, implementation, and consequences of surveillance (Martin, 2012, p. 421).

While social media offers its users a free communication environment, it should be noted that this freedom may be restricted if it infringes on the rights of other users, as is the case in offline life. The freedom of communication offered by the virtual environment is regulated by legal regulations on socially sensitive issues such as bullying or hate speech. Governments are conducting studies within the framework of internet law and protecting the personal rights of individuals in virtual environments. Attitudes and behaviors displayed on social media impose responsibilities on individuals in the context of digital identity, making it mandatory to avoid behaviors that violate laws and regulations. However, social media is designed as an environment where users can express themselves freely; individuals can communicate within the scope of freedom of expression as long as they do not violate the rights of other users (Engin, 2015, pp. 20–21).

The changeable and disembodied nature of digital identities leads users to perceive themselves as invisible compared to the offline world. This situation may cause individuals to be careless in their behavior on social networks and occasionally participate in cyberbullying or hate speech. Research links social media users' tendency toward such actions to their perception of anonymity (Dursun & Tugtekin, 2016, p. 545).

Advances in communication technologies and the transfer of daily life practices to the digital environment have led to significant changes in individuals' perceptions of social visibility and privacy. Social media allows users to be more courageous in terms of freedom of expression and self-presentation, enabling them to voluntarily share their personal information, photos, and videos. These shares reinforce individuals' sense of gaining social visibility while constructing their digital identities; likes and comments on these shares enable individuals to make inferences about their own values and perceptions of social acceptance. As a result, the boundaries of the concepts of private space and privacy are becoming increasingly blurred (Yavuz, 2019).

In our era, the lack of common values regarding individuals' life choices increases the tendency to monitor the lives of other individuals. The effort to make inferences by observing the lives of other users in the process of constructing one's own identity often results in privacy violations (Kete, 2011, p. 66). The digitization of life practices has led to speed taking center stage in banking, shopping, work life, and personal relationships, while also blurring the boundaries between public and private spaces. The ability to access the world from a small screen without time and space constraints creates an illusion of freedom in individuals. This illusion of freedom can result in individuals transferring their personal information to digital environments without question. In digital environments, the sharing of highly personal information such as names, surnames, addresses, and phone numbers has become increasingly normalized. The public disclosure of private information makes surveillance inevitable for individuals. Social media and other virtual networks offer certain prerequisites for individuals to engage in virtual activity, including the processes of creating an account and registering for a network. Individuals who wish to participate in online environments register with networks by sharing their identity information, and their identities within the information flow may be compromised. Recent examples show that social network servers share user information with governments or commercial companies (Kalaman, 2016, p. 13).

In social media environments, individuals exist through virtual representations rather than physical representations. Digital identities consist of specific and consciously organized information. Just as in offline identity construction, peer interaction plays an important role in digital identity construction. Within the framework of the self-perception that develops as a result of these interactions, individuals construct their digital identities and present themselves in a public process on social media. The individual characteristics displayed on social media accounts shape the construction of digital identities in a positive or negative way, depending on the interactions of other users (Boz, 2012, pp. 31–35).

Changes in communication technologies have also transformed the ways in which individuals present themselves in society. Throughout history, technological developments have led to transformations in communication forms and cultural elements, changing individuals' strategies for visually constructing and presenting their identities. With internet technology, individuals have encountered environments with unlimited informational richness, and methods of gaining social visibility have transformed accordingly. The surveillance society created by individuals who enjoy watching and being watched has made it easier for those in power to control the masses. In communication environments dominated by power, visibility means being controlled by the state's "instruments of violence" in the context of political activities. Surveillance systems, which are a component of the state's apparatus of violence, are referred to as "white violence," and the state instrumentalizes them to silence dissenting voices or exert pressure (Çoban, 2014, pp. 305–307).

Social networks are spaces where individuals share almost all the details of their private lives. Users try to convey the message "I am living a wonderful life and everything is fine" through posts such as exaggerated dinner table photos, coffee cups beautified with filters, or luxury location tags. Often, bad photos or sad moments are not shared on social media accounts. Individuals who construct their identities through posts and interactions adopt lives on social media that are inconsistent with their offline lives, leading to alienation from offline life standards (Akgül & Hekimoğlu Toprak, 2019).

Social media networks allow individuals to construct digital identities through fake identities or pseudonyms, and this fake individualization increasingly shapes offline reality. Social relationships are shaped around these fake identities, and social media has gained a central position beyond influencing offline reality (Çoban, 2014, pp. 309–313).

The identity characteristics displayed in social media environments may vary depending on the nature of the environment in which communication takes place. The identity displayed when discussing public issues in media seen as public spaces may differ from the identity displayed in chat rooms. At this point, the changeable and reconstructable nature of digital identities is decisive (Boz, 2012, p. 37).

CONCLUSION

Contemporary social life has become a sphere in which individuals reconstruct, transform, and often produce their identities under surveillance through the opportunities provided by digitalization. The structure of identity, which historically gained meaning through social status, belonging, and cultural values, has evolved into a different dimension in the digital age. Today, identity is not only constructed through the relationships an individual establishes within their social environment but also through the performances displayed on virtual platforms, the digital traces left behind, and the representations they choose to make visible. In this sense, identity has ceased to be limited to physical reality and has begun to exist in the virtual world in a plural, fragmented, and fluid form. One of the most significant effects of digitalization on identity is that it offers individuals the opportunity to re-experience their self and to create different versions of it. Social media platforms provide users with a space of liberation where they can display their "ideal self" through visual, textual, and symbolic representations, something that is often not possible in everyday life. However, this freedom is frequently intertwined with the pressure of visibility imposed by surveillance mechanisms, transforming individuals into subjects who are both "free" and "monitored." Digital identities shaped by likes, follower counts, and algorithms not only meet individuals' need for social acceptance but also make them part of a system that keeps them under constant observation.

With the advancement of virtual reality technologies, the experience of identity has moved beyond being merely a representation constructed through a screen. Individuals transcend the boundaries of physical space through avatars and digital bodies, gaining the opportunity to experience different social roles and to redefine their identities. However, this process demonstrates that identity is no longer a "fixed" and "essential" concept but rather a phenomenon that is constantly reconstructed, variable, and experiential. Therefore, in the contemporary world, identity gains existence through "phygital" experiences that are simultaneously real, virtual, and situated in between. The phenomenon of digital surveillance constitutes the most critical dimension of this process. Individuals, by voluntarily sharing information on social media and web-based platforms, erode the boundaries of their privacy and render what is private into something public. Surveillance, unlike the unilateral control of the classical panopticon, has today assumed a more invisible, internalized, and routinized form. Users simultaneously take on the roles of both the surveillant and the surveilled, making surveillance an ordinary part of social interaction. However, this "normality" leads individuals to present their identities in censored, controlled, or idealized forms, where a powerful mechanism of control operates behind the illusion of freedom.

In this context, the digitalization of identity encompasses a dual dynamic. On the one hand, it offers individuals the opportunity to express themselves, to become visible, and to experiment with multiple identities, while on the other hand, it places them within the surveillance domain of data-driven algorithms, states, and corporations. This dual structure clearly demonstrates that identity is not merely a matter of individual choice or social belonging but also a process shaped by power relations, economic interests, and technological infrastructures. As a result, the construction of identity in the digital age is neither entirely a practice of free subjectivity nor solely the outcome of imposed surveillance. Rather, it is a multi-layered and fluid phenomenon that is continuously reproduced through the relationships individuals establish within digital networks, the representations they perform, and the algorithmic regulations to which they are exposed. This situation has weakened the "stable" and "fixed" nature of identity in the modern era and has instead replaced it with temporary, performative, and fragile forms of identity.

It is clear that digital identities will become even more important in the future. Artificial intelligence, augmented reality, biometric verification, and blockchain technologies will make identity construction both more secure and more traceable. At this point, the balance between individuals' ability to freely express their digital identities and the protection of their privacy will remain the central issue of the digital society. Therefore, the digitalization of identity stands before us as a contemporary matter that must be discussed in depth not only on individual and societal levels, but also in ethical, legal, and political dimensions.

REFERENCES

Agger, B. (2004). *The virtual self.* Blackwell Publishing.

Akgül, M., & Hekimoğlu Toprak, H. (2019). The transformation of privacy on social networks: The case of Instagram [Sosyal ağlarda mahremiyetin dönüşümü: Instagram örneği]. *Anadolu Üniversitesi Sosyal Bilimler Dergisi, 10*(38), 75–114. DOI: 10.5824/1309-1581.2019.3.004.x

Akkaş, İ. (2016). Identities and virtual communities in a multi-faced network of relations [Çok yüzlü ilişkiler ağında kimlikler ve sanal cemaatler]. *Düzce Üniversitesi Sosyal Bilimler Dergisi, 3*(2), 37–53.

Akyazı, E., & Ateş, A. (2012). The role of social networks in creating cultural identity awareness: A study on Manav Turks. [Kültürel kimlik farkındalığı yaratmada sosyal ağların rolü: Manav Türkleri üzerine bir araştırma] In Kara, T., & Özgen, E. (Eds.), *Social media, academy: Communication, marketing communication, network society, technology* [Sosyal medya, akademi: İletişim, pazarlama iletişimi, ağ toplumu, teknoloji]. (pp. 173–192). Beta Publication.

Augusto, F. R., & Simões, M. J. (2017). To see and be seen, to know and be known: Perceptions and prevention strategies on Facebook surveillance. *Social Sciences Information. Information Sur les Sciences Sociales, 56*(4), 596–618. DOI: 10.1177/0539018417734974

Baban, E. (2012). McLuhan and Baudrillard's perspective on social media: The captivity of expression, the surveilled society, and the lost identity syndrome. [Mc Luhan ve Baudrillard'ın penceresinden sosyal medyanın etkisi: İfadenin esareti, gözetlenen toplum ve kayıp kimlik sendromu] In Kara, T., & Özgen, E. (Eds.), *Social Media Academy* [Sosyal Medya Akademi]. (pp. 57–83). Beta Press.

Başaran, F. (2005). The political economy of the Internet. [İnternetin ekonomi politiği] In Toplum, M. (Ed.), *Internet, society, culture* [*İnternet, toplum, kültür*]. (pp. 32–52). Epos Publication.

Baudrillard, J. (2015). *The spirit of terrorism and reign of evil* [*Şeytana satılan ruh ya da kötülüğün egemenliği*]. (Adanır, O., Trans.). Doğu Batı Publication.

Boyd, D. M., & Ellison, N. B. (2007). Social network sites: Definition, history, and scholarship. *Journal of Computer-Mediated Communication, 13*(1), 210–230. DOI: 10.1111/j.1083-6101.2007.00393.x

Boz, N. (2012). *Digital identity and self-presentation in new communication environments* [*Yeni iletişim ortamlarında dijital kimlik ve benlik sunumu*] (Doctoral dissertation). Istanbul.

Çakır, M. (2015). *Performance and surveillance on the Internet: A critical reading* [*İnternette gösteri ve gözetim: Eleştirel bir okuma*]. Ütopya Publication.

Castells, M. (2008). *The rise of the network society: The information age, economy, society and culture* (Vol. 1; Kılıç, E., Trans.). Istanbul Bilgi University Publication. [*Ağ toplumunun yükselişi enformasyon çağı: Ekonomi, toplum ve kültür*]

Castells, M. (2016). *Communication power* [*İletişim gücü*]. Istanbul Bilgi University Publication.

Çelik, H. (2010). Identity debates in the globalization process and the role of media: The case of Kosovo [*Küreselleşme sürecinde kimlik tartışmaları ve medyanın rolü: Kosova örneği*]. *İstanbul Arel Üniversitesi Yayınları, 3*(7), 21–44.

Chambers, I. (2005). *Migration, culture, identity* [*Göç, kültür, kimlik*]. (Türkmen, İ., & Beşikçi, M., Trans.). Ayrıntı Publication.

Chatfield, T. (2013). *How to survive in the digital age* [*Dijital çağa nasıl uyum sağlarız*]. (Konca, L., Trans.). Sel Publishing.

Clarke, R. (2005, Aprıl 30). Have we learnt to love Big Brother? Xamax Consultancy Pty Ltd. https://www.rogerclarke.com/DV/DV2005.html

Çoban, B. (2014). The new panopticon: Power of surveillance and Facebook. [Yeni panoptikon gözü iktidarı ve Facebook] In Çoban, B. (Ed.), *Social media revolution* [*Sosyal medya devrimi*]. (pp. 303–319). Su Publication.

Coleman, B. (2011). *Hello Avatar: Rise of the networked generation* [*Hello Avatar: Dijital neslin yükselişi*]. MediaCat Publication.

Cover, R. (2015). *Digital identities: Creating and communicating the online self.* Academic Press.

Çuhacı, G. (2007). Body in digital arts / Dijital sanatlarda bedenin kullanımı (Doctoral dissertation). Marmara University, Institute of Social Sciences, Department of Communication, Istanbul.

Dijk, J. V. (2018). *The network society* [*Ağ toplumu*]. (Sakin, Ö., Trans.). Epsilon Publication.

Dolgun, U. (2008). *Transparent prison or surveillance society: Surveillance, social control and power relations in a globalizing world* [*Şeffaf hapishane yahut gözetim toplumu: Küreselleşen dünyada gözetim, toplumsal denetim ve iktidar ilişkileri*]. Ötüken Publication.

Durante, M. (2011). The online construction of personal identity through trust and privacy. *Information (Basel)*, *2*(4), 594–620. DOI: 10.3390/info2040594

Dursun, Ö. Ö., & Tugtekin, E. B. (2016). The new problem of social media: Virtual identities. [Sosyal medyanın yeni sorunsalı: Sanal kimlikler] In İşman, A., Odabaşı, H. F., & Akkoyunlu, B. (Eds.), *Readings in educational technology* [*Eğitimde teknoloji okumaları*]. 1st ed., pp. 535–552). TOJET.

Engin, Y. (2015). The phenomenon of digital identity among social media users and its examination in the context of social events [*Sosyal medya kullanıcılarında dijital kimlik olgusu ve toplumsal olaylar bağlamında incelenmesi*] (Master's thesis, Istanbul University, Institute of Social Sciences, Department of Journalism). Istanbul.

Erdoğan, İ. (2011). *Understanding communication* [*İletişimi anlamak*]. Pozitif Press.

Esgin, M. S. (2015). New trends in the world of web technologies. [Web teknolojileri dünyasında yeni trendler] In Baloğlu, A. (Ed.), *Social media mining* [*Sosyal medya madenciliği*]. (pp. 5–17). Beta Publication.

Ferhat, S. (2016). Temmuz). The reality of the digital world, the virtuality of the real world: Virtual reality as a digital media product [Dijital dünyanın gerçekliği, gerçek dünyanın sanallığı: Bir dijital medya ürünü olarak sanal gerçeklik]. *TRT Akademi*, *1*(2), 724–746.

Fire, M., Goldschmidth, R., & Elovici, Y. (2014). Online social networks: threats and solutions. *IEEE Communication Survey&Tutorials, Fourth Quarter*, 2019-2036.

Foucault, M. (2006). *Discipline and punish: The birth of the prison* [*Hapishanenin doğuşu*]. (Kılıçbay, M. A., Trans.). İmge Publication.

Funk, R. (2013). *Me and us: Psychoanalysis of the postmodern human* [*Ben ve biz: Postmodern insanın psikanalizi*]. (Tanyeri, Ç., Trans.). Yapı Kredi Publication.

Geray, H. (2019). *Corporate communication in the new economy of media: Digital transformation in newspapers, television, advertising, and public relations* [*Medyanın yeni ekonomisinde kurumsal iletişim: Gazeteler, televizyonlar, reklamcılık ve halkla ilişkilerde dijital dönüşüm*]. Ütopya Publication.

Gibson, W. (2012). *Neuromancer*. Altıkırkbeş Press. DOI: 10.2307/j.ctv1168ch3.12

Gilliom, J., & Monahan, T. (2013). *Supervision: An introduction to the surveillance society*. University of Chicago Press.

Goffman, E. (2004). *The presentation of self in everyday life* [*Günlük yaşamda benliğin sunumu*]. Metis Publication.

Gopalakrishnan, M. S. (2017, Haziran 27). What awaits humans in the digital age [Dijital çağın insanlarını neler bekliyor]. *DW Türkçe*. https://www.dw.com/tr/dijital-%C3%A7a%C4%9F%C4%B1n-insanlar%C4%B1n%C4%B1-neler-bekliyor/a-39395314

Guga, J. (2015). Beyond artificial intelligence. In *Cyborg tales: The reinvention of the human in the information age* (pp. 45–62). Springer.

Güney, S. (2017). *Social psychology* [*Sosyal psikoloji*]. Nobel Akademi Publishing.

Haggerty, K. D. (2006). Tear down the walls: On demolishing the panopticon. In D. Lyon (Ed.), *Theorizing surveillance: The panopticon and beyond* (pp. 23-45). Willan Publishing.

İlhan, S. (2013). Identity construction in the liquid society: Fluid, eclectic, self-centered identities [Akışkan toplumda kimlik inşası: Geçişken, eklektik, ben odaklı kimlikler]. *Fırat Üniversitesi Sosyal Bilimler Dergisi*, *23*(2), 233–246.

Işıklı, Ş., & Küçükvardar, M. (2016). *Information technology revolution* [*Bilişim devrimi*]. Birleşik Press.

Kalaman, S. (2016). Transformation of privacy in new media: Sociocultural, economic, and political dimensions the case of Facebook [Sosyokültürel, ekonomik ve siyasi boyutlarıyla yeni medyada mahremiyetin dönüşümü: Facebook örneği] (Doctoral dissertation, Ege University, Institute of Social Sciences, Department of Radio, Television, and Cinema).

Kalaman, S. (2019). New media and digital surveillance: A study on social media users in Turkey [Yeni medya ve dijital gözetim: Türkiye'deki sosyal medya kullanıcıları üzerine bir araştırma]. *Yönetim ve Ekonomi Dergisi*, *26*(2), 575–594. DOI: 10.18657/yonveek.556868

Kellner, D. (2001, May). Popular culture and the construction of postmodern identities [Popüler kültür ve postmodern kimliklerin inşası]. *Doğu Batı Üç Aylık Düşünce Dergisi*, 187–219.

Kete, N. (2011). Reading poverty, privacy, and death relations through media. [Yoksulluk, mahremiyet ve ölüm ilişkisini medya üzerinden okumak] In Köse, H. (Ed.), *Media privacy: The phenomenon of privacy in media and a transparent life* [*Medya mahrem: Medyada mahremiyet olgusu ve transparan bir yaşamdan*]. (pp. 61–84). Ayrıntı Publication.

Kramer, N. C., & Winter, S. (2008). Impression management 2.0: The relationship of self-esteem, extraversion, self-efficacy, and self-presentation within social network sites. *Journal of Media Psychology, 20*(3), 106–116. DOI: 10.1027/1864-1105.20.3.106

Kulga, C. E. (2014). A study on self-presentation in everyday life [Günlük yaşamda benlik sunumları üzerine bir inceleme] (Master's thesis, Gazi University, Institute of Social Sciences, Department of Public Relations and Promotion, Ankara).

Lyon, D. (1997). *Electronic eye* [*Elektronik göz*]. (Hattatoğlu, D., Trans.). Sarmal Press.

Lyon, D. (2006). *The surveilled society* [*Gözetlenen toplum*]. (Soykan, G., Trans.). Kalkedon Publishing.

Lyon, D. (2013). *Surveillance studies* [*Gözetim çalışmaları*]. (Toprak, A., Trans.). Kalkedon Publishing.

Manago, A. M. (2015). Identity development in the digital age: The case of social networking sites. In McLean, K. C., & Syed, M. (Eds.), *The Oxford handbook of identity development* (pp. 508–526). Oxford University Press., DOI: 10.1093/oxfordhb/9780199936564.013.031

Martin, J. (2012). Second Life surveillance: Power to the people or virtual surveillance society? *Surveillance & Society*, 9(4), 408–423. DOI: 10.24908/ss.v9i4.4346

Özçetin, B. (2019). *Mass communication theories: Concepts, schools, and models* [*Kitle iletişim kuramları: Kavramlar, okullar ve modeller*]. İletişim Publication.

Özkan, K. D. (2021). Privacy issues in the context of globalization, social networks, and the surveillance society: An Instagram content analysis [Küreselleşme, sosyal ağlar ve gözetim toplumu bağlamında mahremiyet sorunları: Instagram içerik analizi]. *Akademi Sosyal Bilimler Dergisi*, 8(22), 69–88.

Rheingold, H. (1993). *The virtual community: Homesteading on the electronic frontier*. Addison-Wesley.

Robins, K. (1999). *Image: The culture and politics of seeing* [*İmaj: Görmenin kültür ve politikası*]. (Türkoğlu, N., Trans.). Ayrıntı Publication.

Rose, N. (1999). *Powers of freedom: Reframing political thought.* Cambridge University Press. DOI: 10.1017/CBO9780511488856

Schmidt, E., & Cohen, J. (2013). *The new digital age: Reshaping the future of people, nations, and business.* Alfred A. Knopf.

Thomas, A. (2007). *Youth online: Identity and literacy in the digital age.* Peter Lang International Academic Publishers.

Timisi, N. (2005). The reality of virtuality: The Internet's entry into identity and community spaces. [Sanallığın gerçekliği: İnternetin kimlik ve topluluk alanlarına girişi] In Binark, M., & Kılıçbay, B. (Eds.), *Internet, society, culture* [*İnternet toplum kültür*]. (pp. 89–106). Epos Publication.

Toffler, A. (1992). *Powershift: Knowledge, wealth, and violence at the edge of the 21st century* [*Yeni güçler yeni şoklar*]. (Çorakçı, B., Trans.). Altın Kitaplar Press.

Turkle, S. (1995). *Life on the screen: Identity in the age of the Internet.* Simon & Schuster.

Turkle, S. (1999). Cyberspace and identity. *Contemporary Sociology, 28*(6), 643–648. DOI: 10.2307/2655534

Ünsal, R. (2022). Super connected: Internet, digital media, and techno-social life [Süper bağ(lantı)lı: İnternet, dijital medya ve tekno-sosyal hayat]. *Hacı Bayram Veli Üniversitesi Yeni Medya Dergisi, 13*, 517–521.

Utma, S. (2024). The concept of surveillance and internalization of surveillance on social media [*Gözetim kavramı ve sosyal medyada gözetimin içselleştirilmesi*]. *Journal of Social* [JOSHAS]. *Humanities and Administrative Sciences, 9*(61), 2276–2283. DOI: 10.29228/JOSHAS.66357

Yavuz, C. (2019). Self-presentation on social media in the context of privacy: The case of Instagram [Mahremiyet bağlamında sosyal medyada benliğin sunumu: Instagram örneği] (Master's thesis, Marmara University, Institute of Social Sciences, Department of Public Relations, Interpersonal Communication Program). Istanbul.

ADDITIONAL READING

Armağan, A. (2013). *Changes in identity structures and virtualized identity presentations: A study on students* [Kimlik yapılarında değişim ve sanallaşan kimlik sunumları: Öğrenciler üzerinde bir araştırma]. Uluslararası Hakemli Sosyal Bilimler E-Dergisi.

Jenkins, H. (2018). *Convergence culture: Technologies and fan culture* [*Cesur yeni medya: Teknolojiler ve hayran kültürü*]. İletişim Publication.

Kellner, D. M., & Durham, M. G. (2006). *Media and cultural studies: KeyWorks*. Blackwell Publishing.

Kesim Güven, S. (2016). Social legitimacy of surveillance. [Gözetimin toplumsal meşruiyeti] In Çoban, B., & Ataman, B. (Eds.), *Surveillance society: Panopticon* [*Gözetim toplumu: Panoptikon*]. (pp. 15–31). Ege Press.

Koşar, A. F. (2024). Social media imprisons people in their likes: The example of YouTube and the surveillance society [YouTube örneği ve gözetim toplumu]. *Journal of Social Perspective Studies*, *1*(1), 14–19. DOI: 10.5281/zenodo.10928519

Morley, D., & Robins, K. (1997). *Spaces of identity, global media, electronic environments, and cultural boundaries* [*Kimlik mekânları, küresel medya, elektronik ortamlar ve kültürel sınırlar*]. E. Zeybekoğlu, Çev.

Özdemir, Z. (2015). A new trend in identity construction on social media: Selfie use [Sosyal medyada kimlik inşasında yeni akım: Özçekim kullanımı]. *Maltepe Üniversitesi İletişim Fakültesi Dergisi*, *2*(1), 112–131.

Shavers, B. (2016). Digital identity. In Shavers, B. (Ed.), *Hiding behind the keyword: Uncovering covert communication methods with forensic analysis* (pp. 187–202). Syngress. DOI: 10.1016/B978-0-12-803340-1.00009-4

Tanrıbilir, R. N. (2015). *New media and communication approaches* [*Yeni medya ve iletişimsel yaklaşımlar*]. Kriter Publication.

Tredinnick, L. (2008). *Digital information culture: The individual and society in the digital age*. Chandos Publishing. DOI: 10.1533/9781780631677

Chapter 11

The Future of Web Technologies and Their Implications for the Digital Society

Prianto Roito Siregar
Universitas Esa Unggul, Indonesia

Binastya Anggara Sekti
https://orcid.org/0000-0001-5489-4888
Universitas Esa Unggul, Indonesia

ABSTRACT

The development of web technology from Web 1.0 to Web 5.0 has revolutionized the way humans interact digitally, influencing identity, autonomy, employment, government, education, and culture. The modern web is now intelligent, contextual, and emotional, powered by AI, IoT, blockchain, and quantum computing. Digital identities are evolving towards decentralized models such as Self-Sovereign Identity (SSI), while governance is beginning to implement Decentralized Autonomous Organizations (DAOs). The world of work is changing through the gig economy and the token economy, although it comes with challenges in the form of digital divides and algorithmic manipulation. Education and cultural preservation are also digitized through adaptive learning and immersive technology. With this great opportunity also arises the issue of ethics, digital rights, and the need for inclusive and visionary policies. The web of the future must be not only smart, but also fair, ethical, and humane.

DOI: 10.4018/979-8-3373-5167-4.ch011

1. INTRODUCTION

The rapid evolution of web technologies is reshaping the way societies function across all levels, encompassing the economic, social, cultural, political, and educational domains. The internet, once a passive tool for accessing static information, is now emerging as an intelligent, context-aware, and emotionally responsive ecosystem. From the early foundations of Web 1.0 to the current and anticipated developments of Web 4.0 and Web 5.0, the web has undergone a profound metamorphosis. This shift is not merely technical but represents a transformation in human experience and agency in the digital space. The future of the internet lies in its ability to understand, interpret, and even empathize with human intention, creating a space that is not just informative but intuitive and emotionally intelligent. This paper explains how data taken from dislocation dynamics simulations can be changed or modified using semantic web technology through data annotation with ontology (Ihsan et al., 2025)

The transition from Web 2.0 to Web 3.0, and further into Web 4.0 and Web 5.0, marks a significant progression in web capability and human-computer interaction. Web 2.0 introduced a participatory culture where users became active contributors through blogs, social media, and collaborative platforms such as Wikipedia. However, Web 3.0 expanded upon this by introducing the Semantic Web, where data is machine-readable and contextually meaningful, thus enabling personalized services, intelligent agents, and AI-driven applications. Research conducted in the long-term development of Web technology is conducted in a theoretically and empirically grounded manner (Priestley et al., 2020). Web 4.0, sometimes referred to as the "symbiotic web," is characterized by real-time decision-making capabilities using data from IoT devices, while Web 5.0 is conceptualized as an empathetic and human-centric web. Here, digital platforms not only respond to data but to the user's emotions, thoughts, and consciousness. In digital platforms, an abnormal event involves multiple data sources and complex types of information, and the difficulty of tracking it increases due to the similarity and interaction between components, operations, and user behaviour (Zhou et al., 2025).

The impact of this web evolution extends deeply into digital society. However, the next generation of Web evolution (Web 3.0) is here and shaping our lives. Web 3.0 is a decentralized Web architecture that is smarter and more secure than previous versions (Gan et al., 2023). Digital identity, for instance, has transformed from simple login credentials to complex, decentralized systems that emphasize user control and privacy. Self-Sovereign Identity (SSI) models are now enabling individuals to manage their identity data across platforms without relying on centralized authorities. This transformation aligns with the increasing emphasis on autonomy, data ownership, and digital dignity in a surveillance-prone era. Additionally, virtual and augmented reality are converging with AI to produce digital twins—virtual representations of individuals that can operate within digital environments on behalf of their real-world counterparts. This evolution raises pressing questions about surveillance, autonomy, and consent in digital spaces.

A decentralized autonomous organization (DAOs) can be thought of as an organization or community where its design, processes, and operational tasks are encoded into agreements or smart contracts, adhering to collective guidelines, values, and consensus (Saurabh et al., 2025). Governance models are also being challenged and reimagined in the future web. Blockchain-based Decentralized Autonomous Organizations (DAOs) are introducing new models for participatory governance that transcend geographic boundaries. Unlike traditional governance systems, DAOs are governed by smart contracts and collective consensus, making decision-making processes more transparent and democratic. Meanwhile, e-government platforms are leveraging Web 3.0 and 4.0 tools to increase transparency, foster civic participation, and enhance accountability in public service delivery. However, the promise of technological empowerment comes with new risks: regulatory gaps, algorithmic governance, and the potential for digital authoritarianism. Thus, the digital polity must evolve in tandem with the technology it governs.

In light of these developments, this chapter provides an overview of the future web paradigms and their multifaceted implications for identity, governance, education, economy, and culture. It synthesizes current trends and future possibilities while drawing on interdisciplinary research from computer science, digital ethics, policy studies, and social theory. As we move into an era marked by emotional intelligence, ubiquitous connectivity, and decentralized control, we must critically examine both the benefits and the challenges posed by emerging web technologies. This includes ensuring ethical design, regulatory foresight, and inclusive participation in shaping the digital future. The web must not only become more intelligent but more just, empathetic, and equitable.

2. DEFINING THE INTELLIGENT WEB

The rapid development of the transformation of Web 1.0 technology to Web 2.0, internet users are given various opportunities to express their thoughts, opinions, emotions, or statements throughout the world in the public domain (Santra et al., 2024). Web technologies have undergone significant transformations since their inception, evolving from static content delivery systems to emotionally intelligent and context-aware platforms. This continuum reflects not only technological advancements but also the shifting relationship between humans and digital systems.

Understanding this trajectory is essential to framing the rise of the "Intelligent Web," broadly encompassing Web 3.0, Web 4.0, and Web 5.0.

Web 1.0 (roughly 1990–2004) marked the earliest stage of the internet, often referred to as the "read-only web." In this phase, web pages were static, content was centrally produced, and user interaction was minimal. Websites were essentially digital brochures. There were no personalized experiences, and interactivity was limited to basic hyperlinks and guestbooks.

Web 2.0 (2004–2015) revolutionized online interaction by introducing dynamic content, user-generated platforms, and social networking. This "read-write web" enabled people to share content and collaborate globally, giving rise to blogs, social media, wikis, and platforms like YouTube and Facebook. Participation and community became key pillars of this phase, paving the way for collective intelligence.

Web 3.0, also known as the *Semantic Web*, introduced machine-understandable content, artificial intelligence (AI), and personalized services. It focuses on structuring data in a way that machines can interpret relationships between concepts. AI-driven assistants, recommendation systems, and ontologies are foundational here, marking the transition toward intelligence in the web ecosystem.

Web 4.0 advances further into *context-aware computing*. By leveraging IoT devices, big data, and real-time analytics, Web 4.0 systems can autonomously interpret user environments and act proactively. This stage emphasizes ubiquitous connectivity and autonomous agent interaction . Examples include smart cities, autonomous vehicles, and predictive healthcare platforms.

Web 5.0, though still largely conceptual, is described as an *emotive and human-centric web*. It aspires to create emotionally responsive systems that understand and adapt to user emotions through affective computing, brain-computer interfaces, and immersive technologies. This phase marks a potential convergence of consciousness and technology, opening ethical, philosophical, and technical debates.

Table 1. Comparison of web evolution phases

Web Version	Period	Key Features	User Role	Technologies Involved
Web 1.0	1990–2004	Static pages, read-only	Consumer	HTML, HTTP, static websites
Web 2.0	2004–2015	Dynamic content, social media	Contributor	JavaScript, AJAX, social platforms
Web 3.0	2015–Present	Semantic web, AI, personalization	Collaborator	RDF, OWL, NLP, machine learning
Web 4.0	Emerging	Context-aware, autonomous agents	Participant	IoT, big data, real-time analytics, edge computing
Web 5.0	Conceptual	Emotion-aware, human-centric, immersive	Cognitive Being	Affective computing, BCI, emotional AI

As the web continues to evolve toward more intelligent, intuitive, and autonomous forms, the shift from information retrieval to emotion recognition highlights a crucial redefinition of human-computer interaction. The Web has evolved in its own unique way. From the static, informative characteristics of Web 1.0, it has evolved into the interactive experiences offered by Web 2.0. Web 3.0 through Web 5.0 represent a continuum in which technology not only processes meaning but responds empathetically and proactively to human needs. This transformation is the foundation of the *Intelligent Web*, an environment where AI, context-awareness, and emotional intelligence converge to produce deeply integrated digital experiences.

Figure 1. Web evolution timeline

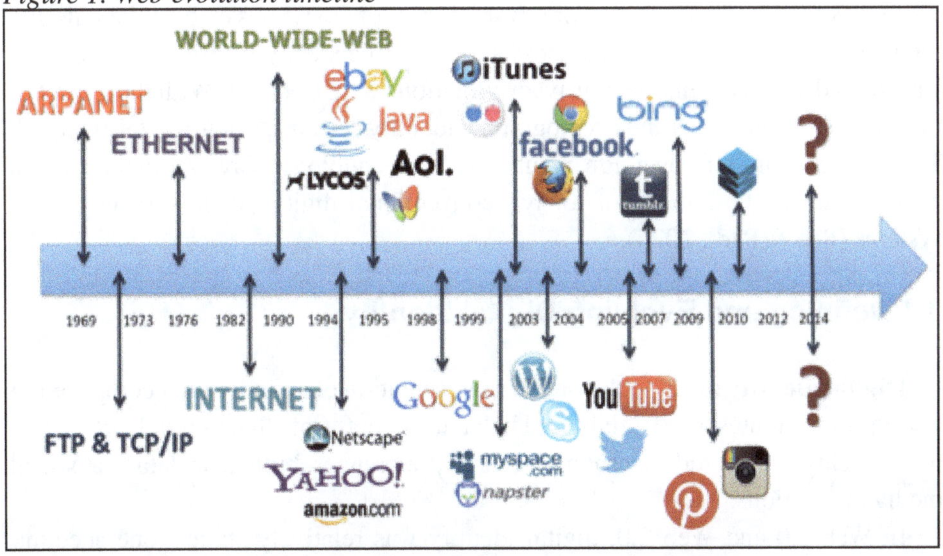

3. IMPACTS ON DIGITAL IDENTITY AND AUTONOMY

As web technologies evolve toward intelligence and emotional responsiveness, the nature of digital identity is being redefined in profound ways. Identity in the digital realm is no longer just a set of login credentials—it encompasses behavioral patterns, emotional states, biometric data, and digital interactions across platforms. The shift from centralized to decentralized identity systems marks a fundamental change in how individuals assert, control, and protect their digital selves. Current approaches to managing digital identities struggle to meet the demands of ongoing digital transformation (Babel et al., 2025).

The rise of the Intelligent Web, driven by the convergence of Artificial Intelligence (AI), Semantic Web technologies, the Internet of Things (IoT), and machine learning, is fundamentally reshaping the way digital identity is defined and how personal autonomy is exercised online. As the web becomes more "intelligent," it no longer acts as a passive medium for communication and information retrieval. It evolves into an active agent—interpreting, predicting, and even influencing user behavior. These transformations have profound implications on both the construct of digital identity and the autonomy of individuals in the digital space.

In the early days of the web, identity was managed by centralized service providers (e.g., social media platforms or government portals) who issued credentials and retained user data. This created ecosystems of dependency where user autonomy was limited, and data misuse or privacy violations were frequent. With the advent of blockchain technologies and cryptographic identity systems, a new model emerged: The presence of self-sovereign identity (SSI) technology plays a crucial role in overcoming the limitations of today's conventional digital identity management systems (Seo & Park, 2025).

3.1 Defining and Evolving Digital Identity

Digital identity refers to the online representation of an individual composed of a series of attributes, credentials, and behavioral footprints that uniquely identify a person. This may include usernames, search preferences, biometric data, and social media interactions.

In Web 1.0 and Web 2.0, digital identity was relatively static—one account, one password, one online profile. However, with the transition to Web 3.0, 4.0, and even 5.0, digital identity has become dynamic, contextual, and decentralized. An individual no longer fully controls how their identity is constructed; algorithms now interpret, infer, and even augment digital identities in real time.

Key Concepts in Modern Digital Identity:

1. Decentralized Identity (DID): Uses blockchain/distributed ledger technologies to anchor identity credentials. Users store identifiers in their digital wallets and share them only when necessary.
2. Self-Sovereign Identity (SSI): A user-centric model where the individual holds complete control over personal identity data and can present verifiable credentials without involving third-party verifiers.

3. Digital Twins: Virtual representations of individuals—often enhanced by AI and IoT—that mirror a user's behavior, preferences, and interactions in digital environments. These twins may be used for simulation, personalization, or even delegation of decision-making. Table 2. Shows Comparison of Web Evolution Phases.

Table 2. Comparison of digital identity models

Aspect	Centralized Identity	Federated Identity	Decentralized/SSI
Ownership	Service provider	Shared among trusted providers	Individual (user-controlled)
Trust Model	Centralized authority	Trust in federation	Blockchain-based verification
Privacy	Low	Medium	High
Interoperability	Limited	Moderate	High (via standards like DID/VC)
Data Portability	Minimal	Moderate	Full user portability
Examples	Facebook Login, Google ID	SSO (e.g., eduGAIN)	Sovrin, uPort, Microsoft Entra

These developments offer significant gains in autonomy and privacy, empowering individuals to become stewards of their own identity. However, they also introduce new risks and challenges. For instance, digital twins—while useful for automation and personalization—raise concerns about surveillance, consent, and the boundary between human and digital selves (Risser & Stilgoe, 2020). The more identity becomes machine-readable and emotionally responsive, the more vulnerable it becomes to manipulation and profiling.

Moreover, regulatory and ethical gaps persist. While frameworks such as the EU's *General Data Protection Regulation* (GDPR) and the emerging *Decentralized Identifiers (DID)* standards from W3C aim to establish user rights, the implementation of these principles is still uneven globally. The future of digital identity thus hinges on international cooperation, robust cryptographic standards, and digital literacy to ensure that autonomy is meaningful, not merely symbolic.

In sum, the evolution of digital identity systems represents both an opportunity and a responsibility. It offers pathways to empower users, dismantle data monopolies, and protect individual dignity in digital environments. However, achieving true digital autonomy requires ongoing efforts in regulation, technical design, and public awareness. Figure 2. Shows Architecture of Self-Sovereign Identity (SSI).

Figure 2. Architecture of Self-Sovereign Identity (SSI)

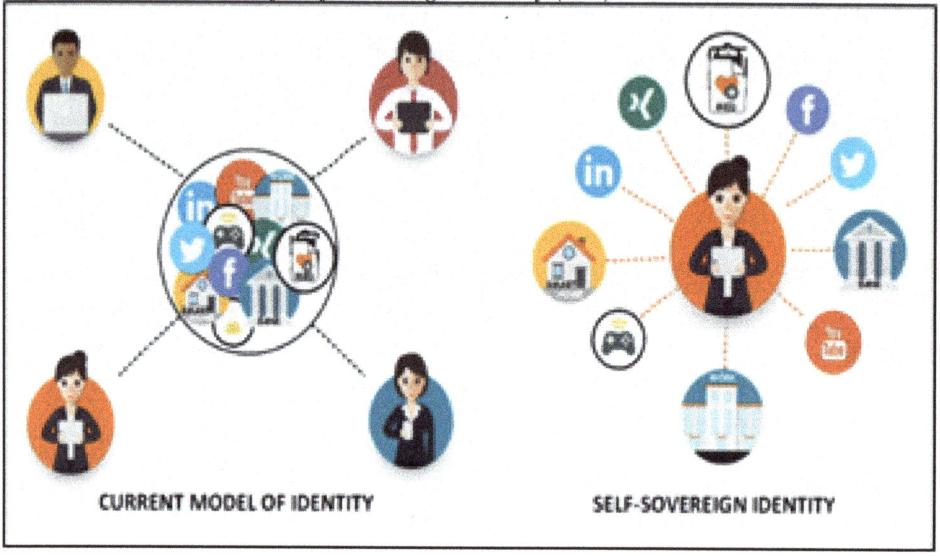

3.2 Intelligent Web's Impact on Digital Identity

a. Personalization and Identity Fragmentation

The Intelligent Web leverages machine learning to personalize user experiences based on preferences, search history, location, and even facial expressions. However, this leads to **identity** fragmentation, where individuals possess multiple "digital personas" across platforms.

Example: A person may be recognized as a cybersecurity expert on LinkedIn, a gamer on Twitch, and a lifestyle influencer on Instagram. These personas coexist but may present contradictory facets of the same person.

b. Algorithmic Profiling and Inference

Modern intelligent systems can infer user attributes never explicitly shared—such as sexual orientation, mental health, or political views—based solely on patterns of interaction. This leads to the emergence of predictive identities, constructed by algorithms, not the users themselves. Modern intelligent technologies provide support in the form of automatic adaptation of mixed protocols, and ensure smooth communication between various industrial equipment (He & Bhatti, 2025).

3.3 Impacts on Digital Autonomy

Digital autonomy refers to the capacity of individuals to make free and informed decisions regarding their digital interactions, including control over data, access, and visibility. The core of the traditional adoption model, does not provide significant effects, to show a generational shift towards digital autonomy (Maria Koziel et al., 2025). The Intelligent Web presents new challenges to this autonomy:

a. Filter Bubbles and Echo Chambers

Personalized recommendation systems create informational echo chambers, where users are only exposed to ideas and content aligned with their existing beliefs. This restricts exposure to diverse perspectives and reinforces cognitive biases.

b. Algorithmic Nudging

Digital platforms increasingly use behavioral data to nudge users into specific decisions: buying products, watching certain videos, even forming political opinions. This undermines user autonomy by influencing decisions through opaque algorithmic processes.

c. Surveillance and Data Ownership

The Intelligent Web is often accompanied by pervasive surveillance, with data collected via IoT sensors, geolocation, browser fingerprints, and voice assistants. Most of this data is harvested without full user awareness, weakening user control over their own digital footprints. Table 3. Shows Dual effects of Intelligent Web on identity and autonomy.

Table 3. Dual effects of intelligent web on identity and autonomy

Aspect	Positive Impact	Negative Impact
Personalization	More relevant, efficient user experience	Information isolation, filter bubbles
Context-aware systems	Adaptive, natural interactions	Excessive behavioral influence
Data profiling	Accurate predictions and insights	Privacy invasion, identity manipulation
Service automation	Time-saving and reduced manual effort	Dependence and loss of control
Predictive analytics	Supports decision-making and personalization	Behavior manipulation and ethical concerns

4. GOVERNANCE, DEMOCRACY, AND DIGITAL CITIZENSHIP

The evolution of web technologies has transformed not only communication and commerce but also the very mechanisms of governance and civic engagement. As societies become increasingly digitized, governance models must adapt to support transparency, inclusivity, and citizen participation in a distributed, real-time, and borderless world. In a study, there is a discussion of further implementation by developing and applying a contextual mobile game approach based on decision trees appropriately to foster digital citizenship competencies (Panjaburee et al., 2025). The concept of digital citizenship—defined as the ability to engage in society online responsibly and effectively—is now foundational to democratic participation in the 21st century.

Traditional governance systems are often hierarchical, slow-moving, and geographically constrained. In contrast, digital governance leverages web technologies to facilitate faster decision-making, greater citizen involvement, and more efficient public service delivery. E-Government platforms allow citizens to interact with the state through online portals for tax filing, licensing, and consultations. In other circumstances, various participatory tools such as digital voting, online petitions, and citizen engagement apps can greatly enable deeper democratic processes (Azad & Zablith, 2022).

Emerging models like Decentralized Autonomous Organizations (DAOs) and smart contracts further push the boundaries of governance by distributing control across peer-to-peer networks. DAOs use blockchain-based consensus mechanisms to make collective decisions without central leadership, enabling transparent and tamper-proof governance. These models can be applied to cooperatives, public funding, policy experimentation, and even parliamentary simulations (Hassan et al., 2020). Table 4. Shows Comparison of Governance Models in the Digital Era.

Table 4. Comparison of governance models in the digital era

Model	Features	Examples	Limitations
Traditional Governance	Hierarchical, bureaucratic, centralized decision-making	Ministries, municipal governments	Slow processes, limited participation
E-Government	Digital public services, centralized platforms	e-Residency (Estonia), GOV.UK	Central control, potential privacy issues
Digital Democracy	Online voting, citizen engagement platforms	Decide Madrid, Taiwan vTaiwan platform	Low digital literacy, risk of manipulation

continued on following page

Table 4. Continued

Model	Features	Examples	Limitations
DAO (Blockchain-Based)	Code-based, decentralized, token voting	Aragon, Gitcoin, ConstitutionDAO	Governance complexity, legal recognition challenges
Smart Contracts	Automated, self-executing rules	Ethereum governance contracts	Inflexibility, susceptibility to code bugs

These governance innovations redefine the relationship between citizens and institutions. Digital citizenship is no longer limited to voting every few years; it includes daily micro-engagement in policy discourse, participatory budgeting, and community moderation. This also gives rise to liquid democracy, where voting power can be delegated fluidly among trusted peers depending on issue area.

However, the emergence of algorithmically mediated governance also presents challenges: Who will set the rules encoded in smart contracts? How will a DAO handle conflict resolution? What about unequal access for digitally marginalized groups? These questions may point to the need for hybrid governance models that combine the transparency and inclusivity of digital systems with human ethical judgment and regulatory oversight (Khan et al., 2025).

Global governance frameworks must evolve to address these dynamics. Regulatory bodies must grapple with cross-border jurisdiction, AI accountability, and identity verification in decentralized spaces. At the same time, education systems must promote digital literacy and civic competence to ensure that all individuals can meaningfully participate in the digital public sphere. Figure 3. Shows Architecture of a Decentralized Autonomous Organization (DAO).

Figure 3. Architecture of a Decentralized Autonomous Organization (DAO)

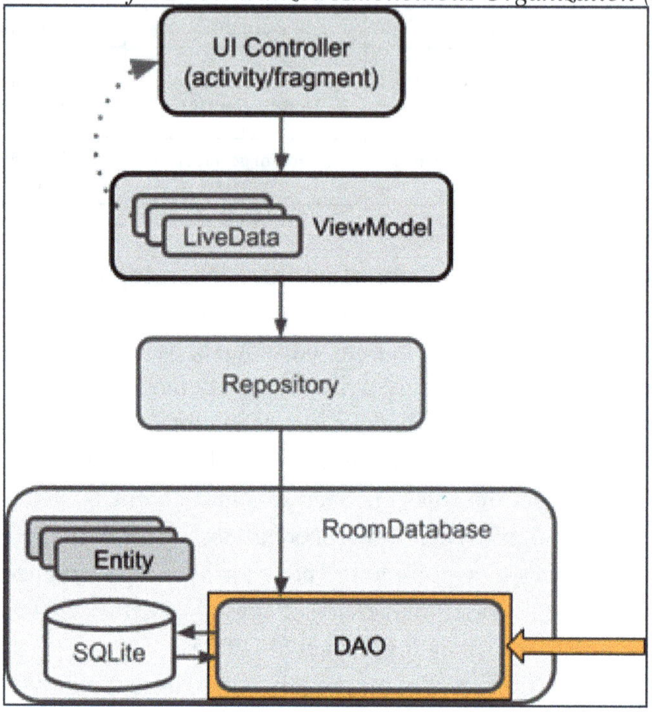

5. SOCIO-ECONOMIC TRANSFORMATION AND THE FUTURE OF WORK

The evolution of web technologies, especially the transition from Web 3.0 to Web 5.0, is not only reshaping the internet but also revolutionizing societies and economies worldwide. These technological advancements are fundamentally altering how we work, produce, and distribute value. At the intersection of artificial intelligence (AI), blockchain, the Internet of Things (IoT), and decentralized platforms, the socio-economic landscape is being reimagined. This transformation raises urgent questions regarding employment, education, inequality, labor rights, and governance in the digital age. This shift creates opportunities for flexibility, innovation, and global collaboration, but also introduces risks of inequality, digital precarity, and skill obsolescence. The key emerging and enabling technologies are 6G networks positioned to be applicable in the areas of value creation and capture, and an outline of the proposed technological innovation transformation considering the available 6G system architecture layers (Yrjola et al., 2022).

5.1 The Changing Nature of Work

Traditionally, work has been defined by physical presence, repetitive tasks, and hierarchical structures. However, digital technologies have disrupted this model. AI-powered automation, smart contracts, remote collaboration tools, and the gig economy have introduced flexibility and efficiency—while also threatening job security and long-standing professions.

Table 5. Comparison of traditional vs. future work models

Aspect	Traditional Work Model	Future Work Model (Web 4.0/5.0)
Work Location	Onsite (office/factory)	Remote/Hybrid/Virtual (Metaverse, cloud)
Job Type	Full-time, linear career path	Freelance, gig, decentralized employment
Skill Demand	Routine, repetitive	Cognitive, creative, tech-driven
Decision-making	Top-down hierarchy	Decentralized, AI-assisted
Employment Relationship	Long-term contracts	Smart contracts, token-based incentives

One of the most visible transformations is the rise of the gig and platform economy, where digital platforms such as Uber, Upwork, and Tokopedia match labor supply with demand in real time. This ecosystem, supported by Web 2.0 and Web 3.0 technologies, promotes flexibility and autonomy but often lacks traditional labor protections like healthcare, contracts, or collective bargaining. Meanwhile, platform work is increasingly influenced by AI algorithms that determine task distribution, pricing, and worker evaluation.

Another major development is the emergence of token economies driven by blockchain technologies. These systems reward users, creators, and contributors with cryptocurrencies or tokens for their participation in decentralized platforms. Through models like *play-to-earn*, *learn-to-earn*, or *contribute-to-earn*, new types of micro-economies are being formed—some empowering, others speculative and volatile. Digital identity and wallet infrastructure are crucial enablers of this new economic landscape.

At the same time, lifelong learning and digital upskilling have become essential as the pace of technological change accelerates. Web-based learning platforms such as Coursera, Khan Academy, and decentralized education models (e.g., blockchain-verified credentials) enable individuals to continuously adapt. Intelligent tutoring systems, AI mentors, and adaptive learning engines personalize education based on user behavior and performance. The development of AI technology can address various critical social challenges, such as inequality, accessibility, and personalized learning (Leddy & McCreanor, 2024).

While these technological transformations present new pathways for economic participation, they also raise important equity concerns. Access to high-speed internet, advanced digital tools, and quality education is still uneven globally, creating a digital divide. Furthermore, workers in the gig and token economy are often exposed to algorithmic management, which lacks transparency and may replicate systemic biases.

In response, policymakers and organizations are exploring new social protection models such as portable benefits, universal basic income (UBI), and recognition of DAO-based work in labor law. Education systems must also adapt, embedding digital literacy, ethical tech use, and entrepreneurial thinking from early stages. Businesses must embrace human-centered design and responsible automation to avoid widening inequality.

The future of work, therefore, is not just about technology—it is about rethinking socioeconomic contracts in a world where value creation, labor, and identity are digital. Embracing the full potential of Web 3.0–5.0 requires inclusive strategies that empower workers, protect rights, and ensure that transformation leads to equity, not exclusion.

5.2 Automation, AI, and Employment Shifts

Automation and AI are replacing repetitive and rule-based jobs at an accelerating pace. A 2023 McKinsey report estimates that by 2030, up to 800 million jobs could be displaced globally due to AI and robotics, but new roles will also emerge, many of which are not yet defined today. The development of Artificial Intelligence (AI) has revolutionized traditional methods and improved decision-making and automation (Sularso et al., 2025). Figure 4: shows Job Displacement and Creation Trends by Sector.

Figure 4. Job displacement and creation trends by sector

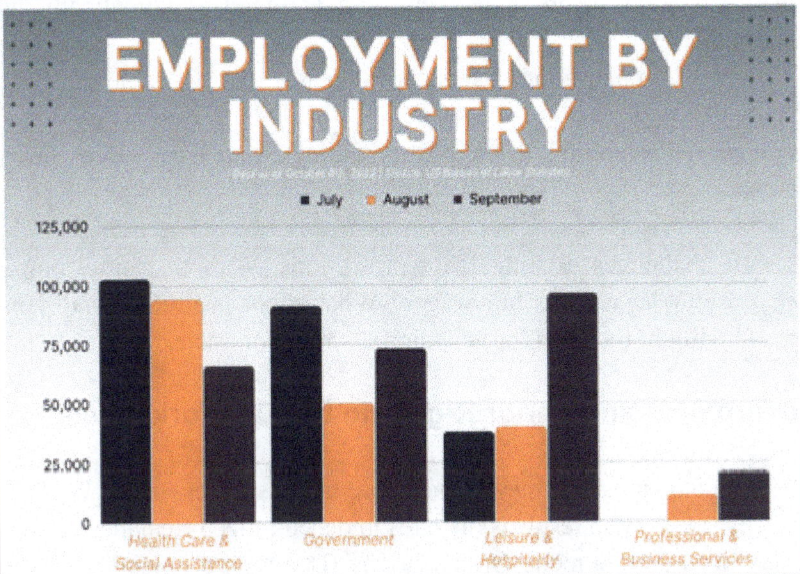

Jobs most at risk include:

- Data entry and bookkeeping
- Manufacturing line workers
- Basic customer service

Emerging job areas:

- AI ethics and safety analysts
- Data curators and digital librarians
- Metaverse designers and digital architects
- Quantum computing engineers

5.3 Rise of the Gig and Platform Economy

The gig economy—empowered by platforms such as Upwork, Fiverr, and Uber—is reshaping labor markets. In Web 3.0 and beyond, blockchain-based platforms introduce decentralized gig economies, where workers own their reputations and earn through cryptocurrencies or NFTs.

Key characteristics of Web 5.0-driven gig work:

- Decentralized Identity: Workers carry verified credentials across platforms.
- Smart Contracts: Work agreements are enforced a utomatically without intermediaries.
- Tokenized Compensation: Users earn tokens, often tradeable or convertible into equity.
- Reputation Portability: Work history, ratings, and trust scores are stored on-chain.

This shift challenges existing labor protections. Without central employers, questions arise: Who ensures fair wages? What about healthcare and pensions? These gaps highlight the need for new digital social contracts.

5.6 Governance and Labor Rights in Digital Workspaces

In the Web 5.0 landscape, new governance models are essential. Who governs digital workspaces? Who resolves disputes in decentralized freelance platforms?

Decentralized Autonomous Organizations (DAOs) are emerging as possible frameworks for labor governance. They use blockchain-based voting, community moderation, and transparent smart contract enforcement.

However, this raises legal, ethical, and regulatory dilemmas:

- Are DAO workers employees or contributors?
- Can smart contracts be modified to reflect changing work needs?
- Who ensures compliance with labor standards in a borderless, code-driven environment?

Policy-makers, trade unions, and tech communities must collaborate to redesign labor laws that align with digital realities, ensuring rights without stifling innovation.

5.5 Socio-economic Inequality and Inclusion

One of the most critical challenges is the risk of digital inequality. While digitalization can drive productivity and innovation, it may also deepen socio-economic gaps between:

- Tech-savvy urban elites and digitally marginalized rural communities
- Highly skilled AI experts vs. displaced manual workers
- Developed economies vs. emerging economies

Web 5.0, however, presents a dual-edged sword. On one hand, it can decentralize opportunities through:

- Global micro-tasking platforms
- Universal basic income (UBI) pilots via smart contracts
- Peer-to-peer digital cooperatives

On the other hand, unequal access to infrastructure, connectivity, and digital literacy risks excluding millions. Digital transformation must therefore be accompanied by inclusive policies, such as:

- Public funding for rural connectivity
- Digital skills training programs for vulnerable populations
- Portable digital wallets for universal access to social welfare

The socio-economic transformation ushered in by advanced web technologies presents both immense opportunities and unprecedented challenges. The future of work will be decentralized, digital, and dynamic—but must also be equitable, ethical, and human-centric.

6. ETHICAL CONSIDERATIONS AND DIGITAL RIGHTS

The rise of intelligent and emotionally responsive web technologies brings not only innovation but also complex ethical challenges. As we enter the era of Web 4.0 and Web 5.0—featuring autonomous agents, real-time analytics, and emotionally aware AI—our digital lives become increasingly intertwined with systems capable of sensing, predicting, and influencing behavior. This transformation necessitates urgent and thoughtful attention to ethical frameworks and the protection of digital rights. Regarding the future of AI ethics, it is important to emphasize a balanced approach that embraces innovation while prioritizing ethical considerations in the development and application of AI (Chakrabarti et al., 2025).

One of the foundational ethical issues is data ownership and informed consent. In legacy web systems, personal data is often collected passively and monetized without the user's full awareness. While regulations like the EU's General Data Protection Regulation (GDPR) have pushed for greater transparency, real-world implementation still falls short. The shift to self-sovereign identity (SSI) and decentralized data wallets in Web 3.0 and beyond offers a path toward user empowerment, allowing individuals to store, control, and selectively share their personal data. However, these systems must be designed with usability and accessibility in mind to avoid reinforcing digital exclusion.

Another critical concern is algorithmic bias and the lack of accountability in automated decision-making systems. AI-driven platforms increasingly shape decisions in hiring, credit, healthcare, and law enforcement. When these systems are trained on biased datasets or built without transparency, they can reinforce systemic discrimination. It is worth highlighting the challenges posed by AI in complying with the "5 Ps of ethical data handling" (origin, protection, purpose, preparation, and privacy) and emphasizing the need for supplementary regulations such as the GDPR to fully ensure ethical data practices (Hähnel, 2025). With Web 5.0 expected to include emotionally responsive systems, the stakes are even higher: how can we ensure that systems interpreting human emotions do not misjudge, stereotype, or manipulate users? Ethical design in this context requires not only technical fixes but also diverse participation in algorithm development, ongoing audits, and mechanisms for redress.

Equally important is the question of mental health and digital wellbeing. As immersive technologies such as augmented reality (AR), virtual reality (VR), and emotionally intelligent agents become mainstream, users may experience overstimulation, social comparison, or emotional manipulation. Studies have shown that excessive screen time, algorithmic content curation, and emotionally persuasive design can increase anxiety, depression, and addictive behavior—especially among younger populations. Thus, ethical digital environments must prioritize wellbeing through intentional design choices like time-limiting features, nudging for offline activities, and emotional transparency.

The future web also demands attention to digital inclusion and accessibility. While digital tools have the potential to reduce inequalities, they often reproduce them due to gaps in infrastructure, education, and language. For example, Web 4.0 systems powered by real-time AI may exclude those with limited internet access or cognitive impairments if not built inclusively. Universal design principles, multilingual support, and offline-accessible services are crucial for ensuring that no one is left behind in the digital transformation. Digital resources are valuable in socio-educational interventions with vulnerable migrant women for developing creative skills (Díaz-Pereira et al., 2025).

Finally, there is a growing movement toward recognizing digital rights as fundamental human rights. This includes the right to privacy, the right to access digital services, the right to be forgotten, the right to explanation of algorithmic decisions, and the right to not be emotionally manipulated by AI. These rights are now being codified in international frameworks such as the OECD AI Principles, UNESCO AI Ethics Guidelines, and Digital Bill of Rights proposals). However, enforcing these rights globally remains a challenge due to disparities in political will, legal infrastructure, and technological capacity.

Table 6. Ethical challenges in the intelligent web and mitigation strategies

Ethical Challenge	Description	Proposed Solutions
Data Ownership & Consent	Lack of user control over personal data	Self-sovereign identity (SSI), data transparency, GDPR-style regulation
Algorithmic Bias	Discrimination in AI outcomes due to biased datasets or opaque models	Inclusive AI development, bias audits, explainable AI
Emotional Manipulation	AI systems exploit user emotions for profit or influence	Ethical AI guidelines, affective computing standards, emotional consent mechanisms
Digital Wellbeing	Overuse, addiction, or mental health deterioration due to persuasive design	Wellbeing-centric UX design, time-use limits, mental health alerts
Exclusion & Accessibility	Unequal access to digital tools and benefits	Universal design, multilingual systems, affordable access initiatives
Governance and Oversight	Weak legal and institutional mechanisms to oversee digital systems	Multistakeholder regulation, digital ethics boards, international tech governance

Addressing these challenges requires moving beyond compliance to adopt an "ethics by design" approach—embedding moral values such as fairness, inclusivity, transparency, and sustainability into the design, deployment, and governance of web technologies. This includes interdisciplinary collaboration between engineers, designers, ethicists, policymakers, and affected communities. Ethical audits, algorithmic impact assessments, and participatory design processes can help anticipate harms before they scale.

The intelligent web is not ethically neutral. It can either enhance autonomy, dignity, and equity—or amplify surveillance, manipulation, and injustice. The direction it takes depends on collective choices made now by developers, regulators, institutions, and users. Ensuring a humane and just digital future means anchoring technological innovation in democratic values and human rights from the start.

7. EDUCATIONAL AND CULTURAL IMPLICATIONS

The evolution of web technologies—from Web 3.0 through Web 5.0—has profoundly impacted education and cultural preservation worldwide. Web 3.0 previously represented the next stage of the Internet's evolution, with the goal of empowering users with increased autonomy, efficiency, quality, security, and privacy (Hassan et al., 2025).This transformation is not solely technical but also affects how knowledge is created, accessed, and experienced. In education, these technologies are reshaping how learners engage with content, how teachers facilitate instruction, and how institutions deliver credentials. In the cultural realm, the web has opened new opportunities for the digitization, dissemination, and revitalization of diverse cultural expressions across borders.

Web 3.0, also known as the Semantic Web, enabled machines to interpret and connect data meaningfully. In education, this advancement laid the foundation for personalized and adaptive learning systems. Platforms like Coursera, Khan Academy, and EdX use artificial intelligence (AI) to tailor content and assessments based on individual performance and preferences. Moreover, blockchain technology has emerged in the education sector to provide secure and verifiable digital credentials, learning portfolios, and transparent academic records. These technologies offer learners autonomy, verifiability, and lifelong learning opportunities.

As we move into the era of Web 4.0, education is becoming increasingly context-aware and **immersive**. Technologies such as augmented reality (AR), virtual reality (VR), and Internet of Things (IoT) allow students to engage with content through experiential simulations—ranging from virtual field trips to interactive science experiments. These tools enhance student engagement, emotional connection, and knowledge retention. Real-time learning analytics and sensor-based environments also allow educators to respond to students' needs dynamically, enhancing learning outcomes at both individual and institutional levels.

Looking ahead, Web 5.0 introduces emotionally intelligent and empathetic systems that recognize and respond to human feelings. Through affective computing, educational systems can detect learners' emotional states—such as frustration, boredom, or confusion—via facial expressions, voice tone, and physiological data. These insights allow adaptive systems to modify instruction styles, suggest breaks, or offer motivational support. While this innovation promises to humanize learning, it also raises serious concerns about emotional data privacy, consent, and the ethical use of biometric information.

On the cultural front, the intelligent web fosters a new era of digital heritage preservation and intercultural exchange. Museums, archives, and cultural institutions are digitizing rare manuscripts, artifacts, and oral histories, making them globally accessible via platforms like Google Arts & Culture, Europeana, and UNESCO's World Digital Library. AI is also being used to translate ancient texts, revive extinct languages, and reconstruct damaged artworks, thus enabling broader participation in cultural memory and storytelling. These initiatives democratize access to cultural heritage while promoting diversity and inclusion.

However, these advances also come with critical challenges. The digital divide remains a major barrier, particularly in low-income countries or remote areas where internet access, digital literacy, and educational resources are limited. Without equitable infrastructure and support, there is a risk that digital education technologies will reinforce existing inequalities. Furthermore, educational systems in many countries are not yet prepared—pedagogically or ethically—to integrate these technologies responsibly. Government policies, teacher training, and community engagement must be prioritized to ensure inclusive and effective implementation.

Another implication of the intelligent web is the rise of global learning communities. With the growth of MOOCs (Massive Open Online Courses), collaborative platforms like GitHub, and real-time virtual classrooms, learners and educators from diverse cultural and linguistic backgrounds can now co-create knowledge and solve problems together. This encourages not only access to education but also intercultural dialogue, empathy, and global citizenship—skills that are crucial in an interconnected, digitally mediated world.

In the future, education will no longer be defined solely by physical classrooms or standardized testing. Instead, it will evolve into a continuous, multimodal, and emotionally aware **process**—tailored to the learner's identity, goals, and context. Similarly, culture will no longer be confined to national borders or static representations; it will become living and dynamic, shaped collaboratively in digital spaces. To guide this transformation ethically and sustainably, we must design digital educational and cultural ecosystems that reflect human dignity, equity, and pluralism.

8. TECHNOLOGICAL TRENDS SHAPING THE FUTURE WEB

As we transition from Web 3.0 into the more autonomous and emotionally intelligent realms of Web 4.0 and Web 5.0, several technological advancements are driving this evolution. These trends are not isolated innovations but interconnected systems that collectively enhance the intelligence, adaptability, and emotional responsiveness of the web. Understanding these technologies is crucial for anticipating the challenges and opportunities of future digital societies.

One of the most foundational trends is the deployment of 5G and beyond—including upcoming 6G frameworks. These ultra-fast wireless networks are key to enabling low-latency, real-time interactions across a vast range of connected devices. From smart cities to autonomous vehicles to augmented reality classrooms, 5G ensures that devices and applications can process and exchange data almost instantaneously. This is critical for the seamless functioning of Web 4.0 systems, where responsiveness and context-awareness are core.

Another emerging trend is the Quantum Web, which refers to a future internet architecture built on the principles of quantum computing and quantum communication. Unlike classical systems, quantum networks promise unbreakable encryption, ultra-secure communication, and exponentially faster processing power. Quantum key distribution (QKD) could redefine cybersecurity protocols and data sovereignty by ensuring that even powerful AI agents cannot eavesdrop or tamper with communications.

Edge computing and fog networking are also shaping the web's infrastructure by shifting computation closer to the data source. Rather than relying solely on centralized cloud servers, edge computing allows devices such as sensors, smartphones, and IoT systems to process data locally. This reduces latency, saves bandwidth, and enhances privacy by keeping sensitive information on the edge devices themselves. These architectures support the distributed intelligence required in smart environments such as factories, hospitals, and homes.

Perhaps the most transformative—and controversial—development is the rise of emotional AI and sentient web interfaces. These systems are designed to detect and interpret human emotions through voice, facial expressions, biometric signals, or behavioral patterns. Applications range from emotionally aware digital assistants (e.g., Replika, Woebot) to adaptive user interfaces that change tone and content based on the user's mood. In Web 5.0, such interfaces aim not only to serve but to empathize and connect, raising questions about consent, ethics, and emotional manipulation.

These technologies are converging into what many scholars describe as the Intelligent Web—a digital ecosystem capable of understanding, predicting, and even emotionally relating to users. While these trends offer immense potential for personalization, accessibility, and automation, they also introduce risks related to surveillance, bias, digital addiction, and loss of agency. As such, it is imperative that these technologies be guided by robust governance, inclusive policy frameworks, and ethics-by-design principles.

Table 7. Key technological trends driving the future web

Trend	Description	Implication
5G / 6G Networks	High-speed, low-latency communication	Enables real-time, immersive digital services
Quantum Web	Quantum-based internet and encryption	Ultra-secure communication, next-gen cryptography
Edge & Fog Computing	Decentralized data processing near data sources	Reduces latency, increases privacy, supports autonomous systems
Emotional AI	AI systems that detect and respond to human emotion	Personalized interfaces, empathy-based agents, ethical challenges
Brain-Computer Interfaces (BCI)	Neural input-output systems between brain and devices	New human-machine interaction models, accessibility breakthroughs
AI at Scale	Large-scale, generative, and multimodal AI models	Content generation, real-time language translation, emotional modeling

As these trends mature, they will reshape core human experiences: from how we learn, work, and govern, to how we feel, trust, and **relate** in digital environments. For instance, emotional AI in education may increase engagement, but if used without consent, it can violate personal boundaries. Similarly, edge computing enhances privacy by decentralization, yet it may reduce oversight and standardization. These paradoxes must be acknowledged in the policy discourse.

Moreover, AI at scale—such as GPT-like models—raises concerns about deepfakes, misinformation, and intellectual property. In the cultural sector, generative AI might replicate artistic styles or voices, creating tension between innovation and authenticity. The same tools that empower can also exploit, making ethical governance non-negotiable.

The future web is not a single invention but a convergence of intelligent, connected, and emotionally aware systems. These technologies—5G, quantum, AI, edge computing, and emotional interfaces—are building a web that sees, listens, learns, and feels. While this opens vast possibilities for human advancement, it also challenges us to redefine our values, rights, and responsibilities in the digital age. Only with thoughtful design, inclusive dialogue, and proactive governance can we ensure that the future web is not only intelligent—but also ethical, equitable, and human-centric.

9. POLICY AND REGULATION IN THE FUTURE WEB

As the web evolves from static content delivery to an emotionally intelligent, autonomous, and highly interactive environment in Web 5.0, the need for proactive, adaptive, and ethically grounded policies becomes increasingly urgent. Future web ecosystems will operate at the intersection of AI, blockchain, quantum computing, and human emotion. Without thoughtful governance, these technologies could exacerbate inequalities, compromise digital rights, and erode public trust in digital infrastructure.

One of the foundational challenges in governing the future web lies in establishing legal clarity over decentralized systems. Technologies like blockchain, Decentralized Autonomous Organizations (DAOs), and Self-Sovereign Identity (SSI) resist traditional jurisdictional boundaries. These systems empower users by removing intermediaries but complicate accountability and legal recourse. As DAOs begin to manage real-world assets and make governance decisions algorithmically, states must develop regulatory frameworks that both recognize these entities and ensure transparency and due process.

Furthermore, with the rise of emotional AI and sentient interfaces, new regulatory domains emerge around emotional privacy, data ethics, and psychological safety.

These systems collect sensitive emotional data—voice tone, facial expressions, stress levels—that are far more personal than traditional behavioral metrics. Without strict guidelines, such data could be used for manipulation, surveillance, or biased profiling. Governments and international organizations, such as the EU's AI Act and UNESCO's AI Ethics Framework, have emphasized the need for explainable, transparent, and human-centric AI regulation.

Another critical domain is cross-border data governance. As data flows increasingly transcend national boundaries, conflicts over data localization, digital sovereignty, and cloud jurisdiction intensify. The General Data Protection Regulation (GDPR) in Europe and similar frameworks in Brazil (LGPD), India (DPDP Act), and Indonesia (UU PDP) set precedents for enforcing user consent, data portability, and the right to be forgotten. However, in a global web powered by autonomous agents, harmonizing these laws across jurisdictions remains a complex geopolitical challenge.

Cybersecurity in Web 5.0 also demands upgraded regulation. As IoT, AI, and quantum systems become deeply embedded in public infrastructure, the attack surface expands exponentially. Governments must move from reactive postures to preventive, resilient cybersecurity architectures, possibly coordinated through multi-stakeholder collaborations involving public sectors, tech companies, and civil society. The NIST Cybersecurity Framework, ENISA guidelines, and Global Forum on Cyber Expertise (GFCE) have all promoted such participatory models to ensure shared responsibility and trust.

Finally, ensuring digital equity and inclusion must become a regulatory priority. Without policies that guarantee universal access to high-speed internet, digital literacy, and inclusive design, the future web may deepen existing divides. Marginalized communities—rural, elderly, disabled, or indigenous—risk being excluded from critical innovations in education, governance, and employment. As such, policies must go beyond technological regulation to include social and economic justice, ensuring that Web 5.0 is not only intelligent, but inclusive and fair. Table 8. shows Key Policy Domains for Future Web Governance.

Table 8. Key policy domains for future web governance

Policy Domain	Key Concerns	Regulatory Examples
Decentralized Governance	DAO legitimacy, blockchain-based voting, algorithmic decision-making	MiCA (EU), SEC guidance on token classification
AI & Emotional Privacy	Emotional data ethics, manipulative interfaces, transparency	EU AI Act, UNESCO AI Ethics Guidelines
Cross-Border Data Flows	Data localization, cloud sovereignty, compliance conflicts	GDPR, LGPD (Brazil), UU PDP (Indonesia)

continued on following page

Table 8. Continued

Policy Domain	Key Concerns	Regulatory Examples
Cybersecurity	IoT vulnerabilities, quantum threats, critical infrastructure protection	NIST Framework, ENISA, GFCE
Digital Equity & Access	Infrastructure gaps, digital literacy, inclusive design	UN SDG Goal 9, ITU Digital Inclusion Guidelines

To effectively regulate the future web, governance must go beyond technical standards and embrace normative ethical principles such as:

- Transparency: Users should understand how algorithms affect their experience.
- Accountability: Developers and institutions must be answerable for unintended harms.
- Inclusivity: Policies must reflect diverse voices, especially marginalized groups.
- Proportionality: Regulation should balance innovation and protection without stifling progress.
- Global Cooperation: Harmonization across jurisdictions is vital to govern borderless technologies.

These principles are echoed in recent global charters such as the GPAI (Global Partnership on AI) and the OECD AI Principles, which advocate for human-centered, rights-respecting innovation at scale. Figure 4. shows Policy Architecture for the Future Web.

Figure 5. Policy architecture for the future web

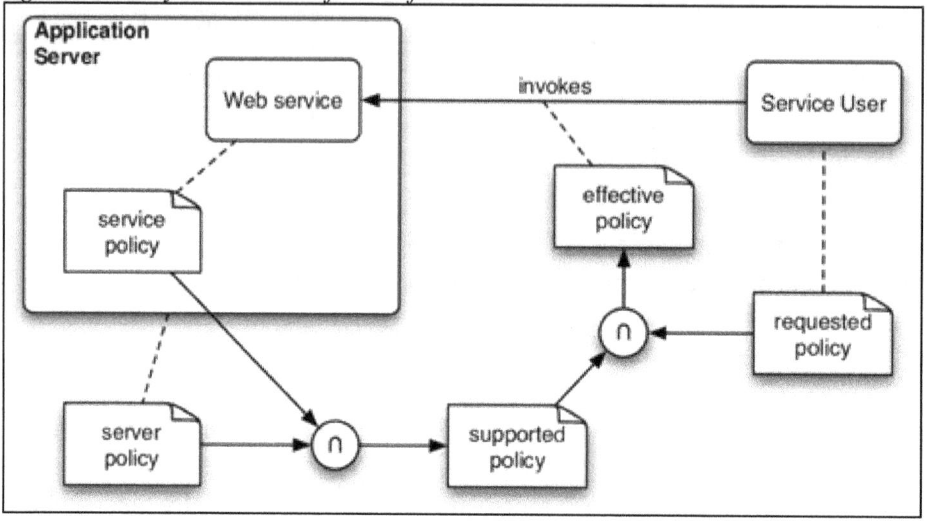

10. CONCLUSION

The evolution of web technologies from Web 1.0 to Web 5.0 represents far more than a technological shift—it signifies a transformation in how humans interact with information, institutions, and one another. Each stage in this trajectory has deepened digital integration into society, from the static content of the early web to the semantic intelligence of Web 3.0, the contextual awareness of Web 4.0, and now the emotionally responsive, human-centric vision of Web 5.0. As a result, our digital experiences are no longer passive but increasingly personal, predictive, and participatory.

The promise of the future web lies in its ability to empower individuals, enhance collective intelligence, and enable new forms of governance, learning, and cultural expression. Innovations such as decentralized identity, affective computing, immersive education, and global knowledge networks offer powerful tools for inclusion and equity. If designed thoughtfully, these systems can amplify human potential and bring underserved communities into the digital fold.

However, the same technologies carry significant risks. Emotional AI, quantum networks, and AI governance models challenge traditional notions of privacy, autonomy, and accountability. Without robust policy frameworks, inclusive design, and ethical safeguards, the future web could replicate or even worsen existing inequalities, exploit vulnerabilities, or centralize control in the hands of a few. Regulatory foresight, multi-stakeholder collaboration, and civic engagement will be crucial to ensuring that digital rights and human dignity are protected.

Furthermore, the future web must not only be intelligent but also empathetic, ethical, and inclusive. Governance models must evolve to keep pace with innovation—emphasizing transparency, accountability, and fairness across jurisdictions and cultures. Education systems must foster critical digital literacy and emotional resilience, while cultural policies must support preservation, diversity, and respectful exchange in a global digital society.

Ultimately, shaping the web of the future is not merely a technological task—it is a social responsibility. Policymakers, developers, educators, and users alike must commit to building a web that serves the public good, enhances democratic participation, and uplifts human potential. By doing so, we can ensure that the web remains not only a tool for innovation, but a force for just, sustainable, and inclusive digital progress.

REFERENCES

Azad, B., & Zablith, F. (2022). An emergent mechanism of inclusive e-Government design: The interplay of user design input and provider response. *Information Polity, 27*(4), 433–453. DOI: 10.3233/IP-220010

Babel, M., Willburger, L., Lautenschlager, J., Völter, F., Guggenberger, T., Körner, M.-F., Sedlmeir, J., Strüker, J., & Urbach, N. (2025). Self-sovereign identity and digital wallets. *Electronic Markets, 35*(1), 28. Advance online publication. DOI: 10.1007/s12525-025-00772-0

Chakrabarti, M., Fabozzi, F. J., Narain, A., & Sood, A. (2025). Ethical AI in Asset Management: Frameworks for Transparency, Compliance, and Trust. *The Journal of Financial Data Science, 7*(1), 18–35. DOI: 10.3905/jfds.2025.7.1.018

Díaz-Pereira, M. P. M. D. P., Delgado-Parada, J. J., Ricoy, M.-C. M.-C., & Fernández-Iglesias, M. J. M. J. (2025). Design and evaluation of a repository of toolkits based on design thinking for socio-educational intervention with vulnerable migrant women. *Computers & Education, 231*, 105294. Advance online publication. DOI: 10.1016/j.compedu.2025.105294

Gan, W., Ye, Z., Wan, S., & Yu, P. S. (2023). Web 3.0: The Future of Internet. *ACM Web Conference 2023 - Companion of the World Wide Web Conference, WWW 2023*, 1266–1275. DOI: 10.1145/3543873.3587583

Hähnel, M. (2025). Ethical challenges and solutions in AI-driven medical data management: A focus on distributed machine learning. *Discover Artificial Intelligence, 5*(1), 53. Advance online publication. DOI: 10.1007/s44163-025-00266-0

Hassan, M. A., Jamshidi, M. B., Manh, B. D., Chu, N. H., Nguyen, C.-H., Hieu, N. Q., Nguyen, C. T., Hoang, D. T., Nguyen, D. N., Van Huynh, N., Alsheikh, M. A., & Dutkiewicz, E. (2025). Enabling technologies for Web 3.0: A comprehensive survey. *Computer Networks, 264*, 111242. Advance online publication. DOI: 10.1016/j.comnet.2025.111242

He, B., & Bhatti, U. A. (2025). Smart Cities and Smart Networks: AI Applications in Urban Geography and Industrial Communication. *International Journal of High Speed Electronics and Systems, 34*(3), 2440122. Advance online publication. DOI: 10.1142/S0129156424401220

Ihsan, A. Z., Fathalla, S., & Sandfeld, S. (2025). Modeling dislocation dynamics data using semantic web technologies. *Neural Computing & Applications, 37*(18), 11737–11753. DOI: 10.1007/s00521-024-10674-5 PMID: 40538984

Khan, F. S., Mazhar, S. S., Mazhar, K. A., AlSaleh, D., & Mazhar, A. (2025). Model-agnostic explainable artificial intelligence methods in finance: A systematic review, recent developments, limitations, challenges and future directions. *Artificial Intelligence Review*, *58*(8). Advance online publication. DOI: 10.1007/s10462-025-11215-9

Leddy, M., & McCreanor, N. (2024). Exploring how Education can Leverage Artificial Intelligence for Social Good. *Proceedings of the European Conference on Innovation and Entrepreneurship, ECIE, 19*(1), 1041–1048. DOI: 10.34190/ecie.19.1.2906

Maria Koziel, A., Shen, C.-W., Djailani, I., & Chang, Y.-L. (2025). Beyond Social Norms: Psychological and Hedonic Drivers of Metaverse Adoption Among Generation Y. *IEEE Access : Practical Innovations, Open Solutions*, *13*, 78441–78460. DOI: 10.1109/ACCESS.2025.3563758

Panjaburee, P., Intarakamhang, U., Srisawasdi, N., Poompimol, S., & Tapingkae, P. (2025). Predictors of active and inactive learners' intention to use decision tree-based contextual mobile games for cultivating digital citizenship behaviour. *International Journal of Mobile Learning and Organisation*, *19*(1), 1–32. DOI: 10.1504/IJMLO.2025.143022

Priestley, M., Sluckin, T. J., & Tiropanis, T. (2020). Innovation on the web: The end of the S-curve? *Internet Histories*, *4*(4), 390–412. DOI: 10.1080/24701475.2020.1747261

Santra, A., Chakrabarty, D., Giri, A., & Dhara, S. K. (2024). Analyzing the Customer Sentiment of Reels and Short Video Viewers of Facebook Using Social Media Analysis. *Lecture Notes in Networks and Systems, 949 LNNS*, 159–167. DOI: 10.1007/978-981-97-1313-4_14

Saurabh, K., Upadhyay, P., & Rani, N. (2025). Towards Blockchain Decentralized Autonomous Organizations (DAO) Design. *Information Systems Frontiers*, *27*(2), 659–681. DOI: 10.1007/s10796-023-10455-w

Seo, J., & Park, S. (2025). Self-sovereign identity framework with user-friendly private key generation and rule table. *Future Generation Computer Systems*, *167*, 107757. Advance online publication. DOI: 10.1016/j.future.2025.107757

Sularso, S., Wadiyo, W., Cahyono, A., Suharto, S., & Pranolo, A. (2025). A Comprehensive Visualization for Music Education and Artificial Intelligence. *JOIV: International Journal on Informatics Visualization*, *9*(2), 718–727. DOI: 10.62527/joiv.9.2.2500

Yrjola, S., Ahokangas, P., & Matinmikko-Blue, M. (2022). Value Creation and Capture from Technology Innovation in the 6G Era. *IEEE Access : Practical Innovations, Open Solutions*, *10*, 16299–16319. DOI: 10.1109/ACCESS.2022.3149590

Zhou, D., Tan, Q., Huang, H., Huang, Q., & Qin, N. (2025). A Study of Knowledge Graph and IoT Integration-Based Anomalous Event Tracking Method for Digital Platforms. *International Journal of High Speed Electronics and Systems*, *34*(4), 2540314. Advance online publication. DOI: 10.1142/S0129156425403146

Compilation of References

Abrahams, T. O., Ewuga, S. K., Kaggwa, S., Uwaoma, P. U., Hassan, A. O., & Dawodu, S. O. (2024). Mastering compliance: A comprehensive review of regulatory frameworks in accounting and cybersecurity. Comput. Sci. IT Res. j., 5(1), 120–140.

Abul Khair, M., Mangal, A., & Singiri, S. (2023). Advanced security features in Oracle HCM Cloud. *Universal Research Reports*, *10*(4), 493–511. DOI: 10.36676/urr.v10.i4.1360

Afolabi, S. O., Malachi, I. O., Olawumi, A. O., & Oladapo, B. I. (2025). Data Process of Net-Zero Revolution for Transforming Earth and Beyond Sustainably. *Sustainability (Basel)*, *17*(12), 5367. Advance online publication. DOI: 10.3390/su17125367

Agbeyangi, A., & Suleman, H. (2024, November). Advances and challenges in low-resource-environment software systems: A Survey. In *Informatics* (Vol. 11, No. 4, p. 90). MDPI. DOI: 10.3390/informatics11040090

Agger, B. (2004). *The virtual self.* Blackwell Publishing.

Agustina, L., & Roisatin, U. (2024). The efficacy of case-based learning model integrated with critical thinking skills to improve efl learners' reading comprehension. *Journal of Languages and Language Teaching*, *12*(3), 1443. DOI: 10.33394/jollt.v12i3.11619

Akgül, M., & Hekimoğlu Toprak, H. (2019). The transformation of privacy on social networks: The case of Instagram [Sosyal ağlarda mahremiyetin dönüşümü: Instagram örneği]. *Anadolu Üniversitesi Sosyal Bilimler Dergisi*, *10*(38), 75–114. DOI: 10.5824/1309-1581.2019.3.004.x

Akkaş, İ. (2016). Identities and virtual communities in a multi-faced network of relations [Çok yüzlü ilişkiler ağında kimlikler ve sanal cemaatler]. *Düzce Üniversitesi Sosyal Bilimler Dergisi*, *3*(2), 37–53.

Akyazı, E., & Ateş, A. (2012). The role of social networks in creating cultural identity awareness: A study on Manav Turks. [Kültürel kimlik farkındalığı yaratmada sosyal ağların rolü: Manav Türkleri üzerine bir araştırma] In Kara, T., & Özgen, E. (Eds.), *Social media, academy: Communication, marketing communication, network society, technology* [Sosyal medya, akademi: İletişim, pazarlama iletişimi, ağ toplumu, teknoloji]. (pp. 173–192). Beta Publication.

Alamri, B., Crowley, K., & Richardson, I. (2022). Cybersecurity risk management framework for blockchain identity management systems in health IoT. *Sensors (Basel)*, *23*(1), 218. DOI: 10.3390/s23010218 PMID: 36616816

Al-Barakati, A. (2021). Leveraging Artificial Intelligence-enabled Workflow Framework for Legacy Transformation. *International Journal of Advanced Computer Science andApplications*, *12*(12), 297–303. DOI: 10.14569/IJACSA.2021.0121239

Albashtawi, A., & Bataineh, K. (2020). The effectiveness of google classroom among efl students in jordan: An innovative teaching and learning online platform. *International Journal of Emerging Technologies in Learning*, *15*(11), 78. DOI: 10.3991/ijet.v15i11.12865

AlDahoul, N., Hong, J., Varvello, M., & Zaki, Y. (2025). Towards a World Wide Web powered by generative AI. *Scientific Reports*, *15*(1), 7251. Advance online publication. DOI: 10.1038/s41598-024-77301-0 PMID: 40021676

Alevizos, L., Eiza, M. H., Ta, V. T., Shi, Q., & Read, J. (2022). Blockchain-enabled intrusion detection and prevention system of APTs within zero trust architecture. *IEEE Access : Practical Innovations, Open Solutions*, *10*, 89270–89288. DOI: 10.1109/ACCESS.2022.3200165

Alexopoulos, K., Nikolakis, N., & Xanthakis, E. (2022). *Digital Transformation of Production Planning and Control in Manufacturing SMEs-The Mold Shop Case. Laboratory for Manufacturing Systems & Automation (LMS)*. Department of Mechanical Engineering & Aeronautics, University of Patras., DOI: 10.3390/app122110788

Algouzi, S., Alzubi, A., & Nazim, M. (2023). Enhancing efl students' critical thinking skills using a technology-mediated self-study approach: Efl graduates and labor market in perspective. *PLoS One*, *18*(10), e0293273. DOI: 10.1371/journal.pone.0293273 PMID: 37856514

Alharbi, A. (2020). Wikis in language learning: Merits and limitations. *Journal of English Language Teaching and Applied Linguistics*, *2*(4), 79–88. DOI: 10.32996/jeltal.2020.2.4.9

Alharbi, M., & Alqefari, A. (2021). The impact of teacher feedback via google doc in l2 learners' writing. *International Journal of Learning Teaching and Educational Research, 20*(11), 170–194. DOI: 10.26803/ijlter.20.11.10

Ali, I., Azim, M., & Rehman, A. (2024). Translanguaging as a tool to decolonize english language teaching in pakistan: Opportunities and challenges. *Pakistan Social Sciences Review, 8*(I). Advance online publication. DOI: 10.35484/pssr.2024(8-I)23

Alnaser, A. A., & Elmousalami, H. (2025). Benefits and Challenges of AI-Based Digital Twin Integration in the Saudi Arabian Construction Industry: A Correspondence Analysis (CA) Approach. *Applied Sciences (Basel, Switzerland), 15*(9), 4675. Advance online publication. DOI: 10.3390/app15094675

Alomari, G. (2025). Intersection of AI and cybersecurity: Protecting healthcare data in a connected world. *Glob. Insights Artif. Intell. Comput., 1*(2), 37–56. DOI: 10.70445/giaic.1.2.2025.37-56

Amin, E. (2020). A review of research into google apps in the process of english language learning and teaching. *Arab World English Journal, 11*(1), 399–418. DOI: 10.24093/awej/vol11no1.27

Amouei, M., Rezvani, M., & Fateh, M. (2021). RAT: Reinforcement-learning-driven and adaptive testing for vulnerability discovery in web application firewalls. IEEE Trans. Dependable Secure Comput., 1.

Anis, A., & Zulkernine, M., Iqbal Shahrear and Liem, C., & Chambers, C. (2018, August). Securing web applications with secure coding practices and integrity verification. 2018 IEEE 16th Intl Conf on Dependable, Autonomic and Secure Computing, 16th Intl Conf on Pervasive Intelligence and Computing, 4th Intl Conf on Big Data Intelligence and Computing and Cyber Science and Technology(DASC/PiCom/DataCom/CyberSciTech).

Ao, J. (2025). Research on the impact of artificial intelligence on corporate sustainability performance and its mechanisms: An empirical analysis based on text analysis. *Discover Artificial Intelligence, 5*(1), 122. Advance online publication. DOI: 10.1007/s44163-025-00359-w

Appelt, D., Nguyen, C. D., Panichella, A., & Briand, L. C. (2018). A machine-learning-driven evolutionary approach for testing web application firewalls. *IEEE Transactions on Reliability, 67*(3), 733–757. DOI: 10.1109/TR.2018.2805763

Arceneaux, P. (2024). Value creation through organizational storytelling: Strategic narratives in foreign government public relations. *Public Relations Review, 50*(2), 102433. DOI: 10.1016/j.pubrev.2024.102433

Armbrust, M., Fox, A., Griffith, R., Joseph, A. D., Katz, R., Konwinski, A., Lee, G., Patterson, D., Rabkin, A., Stoica, I., & Zaharia, M. (2010). A view of cloud computing. *Communications of the ACM*, *53*(4), 50–58. DOI: 10.1145/1721654.1721672

Arya, L. (2024). Securing healthcare data and cybersecurity innovations in the era of Industry 5.0. In *Cybersecurity and Data Management Innovations for Revolutionizing Healthcare* (pp. 132–147). IGI Global. DOI: 10.4018/979-8-3693-7457-3.ch006

Asplund, S. B., Ljung Egeland, B., & Olin-Scheller, C. (2024). Sharing is caring: Young people's narratives about BookTok and volitional reading. *Language and Education*, *38*(4), 635–651. DOI: 10.1080/09500782.2024.2324947

Asrianti, A., Iskandar, I., & Patak, A. (2022). The implementation of multicultural-based english language teaching in a language institution. *International Journal of Humanities and Innovation (Ijhi)*, *5*(2), 67–73. DOI: 10.33750/ijhi.v5i2.150

Augusto, F. R., & Simões, M. J. (2017). To see and be seen, to know and be known: Perceptions and prevention strategies on Facebook surveillance. *Social Sciences Information. Information Sur les Sciences Sociales*, *56*(4), 596–618. DOI: 10.1177/0539018417734974

Azad, B., & Zablith, F. (2022). An emergent mechanism of inclusive e-Government design: The interplay of user design input and provider response. *Information Polity*, *27*(4), 433–453. DOI: 10.3233/IP-220010

Baban, E. (2012). McLuhan and Baudrillard's perspective on social media: The captivity of expression, the surveilled society, and the lost identity syndrome. [Mc Luhan ve Baudrillard'ın penceresinden sosyal medyanın etkisi: İfadenin esareti, gözetlenen toplum ve kayıp kimlik sendromu] In Kara, T., & Özgen, E. (Eds.), *Social Media Academy* [Sosyal Medya Akademi]. (pp. 57–83). Beta Press.

Babel, M., Willburger, L., Lautenschlager, J., Völter, F., Guggenberger, T., Körner, M.-F., Sedlmeir, J., Strüker, J., & Urbach, N. (2025). Self-sovereign identity and digital wallets. *Electronic Markets*, *35*(1), 28. Advance online publication. DOI: 10.1007/s12525-025-00772-0

Balagopalan, A., Jacobs, A. Z., & Biega, A. J. (2023). The Role of Relevance in Fair Ranking. *SIGIR 2023 - Proceedings of the 46th International ACM SIGIR Conference on Research and Development in Information Retrieval*, 2650–2660. DOI: 10.1145/3539618.3591933

Barszcz, M., Dziedzic, K., Skublewska-Paszkowska, M., & Powroznik, P. (2023). 3D scanning digital models for virtual museums. *Computer Animation and Virtual Worlds*, *34*(3-4), e2154. DOI: 10.1002/cav.2154

Başaran, F. (2005). The political economy of the Internet. [İnternetin ekonomi politiği] In Toplum, M. (Ed.), *Internet, society, culture* [*İnternet, toplum, kültür*]. (pp. 32–52). Epos Publication.

Batam, U. I., Haeruddin, H., Prasetyo, S. E., Batam, U. I., Kaharuddin, A. W., & Batam, U. I. (2024). Optimalisasi Keamanan Jaringan Di Era Digital menggunakan metode Zero Trust. *Journal of Information System and Technology*, *5*(3), 15–24. DOI: 10.37253/joint.v5i3.9986

Baudrillard, J. (2015). *The spirit of terrorism and reign of evil* [*Şeytana satılan ruh ya da kötülüğün egemenliği*]. (Adanır, O., Trans.). Doğu Batı Publication.

Baumgartner, A., Rohrbach, T., & Schönhagen, P. (2023). 'If the phone were broken, I'd be screwed': Media use of people with disabilities in the digital era. *Disability & Society*, *38*(1), 73–97. DOI: 10.1080/09687599.2021.1916884

Belkhamza, Z. (2023). Cybersecurity in digital transformation applications: Analysis of past research and future directions. *Iccws*, *18*(1), 19–24. DOI: 10.34190/iccws.18.1.1005

Benlhabib, H., & Berrado, A. (2025). Towards a digital platform for performance management and systemic improvement of education systems: Evidence from Morocco. *Discover Education*, *4*(1), 15. Advance online publication. DOI: 10.1007/s44217-024-00317-1

Bercaru, V., & Popescu, N. (2024). A Systematic Review of Accessibility Techniques for Online Platforms: Current Trends and Challenges. *Applied Sciences (Basel, Switzerland)*, *14*(22), 10337. Advance online publication. DOI: 10.3390/app142210337

Bezus, S., Akbilek, E., & Mekeko, N. (2021). Web Technologies in Distance Learning: Student Perception on the Advantages and Disadvantages. *2021 IEEE International Conference on Educational Technology, ICET 2021*, 85-89. Retrieved from DOI: 10.1109/ICET52293.2021.9563134

Bian, X., Wang, B., Li, K., & Du, Z. (2025). Navigating ethical decision-making in digital transformation: Ethical climate, digital competence, and person-organization fit in China's banking sector. *Humanities & Social Sciences Communications*, *12*(1), 920. Advance online publication. DOI: 10.1057/s41599-025-05184-1

Binkley, C. E., Bouslov, D., Zaidi, A., Kaye, L., Whalen, R., Sethi, S., & Azar, J. (2025). An early pipeline framework for assessing vendor AI solutions to support return on investment. *NPJ Digital Medicine*, *8*(1), 368. Advance online publication. DOI: 10.1038/s41746-025-01767-z PMID: 40523928

Bocean, C. G., & Vărzaru, A. A. (2025). Health status in the era of digital transformation and sustainable economic development. *BMC Health Services Research*, *25*(1), 343. Advance online publication. DOI: 10.1186/s12913-025-12498-y PMID: 40045359

Bogdanova, G., Todorov, T., Dochkova-Todorova, J., Noev, N., & Sabev, N. (2024). Design and Development Model of a Web Accessibility Ecosystem. *Information (Basel)*, *15*(10), 613. DOI: 10.3390/info15100613

Bokolo, A. J. (2025). Implementing Digital Sovereignty to Accelerate Smarter Mobility Solutions in Local Communities. *Smart Cities*, *8*(4), 106. DOI: 10.3390/smartcities8040106

Boniotti, C. (2023). The public-private-people partnership (P4) for cultural heritage management purposes. *Journal of Cultural Heritage Management and Sustainable Development*, *13*(1), 1–14. DOI: 10.1108/JCHMSD-12-2020-0186

Boopathi, S., & Khang, A. (2023). AI-integrated technology for a secure and ethical healthcare ecosystem. In *AI and IoT-Based Technologies for Precision Medicine* (pp. 36–59). IGI Global. DOI: 10.4018/979-8-3693-0876-9.ch003

Boyd, D. M., & Ellison, N. B. (2007). Social network sites: Definition, history, and scholarship. *Journal of Computer-Mediated Communication*, *13*(1), 210–230. DOI: 10.1111/j.1083-6101.2007.00393.x

Boz, N. (2012). *Digital identity and self-presentation in new communication environments* [*Yeni iletişim ortamlarında dijital kimlik ve benlik sunumu*] (Doctoral dissertation). Istanbul.

Buragohain, D., Buragohain, D., Meng, Y., Deng, C., & Chaudhary, S. (2025). A metaverse based digital preservation of temple architecture and heritage. *Scientific Reports*, *15*(1), 15484. DOI: 10.1038/s41598-025-00039-w PMID: 40319075

Burrell, D. N., & Burton, S. L. Nobles Calvin and Springs, D., Huff, A. J., Brown-Jackson, K. L., Richardson, K., Wright, J. B., Muller, S. R., & Jones, A. J. (2023). The managerial ethical and operational challenges of hospital cybersecurity. In Transformational Interventions for Business, Technology, and Healthcare (pp. 444–458). IGI Global.

Butterworth, J., & van Schaik, S. (2024). Reflections on Two Decades of the Endangered Archives Programme. *Preservation in Perspective: International Strategies for the Preservation of Written Cultural Heritage*, 29.

Bychkov, I., Ruzhnikov, G., Fedorov, R., Popova, A., Avid, B., Batgerel, B., & Dulamrchaga, U. (2022). Digital transformation of the environmental monitoring for Lake Khubsugul and Prikhubsugulye. *Journal of Computational Technologies*, 14 - 29. doi:DOI: 10.25743/ICT.2022.27.5.003

Çakır, M. (2015). *Performance and surveillance on the Internet: A critical reading* [*İnternette gösteri ve gözetim: Eleştirel bir okuma*]. Ütopya Publication.

Camilleri, M. A., Troise, C., Strazzullo, S., & Bresciani, S. (2023). Creating shared value through open innovation approaches: Opportunities and challenges for corporate sustainability. *Business Strategy and the Environment*, *32*(7), 4485–4502. DOI: 10.1002/bse.3377

Capurro, C., & Severo, M. (2023). Mapping European Digital Heritage Politics: An Empirical Study of Europeana as a Web-based Network. *Heritage & Society*, •••, 1–21. DOI: 10.1080/2159032X.2023.2266801

Cárdenas Rosero, G. E., Guevara Vega, C. P., & Landeta-López, P. (2025). Website protection: An evaluation of the Web Application Firewall. *Data and Metadata*, *4*, 190. DOI: 10.56294/dm2025190

Casanova, J., & Savoie, M. (2019). Navigating the EU regulatory landscape for payments. *Journal of Payments Strategy and Systems*, *13*(3), 242–254. DOI: 10.69554/BKTB9869

Castells, M. (2008). *The rise of the network society: The information age, economy, society and culture* (Vol. 1; Kılıç, E., Trans.). Istanbul Bilgi University Publication. [*Ağ toplumunun yükselişi enformasyon çağı: Ekonomi, toplum ve kültür*]

Castells, M. (2016). *Communication power* [*İletişim gücü*]. Istanbul Bilgi University Publication.

Çelik, H. (2010). Identity debates in the globalization process and the role of media: The case of Kosovo [*Küreselleşme sürecinde kimlik tartışmaları ve medyanın rolü: Kosova örneği*]. *İstanbul Arel Üniversitesi Yayınları, 3*(7), 21–44.

Cerezo, E., Coma-Roselló, T., Aguelo, A., Blasco-Serrano, A. C., & Garrido, M. Á. (2023). Exploring intergenerational interactions through an online storytelling experience. *IEEE Transactions on Learning Technologies*, *17*, 157–171. DOI: 10.1109/TLT.2023.3260955

Chakrabarti, M., Fabozzi, F. J., Narain, A., & Sood, A. (2025). Ethical AI in Asset Management: Frameworks for Transparency, Compliance, and Trust. *The Journal of Financial Data Science*, *7*(1), 18–35. DOI: 10.3905/jfds.2025.7.1.018

Chambers, I. (2005). *Migration, culture, identity* [*Göç, kültür, kimlik*]. (Türkmen, İ., & Beşikçi, M., Trans.). Ayrıntı Publication.

Chandramouli, R. (2022). *Guide to a secure enterprise network landscape*. National Institute of Standards and Technology.

Chatfield, T. (2013). *How to survive in the digital age* [*Dijital çağa nasıl uyum sağlarız*]. (Konca, L., Trans.). Sel Publishing.

Chen, D., & Huang, Y. (2025). Integrating reinforcement learning and large language models for crop production process management optimization and control through a new knowledge-based deep learning paradigm. *Computers and Electronics in Agriculture, 232*, 110028. Advance online publication. DOI: 10.1016/j.compag.2025.110028

Cheng, P., & Chen, D. (2025). Cultural gene decoding: Digital protection of intangible paper-cut and construction of gene bank. *Digital Scholarship in the Humanities, 40*(1), 54–63. DOI: 10.1093/llc/fqaf008

Chen, S., Yang, L., Zhang, Y., Zhang, M., Xie, Y., Zhu, Z., & Li, J. (2025). Digital Human Technology in E-Learning: Custom Content Solutions. *Applied Sciences (Basel, Switzerland), 15*(7), 3807. Advance online publication. DOI: 10.3390/app15073807

Chen, Y., Chuang, H., & Lacaste, A. (2021). A pedagogical framework of cross-cultural online collaborative projects in english as foreign language (efl) classrooms. *Journal of Education and Learning (Edulearn), 15*(2), 223–233. DOI: 10.11591/edulearn.v15i2.19950

Chirumalla, K., Oghazi, P., Nnewuku, R. E., Tuncay, H., & Yahyapour, N. (2025). Critical factors affecting digital transformation in manufacturing companies. *The International Entrepreneurship and Management Journal, 21*(1), 54. Advance online publication. DOI: 10.1007/s11365-024-01056-3

Clarke, R. (2005, Aprıl 30). Have we learnt to love Big Brother? Xamax Consultancy Pty Ltd. https://www.rogerclarke.com/DV/DV2005.html

Çoban, B. (2014). The new panopticon: Power of surveillance and Facebook. [Yeni panoptikon gözü iktidarı ve Facebook] In Çoban, B. (Ed.), *Social media revolution* [*Sosyal medya devrimi*]. (pp. 303–319). Su Publication.

Coleman, B. (2011). *Hello Avatar: Rise of the networked generation* [*Hello Avatar: Dijital neslin yükselişi*]. MediaCat Publication.

Cover, R. (2015). *Digital identities: Creating and communicating the online self.* Academic Press.

Cowie, M. R., Blomster, J. I., Curtis, L. H., Duclaux, S., Ford, I., Fritz, F., Goldman, S., Janmohamed, S., Kreuzer, J., Leenay, M., Michel, A., Ong, S., Pell, J. P., Southworth, M. R., Stough, W. G., Thoenes, M., Zannad, F., & Zalewski, A. (2017). Electronic health records to facilitate clinical research. *Clinical Research in Cardiology; Official Journal of the German Cardiac Society, 106*(1), 1–9. DOI: 10.1007/s00392-016-1025-6 PMID: 27557678

Çuhacı, G. (2007). Body in digital arts / Dijital sanatlarda bedenin kullanımı (Doctoral dissertation). Marmara University, Institute of Social Sciences, Department of Communication, Istanbul.

Cui, T., Liu, L., Cheng, H., Chang, S., & Feng, Y. (2024). Crowdsourcing for innovation: Effects of idea content and competition intensity on idea success. *The Journal of Strategic Information Systems, 33*(2), 101839. DOI: 10.1016/j.jsis.2024.101839

Çınar, A., Erişen, Y., & Çeliköz, M. (2022). A mixed-method research on the effectiveness of using gamification elements in an online english course. *International Journal of Educational Research Review, 7*(4), 280–291. DOI: 10.24331/ijere.1140960

Da Milano, C., Falchetti, E., Migone, P., & Nisi, V. (2023). Digital storytelling, cultural heritage, and social inclusion: The MEMEX project. In *Digital Approaches to Inclusion and Participation in Cultural Heritage* (pp. 8–26). Routledge. DOI: 10.4324/9781003277606-2

Dahiya, R. (2024). A Blockchain Based Security system framework in Healthcare Domain using IoT. *J. Electr. Syst., 20*(3s), 2039–2050. DOI: 10.52783/jes.1805

Damberg, A. (2022). The influence of health consciousness on fitness app usage in the UK market. *Journal of Regional Fitness Research, 10*(4), 44–58.

Dargan, S., Bansal, S., Kumar, M., Mittal, A., & Kumar, K. (2023). Augmented reality: A comprehensive review. *Archives of Computational Methods in Engineering, 30*(2), 1057–1080. DOI: 10.1007/s11831-022-09831-7

Davenport, T. H., & Bean, R. (2018). Big companies are embracing analytics, but most still don't have a data-driven culture. *Harvard Business Review, 6*, 1–4.

Denzel, K. (2025). A survey of security in zero trust network architectures. *GSC Adv. Res. Rev., 22*(2), 182–214. DOI: 10.30574/gscarr.2025.22.2.0036

Dergaa, I.. (2024). Using artificial intelligence for exercise prescription in personalised health promotion: A critical evaluation of OpenAI's GPT-4 model. *Biology of Sport*, *41*(2), 221–241. DOI: 10.5114/biolsport.2024.133661 PMID: 38524814

Deri, M. G., Chiti, L., & Ciuffoletti, A. (2023). A Sustainable Approach to Tourist Signage on Heritage Trails. *Sustainability (Basel)*, *15*(23), 16251. DOI: 10.3390/su152316251

Desmal, A. J., Alsaeed, M., Zolait, A. H., & Hamid, S. (2023). Feedback for Excellence: Improving mGovernment Services Through User Insights. *2023 International Conference on Innovation and Intelligence for Informatics, Computing, and Technologies, 3ICT 2023*, 181–187. DOI: 10.1109/3ICT60104.2023.10391312

Deveci, M., Pamucar, D., Vasilateanu, A., Datta, G., Goga, N., Marian, C. V., Bratosin, I.-A., & Cali, U. (2025). Prioritization of health distributed ledger technology use cases using fuzzy sine trigonometric based decision-making model. *Expert Systems with Applications*, *294*, 128794. Advance online publication. DOI: 10.1016/j.eswa.2025.128794

Díaz-Pereira, M. P. M. D. P., Delgado-Parada, J. J., Ricoy, M.-C. M.-C., & Fernández-Iglesias, M. J. M. J. (2025). Design and evaluation of a repository of toolkits based on design thinking for socio-educational intervention with vulnerable migrant women. *Computers & Education*, *231*, 105294. Advance online publication. DOI: 10.1016/j.compedu.2025.105294

Dib, O., & Toumi, K. (2020). Decentralized identity systems: Architecture, challenges, solutions and future directions. *Ann. Emerg. Technol. Comput.*, *4*(5), 19–40. DOI: 10.33166/AETiC.2020.05.002

Dijk, J. V. (2018). *The network society* [*Ağ toplumu*]. (Sakin, Ö., Trans.). Epsilon Publication.

Djatmiko, G. H., Sinaga, O., & Pawirosumarto, S. (2025). Digital Transformation and Social Inclusion in Public Services: A Qualitative Analysis of E-Government Adoption for Marginalized Communities in Sustainable Governance. *Sustainability (Basel)*, *17*(7), 2908. Advance online publication. DOI: 10.3390/su17072908

Dogan, B., & Gogus, A. (2025). The Effect of the 'Instructional Technologies' Course on the Competencies of Teacher Candidates in Using Web 2.0 Tools: The Case of Early Childhood Education Program. *Springer Science and Business Media B.*, *30*(2), 883–910. DOI: 10.1007/s10758-025-09842-w

Dolgun, U. (2008). *Transparent prison or surveillance society: Surveillance, social control and power relations in a globalizing world* [*Şeffaf hapishane yahut gözetim toplumu: Küreselleşen dünyada gözetim, toplumsal denetim ve iktidar ilişkileri*]. Ötüken Publication.

Dreyfus, S., & Hellwig, A. F. (2023). Meaningful Rituals: A Linguistic Analysis of Acknowledgements of Country. *Journal of Australian Studies*, *47*(3), 590–610. DOI: 10.1080/14443058.2023.2236618

Dundua, E. (2024). Digital Marketing and Corporate Social Responsibility: Strategies for Brand Building and Stakeholder Engagement. *Springer Proceedings in Business and Economics*, 269–282. DOI: 10.1007/978-3-031-66517-2_21

Duque, J., & Garzón, A. (2024). Exploring the transformative impact of ict integration in the efl classroom. *Religación : Revista de Ciencias Sociales y Humanidades*, 9(40), e2401172. DOI: 10.46652/rgn.v9i40.1172

Durante, M. (2011). The online construction of personal identity through trust and privacy. *Information (Basel)*, *2*(4), 594–620. DOI: 10.3390/info2040594

Dursun, Ö. Ö., & Tugtekin, E. B. (2016). The new problem of social media: Virtual identities. [Sosyal medyanın yeni sorunsalı: Sanal kimlikler] In İşman, A., Odabaşı, H. F., & Akkoyunlu, B. (Eds.), *Readings in educational technology* [*Eğitimde teknoloji okumaları*]. 1st ed., pp. 535–552). TOJET.

Egorov, M., Wilkison, M., & Nunez, D. (2017). NuCypher KMS: Decentralized key management system.

Engin, Y. (2015). The phenomenon of digital identity among social media users and its examination in the context of social events [*Sosyal medya kullanıcılarında dijital kimlik olgusu ve toplumsal olaylar bağlamında incelenmesi*] (Master's thesis, Istanbul University, Institute of Social Sciences, Department of Journalism). Istanbul.

Erdoğan, İ. (2011). *Understanding communication* [*İletişimi anlamak*]. Pozitif Press.

Esgin, M. S. (2015). New trends in the world of web technologies. [Web teknolojileri dünyasında yeni trendler] In Baloğlu, A. (Ed.), *Social media mining* [*Sosyal medya madenciliği*]. (pp. 5–17). Beta Publication.

Eskandarzadeh, A. (2023). The future of web 3: A roadmap for the decentralized web. *Concepts, Technologies, Challenges, and the Future of Web 3*, 511-523. DOI: 10.4018/978-1-6684-9919-1.ch025

Eswaran, U., & Eswaran, V. (2024). AI-Driven Cross-Platform Design: Enhancing Usability and User Experience. *Navigating Usability and User Experience in a Multi-Platform World*, 19-48. DOI: 10.4018/979-8-3693-2337-3.ch002

Evenson, K. R., Goto, M. M., & Furberg, R. D. (2018). Using fitness trackers and smartwatches to measure physical activity in research: Analysis of consumer wrist-worn wearables. *Journal of Medical Internet Research*, *20*(3), e110. DOI: 10.2196/jmir.9157 PMID: 29567635

Far, I. K.. (2023). Fitness applications for home-based training. *Journal of Mobile Fitness Technology*, *18*(3), 112–126.

Farnel, S., Shiri, A., Gruben, E. J., Amos, B. S., & Kotokak, L. (2024). Enhancing Digital Libraries through Digital Storytelling: The Case of the Inuvialuit Digital Library. In *Library and Information Sciences in Arctic and Northern Studies* (pp. 209–226). Springer International Publishing., DOI: 10.1007/978-3-031-54715-7_10

Farshad, S., & Fortin, C. (2023). Active engagement in collaborative engineering design: How to measure and use it in a feedback system? *Proceedings of the Design Society*, *3*, 455–464. DOI: 10.1017/pds.2023.46

Fayyaz, S. (2019). A review on measuring digital trade & e-commerce as new economic statistics products. *Statistika, 99*(1), 57–68. https://www.scopus.com/inward/record.uri?eid=2-s2.0-85065500011&partnerID=40&md5=786eeace3689f08a2cea99eb55c6dc0b

Felipe, T., Torres de Oliveira, R., Toth-Peter, A., Mathews, S., & Dulleck, U. (2025). Digital transformation in commercial banks: Unraveling the flow of Industry 4.0. *Digital Business*, *5*(2), 100129. Advance online publication. DOI: 10.1016/j.digbus.2025.100129

Feng, Z., Luo, N., Wu, S., & Yan, Z. J. (2025). Trade-in marketing strategies in gaming industry: The effect of digital transformation. *Electronic Markets*, *35*(1), 58. Advance online publication. DOI: 10.1007/s12525-025-00800-z

Ferhataj, A., Memaj, F., Sahatcija, R., Ora, A., & Koka, E. (2025). Ethical concerns in AI development: Analyzing students' perspectives on robotics and society. *Journal of Information. Communication and Ethics in Society*, *23*(2), 165–187. DOI: 10.1108/JICES-08-2024-0111

Ferhat, S. (2016). Temmuz). The reality of the digital world, the virtuality of the real world: Virtual reality as a digital media product [Dijital dünyanın gerçekliği, gerçek dünyanın sanallığı: Bir dijital medya ürünü olarak sanal gerçeklik]. *TRT Akademi*, *1*(2), 724–746.

Fielding, N. (2000). The shared fate of two innovations in qualitative methodology: The relationship of qualitative software and secondary analysis of archived qualitative data. In *Forum: Qualitative Social Research* (Vol. 1, No. 3).

Fife, K., Flinn, A., & Nyhan, J. (2023). Documenting resistance, conflict and violence: A scoping review of the role of participatory digital platforms in the mobilisation of resistance. *Archival Science*, *23*(3), 471–499. DOI: 10.1007/s10502-023-09416-8

Fire, M., Goldschmidth, R., & Elovici, Y. (2014). Online social networks: threats and solutions. *IEEE Communication Survey&Tutorials, Fourth Quarter*, 2019-2036.

Firliantama, M. and Rokhayani, A. (2023). Young learners' engagement in vocabulary learning taught by games and learning application: systematic review. simple, 1(1), 1-6. https://doi.org/DOI: 10.24176/simple.v1i1.10585

Foucault, M. (2006). *Discipline and punish: The birth of the prison* [*Hapishanenin doğuşu*]. (Kılıçbay, M. A., Trans.). İmge Publication.

Fowler, M., & Foemmel, M. (2006). *Continuous integration.*

Francesconi, E. (2018). On the future of legal publishing services in the Semantic Web. *Future Internet*, *10*(6), 48. Advance online publication. DOI: 10.3390/fi10060048

Freie Universität Berlin. Brynjolfsson, E., & McAfee, A. (2014). The second machine age: Work, progress, and prosperity in a time of brilliant technologies. W. W. Norton & Company.

Funk, R. (2013). *Me and us: Psychoanalysis of the postmodern human* [*Ben ve biz: Postmodern insanın psikanalizi*]. (Tanyeri, Ç., Trans.). Yapı Kredi Publication.

Fu, Y., Shi, K., & Xi, L. (2025). Artificial intelligence and machine learning in the preservation and innovation of intangible cultural heritage: Ethical considerations and design frameworks. *Digital Scholarship in the Humanities*, *40*(2), 487–508. DOI: 10.1093/llc/fqaf034

Gan, W., Ye, Z., Wan, S., & Yu, P. S. (2023). Web 3.0: The Future of Internet. *ACM Web Conference 2023 - Companion of the World Wide Web Conference, WWW 2023*, 1266–1275. DOI: 10.1145/3543873.3587583

Garbis, J., & Chapman, J. W. (2021). Network access control. In *Zero Trust Security* (pp. 105–116). Apress. DOI: 10.1007/978-1-4842-6702-8_7

García-Mieres, H., Parra, L., Paz-Vázquez, L. M., Castaño, E., & Pedrosa, I. (2024). Bridging generations: The power of digitization and social innovation in preserving rural cultural heritage. *Innovation (Abingdon)*, •••, 1–14. DOI: 10.1080/13511610.2024.2424773

Gartner. (2022). Digital capability frameworks for transformation. Gartner Research

Gazzawe, F., Mayouf, M., Lock, R., & Alturki, R. (2022). The Role of Machine Learning in E-Learning Using the Web and AI-Enabled Mobile Applications. *Mobile Information Systems, 2022*, 1–10. Advance online publication. DOI: 10.1155/2022/3696140

Gençer, S., Oluk, N., Kadayifçi, H., & Çelik, A. (2023). The purposes and justifications for preferences of web 2.0 tools used by pre-service chemistry teachers in their teaching practices in distance education environment. Shanlax International Journal of Education, 11(S1-Jan), 61-75. https://doi.org/DOI: 10.34293/education.v11iS1-Jan.5908

Geray, H. (2019). *Corporate communication in the new economy of media: Digital transformation in newspapers, television, advertising, and public relations* [*Medyanın yeni ekonomisinde kurumsal iletişim: Gazeteler, televizyonlar, reklamcılık ve halkla ilişkilerde dijital dönüşüm*]. Ütopya Publication.

Giang, H. T. T., & Dung, L. T. (2025). Sharing economy and retailer sustainable performance: The mechanisms via business model innovation and digital capabilities. *Journal of Innovation and Entrepreneurship, 14*(1), 27. Advance online publication. DOI: 10.1186/s13731-025-00492-x

Gibson, W. (2012). *Neuromancer*. Altıkırkbeş Press. DOI: 10.2307/j.ctv1168ch3.12

Gilliom, J., & Monahan, T. (2013). *Supervision: An introduction to the surveillance society*. University of Chicago Press.

Goffman, E. (2004). *The presentation of self in everyday life* [*Günlük yaşamda benliğin sunumu*]. Metis Publication.

González, C. S., Toledo, P., Muñoz, V., Noda, M. A., Bruno, A., & Moreno, L. (2013). Inclusive educational software design with agile approach. *ACM International Conference Proceeding Series*, 149–155. DOI: 10.1145/2536536.2536559

Gopalakrishnan, M. S. (2017, Haziran 27). What awaits humans in the digital age [Dijital çağın insanlarını neler bekliyor]. *DW Türkçe*. https://www.dw.com/tr/dijital-%C3%A7a%C4%9F%C4%B1n-insanlar%C4%B1n%C4%B1-neler-bekliyor/a-39395314

Graham, M. (Ed.). (2019). *Digital economies at global margins*. MIT Press. DOI: 10.7551/mitpress/10890.001.0001

Grewal, D., Kroschke, M., Mende, M., Roggeveen, A. L., & Scott, M. L. (2020). Frontline cyborgs at your service: How human enhancement technologies affect customer experiences in retail, sales, and service settings. *Journal of Interactive Marketing*, *51*(1), 9–25. DOI: 10.1016/j.intmar.2020.03.001

Guga, J. (2015). Beyond artificial intelligence. In *Cyborg tales: The reinvention of the human in the information age* (pp. 45–62). Springer.

Guiñez-Molinos, S., González, J., Gomar-Sancho, C., Espinoza, P., & Constenla, G. (2021). A web platform (mosaico) to design, perform, and assess collaborative clinical scenarios for medical students: Viewpoint. *JMIR Medical Education*, *7*(1), e23370. DOI: 10.2196/23370 PMID: 33496676

Güney, S. (2017). *Social psychology* [*Sosyal psikoloji*]. Nobel Akademi Publishing.

Gupta, K., Takaki, K., Tsutsui, A., Teramoto, K., & Ryskeldiev, B. (2025). AccessibleShip: Exploring Packaging and Shipping Barriers for Visually Impaired Users in C2C E-Commerce. *Conference on Human Factors in Computing Systems - Proceedings*. DOI: 10.1145/3706599.3706665

Gurbuxani, S., Gupta, L., & Madan, K. (2024). Virtual fitness trainer using artificial intelligence. In *Proceedings of the Sixteenth International Conference on Contemporary Computing (IC3-2024)* (pp. 226–233). Noida, India.

Haggerty, K. D. (2006). Tear down the walls: On demolishing the panopticon. In D. Lyon (Ed.), *Theorizing surveillance: The panopticon and beyond* (pp. 23-45). Willan Publishing.

Hähnel, M. (2025). Ethical challenges and solutions in AI-driven medical data management: A focus on distributed machine learning. *Discover Artificial Intelligence*, *5*(1), 53. Advance online publication. DOI: 10.1007/s44163-025-00266-0

Hansen, D. L.. (2020). A review of gamified fitness tracker apps and future directions. In *Proceedings of the Annual Symposium on Computer–Human Interaction in Play (CHI PLAY '20)*.

Hardy, P., & Dobson, S. (2024). Voice, Belonging, Storytelling and Transformation in Digital Storytelling Workshop Settings—Some Philosophical Considerations. In *Learning Inclusion in a Digital Age: Belonging and Finding a Voice with the Disadvantaged* (pp. 95–105). Springer Nature Singapore., DOI: 10.1007/978-981-99-7196-1_7

Hassan, A. O., Ewuga, S. K., Abdul, A. A., Abrahams, T. O., Oladeinde, M., & Dawodu, S. O. (2024). Cybersecurity in banking: A Global Perspective with a focus on Nigerian practices. Comput. Sci. IT Res. j., 5(1), 41–59.

Hassan, I., Nasidi, Q., Azmi, M., & Gamji, M. (2021). Challenges and benefits of web 2.0-based learning among international students of english during the covid-19 pandemic in cyprus. https://doi.org/DOI: 10.31235/osf.io/fm5c6

Hassan, M. A., Jamshidi, M. B., Manh, B. D., Chu, N. H., Nguyen, C.-H., Hieu, N. Q., Nguyen, C. T., Hoang, D. T., Nguyen, D. N., Van Huynh, N., Alsheikh, M. A., & Dutkiewicz, E. (2025). Enabling technologies for Web 3.0: A comprehensive survey. *Computer Networks*, *264*, 111242. Advance online publication. DOI: 10.1016/j.comnet.2025.111242

Hastomo, T., Istiara, F., & Nurchurifiani, E. (2021). Google classroom: An online platform for teaching english. *Aksara Jurnal Bahasa Dan Sastra*, *22*(2). Advance online publication. DOI: 10.23960/aksara/v22i2.pp300-308

He, B., & Bhatti, U. A. (2025). Smart Cities and Smart Networks: AI Applications in Urban Geography and Industrial Communication. *International Journal of High Speed Electronics and Systems*, *34*(3), 2440122. Advance online publication. DOI: 10.1142/S0129156424401220

Hernández-Barrera, E., Alfonso-Francia, G., Badillo-Fernández, M., & Tovar-Arriaga, S. (2025). Advanced AI strategies for accurate detection and localization of retinal nerve fiber layer defects: Employing multifaceted analysis across various color spaces. *Network Modeling and Analysis in Health Informatics and Bioinformatics*, *14*(1), 11. Advance online publication. DOI: 10.1007/s13721-025-00507-3

Hsu, C.-C., & Kuo, Z.-H. (2005). An adaptive interface for customer transaction assistant in electronic commerce. *Proceedings of the International Conference on Electronic Business (ICEB)*, 962–966. https://www.scopus.com/inward/record.uri?eid=2-s2.0-84873553119&partnerID=40&md5=7829134c4536d5466065112a16a09cd3

Huang, R., Shuai, Q., Zhang, Y., Chen, Y., & Zhang, Q. (2025). The impact of digital education on household allocation of risky financial assets in China. *Scientific Reports*, *15*(1), 21840. Advance online publication. DOI: 10.1038/s41598-025-01140-w PMID: 40594050

Huong, N. and Ngoc, N. (2024). An investigation into english –majored sophomores' perceptions of english movies to improve vocabulary at huit. Journal of Knowledge Learning and Science Technology Issn 2959-6386 (Online), 3(1), 52-62. https://doi.org/DOI: 10.60087/jklst.vol3.no1.p62

Hussain, M. I., He, J., Zhu, N., Sabah, F., Zardari, Z. A., Hussain, S., & Razque, F. (2021). AAAA: SSO and MFA implementation in multi-cloud to mitigate rising threats and concerns related to user metadata. *Applied Sciences (Basel, Switzerland)*, *11*(7), 3012. DOI: 10.3390/app11073012

Hutson, J. (2024). Digital Cultural Heritage Preservation. In *Art and Culture in the Multiverse of Metaverses: Immersion, Presence, and Interactivity in the Digital Age* (pp. 99-141). Cham: Springer Nature Switzerland. DOI: 10.1007/978-3-031-66320-8_4

Idrissov, Y. and Tussupbekova, M. (2021). Using of wiki-technologies in the process of learning english for students of non-language specialties., 58-63. https://doi.org/ DOI: 10.46656/proceeding.2021.foreign.language(12)

Ifenthaler, D., & Yau, J. Y. K. (2020). Utilising learning analytics to support study success in higher education: A systematic review. *Educational Technology Research and Development, 68*(4), 1961–1990. DOI: 10.1007/s11423-020-09788-z

Ihsan, A. Z., Fathalla, S., & Sandfeld, S. (2025). Modeling dislocation dynamics data using semantic web technologies. *Neural Computing & Applications, 37*(18), 11737–11753. DOI: 10.1007/s00521-024-10674-5 PMID: 40538984

İlhan, S. (2013). Identity construction in the liquid society: Fluid, eclectic, self-centered identities [Akışkan toplumda kimlik inşası: Geçişken, eklektik, ben odaklı kimlikler]. *Fırat Üniversitesi Sosyal Bilimler Dergisi, 23*(2), 233–246.

Independent Researcher United States, & Ahmadi, S. (2024). Challenges and solutions in network security for serverless computing. Ijcsrr, 07(01).

Indravathy, K., & Abd Rahim, N. (2025). How ambidextrous entrepreneurial leaders react to the artificial intelligence boom. *IAES International Journal of Artificial Intelligence, 14*(3), 1708–1718. DOI: 10.11591/ijai.v14.i3.pp1708-1718

Işıklı, Ş., & Küçükvardar, M. (2016). *Information technology revolution* [*Bilişim devrimi*]. Birleşik Press.

Jeseo, V., & Lindsey Hall, K. K. (2025). A framework for inclusive service experiences (FISE): Bridging the gap between traditional and immersive offerings. *Journal of Service Theory and Practice, 35*(5), 805–831. Advance online publication. DOI: 10.1108/JSTP-12-2024-0468

Jia, Y., & Guo, W. (2023, July). Museum Blended Learning Through Digital Learning Platform: The Case of Smithsonian Learning Lab. In *International Conference on Blended Learning* (pp. 224-235). Cham: Springer Nature Switzerland. DOI: 10.1007/978-3-031-35731-2_20

Jian-chun, D., Wang, L., & He, Y. (2023). Exploring the effect of wiki-based writing instruction on writing skills and writing self-efficacy of chinese english-as-a-foreign language learners. *Frontiers in Psychology, 13*, 1069832. Advance online publication. DOI: 10.3389/fpsyg.2022.1069832 PMID: 36704680

Jiang, C., Niu, Z., Qu, J., Zhao, Y., & Rezaeipanah, A. (2025). Overlapping community-based fair influence maximization under a multi-transformation optimization algorithm. *Journal of Big Data*, *12*(1), 133. Advance online publication. DOI: 10.1186/s40537-025-01181-y

Jiang, J. (2024). Emotions are what will draw people in: A study of critical affective literacy through digital storytelling. *Journal of Adolescent & Adult Literacy*, *67*(4), 253–263. DOI: 10.1002/jaal.1322

Jofre, M., Navarro-Llobet, D., Agulló, R., Puig, J., Gonzalez-Granadillo, G., Mora Zamorano, J., & Romeu, R. (2021). Cybersecurity and privacy risk assessment of point-of-care systems in healthcare—A use case approach. *Applied Sciences (Basel, Switzerland)*, *11*(15), 6699. DOI: 10.3390/app11156699

Judijanto, L., & Lubis, A. F. (2025). Mapping a legal study on cybersecurity and data protection: A bibliometric review and its implications for regulation in the digital age. *West Science Law and Human Rights*, *3*(01), 34–41. DOI: 10.58812/wslhr.v3i01.1598

Jumariati, J., Elyani, E., Nawal, N., & Larasati, S. (2022). Developing an instrument to assess efl learners' critical thinking skills in writing expository problem-solution essays. *International Journal of English Language Teaching*, *10*(5), 30–37. DOI: 10.37745/ijelt.13/vol10n53037

Kalaman, S. (2016). Transformation of privacy in new media: Sociocultural, economic, and political dimensions the case of Facebook [Sosyokültürel, ekonomik ve siyasi boyutlarıyla yeni medyada mahremiyetin dönüşümü: Facebook örneği] (Doctoral dissertation, Ege University, Institute of Social Sciences, Department of Radio, Television, and Cinema).

Kalaman, S. (2019). New media and digital surveillance: A study on social media users in Turkey [Yeni medya ve dijital gözetim: Türkiye'deki sosyal medya kullanıcıları üzerine bir araştırma]. *Yönetim ve Ekonomi Dergisi*, *26*(2), 575–594. DOI: 10.18657/yonveek.556868

Kaur, N., & Rai, M. (2024). Role of Digital Technology and Education for Transformation of Cultural Heritage. In *Digital Cultural Heritage* (pp. 206–221). CRC Press. DOI: 10.1201/9781032630564-11

Keesara, S., Jonas, A., & Schulman, K. (2020). Covid-19 and health care's digital revolution. *The New England Journal of Medicine*, *382*(23), e82. DOI: 10.1056/NEJMp2005835 PMID: 32240581

Kellner, D. (2001, May). Popular culture and the construction of postmodern identities [Popüler kültür ve postmodern kimliklerin inşası]. *Doğu Batı Üç Aylık Düşünce Dergisi*, 187–219.

Kesavan, S., Saravana, K., Kumar, A., & Vengatesan K. (2021). An investigation on adaptive HTTP media streaming Quality-of-Experience (QoE) and agility using cloud media services. *International Journal of Computers and Applications*, 431 - 444. DOI: 10.1080/1206212X.2019.1575034

Kete, N. (2011). Reading poverty, privacy, and death relations through media. [Yoksulluk, mahremiyet ve ölüm ilişkisini medya üzerinden okumak] In Köse, H. (Ed.), *Media privacy: The phenomenon of privacy in media and a transparent life* [*Medya mahrem: Medyada mahremiyet olgusu ve transparan bir yaşamdan*]. (pp. 61–84). Ayrıntı Publication.

Kew, S. (2021). Japanese students' english language learning experience through computer game-based student response systems. *Turkish Journal of Computer and Mathematics Education (Turcomat)*, *12*(3), 1993–1998. DOI: 10.17762/turcomat.v12i3.1036

Khan, F. S., Mazhar, S. S., Mazhar, K. A., AlSaleh, D., & Mazhar, A. (2025). Model-agnostic explainable artificial intelligence methods in finance: A systematic review, recent developments, limitations, challenges and future directions. *Artificial Intelligence Review*, *58*(8). Advance online publication. DOI: 10.1007/s10462-025-11215-9

Khan, M. (2024). Safeguarding IoT networks against DDoS attacks using deep learning based zero trust network access. *Electronics Letters*, *60*(21), e70075. DOI: 10.1049/ell2.70075

Khaskheli, F., Aijaz, S., Syed, M., & Shah, W. (2021). *Attitudes of foreign language teaching assistants towards teaching of english in pakistani context*. JLLL., DOI: 10.7176/JLLL/78-03

Kılınç, H., & Altınpulluk, H. (2021). Discussion forums as a learning material in higher education institutions. *International Journal of Higher Education Pedagogies*, *2*(1), 1–9. DOI: 10.33422/ijhep.v2i1.25

Kim, J., Oh, J., Gim, G., & Kim, Y. (2024). An Empirical Study on E-Government Service Using Web Standard Policy. *Studies in Computational Intelligence*, *1160*, 75–85. DOI: 10.1007/978-3-031-61163-6_7

Kim, Y., Trimi, S., & Chung, J. H. (2014). Big-data applications in the government sector. *Communications of the ACM*, *57*(3), 78–85. DOI: 10.1145/2500873

Knapik, W., & Król, K. (2023). Inclusion of vanishing cultural heritage in a sustainable rural development strategy–prospects, opportunities, recommendations. *Sustainability (Basel), 15*(4), 3656. DOI: 10.3390/su15043656

Korać, D., Damjanović, B., Simić, D., & Pu, C. (2025). Management of evaluation processes and creation of authentication metrics: Artificial intelligence-based fusion framework. *Information Processing & Management, 62*(6), 104233. Advance online publication. DOI: 10.1016/j.ipm.2025.104233

Koutsabasis, P. (2010). E-Business and Web Accessibility. In *Encyclopedia of E-Business Development and Management in the Global Economy* (pp. 570–577). DOI: 10.4018/978-1-61520-611-7.ch056

Kramer, N. C., & Winter, S. (2008). Impression management 2.0: The relationship of self-esteem, extraversion, self-efficacy, and self-presentation within social network sites. *Journal of Media Psychology, 20*(3), 106–116. DOI: 10.1027/1864-1105.20.3.106

Kulga, C. E. (2014). A study on self-presentation in everyday life [Günlük yaşamda benlik sunumları üzerine bir inceleme] (Master's thesis, Gazi University, Institute of Social Sciences, Department of Public Relations and Promotion, Ankara).

Kulkarni, S., & Kulkarni, A. (2024). Review on use of Immersive Technologies in Tourism. In *2024 International Conference on Intelligent Computing and Emerging Communication Technologies (ICEC)* (pp. 1-7). IEEE. DOI: 10.1109/ICEC59683.2024.10837334

Kumar, P., Sharma, R., Singh, D. K., & Arora, P. (2025). Tracing the digital threads: A bibliometric analysis of cultural heritage digitization efforts. In *Advances in Science, Engineering and Technology* (pp. 435-439). CRC Press.

Leddy, M., & McCreanor, N. (2024). Exploring how Education can Leverage Artificial Intelligence for Social Good. *Proceedings of the European Conference on Innovation and Entrepreneurship, ECIE, 19*(1), 1041–1048. DOI: 10.34190/ecie.19.1.2906

Lee, I., & Lee, K. (2015). The Internet of Things (IoT): Applications, investments, and challenges for enterprises. *Business Horizons, 58*(4), 431–440. DOI: 10.1016/j.bushor.2015.03.008

Leffingwell, D. (2016). *SAFe® 4.0 reference guide: scaled agile framework® for lean software and systems engineering*. Addison-Wesley Professional.

Lemon, K. N., & Verhoef, P. C. (2016). Understanding customer experience throughout the customer journey. *Journal of Marketing, 80*(6), 69–96. DOI: 10.1509/jm.15.0420

Lewandowski, M., & Czech, F. (2024). How universities and NGOs see each other: Review of literature on partnership concepts. *Universities and Non-Governmental Organisations*, 24-46.

Li, S., Abel, M., & Negre, E. (2020). Managing and recommending resources in web-based collaborative working environments.. https://doi.org/DOI: 10.1109/WETICE49692.2020.00063

Liang, X., Tao, M., Xia, Y., Wang, J., Li, K., Wang, Y., He, Y., Yang, J., Shi, T., Wang, Y., Zhang, M., & Wang, X. (2025). SAGE: Self-evolving Agents with Reflective and Memory-augmented Abilities. *Neurocomputing*, *647*, 130470. Advance online publication. DOI: 10.1016/j.neucom.2025.130470

Lian, Y., & Xie, J. (2024). The evolution of digital cultural heritage research: Identifying key trends, hotspots, and challenges through bibliometric analysis. *Sustainability (Basel)*, *16*(16), 7125. DOI: 10.3390/su16167125

Liashenko, M., & Öztok, M. (2024). The acceptance of a wiki site as a learning platform in english exam training. *NLC*, *12*, 26–29. DOI: 10.54337/nlc.v12.8629

Liebig, L., Güttel, L., Jobin, A., & Katzenbach, C. (2024). Subnational AI policy: shaping AI in a multi-level governance system. *ZeMKI, Centre for Media, Communication and Information Research*, 1477 - 1490. DOI: 10.1007/s00146-022-01561-5

Li, J., Zheng, X., Watanabe, I., & Ochiai, Y. (2024). A systematic review of digital transformation technologies in museum exhibition. *Computers in Human Behavior*, *108407*, 108407. Advance online publication. DOI: 10.1016/j.chb.2024.108407

Li, S., Yang, Y., Han, C., Sun, Y., Attar, R. W., & Gupta, B. B. (2025). Addressing consumer needs: Effects of firms remediation strategies on satisfaction and brand usage intent in AI-powered voice assistant service failures. *International Journal of Information Management*, *85*, 102951. Advance online publication. DOI: 10.1016/j.ijinfomgt.2025.102951

Liu, D., Sun, N., & Zhu, X. (2025). ESG ratings empower high-quality development of logistics enterprises through digital transformation and green innovation. *Scientific Reports*, *15*(1), 22861. Advance online publication. DOI: 10.1038/s41598-025-06029-2 PMID: 40596363

Liu, J., Jiang, F., Tashiro, S., Chen, S., & Tanaka, M. (2025). A physics-informed and data-driven framework for robotic welding in manufacturing. *Nature Communications*, *16*(1), 4807. Advance online publication. DOI: 10.1038/s41467-025-60164-y PMID: 40410176

Liu, Z., Duan, P., Chu, Q., Kuhlmann, L., Zhang, C., Yue, W., Tang, X., & Zhang, B. (2026). An attributed multiplex network enabled GNN-based stock predictor with observable and non-observable information. *Expert Systems with Applications, 296*, 129018. Advance online publication. DOI: 10.1016/j.eswa.2025.129018

Loi, M., Christen, M., Kleine, N., & Weber, K. (2019). Cybersecurity in health – disentangling value tensions. *J. Inf. Commun. Ethics Soc., 17*(2), 229–245. DOI: 10.1108/JICES-12-2018-0095

Lo, P. (2024). Healthcare innovations: Enhancing patient privacy and security in the digital era. *Healthcare Management Forum, 37*(5), 8404704241254820. DOI: 10.1177/08404704241254820 PMID: 38775093

Ludvigsen, K. R. (2023). The role of cybersecurity in medical devices regulation: Future considerations and solutions. *Law Tech Hum, 5*(2), 59–77. DOI: 10.5204/lthj.3080

Lukitasari, M., Hasan, R., Sukri, A., & Handhika, J. (2021). Developing student's metacognitive ability in science through project-based learning with e-portfolio. *International Journal of Evaluation and Research in Education (Ijere), 10*(3), 948. DOI: 10.11591/ijere.v10i3.21370

Lyon, D. (1997). *Electronic eye* [*Elektronik göz*]. (Hattatoğlu, D., Trans.). Sarmal Press.

Lyon, D. (2006). *The surveilled society* [*Gözetlenen toplum*]. (Soykan, G., Trans.). Kalkedon Publishing.

Lyon, D. (2013). *Surveillance studies* [*Gözetim çalışmaları*]. (Toprak, A., Trans.). Kalkedon Publishing.

Mahroof, J., Rafi, D. A., & Ahmad, D. A. (2025). Talent management during digital transformation: Role of transformational leadership and resistance to change. *Technology in Society, 83*, 102964. Advance online publication. DOI: 10.1016/j.techsoc.2025.102964

Mahyoob, M. (2020). Challenges of e-learning during the covid-19 pandemic experienced by efl learners. *Arab World English Journal, 11*(4), 351–362. DOI: 10.24093/awej/vol11no4.23

Maietti, F. (2023). Heritage enhancement through digital tools for sustainable fruition: A conceptual framework. *Sustainability (Basel), 15*(15), 11799. DOI: 10.3390/su151511799

Malik, S., Huang, Q., & Oteir, I. (2021). Perceived psychological, linguistic and socio-cultural obstacles: An investigation of english communication apprehension in efl learners. *International Journal of Instruction*, *14*(4), 733–752. DOI: 10.29333/iji.2021.14442a

Manago, A. M. (2015). Identity development in the digital age: The case of social networking sites. In McLean, K. C., & Syed, M. (Eds.), *The Oxford handbook of identity development* (pp. 508–526). Oxford University Press., DOI: 10.1093/oxfordhb/9780199936564.013.031

Manipuspika, Y. (2020). Learning styles of indonesian efl students: culture and learning. https://doi.org/DOI: 10.31235/osf.io/j8vwe

Mantzou, P., Bitsikas, X., & Floros, A. (2023). Enriching cultural heritage through the integration of art and digital technologies. *Social Sciences (Basel, Switzerland)*, *12*(11), 594. DOI. 10.3390/socsci12110594

Margaretha, W., Ariesia, K., & Yustian, O. R. (2025). ARTIFICIAL INTELLIGENCE AND ENTREPRENEURSHIP EDUCATION: INCREASING ENTREPRENEURIAL INTENTIONS AMONG FUTURE ENTREPRENEURS IN BANDUNG CITY. *Journal of Theoretical and Applied Information Technology*, *103*(7), 2813–2824. https://www.scopus.com/inward/record.uri?eid=2-s2.0-105002738499&partnerID=40&md5=bc240b968dd23a1966e8c423140102df

Maria Koziel, A., Shen, C.-W., Djailani, I., & Chang, Y.-L. (2025). Beyond Social Norms: Psychological and Hedonic Drivers of Metaverse Adoption Among Generation Y. *IEEE Access : Practical Innovations, Open Solutions*, *13*, 78441–78460. DOI: 10.1109/ACCESS.2025.3563758

Marsh, E. (2023). *Creating Digital Exhibits for Cultural Institutions: A Guide*. Routledge. DOI: 10.4324/9781003301493

Martin, J. (2012). Second Life surveillance: Power to the people or virtual surveillance society? *Surveillance & Society*, *9*(4), 408–423. DOI: 10.24908/ss.v9i4.4346

Martins, B., & Duarte, C. (2024). A large-scale web accessibility analysis considering technology adoption. *Universal Access in the Information Society*, *23*(4), 1857–1872. DOI: 10.1007/s10209-023-01010-0

Masciotta, M. G., Sanchez-Aparicio, L. J., Oliveira, D. V., & Gonzalez-Aguilera, D. (2023). Integration of laser scanning technologies and 360° photography for the digital documentation and management of cultural heritage buildings. *International Journal of Architectural Heritage*, *17*(1), 56–75. DOI: 10.1080/15583058.2022.2069062

Means, B., Bakia, M., & Murphy, R. (2014). *Learning online: What research tells us about whether, when and how*. Routledge. DOI: 10.4324/9780203095959

Meng, L., Ding, L., Atli, M., Khan, A. M., Shan, Y., & Farooq, M. U. (2025). Enhancing two dimensional irregular pattern packing using a modified genetic algorithm and image processing. *Engineering Applications of Artificial Intelligence, 155*, 111040. Advance online publication. DOI: 10.1016/j.engappai.2025.111040

Meng, Y., Chu, M. Y., & Chiu, D. K. (2023). The impact of COVID-19 on museums in the digital era: Practices and challenges in Hong Kong. *Library Hi Tech, 41*(1), 130–151. DOI: 10.1108/LHT-05-2022-0273

Mijwil, M., Filali, Y., Aljanabi, M., Bounabi, M., & Al-Shahwani, H. (2023). The purpose of cybersecurity governance in the digital transformation of public services and protecting the digital environment. *Mesopotamian Journal of CyberSecurity, 2023*, 1–6. DOI: 10.58496/MJCS/2023/001

Mishra, S., & Sharma, S. (2025). User Experience for Inclusion: Analysis of WCAG 2.2 in Pharmacy App for Visually Impaired Group. *Communications in Computer and Information Science, 2338 CCIS*, 187–201. DOI: 10.1007/978-3-031-80832-6_14

Mishra, D., & Maheshwari, N. (2023). Effective governance through crowdsourcing: A strategic framework for empowered participation. *IEEE Transactions on Engineering Management, 71*, 4647–4664. DOI: 10.1109/TEM.2022.3218188

Mohammadi, F., Panou, A., Ntantogian, C., Karapistoli, E., Panaousis, E., & Xenakis, C. (2019, October). CUREX: seCUre and pRivate hEalth data eXchange. IEEE/WIC/ACM International Conference on Web - Companion Volume. DOI: 10.1145/3358695.3361753

Moss, M. S., & Gollins, T. J. (2023). Our digital legacy: an archival perspective. In *Michael Moss on Archives* (pp. 160–184). Routledge. DOI: 10.4324/9781003407188-19

Murrar, A., Paz, V., Batra, M., & Yerger, D. (2025). Strategies for driving customer adoption of AI-powered mobile apps: Insights from structural equation modeling in the water sector. *Journal of Systems and Information Technology, 27*(3), 343–364. DOI: 10.1108/JSIT-12-2023-0335

Mustafa, S., Zhang, W., & Naveed, M. M. (2023). What motivates online community contributors to contribute consistently? A case study on Stackoverflow netizens. *Current Psychology (New Brunswick, N.J.), 42*(13), 10468–10481. DOI: 10.1007/s12144-022-03307-4 PMID: 35789627

Nabhan, S., & Sa'diyah, H. (2021). Collaborative writing using google docs in an efl classroom: Voices from high school students. *Veles Voice of English Language Education Society*, *5*(2), 156–166. DOI: 10.29408/veles.v5i2.3863

Naepi, S., Atuatasi, B., Naepi, G., De Stefani, S., Kingston, A., & Banaś, P. (2025). Pride, belonging, and identity: Pacific peoples and museums in Aotearoa New Zealand. In *The Visitor Studies Guide* (pp. 71–81). Routledge.

Namsaeng, P., & Sukying, A. (2021). The effect of group reading strategy on critical thinking skills in thai efl university learners. *Journal of English Language Teaching and Applied Linguistics*, *3*(2), 30–40. DOI: 10.32996/jeltal.2021.3.2.4

Nazarenko, V., Zazymko, O., Funderburk, M., & Klikh, L. (2024). Web information educational assistant service with focus on artificial intelligence and smart systems technologies. *CEUR Workshop Proceedings*, *3781*, 175–191. https://www.scopus.com/inward/record.uri?eid=2-s2.0-85207073925&partnerID=40&md5=36acf26d32f0374aaf7fe0aae07e309e

Nethercote, M. (2023). Platform landlords: Renters, personal data and new digital footholds of urban control. *Digital Geography and Society*, *5*, 100060. DOI: 10.1016/j.diggeo.2023.100060

Newman, S. (2015). *Building microservices: Designing fine-grained systems*. O'Reilly Media.

Niaz, S., Buriro, G., & Soomro, N. (2022). Web-based english language learning: A review from web 1.0 to web 3.0. *Pakistan Journal of Humanities and Social Sciences*, *10*(2). Advance online publication. DOI: 10.52131/pjhss.2022.1002.0246

Ning, C. (2024). Modern software and physical education: Can online training improve squat jump and sprint performance? *BMC Medical Education*, *24*(1), 5345.

Noordin, M. F., & Othman, R. (2005). Challenges to an E-business model: Pre- and post-adoption. *Internet and Information Technology in Modern Organizations: Challenges and Answers - Proceedings of the 5th International Business Information Management Association Conference, IBIMA 2005, 1*. https://www.scopus.com/inward/record.uri?eid=2-s2.0-84903648466&partnerID=40&md5=fbdc6410f4674496b3d66763f46e79c9

Oeamoum, N., & Sriwichai, C. (2020). Problems and needs in english language teaching from the viewpoints of pre-service english teachers in thailand. *Asian Journal of Education and Training*, *6*(4), 592–601. DOI: 10.20448/journal.522.2020.64.592.601

OECD. (2020). Digital government in the post-COVID-19 era. *OECD Digital Economy Papers*, (308). Advance online publication. DOI: 10.1787/14e1c5e8-en-fr

Ojo, S., & Covey, A. (2025). Identity and Access Management (IAM) authentication methods: Importance of multi-factor authentication (MFA) and single sign-on (SSO) and access control models. In *Preprints*.

Olca, E., & Can, O. (2022). DICON: A Domain-Independent Consent Management for Personal Data Protection. *IEEE Access*, 95479 - 95497. DOI: 10.1109/ACCESS.2022.3204970

Oluwajana, D., Adeshola, I., & Clement, S. (2021). Does the use of a web-based collaborative platform reduce cognitive load and influence project-based student engagement? *Current Psychology (New Brunswick, N.J.)*, *42*(10), 8265–8278. DOI: 10.1007/s12144-021-02145-0

Özçetin, B. (2019). *Mass communication theories: Concepts, schools, and models* [*Kitle iletişim kuramları: Kavramlar, okullar ve modeller*]. İletişim Publication.

Ozdemir, G., & Zonah, S. (2025). Revolutionising Heritage Interpretation with Smart Technologies: A Blueprint for Sustainable Tourism. *Sustainability (Basel)*, *17*(10), 4330. Advance online publication. DOI: 10.3390/su17104330

Özkan, K. D. (2021). Privacy issues in the context of globalization, social networks, and the surveillance society: An Instagram content analysis [Küreselleşme, sosyal ağlar ve gözetim toplumu bağlamında mahremiyet sorunları: Instagram içerik analizi]. *Akademi Sosyal Bilimler Dergisi*, *8*(22), 69–88.

Panjaburee, P., Intarakamhang, U., Srisawasdi, N., Poompimol, S., & Tapingkae, P. (2025). Predictors of active and inactive learners' intention to use decision tree-based contextual mobile games for cultivating digital citizenship behaviour. *International Journal of Mobile Learning and Organisation*, *19*(1), 1–32. DOI: 10.1504/IJMLO.2025.143022

Pan, Q.-H., Luo, W.-P., Wang, J., & Dai, J.-P. (2023). A study of legitimacy building and governance of digital platforms. *Studies in Science of Science*, *41*(6), 1076–1084. https://www.scopus.com/inward/record.uri?eid=2-s2.0-85212159063&partnerID=40&md5=ae7a82622eee03b8f512c074157b9fcb

Patrick, G. (2023). Religious rituals, pilgrimages, festivals, and media: Exploring the interface. *The Handbook on Religion and Communication*, 383-397. DOI: 10.1002/9781119671619.ch25

Paulauskas, L., Paulauskas, A., Blažauskas, T., Damaševičius, R., & Maskeliūnas, R. (2023). Reconstruction of industrial and historical heritage for cultural enrichment using virtual and augmented reality. *Technologies*, *11*(2), 36. DOI: 10.3390/technologies11020036

Pentland, A. (2014). *Social physics: How good ideas spread-the lessons from a new science*. Penguin.

Pereira, M. G., de Lima, F. B., de Oliveira, L. F., & de Souza, F. M. (2023). Importance of training volume through the use of step tracker apps in physical activity and body composition. *Physiology & Behavior, 259*, 114038.

Pernarella, M., & Koed Madsen, A. (2023). Urbino belonging: Exploring place-based community heritage with digital & participatory methods. *International Journal of Heritage Studies, 29*(9), 939–960. DOI: 10.1080/13527258.2023.2231909

Peukert, C., & Windisch, M. (2025). The economics of copyright in the digital age. *Journal of Economic Surveys, 39*(3), 877–903. DOI: 10.1111/joes.12632

Picard, R. W. (2010). Emotion research by the people, for the people. *Emotion Review, 2*(3), 250–254. DOI: 10.1177/1754073910364256

Porter, M. E., & Heppelmann, J. E. (2014). How smart, connected products are transforming competition. *Harvard Business Review, 92*(11), 64–88.

Prajwal, R., Pawan, S. J., Nazarian, S., Heller, N., Weight, C. J., Duddalwar, V., & Kuo, C. C. J. (2025). A Study on Energy Consumption in AI-Driven Medical Image Segmentation. *Journal of Imaging, 11*(6), 174. Advance online publication. DOI: 10.3390/jimaging11060174 PMID: 40558774

Prasetya, R. (2021). English teaching based-strategy lms moodle and google classroom. *English Education Journal of English Teaching and Research, 6*(1), 32–44. DOI: 10.29407/jetar.v6i1.15622

Prasetya, R., & Syarif, A. (2023). English language learners' attitude and challenge utilized m-learning: Comparison mobile application moodle and google classroom. *Elt Worldwide Journal of English Language Teaching, 10*(1), 28. DOI: 10.26858/eltww.v10i1.37218

Priestley, M., Sluckin, T. J., & Tiropanis, T. (2020). Innovation on the web: The end of the S-curve? *Internet Histories, 4*(4), 390–412. DOI: 10.1080/24701475.2020.1747261

Privitera, A. G., Fontana, F., & Geronazzo, M. (2024). The Role of Audio in Immersive Storytelling: A Systematic Review in Cultural Heritage. *Multimedia Tools and Applications, 84*(16), 1–39. DOI: 10.1007/s11042-024-19288-4

Prosen, M., & Ličen, S. (2025). Evaluating the digital transformation in health sciences education: A thematic analysis of higher education teachers' perspectives. *BMC Medical Education, 25*(1), 820. Advance online publication. DOI: 10.1186/s12909-025-07420-3 PMID: 40457303

Purwaningtyas, T., Nurkamto, J., & Kristina, D. (2023). Efl teacher intervention in mediating students' interaction in web-based collaborative writing environment using google docs. *Veles Voice of English Language Education Society*, *7*(1), 135–144. DOI: 10.29408/veles.v7i1.7912

Putri, A. N. A., Hermawan, P., Mirzanti, I. R., Meadows, M., & Sadraei, R. (2025). Unpacking green growth in SMEs: A framework for dynamic capabilities, value co-creation, and sustainable performance. *Sustainable Futures : An Applied Journal of Technology, Environment and Society*, *10*, 100840. Advance online publication. DOI: 10.1016/j.sftr.2025.100840

Radosavlevikj, N. (2021). Teachers' and students' perceptions and challenges in communicative language teaching. *Journal of Teaching English for Specific and Academic Purposes*, *307*, 307. Advance online publication. DOI: 10.22190/JTESAP2003307R

Rai, A., Kumar, A., Vyshnav Kumar, A., & Mercy Rajaselvi Beaulah, P. (2026). Visio-Shop: A Technological Solution for Assisting Visually Impaired People in Retail Settings. *Communications in Computer and Information Science, 2608 CCIS*, 362–372. DOI: 10.1007/978-3-032-02537-1_31

Rajaindaran, P., & Abdullah, A. (2023). Google classroom as a tool to enhance english language speaking performance amid the covid-19 pandemic among primary school students. *International Journal of Academic Research in Business & Social Sciences*, *13*(6). Advance online publication. DOI: 10.6007/IJARBSS/v13-i6/16986

Raj, K. R.. (2022). User's perspective about mobile fitness applications. *Journal of User Experience in Fitness Apps*, *15*(2), 98–109.

Ramineni, V., Ingole, B. S., Krishnappa, M. S., Nagpal, A., Jayaram, V., Banarse, A. R., Bidkar, D. M., & Pulipeta, N. K. (2024). AI-Driven Novel Approach for Enhancing E-Commerce Accessibility through Sign Language Integration in Web and Mobile Applications. *Proceedings - 2024 IEEE 17th International Symposium on Embedded Multicore/Many-Core Systems-on-Chip, MCSoC 2024*, 276–281. DOI: 10.1109/MCSoC64144.2024.00053

Rani Bandaru, V. N., Sumalatha, M., Rafee, S. M., Prasadraju, K., & Sri Lakshmi, M. (2024). *Enhancing privacy measures in healthcare within cyber-physical systems through cryptographic solutions. ICST Trans.* Scalable Inf. Syst.

Ranjgar, B., Sadeghi-Niaraki, A., Shakeri, M., Rahimi, F., & Choi, S. M. (2024). *Cultural heritage information retrieval: past, present and future trends*. IEEE., DOI: 10.1109/ACCESS.2024.3374769

Raza, H., Raja, M. J. A. A., Mubeen, R., Masood, Z., & Raja, M. A. Z. (2025). Supervised autoregressive eXogenous Networks with Fractional Grünwald–Letnikov finite differences: Tumor Evolution and Immune Responses under Therapeutic Influence fractals model. *Biomedical Signal Processing and Control, 107*, 107871. Advance online publication. DOI: 10.1016/j.bspc.2025.107871

Reed, M. S., & Rudman, H. (2023). Re-thinking research impact: Voice, context and power at the interface of science, policy and practice. *Sustainability Science, 18*(2), 967–981. DOI: 10.1007/s11625-022-01216-w PMID: 36119558

Reed, R.. (2023). The employer perspective: Insights and practical applications of the 2025 fitness trends. *Journal of Corporate Wellness and Productivity, 11*(1), 34–46.

Rehman, N.. (2023). Gamified experiences and user engagement within fitness apps. *International Journal of Mobile Health, 20*(1), 49–63.

Reis, O., Oliha, J. S., Osasona, F., & Obi, O. C. (2024). Cybersecurity Dynamics in Nigerian banking: Trends and strategies review. Comput. Sci. IT Res. j., 5(2), 336–364.

Reyero Lobo, P., Daga, E., Alani, H., & Fernandez, M. (2023). Semantic Web technologies and bias in artificial intelligence: A systematic literature review. *Semantic Web, 14*(4), 745–770. DOI: 10.3233/SW-223041

Rheingold, H. (1993). *The virtual community: Homesteading on the electronic frontier*. Addison-Wesley.

Ries, E. (2011). *The lean startup: How today's entrepreneurs use continuous innovation to create radically successful businesses.* Crown Currency.

Rizal, R., & Sumaryana, Y. (2021). Peningkatan Keamanan Aplikasi Web Menggunakan Web Application Firewall (WAF) Pada Sistem Informasi Manajemen Kampus Terintegrasi. *Jurnal ICT : Information Communication & Technology, 20*(2), 323–330. DOI: 10.36054/jict-ikmi.v20i2.416

Rizk, N., Nasr, E., & Gheith, M. (2019). Enhancing CREeLS the crowdsourcing based requirements elicitation approach for elearning systems using bi-gram evaluation. *ICENCO 2019 - 2019 15th International Computer Engineering Conference: Utilizing Machine Intelligence for a Better World*, 222 - 226. DOI: 10.1109/ICENCO48310.2019.9027371

Robins, K. (1999). *Image: The culture and politics of seeing* [*İmaj: Görmenin kültür ve politikası*]. (Türkoğlu, N., Trans.). Ayrıntı Publication.

Rodionov, A. (2024). The potential of blockchain technology for creating decentralized identity systems: Technical capabilities and legal regulation. *Irshad J. Law and Policy*, *2*(4), 19–30. DOI: 10.59022/ijlp.170

Rongrong, L., & Ismail, A. I. (2025). AI Innovation in Architectural Design: Enhancing Aesthetic Experience with "Midjourney.". *Journal of Advanced Research Design*, *127*(1), 84–95. DOI: 10.37934/ard.127.1.8495

Rose, N. (1999). *Powers of freedom: Reframing political thought*. Cambridge University Press. DOI: 10.1017/CBO9780511488856

Ross, J. W., Weill, P., & Robertson, D. C. (2006). *Enterprise architecture as strategy: Creating a foundation for business execution*. Harvard Business Review Press.

Roued, H., Castenbrandt, H., & Revuelta-Eugercios, B. A. (2023). Search, save and share: Family historians' engagement practices with digital platforms. *Archival Science*, *23*(2), 187–206. DOI: 10.1007/s10502-022-09404-4 PMID: 36274795

Routman, J. S., Zhang, E. J., Blocker, J. D., Paiste, J., & Tsai, M. H. (2025). Using Performance Frontiers To Evaluate Non-OR Anesthesia (NORA) Efficiency. *Journal of Medical Systems*, *49*(1), 96. Advance online publication. DOI: 10.1007/s10916-025-02229-5 PMID: 40629210

Rusmitaningsih, F. N., Subarjah, H., Yustiana, Y. R., & Saputra, D. R. (2024). Enhancing students' engagement and motivation in physical education: The role of fitness tracker apps. *Edu Sportivo: Indonesian Journal of Physical Education*, *5*(3), 1–10. DOI: 10.25299/esijope.2024.vol5(3).17215

Saari, A., Sinclair, S., Leshinsky, R., & Junnila, S. (2025). Best practices for blockchain-driven digital transformation in cross-industry settings. *Digital Business*, *5*(2), 100127. Advance online publication. DOI: 10.1016/j.digbus.2025.100127

Saeedi, K., Hassan, M. A., Alarifi, S., & Almagwashi, H. (2025). An intuitive approach to cybersecurity risk assessment for non-governmental organizations. *Transforming Government*, *19*(1), 159–182. DOI: 10.1108/TG-08-2024-0201

Saeed, S., Altamimi, S. A., Alkayyal, N. A., Alshehri, E., & Alabbad, D. A. (2023). Digital transformation and cybersecurity challenges for businesses resilience: Issues and recommendations. *Sensors (Basel)*, *23*(15), 6666. DOI: 10.3390/s23156666 PMID: 37571451

Sandhu, K. (2021). Advancing Cybersecurity for Digital Transformation. In Handbook of Research on Advancing Cybersecurity for Digital Transformation (pp. 1–17). IGI Global. DOI: 10.4018/978-1-7998-6975-7.ch001

Santra, A., Chakrabarty, D., Giri, A., & Dhara, S. K. (2024). Analyzing the Customer Sentiment of Reels and Short Video Viewers of Facebook Using Social Media Analysis. *Lecture Notes in Networks and Systems, 949 LNNS*, 159–167. DOI: 10.1007/978-981-97-1313-4_14

Sarkar, S., Choudhary, G., Shandilya, S. K., Hussain, A., & Kim, H. (2022). Security of zero trust networks in cloud computing: A comparative review. *Sustainability (Basel), 14*(18), 11213. DOI: 10.3390/su141811213

Saurabh, K., Upadhyay, P., & Rani, N. (2025). Towards Blockchain Decentralized Autonomous Organizations (DAO) Design. *Information Systems Frontiers, 27*(2), 659–681. DOI: 10.1007/s10796-023-10455-w

Schmidt, E., & Cohen, J. (2013). *The new digital age: Reshaping the future of people, nations, and business*. Alfred A. Knopf.

Scovazzi, T. (2023). Sustainable Development and Intangible Cultural Heritage. In *Cultural Heritage, Sustainable Development and Human Rights* (pp. 213-232). Routledge.

Senan Mahmod Attar Bashi, Z., & Senan, S. (2025). A comprehensive review of zero trust network architecture (ZTNA) and deployment frameworks. *International Journal on Perceptive and Cognitive Computing, 11*(1), 148–153. DOI: 10.31436/ijpcc.v11i1.494

Seo, J., & Park, S. (2025). Self-sovereign identity framework with user-friendly private key generation and rule table. *Future Generation Computer Systems, 167*, 107757. Advance online publication. DOI: 10.1016/j.future.2025.107757

Setiawan, E., & Entusiastik, E. (2022). Online english teaching by using google classroom and its challenges during covid-19 pandemic at sman 1 gedeg mojokerto. *Jurnal Pendidikan Bahasa Inggris Proficiency, 4*(1), 10. DOI: 10.32503/proficiency.v4i1.2244

Shad, A., Abdullah, T., & Butt, U. (2019). Web Accessibility Adoption Framework (WAAF) for Businesses and Web Professionals. *Proceedings of 12th International Conference on Global Security, Safety and Sustainability, ICGS3 2019*. DOI: 10.1109/ICGS3.2019.8688028

Shah, A. M.. (2022). Comparison of cycling path characteristics in South Florida and implications for bicycle infrastructure planning. *International Journal of Sustainable Transportation, 16*(12), 1089–1100.

Shaw, A. M. (2022). Examining user engagement and use of fitness tracking technology: A qualitative study. *Behaviour & Information Technology, 41*(12), 1–13.

Shaw, A. M. (2023). Identifying behavior change techniques in an artificial intelligence-based fitness app: A mixed-methods study. *Health Education & Behavior, 50*(1), 1–10.

Shickel, B., Loftus, T. J., Ozrazgat-Baslanti, T., Ebadi, A., Bihorac, A., & Rashidi, P. (2018). DeepSOFA: a real-time continuous acuity score framework using deep learning. *ArXiv e-prints, 1802.*

Singh, J., Sillerud, B., Yednock, J., Larson, C., Steffen, A., & Singh, A. (2025). Healthcare leaders' attitudes and perceptions on the use of artificial intelligence and artificial intelligence enabled tools in healthcare settings. *Journal of Medical Artificial Intelligence, 8*, 41. Advance online publication. DOI: 10.21037/jmai-24-392

Siregar, T., Luali, N., Vinalistyosari, R., Hanurawan, F., & Anggraini, A. E. (2024). Implementation of vygotsky's constructivism learning theory through project-based learning (pjbl) in elementary science education. *Al Qalam Jurnal Ilmiah Keagamaan Dan Kemasyarakatan, 18*(4), 2586. DOI: 10.35931/aq.v18i4.3620

Soltani, R., Nguyen, U. T., & An, A. (2021). A survey of self-sovereign identity ecosystem. *Security and Communication Networks, 2021*, 1–26. DOI: 10.1155/2021/8873429

Song, S., Bu, J., Wang, Y., Yu, Z., Artmeier, A., Dai, L., & Wang, C. (2018). Reliability aware web accessibility experience metric. *Proceedings of the 15th Web for All Conference : Internet of Accessible Things, W4A 2018.* DOI: 10.1145/3192714.3192836

Song, Y., Gilardi, F., & Lam, C. (2024). Building culturally sustainable communities. Community museums and transmedia storytelling. *Museum Management and Curatorship, 39*(1), 2–19. DOI: 10.1080/09647775.2023.2209868

Southcott, E., & Jooste, J. (2021). Unveiling the impact of mobile fitness applications on motivational orientation in sustaining exercise behaviors. *International Journal of Sport Psychology, 30*(2), 75–91.

Sposato, M. (2025). Artificial intelligence in educational leadership: A comprehensive taxonomy and future directions. *International Journal of Educational Technology in Higher Education, 22*(1), 20. Advance online publication. DOI: 10.1186/s41239-025-00517-1

Sularso, S., Wadiyo, W., Cahyono, A., Suharto, S., & Pranolo, A. (2025). A Comprehensive Visualization for Music Education and Artificial Intelligence. *JOIV: International Journal on Informatics Visualization, 9*(2), 718–727. DOI: 10.62527/joiv.9.2.2500

Thomas, A. (2007). *Youth online: Identity and literacy in the digital age*. Peter Lang International Academic Publishers.

Toffler, A. (1992). *Powershift: Knowledge, wealth, and violence at the edge of the 21st century* [*Yeni güçler yeni şoklar*]. (Çorakçı, B., Trans.). Altın Kitaplar Press.

Topalcengiz, E., & Yıldırım, B. (2020). Teachers' opinions about distance web 2.0 tools training and teachers' ın-class web 2.0 practices. *Journal of Turkish Science Education, 17*(4), 561–577. DOI: 10.36681/tused.2020.45

Turkle, S. (1995). *Life on the screen: Identity in the age of the Internet.* Simon & Schuster.

Turkle, S. (1999). Cyberspace and identity. *Contemporary Sociology, 28*(6), 643–648. DOI: 10.2307/2655534

Unger, R., & Chandler, C. (2023). *A Project Guide to UX Design: For user experience designers in the field or in the making*. New Riders.

Ünsal, R. (2022). Super connected: Internet, digital media, and techno-social life [Süper bağ(lantı)lı: İnternet, dijital medya ve tekno-sosyal hayat]. *Hacı Bayram Veli Üniversitesi Yeni Medya Dergisi, 13*, 517–521.

Urooj, S., & Farooq, P.Dr. Safia UroojProf. Dr. Muhammad Shahid Farooq. (2023). Impact of students' ubiquitous learning through web 2.0 tool on students' 21st century skills: Critical thinking and collaboration. *Sir Syed Journal of Education & Social Research (Sjesr), 6*(3), 29–43. DOI: 10.36902/sjesr-vol6-iss3-2023(29-43)

Utma, S. (2024). The concept of surveillance and internalization of surveillance on social media [*Gözetim kavramı ve sosyal medyada gözetimin içselleştirilmesi*]. *Journal of Social* [JOSHAS]. *Humanities and Administrative Sciences, 9*(61), 2276–2283. DOI: 10.29228/JOSHAS.66357

Valızadeh, M. (2022). Collaborative writing on google docs: Effects on efl learners' descriptive paragraphs. [Indonesian Journal of English Language Teaching and Applied Linguistics]. *Ijeltal, 6*(2), 277. DOI: 10.21093/ijeltal.v6i2.1053

Vélez-Palacios, A., & Ramírez-Ávila, M. (2023). Peer feedback and its impact in the writing process of international baccalaureate students in a public institution. *Yuyay Estrategias Metodologías & Didácticas Educativas, 1*(2), 26–39. DOI: 10.59343/yuyay.v1i2.14

Verhoef, P., Kooge, E., Walk, N., & Wieringa, J. (2021). *Creating value with data analytics in marketing: Mastering data science.* DOI: 10.4324/9781003011163

Viluckienė, J. (2015). Digital divide as social inequality in relation to IT users with disabilities. *Filosofija. Sociologija, 26*(4), 314–321. https://www.scopus.com/inward/record.uri?eid=2-s2.0-84953396407&partnerID=40&md5=425cdbd6c0e9aef2d432cd6ab739f474

Vlase, I., & Lähdesmäki, T. (2023). A bibliometric analysis of cultural heritage research in the humanities: The Web of Science as a tool of knowledge management. *Humanities & Social Sciences Communications, 10*(1), 1–14. DOI: 10.1057/s41599-023-01582-5 PMID: 36909260

Vu-Minh, A., Nguyen-Quy, D., Nguyen-Khanh, H., & Nguyen, T. (2024). AI fitness trainer using 3D human pose estimation and dynamic time warping. In *Proceedings of the 13th Conference on Information Technology and Its Applications (CITA 2024)* (pp. 50–62). DOI: 10.1007/978-3-031-74127-2_5

Wagner, A., & de Clippele, M. S. (2023). Safeguarding cultural heritage in the digital era–A critical challenge. *International Journal for the Semiotics of Law-Revue internationale de Sémiotique juridique, 36*(5), 1915-1923https://.DOI: 10.1007/s11196-023-10040-z

Wang, H., Gao, Z., Zhang, X., Du, J., Xu, Y., & Wang, Z. (2024). Gamifying cultural heritage: Exploring the potential of immersive virtual exhibitions. *Telematics and Informatics Reports, 100150*, 100150. Advance online publication. DOI: 10.1016/j.teler.2024.100150

Wang, H., & Liu, M. (2025). Methods and content innovation strategies of digital education in higher vocational colleges under the background of artificial intelligence. *Journal of Computational Methods in Sciences and Engineering, 25*(3), 2630–2641. DOI: 10.1177/14727978251321337

Wang, J., & Zhao, H. (2025). Enterprise digital transformation and sustainable productivity. *Discover Sustainability, 6*(1), 308. Advance online publication. DOI: 10.1007/s43621-025-01128-6

Wang, Y., Choo, W., Ng, K., Bi, R., & Wang, P. (2025). Evolution of AI enabled healthcare systems using textual data with a pretrained BERT deep learning model. *Scientific Reports, 15*(1), 7540. Advance online publication. DOI: 10.1038/s41598-025-91622-8 PMID: 40038367

Wang, Y., Liu, X., Mao, W., & Wang, W. (2019, May). DCDroid. *Proceedings of the ACM Turing Celebration Conference* - China. DOI: 10.1145/3321408.3326665

Wang, Y., Wang, J., & Chu, Z. (2025). Multi-agent large language models as evolutionary optimizers for scheduling optimization. *Computers & Industrial Engineering*, *206*, 111197. Advance online publication. DOI: 10.1016/j.cie.2025.111197

Wang, Z., Yu, X., Xue, P., Qu, Y., & Ju, L. (2023). Research on medical security system based on zero trust. *Sensors (Basel)*, *23*(7), 3774. DOI: 10.3390/s23073774 PMID: 37050834

Watson, A. (2025). An imperative to innovate? Crisis in the sociotechnical imaginary. *Telematics and Informatics*, *98*, 102229. Advance online publication. DOI: 10.1016/j.tele.2024.102229

Weiglhofer, M., McCully, A., & Bates, J. (2023). Learning about conflict: The role of community museums in educating on difficult heritage in a divided society. *International Journal of Heritage Studies*, *29*(5), 365–381. DOI: 10.1080/13527258.2023.2189741

Wen, L. (2022). Influence of emotional interaction on learners' knowledge construction in online collaboration mode. *International Journal of Emerging Technologies in Learning*, *17*(02), 76–92. DOI: 10.3991/ijet.v17i02.28539

Westerman, G., Bonnet, D., & McAfee, A. (2014). Leading digital: Turning technology into business transformation. Harvard Business Review Press.

Wijaya, K. (2021). Exploring efl teachers perspectives on collaborative learning activities in senior high school contexts. [Journal of English Teaching]. *Jet*, *7*(2), 118–132. DOI: 10.33541/jet.v7i2.2341

World Economic Forum. (2023). Shaping the future of digital economy and new value creation. https://www.weforum.org

World Health Organization. (2022). Telemedicine: Opportunities and developments in member states. https://www.who.int/publications/i/item/9789240027340

Wu, S., & Shafait, Z. (2024). Assessing efl (english as foreign language) education for sustainable development: Exploring the cultural teaching literature. *European Journal of Investigation in Health, Psychology and Education*, *14*(8), 2282–2299. DOI: 10.3390/ejihpe14080152 PMID: 39194946

Wu, X., & Wang, H. (2024). Teacher awareness as professional development: assistant language teachers in a cross-cultural context by nami sakamoto, switzerland: palgrave macmillan. 2022. pp. xiii+ 164. gbp 54.99 (hbk), isbn: 978–3030883997. *International Journal of Applied Linguistics*, *34*(3), 1221–1223. DOI: 10.1111/ijal.12570

Xie, F., Peng, P., Li, D., Xu, Y., & Wu, M. (2025). Uncovering the evolution of digital economy investment networks: A county-level perspective. *Computational Urban Science*, *5*(1), 19. Advance online publication. DOI: 10.1007/s43762-025-00179-9

Xu, E., Wang, W., & Wang, Q. (2023). The effectiveness of collaborative problem solving in promoting students' critical thinking: A meta-analysis based on empirical literature. *Humanities & Social Sciences Communications*, *10*(1), 16. Advance online publication. DOI: 10.1057/s41599-023-01508-1 PMID: 37192950

Yahiaoui, F., Aichouche, R., Chergui, K., Brika, S., Almezher, M., Musa, A., & Lamari, I. (2022). The impact of e-learning systems on motivating students and enhancing their outcomes during covid-19: A mixed-method approach. *Frontiers in Psychology*, *13*, 874181. Advance online publication. DOI: 10.3389/fpsyg.2022.874181 PMID: 35967714

Yamaguchi, S., Nagano, M., Ohira, S., Oshima, R., Oshima, J., Fujihashi, T., Saruwatari, S., & Watanabe, T. (2022). Web services for collaboration analysis with iot badges. *IEEE Access : Practical Innovations, Open Solutions*, *10*, 121318–121328. DOI: 10.1109/ACCESS.2022.3222562

Yang, J., Ge, H., & Cui, Y. (2025). An AI framework for counterattack detection and decision-making evaluation in football. *Journal of Big Data*, *12*(1), 91. Advance online publication. DOI: 10.1186/s40537-025-01128-3

Yang, Y.. (2021). Determinants of fitness app usage and moderating impacts of education, motivation, and gamification-related app features on physical activity intentions. *Journal of Health Psychology*, *27*(5), 124–135. PMID: 34255656

Yan, X., & Sun, T. (2025). Artificial Intelligence Development and Carbon Emission Intensity: Evidence from Industrial Robot Application. *Sustainability (Basel)*, *17*(9), 3867. Advance online publication. DOI: 10.3390/su17093867

Yavuz, C. (2019). Self-presentation on social media in the context of privacy: The case of Instagram [Mahremiyet bağlamında sosyal medyada benliğin sunumu: Instagram örneği] (Master's thesis, Marmara University, Institute of Social Sciences, Department of Public Relations, Interpersonal Communication Program). Istanbul.

Yrjola, S., Ahokangas, P., & Matinmikko-Blue, M. (2022). Value Creation and Capture from Technology Innovation in the 6G Era. *IEEE Access : Practical Innovations, Open Solutions*, *10*, 16299–16319. DOI: 10.1109/ACCESS.2022.3149590

Yüce, E. (2020). Keeping online diaries as an integrated activity for writing skill in efl classes: The case of penzu. *Bartın University Journal of Faculty of Education*, *9*(1), 132–140. DOI: 10.14686/buefad.651004

Yumnam, R. (2021). E-learning: An effective mode of teaching english as a second language. *Journal of Translation and Language Studies*, *2*(2), 1–9. DOI: 10.48185/jtls.v2i2.275

Yu, P., Abdul Hamid, R., Hakim Osman, L., & Liao, J. (2025). Bridging the digital gap: Empirical insights into agri-food supply chain transformation. *Sustainable Futures : An Applied Journal of Technology, Environment and Society*, *10*, 100810. Advance online publication. DOI: 10.1016/j.sftr.2025.100810

Yusup, M., Maisyaroh, M., & Septiana, L. (2020). Securing web application by embedded firewall at gytech Indosantara Mandiri Ltd. *PIKSEL : Penelitian Ilmu Komputer Sistem Embedded and Logic*, *8*(1), 49–58. DOI: 10.33558/piksel.v8i1.2019

Zahrt, O. H., Evans, K., Murnane, E., Santoro, E., Baiocchi, M., Landay, J., Delp, S., & Crum, A. (2023). Effects of wearable fitness trackers and activity adequacy mindsets on affect, behavior, and health: Longitudinal randomized controlled trial. *Journal of Medical Internet Research*, *25*, e40529. DOI: 10.2196/40529 PMID: 36696172

Zaki, A., A., & J. Mohammed, S. (2024). Artificial intelligence for web application firewall (WAF): A comprehensive review. *International Research Journal of Innovations in Engineering And*, *08*(11), 219–224.

Zaki, N., & Adnan, N. (2023). Esl teachers' perceptions of web-based collaborative writing activity. *International Journal of Academic Research in Progressive Education and Development*, *12*(4). Advance online publication. DOI: 10.6007/IJARPED/v12-i4/20153

Zaky, H. (2021). Google docs in undergraduate online composition class: investigating learning styles' impact on writing corrective feedback. Asian Journal of Interdisciplinary Research, 65-84. https://doi.org/DOI: 10.34256/ajir2117

Zeidanloo, H. R., & Špaček, M. (2025). Assessing disruptive potential in the IT sector: A framework for evaluating company-to-company impact. *Journal of Innovation and Entrepreneurship*, *14*(1), 82. Advance online publication. DOI: 10.1186/s13731-025-00541-5

Zhang, H., Li, Y., Zhang, S., Song, L., & Tao, F. (2025). Artificial Intelligence-Enhanced Digital Twin Systems Engineering Towards the Industrial Metaverse in the Era of Industry 5.0. [English Edition]. *Chinese Journal of Mechanical Engineering*, *38*(1), 40. Advance online publication. DOI: 10.1186/s10033-025-01210-0

Zhang, J., & Zhao, Z. (2026). Corporate ESG rating prediction based on XGBoost-SHAP interpretable machine learning model. *Expert Systems with Applications, 295*, 128809. Advance online publication. DOI: 10.1016/j.eswa.2025.128809

Zhang, X., Li, F., Hu, X., & Fang, J. (2025). A lightweight deep learning framework for wild berry detection in complex natural environments. *Engineering Applications of Artificial Intelligence, 154*, 110918. Advance online publication. DOI: 10.1016/j.engappai.2025.110918

Zhang, Z., Li, S., & Yang, Y. (2025). Explorative Policy Optimization for industrial-scale operation of complex process control systems. *Journal of Process Control, 152*, 103471. Advance online publication. DOI: 10.1016/j.jprocont.2025.103471

Zheng, L. (2022). Clustering algorithm in english language learning pattern matching under big data framework. *Computational Intelligence and Neuroscience, 2022*, 1–11. DOI: 10.1155/2022/1380046 PMID: 36110905

Zhou, D., Tan, Q., Huang, H., Huang, Q., & Qin, N. (2025). A Study of Knowledge Graph and IoT Integration-Based Anomalous Event Tracking Method for Digital Platforms. *International Journal of High Speed Electronics and Systems, 34*(4), 2540314. Advance online publication. DOI: 10.1142/S0129156425403146

Zhu, Y., Wan, H., Carlos, L.-A., Ye, J., & Zeng, S. (2025). Evaluating digital maturity in specialized enterprises: A multi-criteria decision-making approach. *The International Entrepreneurship and Management Journal, 21*(1), 28. Advance online publication. DOI: 10.1007/s11365-024-01051-8

Zia, S., Yildiz-Aktas, I. Z., Zia, F., & Parwani, A. V. (2025). An update on applications of digital pathology: Primary diagnosis; telepathology, education and research. *Diagnostic Pathology, 20*(1), 17. Advance online publication. DOI: 10.1186/s13000-025-01610-9 PMID: 39940046

Zohaib, S. M., & Sajjad, S. M. Iqbal Zafar and Yousaf, M., Haseeb, M., & Muhammad, Z. (2024). Zero Trust VPN (ZT-VPN): A cybersecurity framework for modern enterprises to enhance IT security and privacy in remote work environments. In Preprints.

About the Contributors

Arnaldo Santos Professor at the Department of Sciences and Technologies of Portugal Open University. Invited Professor at the Department of Communication and Art of the University of Aveiro. He is a vice director of the doctorate program in web sciences and technology. He is a senior researcher at DIGIMEDIA (Digital Media Communication), and at INESC TEC (Human ISE Center). He completed his PhD studies at the University of Aveiro, where he obtained degrees in Communication Sciences and Technology. He has contributed as author or coauthor to four books and more than 100 papers published in international conferences and journals, as well as in several research projects. He is a specialist in Digital Transformation, Learning Organizations, and Learning Systems. His current research interests include Artificial Intelligence, Learning Organizations, and Knowledge Management. He has more than 30 years of experience in academia and as a consultant, having worked in management in the corporate sector.

José Henrique Pereira São Mamede. Associate Professor with Habilitation in Department of Sciences and Technology of Universidade Aberta (Portuguese Open University). Associate Invited Professor at NOVA IMS - Information Management School in Universidade Nova de Lisboa. Senior Researcher at INESC TEC (HumanISE / ISAC - Information Systems and Applied Computing). Completed the Habilitation in Web Science and Technology in 2021/11/09 in Universidade de Trás-os-Montes e Alto Douro (Vila Real, Portugal). Ph.D. in Information Systems and Technology in 2009/06/26 in Universidade do Minho (Braga, Portugal). M.Sc. in Informatics in 1999/11/05 in Faculdade de Ciências da Universidade de Lisboa (Lisboa, Portugal). B.Sc. in Computer Science and Engineering in 1992/05/11 in Cooperativa de Técnicas Avançadas de Gestão e Informática CRL (COCITE) (Lisboa, Portugal). He is also a collaborator with the Center for Global Studies (CEG) at the Portuguese Open University. He works in the areas of Engineering and Technology with an emphasis on Computer Science and Information Systems. In his curriculum Ciência Vitae the most frequent terms in the context of scientific and technological output are: Information Systems; Enterprise Architecture; Digital Transformation; Internet-of-Things; Higher Education; Computer Security; Information Security; Cybersecurity; Web Accessibility.

***

Syifa Maulida Akmalia is an Information Technology professional with a strong interest in the development and application of Artificial Intelligence (AI) and the Internet of Things (IoT). She focuses on leveraging intelligent systems to support automation, data analytics, and operational efficiency across digital environments. With a solid technical background and practical experience in information technology, Syifa actively keeps pace with emerging technologies and industry trends. Her commitment to continuous learning and technological innovation drives her to contribute to digital transformation initiatives through the implementation of smart, AI- and IoT-based solutions in various domains.

Muhammed Aksoy completed his undergraduate education in 2022 at Ondokuz Mayıs University, Faculty of Communication, Department of Public Relations and Advertising. Since 2023, he has been pursuing his master's degree at Ondokuz Mayıs University, Graduate School of Social Sciences, in the Media and Communication Studies Program. His areas of interest and research include public relations, cinema, advertising, new media, and digital games.

Azamat Ali is an Associate Professor in the School of Liberal and Creative Arts (Journalism and Mass Communication) at Lovely Professional University, Punjab, India. He earned his Ph.D. from Central University of Gujarat, Gandhinagar, and M.Sc. in Science Communication from Devi Ahilya University, Indore. Dr. Ali's research focuses on emerging technologies, development communication, and health and science communication. His work is dedicated to bridging the gap between scientific advancements and societal needs, emphasizing the transformative potential of emerging technologies to drive innovation and benefit communities.

Muhammad Alvin Pratama is a Computer Science professional with key interests in digital technology development, information systems, and innovation aimed at enhancing user experience quality. His strong academic background and technical expertise enable him to contribute to a wide range of projects, including system analysis, software development, modern computing, and the implementation of AI-driven technologies. In practice, Muhammad Alvin Pratama actively develops digital solutions that are efficient, scalable, and user-centered. He places particular focus on areas such as web accessibility, e-business, UI/UX, automation, and digital transformation. His structured, analytical, and creative approach allows him to deliver meaningful contributions in both professional and academic settings. As a dedicated Computer Science practitioner, Muhammad Alvin Pratama is committed to integrating technology with the values of sustainability, inclusivity, and digital ethics. His goal is to create innovative solutions that can be accessed by diverse user groups and support the advancement of a more inclusive and future-ready digital ecosystem.

Kavitha Dhanushkodi is currently working as an Assistant Professor in the School of Computer Science and Engineering(SCOPE) at Vellore Institute of Technology, Chennai Campus, Chennai, Tamil Nadu, India. She has completed Ph.D and Master of Engineering in Computer Science and Engineering from Anna University, Chennai, Her research interests are mainly focused on Software Security, Internet of Things and Cyber Security. She has an overall teaching experience of 14 years in various academic institutions. She has published more than 40 Research papers to her credit in reputed international journals and conferences with high impact factors.

Ankit Dixit is an Assistant Professor in the School of Liberal and Creative Arts (Journalism and Mass Communication) at Lovely Professional University, Phagwara, Punjab, India. He holds a Ph.D. from Babasaheb Bhimrao Ambedkar University, Lucknow, and a Master's degree in Journalism and Mass Communication from Makhanlal Chaturvedi National University of Journalism and Communication, Bhopal, Madhya Pradesh. He completed his Bachelor's degree from Bundelkhand University, Jhansi. Dr. Dixit's areas of expertise include film communication, media law and ethics, advertising and public relations, and event management. He has qualified the UGC-NET with Junior Research Fellowship (JRF). He has published several research papers in UGC CARE-listed and other reputed peer-reviewed journals. Additionally, he has actively participated in numerous national and international seminars and conferences.

Wilson Fabian is affiliated with Esa Unggul University, where he engages in academic and research oriented activities within the field of computer science. His areas of interest include digital systems, emerging technologies, and the integration of computational methods into practical applications. He is committed to contributing to the advancement of knowledge through interdisciplinary research and collaborative academic initiatives. With a strong foundation in technology and analytical thinking, he aims to support innovation and foster the development of effective, future-ready digital solutions. His professional outlook is grounded in continuous learning and the application of ethical, impactful practices in the realm of information technology.

Ilham Firmansyah is an undergraduate student in the Department of Computer Science at Universitas Esa Unggul, Indonesia. He is currently pursuing his studies with an academic focus on information technology and computer science–related fields. His interests include software development, algorithms, and emerging technologies. Ilham is actively engaged in academic activities and aims to contribute to research and innovation in the field of computer science.

Kodrat Mahatma is an Information Technology professional with strong interests and expertise in the development and application of Artificial Intelligence (AI) and the Internet of Things (IoT). He focuses on intelligent system integration, data analytics, and the use of digital technologies to improve system efficiency and performance. With a solid technical background, Kodrat actively keeps up with emerging technologies and explores practical implementations of AI and IoT across various industry contexts. His commitment to continuous learning and technological innovation drives him to contribute to digital transformation initiatives through the design and deployment of smart, scalable, and sustainable technology solutions.

Rudi Heri Marwan is a professional with a strong interest in Visual Communication Design and the Creative Industries. His expertise focuses on visual storytelling, graphic design, branding, and creative content development to support effective communication across digital and print media. Rudi is particularly interested in how visual design can enhance audience engagement, convey meaningful messages, and strengthen brand identity within creative and cultural industries. With a creative mindset and a solid understanding of design principles, he continuously explores innovative approaches in visual communication to adapt to evolving trends in the creative economy. His commitment to creativity and design excellence drives his contributions to projects that integrate aesthetics, functionality, and strategic communication.

Ravikumar R. Natarajan is an experienced academician with over 12+ years of teaching and research expertise across institutions in India, the UAE, and the Maldives. He currently serves as an Assistant Professor at Marwadi University, Rajkot, specializing in Machine Learning, Recommender Systems, and AI-driven applications in healthcare and security. He holds a Ph.D. in Machine Learning and Recommender Systems from Amity University, Jaipur, a Master of Engineering in CSE from VMRF University, Salem, and a Bachelor of Engineering in CSE from Anna University. He also has a MiniMBA from the Swiss eLearning Institute. Dr. Ravikumar has authored more than 8+ multiple SCIE/Scopus-indexed journal articles, 25+ IEEE/Springer conference papers, and co-authored a book on Artificial Intelligence. He has also published 9 patents and contributed 10+ book chapters in emerging domains such as Federated Learning, Blockchain, and Digital Twins for IGI Global, Wiley and Springer publisher. He actively mentors students through initiatives like the Research Activities Club (RAC) and Student Research Internship Training (SRIT), promoting innovation and research culture.

Vivit Rosmayanti, S.Pd.I., M.Pd was born in Botta on June 26, 1987. She has over 10 years of experience teaching at the University. She obtained a bachelor's degree in English Education from Alauddin State Islamic University. She completed her master's and doctoral degrees in English Education from Makassar State University. She is currently a lecturer in the Post Graduate Program, Department of English Education at Makassar State University, South Sulawesi, Indonesia. She is also actively writing research articles to be published in nationally and internationally accredited journals. She has written in some chapter books, monographs, and reference books. She is interested in teaching methods for teaching English. Her research interests include language teaching methodology, ICT instruction, and ESP teaching. She can be contacted at email: rosmayantivivit@gmail.com

Aarthi S is a dedicated Assistant Professor in Computer Science with over six years of teaching experience. She is currently pursuing her Ph.D. at Marwadi University, Gujarat, and holds an M.Phil. and MCA from Bharathiar University, Tamil Nadu. Throughout her academic career, Aarthi has specialized in programming languages such as C++, Java, and C, and contributed to research in recommender systems and AI-related data privacy. She has published journal articles, contributed to book chapters, and actively participated in technical workshops. Known for her student mentorship and engagement in academic events, Aarthi remains committed to fostering innovation and excellence in computer science education.

Binastya Anggara Sekti has been a lecturer at the Faculty of Computer Science, Esa Unggul University, Jakarta, since 2016. He is actively involved in the Artificial Intelligence and Information Security Study Group. He holds a Bachelor's degree in Informatics Engineering from the Bandung Institute of Technology and a Master's degree in Information Systems Management from Trisakti University, Jakarta. Prior to entering academia, he accumulated over 25 years of professional experience as an IT practitioner in various companies across Jakarta. His work focused on developing data centers for internet service providers and delivering IT solutions for the manufacturing and oil & gas sectors. His research interests include artificial intelligence, cybersecurity, and the development of IT infrastructure.

Binastya Anggara Sekti has been a lecturer at the Faculty of Computer Science, Esa Unggul University, Jakarta, since 2016. He is actively involved in the Artificial Intelligence and Information Security Study Group. He holds a Bachelor's degree in Informatics Engineering from the Bandung Institute of Technology and a Master's degree in Information Systems Management from Trisakti University, Jakarta. Prior to entering academia, he accumulated over 25 years of professional experience as an IT practitioner in various companies across Jakarta. His work focused on developing data centers for internet service providers and delivering IT solutions for the manufacturing and oil & gas sectors. His research interests include artificial intelligence, cybersecurity, and the development of IT infrastructure.

Index

L

M

O

P

R

S

T

U

V

W

Z

www.ingramcontent.com/pod-product-compliance
Lightning Source LLC
LaVergne TN
LVHW081536300926
849161LV00006B/1457